The State of Law

d|u|p

The State of Law

*Comparative Perspectives on the
Rule of Law in Germany and Vietnam*

*Ulrich von Alemann/Detlef Briesen/
Lai Quoc Khanh (eds.)*

d|u|p

Gefördert und gedruckt mit Unterstützung der Gerda Henkel Stiftung, der Anton-Betz-Stiftung der Rheinischen Post und der Gesellschaft von Freunden und Förderern der Heinrich-Heine-Universität Düsseldorf e.V. (GFFU).

Bibliografische Information der Deutschen Nationalbibliothek.
Die Deutsche Nationalbibliothek verzeichnet diese Publikation in der Deutschen Nationalbibliografie; detaillierte bibliografische Daten sind im Internet über http://dnb.dnb.de abrufbar.

© düsseldorf university press, Düsseldorf 2017
http://www.dupress.de
Satz und Layout: Duc-Viet Publikationen
Umschlaggestaltung: Marvin P. Klähn
Lektorat, Redaktion: Detlef Briesen
Druck: KN Digital Printforce GmbH, Ferdinand-Jühlke-Straße 7, 99095 Erfurt.
Der Fließtext ist gesetzt in Garamond 3 FV
ISBN: 978-3-95758-053-5

Table of Contents

II. Theoretical Reflections

III. Global Trends and Challenges

IV. Contemporary Debates

8

Introduction

Ulrich von Alemann/Detlef Briesen/Lai Quoc Khanh

This book is the result of an interdisciplinary conference on "the rule of law." Discussions about the topic, especially in the field of development cooperation, are legion. But our approach is somehow unique: It is the outcome of the first meeting of its kind in the Socialist Republic of Vietnam. Our workshop took place in autumn 2014 at the National University of Vietnam, University of Social and Human Sciences, Hanoi (USSH). The conference is thus more than only another document of the intensive German-Vietnamese cooperation; it also indicates the further development of the legal state which can be observed in Vietnam recently: to be able to discuss such an important issue at a university is a distinct sign of the deep transformation process which is currently occurring in the Southeast Asian country. Another element that makes our publication exceptional is that instead of beginning immediately with a highly specialized debate on the state of law in Vietnam from the perspective of one single academic discipline (which will surely emerge in the coming years), we started to discuss numerous facets of the subject "rule of law" arising from a multidisciplinary dialogue. For this reason, the participants and speakers, both at the conference itself and for this present publication, come from various scientific disciplines in Vietnam and Germany: political, historical, social, economic and legal sciences (in which in Europe the topic is discussed most extensively), but also members of Vietnamese governmental and non-governmental organizations.

Our aim for the conference and the conference volume is to open up a dialogue about the rule of law between two very different legal cultures, the German-European and the Vietnamese, which we must locate in the complex setting of Southeast or East Asia. As a result of the complexity of the subject matter, we have therefore refrained from providing a limiting definition of our discourse object "Rechtsstaat." We have learned to operate cautiously in order to avoid the danger of Eurocentrism, as well as too easily dismiss questionable circumstances as country-typical. And in general, caution is necessary, as the constitutional state, however much we may agree on the goal of its worldwide realization, was, on the one hand, always an ideological concept which served issues like the competition between the great powers for colonial possessions and later for the superpowers to expand their zones of influence. The alleged absence of the state of law served only too often to colonize states or to intervene directly in their internal affairs. On the other hand, however, serious violations of the rule of law cannot be so easily explained in terms of a different interpretation of the latter. But by all means different legal traditions have to be taken into account. It cannot be ignored that European states such as Germany follow the Roman tradition of law, while a country like Vietnam is historically and contemporarily deeply influenced by the Confucian tradition of custom and morale.

It is true that we have to accept distinct differences between Roman-European law, and Southeast and East Asian customs and morale, but both traditions also contain many common elements. They make it possible to form an intersection in the definition of the rule of law which is perfectly consistent with today's minimum requirements; in particular the binding of state action to law and justice, the exclusion of state arbitrariness, the principle of proportionality of state action, the division of powers and the independence of the courts, and also to examine the legality of state action, and thus legal certainty.

However, the individual contributions to our volume show that this catalogue is limited or extended by more criteria, or that individual aspects of the rule of law are placed at the center of attention. At the same time, at least three aspects are identified which were of considerable importance for the discussions during the conference:

- the exclusion of state arbitrariness and the principle of proportionality of state action,
- legal certainty and equality of all before the law,
- the enormous international relevance of contemporary trans- and international legal systems.

From the very beginning, we were less likely to document the already established current state of research, since this is more or less non-existent with regard to Vietnam, but to initiate research processes in a way which is appropriate to the relevance of the topic. The legal state is scientifically only adequately researched if it is addressed from various scientific and socio-political angles, also taking into account various perspectives from different legal cultures.

For this reason, our volume is the result of a twofold approach: the contributions from Vietnam stem mainly from the legal, political and historical sciences. They first and foremost document the efforts to improve the connection with international debates and research topics within the framework of the Vietnamese reform process (Doi Moi). Partial aspects of this endeavor then lead to those more specific questions which are addressed by the Vietnamese authors in this volume. They can be specified here briefly as follows.

The contributions by Nguyen Thi Hoi, Pham Duc Anh and Vu Thi Phung deal with the history of Vietnamese law for the period before the middle of the nineteenth century, when the colonization by the European Great Power, France began. The authors question the situation in Vietnam prior to colonization using criteria such as state arbitrariness and proportionality of state action. Since the state in the early modern times, in Europe as well as in Asia, consisted essentially of the ruling monarch and his officials, a discourse on arbitrariness and proportionality always implicitly criticized the ruling monarch. In our context, however, perhaps a more important goal of the contributions is recognizable: to search for pre-colonial traditions and to make these usable for today's societal and political change in Vietnam.

Especially in Vietnam, the division of powers between legislature, executive and judiciary, as defined in most contemporary constitutions, is a decisive feature of the rule of law. This view is at least largely accepted in contemporary debates with particular emphasis on the independence of the judiciary. The contributions by Lai Quoc Khanh and Nguyen Thi Chau Loan therefore focus on the division of powers: Either as an attempt to demonstrate its relevance for the entire constitutional and societal development of Vietnam or to design models for the implementation of a more independent judiciary.

Another focal point is the problems of corruption and low compliance of functionaries in the implementation of legal norms. Such questions are being revived in Vietnam today either with reference to the teachings of the founding father of the nation, Ho Chi Minh, or are more and more addressed in the traditional (Confucian) sense as improvements in the education of officials (Lai Quoc Khanh/Nguyen Ngoc Anh, Nguyen Anh Cuong, Hoang Thi Kim Que, Nguyen Thi Thuy Hang/Phan Duy Anh and Bui Xuan Duc). In addition, a number of contributions (from Dinh Xuan Ly, Duong Xuan Ngoc, Phan Xuan Son and Vu Cong Giao) deal with the contemporary constitution of Vietnam. The two main topics are the problem of whether and to what extent the reform process in the country is adequately secured, and whether the reforms provide the necessary preconditions to ensure especially economic cooperation with Vietnam's neighboring countries.

The contributions from Germany are also an outcome of a respective approximation to the problems of the legal state. They are more generalized and are primarily geared to developing discussions for future cooperation. Since the authors come from various scientific disciplines, these articles reflect the diversity of today's debates about the constitutional state. The contributions from Germany provide key concepts and theories of the scientific discourse about the constitutional state and the development of law, also in transnational and international contexts.

Legal pluralism is such a key concept. Detlef Briesen uses it to describe the various forms of discrimination by law in colonial states, a condition which has also been felt in Vietnam since the conquest by France, and which has had a profound impact until today. Another key concept is that of governing by law. Julian Krüper's contribution is concerned with the question of how the constitutional state can act "constitutionally" in its everyday practice without always referring directly to the idealistic provisions of the constitution. Michael Baurmann and Liu Mengyue focus their article on "trust", a category which at first sight is a non-legal one. They ask how in an East Asian society with many similarities to Vietnam, namely the Chinese society, trust in business relations can be established without formal legal guarantees. Justus Haucap follows a similar approach and points out the importance of institutional and informational requirements for modern market economies. The contributions by Thomas Schmitz and Ulrich von Alemann discuss the development of transnational and international law – on the one hand, the exemplary creation of transnational law by the European Community, on the other hand the increasing role of international organizations in the creation of law.

These terms and theories are certainly of some importance for the future debate on the constitutional state in Vietnam and elsewhere. During the discussions at the conference and in the articles in this volume, the enormous gap in current research has become more visible. For further research we propose to focus on the different periods of modern Vietnamese history and their respective relation to a state of law.

- Before the colonization by France, the Nguyen dynasty's rule in particular was predominantly based on concepts of governance and administration which originated from contemporary China. The rule of law, as well as the entire legal system, were not determined by the formalized European (Roman) law but by the Confucian concept of custom and morale. It was based on trust in the moral integrity of the emperor and his mandarins.

- With the colonization, France established legal pluralism in Indochina, a common concept of colonial rule to discriminate the "native subjects". Consequently, the validity of Confucian-law was increasingly limited to the marginalized Vietnamese village population. The French "Etat légale" was based on arbitrary decisions. It not only failed to create a system of legal certainty and equality but even established systematic discrimination and injustice by law. The French colonial authorities destroyed trust in law to such a degree that the "Etat légale" can even be understood as an essential source of the anti-colonial uprisings since World War I.

- With the August 1945 revolution, a process of enforcing "socialist legality" began, following the model of the Communist Bloc, although the founding father of modern Vietnam, Ho Chi Minh, distanced himself from these ideas, and so Vietnam never developed a theory of socialist legality like the contemporary GDR for example. This was also because Vietnam was constantly involved in wars for almost 50 years, from the Japanese occupation in 1940 until the end of the Third Indochina War in the early 1990s.

- Since the beginning of the reform era (Doi Moi) in the mid-1980s, the Vietnamese government has been seeking to define the rule of law for Vietnam and to implement reforms. A key impetus for the latter is, in particular, the need for legal certainty which is required by national as well as international investors or must be guaranteed in the context of the planned cooperation in ASEAN. The state of law in Vietnam is still in progress

From these four epochs, fascinating perspectives arise for further comparative law research, for which first ideas have been developed here in our volume.

14

This would not have been possible without solving the problem of translating complicated legal terms from Vietnamese into English. Therefore, we would like to express our very great appreciation to the translators, Dr. Dao Duc Thuan, Dr. Lam Minh Chau, and Tran Minh, MA.

I. Traditions

A Brief History of the Idea of the State of Law and Its Basic Indicators

Nguyen Thi Hoi

A Brief History of the Idea of the State of Law

In the history of legal and political ideas of humankind, the idea of legal dominance over a state and society and the notion of a state that rules and controls by law and maintains legal observance werecreated at a time as early as the pre-historical period. The foundation of these ideas is closely tied to the rise of popular sovereignty and democracy as opposed to authoritarian and tyrant individual rulers as well as anarchy and unlawfulness, and requires the state and the society as a whole to depend on law. This is reflected in the ideas of well-known Western and Eastern thinkers.

In the West, the idea of the state of law was founded at an early time and reflected in the works of thinkers and political activities of statesmen. This becomes more apparent when we take a glimpse at the viewpoints of thinkers whose ideas have been famous for many centuries. Solon (c. 638–c. 559 B.C.) was a renowned Greek sophist, poet, legislator and political activist at pre-modern history. In 594 B.C., having been appointed as archon of Athens, Solon passed a number of laws to reform state and society. These included a land reform to return to farmers their lands previously used as mortgages, a slavery reform that gave back bonded slaves their freedom, a class reform to define the rights and responsibilities of each class, and a legislation on the founding of a People's Assembly (ecclesia) and a People's Court (heliala). The introduction of these laws confirmed that Solon was well aware of the role of laws in social governance and control, as he stated that internal peace was based on a firm state and a legal system.[1] He wrote: "Anarchy would generate tons of disasters and bring about the extinction of the city. Only the law is able to establish order and construct unison."[2]

Heraclitus (c. 530–470 B.C.) – the great Greek materialist philosopher, who upheld the law and considered it a means to realize universal harmony, also emphasizes the role of written law and its protection and consolidation. For him, cities are bound to be founded on a legal basis and the law has to be fought for as much as the stability of one's home city.[3]

Socrates (469–399 B.C.), the renowned Greek orator, says that every citizen who has settled in a nation is to be bound by a contract by which he maintains absolute adherence to the law, however good or bad it is. A society cannot function well without efficient laws. The most sacred value is justice, which means to live according to the public law.[4]

Platon (427–347 B.C.), the prominent ancient Greek philosopher and also Socrates' most loyal student, maintains that the state can exist as long as public authorities completely observe the law. He claims to foresee the extinction of the state wherever the law is inefficient and inferior to any personal power. In contrast, wherever the law is superior to the state and public authorities are but its minions, the state and its interests are saved.[5]

Aristotle (384–322 B.C.) is the greatest ancient Greek "encyclopédiste" who is referred to by Karl Marx as the most influential ancient thinker. Friedrich Engels considered him as having the most complete mind among all Greek philosophers. Aristotle states that the law clearly reflects the state's role as it helps to confirm and consolidate civil rights. The law is tasked with facilitating the process by which individuals learn their rights through their relationships. However, there is no right to equalize the members of the society; differences among the rich and the poor necessarily exist. The law is divided by Aristotle into general (natural) law and particular (nationally-bound) laws. The general law is superior to particular laws. In every particular law there are also first the laws that deal with the establishment and organization of city-states

---

[1] See VNU Press (2009).

[2] See Luu Kien Thanh/Pham Hong Thai (1993), 62.

[3] Ibid.

[4] Ibid.

[5] Ibid.

and those that are subordinate to the former. The legal totality makes up political justice which only exists among free and equal people. Aristotle considers legal norms "justice" and to act justly means to follow the laws. Accordingly, he deems states whose authorities rule by law and genuinely in the public interest, pure or original states, while those that favor individual will at the expense of the law and rule only for the sake of individual authorities are corrupt or phony. Regarding the state apparatus, he splits it into three sectors or segments which respectively deal with legislation or decision-making, executive or legal enforcement and jurisdiction or legal judgments. He writes: "Now there are three things in all states which a careful legislator ought well to consider, which are of great consequence to all, and which properly attended to the state must necessarily be happy; and according to the variation of which the one will differ from the other. The first of these is the public assembly; the second the officers of the state, that is, who they ought to be, and with what power they should be entrusted, and in what manner they should be appointed; the third, the judicial department."[6]

In the East the supremacy of the law and the requirement that everyone, including the king, his officials and citizens, has to abide by the law is also manifested in the works of many ancient thinkers.

Kautilya (around the 4th century B.C.) was a chancellor of the powerful Maurya dynasty which is credited with developing a united, wealthy and influential ancient India and was a teacher and friend of King Chandra Gupta. He proposed a plan for national construction based on a stable and ordered society, prosperous economy, formidable army and expanded influence. According to him, for a country to prosper it is first and foremost necessary to establish social order, which requires the first and fundamental role and responsibilities of the king and those of his citizens. However, in order to maintain a lasting reign the king must rule by law and resolutely adhere to it. He advised the king: "However, despite one's position as ruler of a nation, one is not allowed to act according to one's own will. To mobilize popular support for the cause national construction the king is supposed to uphold the law and strictly adhere to public norms. To rule a nation without regard to the law means to give up one's throne without any popular coup."[7]

---

[6] Ellis (1941), Aristotle, 132.

[7] Thích Mãn Giác (1967), 163.

Han Fei (c. 280–233 B.C.) – a prominent representative of the legalistic school, states that the rule by law is necessarily a must for his time. He writes:

"There is no fixed way to rule the people, so it is better to resort to the law. The law has to adapt itself to each particular era, and to be efficient it must be guided by that particular era (...) a ruling principle of wise men is to adapt the law to historical circumstances and make the legislation relevant to historical conditions."[8]

He therefore not only emphasizes the state of law but also calls for the objective adjustment of the law according to each historical era. In addition, he requires everyone, not excluding the king and his officials, to respect and uphold the law; Han Fei supports the equal distribution of law to everyone. He says: "Do whatever is legal and abandon whatever is illegal."[9] Or in another version:

"Thus a lucid king is able to divert his followers from living outside the law, refusing to make good deeds within the law and committing illegal acts. The law is what forbids individual misdeeds to go beyond legal boundaries (...) the king is without safety if the law is unstable, and evil deeds are triumphant without resolute punishments. The law refuses to favor the noble born, just as the plumb-line does not yield to curves. What is assigned by the law, the wise cannot decline and the brave dare not challenge. In applying the law to transgressions, one does not tolerate great ministers; in rewarding good conduct, one does not ignore commoners. Therefore, it is nothing but the law that is capable of correcting ministers' wrongdoings, disciplining commoners' misconducts, removing chaos, righting the wrong and uniting the people's lines."[10]

The above viewpoints show that in ancient ideas on the state and law, the state of law – which is ruled and controlled through legal means, supports the role of the law, respects and adheres to it and considers it an indispensable part of social management – is present. In the "dark ages" humankind had to tolerate the brutal suppression by authoritative monarchies and religiously-fanatical theocracies and live under the domination of feudal regimes – with little or nothing related to the state of law.[11] In Europe

"the missionaries transformed political science and jurisprudence into nothing but the sciences that served theology, and dominant theological principles were jammed into

---

[8] Lã Trấn Vũ (1964), 283.

[9] Lã Trấn Vũ (1964), 288.

[10] Phan Ngoc (2001), 61 ff.

[11] See Dao Tri Uc (2006).

the two former. The teachings of Congregations were at the same time political deter-
minants and religious texts retained as much effect before the court as the law."[12]

Such conditions render democracy, the supreme role of the law and legal compliance, the supreme role of citizens underdeveloped. It was not until the emergence of the capitalist mode of production and the introduction and development of humanism that the idea of the state of law reemerged, as can be seen in different ideas on the state and law by some Western scholars.

Machiavelli (1469–1527), an Italian politician and thinker says that the people are above the prince, since they are better at picking public officials than him, "the people are at all times more prudent, determined and rational than the king."[13] Machiavelli sides with the people, as he argues that a king who can do whatever he wants will become an insane autocrat, and if people can do whatever they want, they will only become mad men. Therefore, the people are better than the king under a legal system; for if unbounded by the law they are likely to commit fewer wrongdoings than the king and are more predisposed to redeeming themselves. This is because any citizen who is corrupted, debased and rebellious can easily listen to advice and return to his right way; while a tyrant king can be stopped by nothing, and it takes nothing other than weapons to let him redo what is wrong.[14]

But more importantly, what is significant is that a legal document that reflects the state of law was created even prior to the Renaissance, the Magna Carta (Great Charter), since it carries the idea of a state that is bounded by the law. The Charter was issued in June, 1215, recognized by King John of England and improved by Edward I in 1297, and can be considered the first important legal document which legitimatized the State of England as a sovereign state of law. The Charter regulated:

"No free man is eligible to being captured or imprisoned, being deprived of his rights and properties, being turned outlaw or forced to go exile and being stripped of his status. The king is in no way permitted to use force against others or to instruct others to use force without the legitimate rulings of his counterpart authorities or unless proper to the law of his kingdom."[15]

---

[12] Truth Publisher (1986), Marx/Engels, 45.

[13] See Pham Huy Chiem (1971), The Prince.

[14] Ibid.

[15] Dao Tri Uc 2006, 116–117.

The Charter is said to be one of first written acts in the West that restricted the king's power, making him bounded by the law and forced to restrain from committing certain actions against the populace without legitimate rationales. These rationales can be found in the decisions of his counterparts or the law.

In the 17th century, given the strong development of the capitalist relations of production, the idea of a state of law is heightened to a new level. The thinkers in this area resort to the idea of natural law to request more freedom and democracy for the people, affirm civil sovereignty, emphasize the role of the law, demand the state to be put under legal supervision and management and bounded by the law, and desire the laws to be in line with a human's natural rights. They argue that the state and law are not created by God, but rather by the conciliation between everyone with respect to a human's rationality. For them, the human being is endowed with certain inherent rights and obligations by its creator, which are associated with his birth and not dependent or given by the state, namely the right to live in freedom and equality, the pursuit of happiness and private ownership. On the other hand, the human being is obliged to refrain from causing damage to others and his community. The resulting demands of the human's will constitute the norms of natural law. "Human law" is supposed to be appropriate to "natural law", meaning the laws created by the state must be in conjunction with a human's intrinsic and natural rights. This idea is embedded in the works of such prominent scholars of this area as Grotius, John Locke, Montesquieu and Rousseau. Locke argues that as soon as he signs the contract to create a state, man has transferred the power to punish individuals to the state, whose authority is thus a congregation of individual power and results from the citizens; state power is limited or restricted by the stipulations of this contract, namely the preservation of freedom, property and life of each individual, but also of a society as a whole. To be sure, Locke's concept of state power resulting from citizens' power is a great scientific and political achievement, and is currently reflected in the constitutions of many contemporary states.

Locke compliments those institutions which are capable of ensuring human freedom, and also confirms that the first and foremost prerequisite is the separation or partition of powers. For him, in a republican state there are the legislative, executive and federative powers; all these powers are authorized to the state by popular will or in other words, the state is granted these powers by the people through a clearly defined agreement. Among these three, the legislative power is supposed to be highest as it is charged with creating mandatory pieces of legislation for every sector and every member of a society. Subsequent to the creation of these pieces, even the legislators are obliged to adhere to them; and the king, who holds the supreme executive or law enforcement power, has to abide by the law.

Locke strongly emphasizes the role of the law in state and social activities, and thus the respect for and compliance with the law by state bodies and personnel. Therefore, whatever leads to state disintegration is for him associated with a lack of respect for and compliance with the law by everyone, including most importantly the state bodies and those who are public authorities. He argues that whenever the legislative organs or the king or all of them violate the laws by, for instance, transgressing their authorized power or abusing power, interfering with the life, freedom and property of the people, state disintegration is likely to occur. This once again confirms that Locke is not only the author of the idea of state of law but also of the idea of separation of powers.

Montesquieu (1689–1755), one of the most prominent French enlighteners, in his famous work "The Spirit of the Laws", provides a definition of the law. He argues that humans are ruled by different kinds of law: natural law, divine law, religious law, international law, political law, civil law, family law, etc. Similar to Locke, Montesquieu is particularly concerned about protecting the freedom of citizens, as he argues that political freedom and civil safety and security can only be achieved with the absence of power abuse. To prevent the abuse of power it is necessary to create an appropriate mechanism to exercise state power. It is the separation of state power and mutual control between the branches of power. According to him, in every administration there are three branches of power: legislative power; the power to exercise that which is allowed by international law (executive power) and the power to perform that which is allowed by civil law (judicial power). Legislative power is the power to create temporary or permanent laws and amend or remove existing laws. Executive power is the power to decide matters regarding war and peace, send or receive ambassadors, increase common security and prevent possible invasive acts. Judicial power is the power to punish criminal acts or settle personal disputes between individuals. These three powers are supposed to be separated or granted to different actors in order to avoid the abuse or mistreatment of power, which ensures the freedom of citizens. For every human is born with the lust for power, he who has power is likely to abuse it. Whenever and wher-

24

ever centralized power is given to a person or an organization, it is likely that it is abused. Montesquieu argues that the separation of state power can guarantee freedom because it prevents authoritarianism and mistreatment of power by the state. He also writes: "The freedom of citizens depends primarily on the validity of criminal laws. A vulnerable innocent citizen's security means the loss of freedom."[16] Therefore, charging a person as guilty must not merely be based on his thoughts, words or poems but on the consideration of his manifested actions. If his words are tied to actions, and his poems contain oppositional motives, then punishment is eligible and regulations must be created to protect his innocence if necessary.

Judging from the ideas of the above thinkers, it can be said that "the state of law" is mentioned by no one although its distinct signs are sketched out. In the 18th century, Immanuel Kant (1724–1804) amended and developed the idea of state of law to a higher plane and Kant himself invented the concept of "state of law". For him, the state is an instrument that connects its member in a legal framework in order to supervise and ensure freedom and equality for every citizen. The state is responsible for addressing social disputes, monitor social relationships and making sure society is constantly improved for the sake of human interests. The state uses the law to assist every citizen in demonstrating his strength and maximizing individual labor and originality. Kant argues that to speak of the state means to speak of a state of law created by the people for the realization of freedom and equality. A person can pursue personal advancement according to his will if he keeps from violating the law. Every citizen is supposed to adhere to the law while enjoying the right and ability to put the state under the law. The state is tasked with protecting the laws and ensuring the reign of the law and freedom. That which promises to bring mutual relations between the state and its citizens is the separation of state powers which distinguishes between executive and legislative ones.[17] Thanks to his ideas, Kant is perceived as one of the prominent theorists on the state of law – a state that is based on individual autonomy and complies with the law in its every activity.

In conclusion, the idea of state of law has a long history which dates back to ancient times and develops alongside the progress of human civilization, re-

---

[16] See Montesquieu (1996), 119, 120.

[17] Nguyễn Văn Huyên (1996), 114.

flecting aspirations of a state and an ideal social order which is capable of ensuring a free life and especially political freedom for everyone.

The Conception and Basic Characteristics of the State of Law

The Concept of State of Law

Since the 19th century, the state of law has no longer just been an idea but has
evolved into a civilized value of humankind, an ideal state model, an inevitable
progress of all democratic states around the world, and a good reference model
for the state shaping and development by contemporary nations. For one, until
now, "the development of human civilization is for the most part regulated by
the progress of civil society and state of law".[18] State of law thus continues to
be a widely researched subject in many countries such as Germany, Russia, the
US and Vietnam that seek to grasp the characteristics of this model according
to which they further improve their respective states. But what is the state of
law? To this question different answers can be proposed, as the state of law is a
complicated, multi-faceted phenomenon which can be viewed from different
angles. This is better vindicated in the conceptions of state of law by contemporary scholars from different countries.

A number of German scholars claim that in modern languages there are
two interchangeable concepts, namely the "state of law" (Rechtsstaat, état de
droit) and the "rule of law", depending on each particular language. These two
in fact share both similar and different points. What they have in common is
that both "state of law" and „rule of law" originate from some basic principles:
the universality of legal norms, the public nature of law and the non-retro-
activeness and transparency of legal norms. The difference is that "rule of law"
is used according to English common law, which puts more emphasis on popular participation in an organized political progress without specifying the
state's role. On the other hand, "state of law" refers to a specific role of a state,
the state, i.e. its real components.

Nevertheless, it is argued by some authors that "the rule of law" is not correctly the equivalent of "nhà nước pháp quyền" in Vietnamese. For one thing,
"the rule of law" refers to a society managed and run on the basis of clearly

---

[18] Vietnam Academy of Social Sciences (1991), 5.

26

identified rights as indicated by human law and natural law, so that the subjects can exercise their rights at their will to improve happiness without violating others' rights; every subject, even the state, has to station itself below the
law. The "rule of law" is therefore not simply a state of law, although it still
plays an important part.[19] Accordingly, I recommend translating "the rule of
law" as "chế độ pháp quyền" instead of "chế độ pháp trị" (which may be translated into English as "rule by law"), as it refers to a higher process compared to
"state of law".

Scholars have different definitions of the state of law. Some authors concep-
tualize state of law as a state that recognizes and respects the supremacy of the
law, makes clear distinctions between the legislative, executive and judicial
branches which are mutually controlled and managed, ensure that its citizens
enjoy full legal safety and their basic liberal rights are protected, and fulfill
international agreements.[20] Another definition says that the "state of law regulates both society and itself according to the law, and the state apparatus is
inferior to the law."[21] Another line of thought says that state of law is not a
specific kind of state but a state model wherein general and particular characteristics coexist and the concept of state of law must be understood in both
dimensions: as a general characteristic of the state as a special organ of political
power, and a particular characteristic of state as part of a triangle made by the
state-the law-civil-society.[22] Other scholars argue that the state of law is a
form of state as its organization and operations are in contrast with those of
authoritarian and dictatorial states; in contrast to those of states that are organized by humanism and also those states that follow legalism.[23]

In addition, there are other conceptions of the state of law. Although the
conceptions of the state of law are different from scholar to scholar, they share
the following common points when contrasting it with authoritarian and totalitarian states or non-state of law:
- First, the state of law is legally founded and its power and operations are
  limited by the law, based on the law and the idea of justice; it must be con-

---

[19] See Nguyen Dang Dung (2007).

[20] Nguyen Duy Quy/Nguyen Tat Vien (2008), 150.

[21] Nguyen Duy Quy/Nguyen Tat Vien (2008), 150.

[22] Nguyen Duy Quy/Nguyen Tat Vien (2008), 151.

[23] Nguyen Duy Quy/Nguyen Tat Vien (2008), 151–152.

trolled by the law; the state is utilized to protect individual freedom and protecting civil interests is its raison d'être.

- Second, the state of law has an advanced legal system which is based on and relevant to a human's natural rights, respects and guarantees the implementation of human rights, civil rights and freedom, and manages to remove authoritarianism, exclusiveness and government's arbitrariness.

- Third, this legal system retains its superiority and is applied equally nationwide; every subject, even the state, is obliged to obey the law and pursue justice, respect human rights and individual freedom. State organization and operations are completely based on legal regulations in order to fulfill these regulations.

- Fourth, the court of law is independent and its rulings must be in conjunction with constitutional principles. It is supposed to safeguard the rights of the people against the violation of any other subject, including the state, and it is followed by all subjects, not excluding state organs.

The above analysis helps us confirm that state of law is first and foremost a state in its fullest sense – an organization that holds political power or a public authority endowed with state characteristics. However, it is not a socio-economic form in the sense of a feudal state or capitalist state, but a state whose organizational structure and operations are different from those of authoritarian or dictatorial states in that it is not an instrument of social and human suppression but one of social benefaction. It does not tamper with individual liberty but serves the public interest, individual freedom and social justice. It is organized and run on the basis of civil sovereignty and separation of powers, as the state and other social subjects always observe and fulfill the law in their behaviors. It is a democratic, just and transparent system that reflects the will of the populace, runs on the basis of and with regard to human's natural rights, respects human basic rights and mutual responsibility between various subjects.

In conclusion: The state of law is a state that is organized and run on the basis of civil sovereignty, the separation of powers and a democratic, transparent and advanced legal system. It is an instrument for the guarantee of individual freedom, social justice and the supremacy of law in state and social activities.

The Basic Features of the State of Law

The above definition of the state of law indicates that apart from the general features, the state of law also possesses these basic characteristics:

First, the state of law is organized and functions on the basis of civil sovereignty.In authoritarian and dictatorial states, the people are always expected to be ruled and suppressed, and can never be said to hold state power but only be subject to it. Whereas in the state of law, the entire state power belongs to them, as they are its highest and sole holders. The people are believed to participate in state activities and supervise the state officials and organs by themselves or through their representatives. They make the supreme and ultimate decisions on the matters pertaining to national being and sovereignty and other important state affairs. Therefore, the state has to serve the interests of its people, and its every policy is supposed to derive from popular demands and interests and serves to meet their appropriate aspirations. The people's sovereignty and various measures to exercise it must be indicated in the Constitution, which is the state's fundamental and original piece of legislation. For example, the current Vietnamese Constitution emphasizes: the State belongs to the People, by the People, for the People; all state power belongs to the People; the People exercise their state power through direct democracy or representative democracy through the National Assembly, People's Councils and through other State organs. The German Constitution also remarks: "All public power derives from the people. They perform this power through elections and public polls as well as through particular legislative, executive and judicial powers."[24]

Second, in the state of law, human rights and civil rights are respected and protected. It can be said that the idea of state of law has its origin from the desire and demand to restrain and control state power in order to ensure individual freedom. Thus, "Freedom, equality, human dignity and other manifestations of human rights assurance are the lasting features of the state of law."[25] The relationship between the state of law and its citizens is based on equality, which means that either side has its rights and obligations in relation to the other. The citizens have both rights and obligations towards the state and vice versa. For this reason, civil freedom is at the same time the limitation of state

[24] Konrad-Adenauer-Stiftung (2002), 88.

[25] Konrad-Adenauer-Stiftung (2002), 51.

power, civil rights are contrary to state rights and citizens' range of freedom is larger than that of the state. While citizens are allowed to do whatever the law does not forbid, state organs and employees are restricted to act within what the law allows. In a state of law, the basic and sacred human rights such as the right to live, to be free and to pursue happiness are expected to be fulfilled because they are acknowledged by the law and ensured; the legitimate rights and benefits, honor and dignity of every citizen are guaranteed and protected by the state through the law. Theoretically, the state of law has to make sure that every individual is equal and free before the law and is provided with ample legal conditions to pursue his personal growth with ease, so that every individual can make the best use of his intrinsic capacity. The fairness and equality among citizens in the state of law are ensured not only in legal terms but also in practice, as the state guarantees every necessary material and spiritual condition for the citizens to exercise them in practice. In addition, the state protects individual freedom from the violation of other actors, including the state organs. Citizens have the rights to replace the authorities should they violate their legitimate rights and interests, to oppose any arbitrary and illegal intervention by the authorities and, at the same time, are obliged to respect and follow the law and fulfill their legal tasks with regard to the state and other actors. In general, in the state of law, the state-individual relationship is directed in a way in which

"The state is a coalition of the masses under the control of the law; humans can in no way be regarded as a means to an end, rather, humans must be an end in itself; every individual and a society as a whole have to respect and protect the law; each citizen is granted the right and ability to pressure those who hold power to respect and adhere to existing laws."[26]

Third, the state of law is a democratic state. The state of law uses law for social management and functions both publicly and democratically. The formal manifestation of democracy in the state of law is that state power stems from its citizens and is authorized by the citizens to the state; therefore it is restricted within the authorized range and by the law. Society is regulated by law and citizens are able to participate in social development, in human rights protection, in economic development and in the assurance of social justice. Democracy and laws are crucial to development and are held in high regard by national

---

[26] Nguyen Van Dong (1996), 21.

decision-makers.[27] The state of law has the full capacity to establish, consolidate and protect democracy. Through the law, the state acknowledges freedom and democracy in every civil sector; acknowledges the intervention in state and social management by social organizations and popular unions; regulates the authority of state organs to restrict their power and keep them from violating civil democracy and freedom. Through the law, the state ensures the implementation of civil rights, preventing illegal acts and creating punitive measures against any actor that violates the legitimate rights and interests of its citizens, so that the established democracy is protected.

Fourth, the state of law has a democratic and transparent legal system which reflects the popular will appropriate to national circumstances and holds the highest position in public and social life. The law can be said to be indispensable to the creation of a state of law but not every legal system is adequate enough to be the law of such a state. Such a legal system has to be democratic, transparent and in conjunction with existing conditions of the country such as its socio-economic level of development, morality, customs, history and traditions, culture, psychological features, international and transnational law which have been recognized or signed by the state. This legal system has to reflect the will of the people, recognize basic human rights, civil sovereignty and mutual responsibility among the subjects. The law of a state of law is supposed to have a universal effect on everyone and their behaviors, and is stable enough to help the subjects anticipate the consequences of their behaviors or the response of the state and other subjects. According to the law, as citizens are held responsible before the state, the state also has responsibilities before its citizens should it violate their legitimate rights and interests; mutual responsibilities are expected of each subject which is involved in legal relations if it violates the interests of other subjects. The democracy of a legal system is reflected not only in its regulations but also in the development of the laws which is expected to conform to popular will. The legal regulations have to be clear and specific and widely and publicly announced so that anyone is able to refer to them to protect his rights. Such a legal system must have feasibility and is primarily reflected in the acts that are developed by capable legislators, among which the constitution is most revered legally. For this reason, the legal

---

[27] Nguyen Duy Quy/Nguyen Tat Vien (2008), 55.

systems of former slavery and feudalistic states are impossible to be rendered as a state of law as they do not meet the above criteria.

The state of law implies that its power or strength resides in the law and the law's supremacy is what constitutes a state of law, so the respect of and compliance with the law is its intrinsic component. The state-law relationship in a state of law is mutual and interactive. Despite being drafted by the state, as long as it takes effect, the law returns to bind the state and becomes the legal framework for the entire organization and functioning of the state apparatus and also a means to restrain and limit state power. The law regulates the establishment, organizational structure, functions, missions and rights of each state organ of every kind and level; standardizes the relations between state organs and between the internal components of an organ. The organization and activities of state apparatus are based on the law and performed within the legal framework for legal purposes. The law becomes a conduit through which the state conveys its will and fulfills its purposes. All state organs and employees have to maintain absolute compliance with the law in their behaviors and are only allowed to do what it permits. They are kept from applying the law in an arbitrary way and instead have to follow the regulated principles and procedures. The state itself should provide necessary institutions and mechanism to supervise its compliance such as the constitutional court, judicial independence, popular supervision and other watchful organizations in the political system. Any state organ or employee who violates the law has to deal with legal responsibility and has to compensate if any individual interest is damaged. The law not only holds a supreme position in the political realm but also in social life. All non-governmental entities and individuals, although permitted to do what the law does not forbid, are obliged to respect and conform to the law and face legal responsibility should they violate it. The essential domination of the law over the state and society is reflected in Locke's remarks:

"Even though the government holds all the rights, because these rights only live to serve social interest and cannot be used arbitrarily and randomly, they must be implemented through the existing and established acts, so that both sides have their responsibilities and safety within the law and even rulers have to be restricted in an adequate range."[28]

---

[28] Konrad-Adenauer-Stiftung (2002), 166.

Fifth, the state of law is organized and functions based on the separation of powers as a means to check and control power. In other words, the state of law is organized and functions in line with the management of state power. Separation of state power is one of the initial features of the state of law. Its aim is to prevent any centralized state power in the hands of an individual or state organ, so that authoritarianism and power abuse can be minimized while state power is performed. The separation allows for the restraining and management of state power and anticipating the behaviors of the government. In a state of law, state power is basically divided into three branches: legislative, executive and judicial branches. Each function is primarily transferred to a state organ. All these functional organs are established based on the purpose and regulations of the law. The constitution endows each organ with a specific set of rights and regulates the mutual relationship between them. As a result, each state organ is able to not only maintain its independent and specialized activities and prevent and restrain other organs so that state power can be limited and controlled, but can also coordinate with other organs to form unity within the state apparatus. This facilitates the effective performance of each state organ and the entire state apparatus. In the practice of organizing state power, legislative power reflects the popular will through the law and is conferred to a congress or parliament. Executive power, which embodies the power to exercise the will of an entire nation through the practical application of the pieces of legislation, is given to the government. Judicial power, the power to judge unconstitutional and unlawful behaviors and to solve civil disputes that threatens justice, civil freedom and social order and safety, is given to the court. The law provides a firm mechanism that involves these three branches in mutual control and checking while also allowing for coordination among them to avoid the abuse of power, maintain the unity of state power and increase the performance of the state apparatus.

Sixth, the state power is closely associated with civil society. The state of law must be developed on the basis of a close relationship with civil society. In a modern sense, civil society is perceived as a relatively autonomous sector in relation to the state, in which social groups and cultural, religious and spiritual organizations exist and function to serve different human interests.[29] Simply put, civil society is composed of non-state and apolitical organizations, and its

---

[29] Nguyen Duy Quy/Nguyen Tat Vien (2008), 61–62.

existence signifies a social sector that is not necessarily dominated by state power. As a social value, civil society indicates a society's innate ability to allow its citizens to establish their organizations to fulfill the aspirations of their members and realize the general social objectives. As an institution, civil society is considered a social entity that exists among the state, families and individuals.[30] Through legal mechanisms, the state regulates the rights and legal responsibilities of itself, individuals and non-state organizations so as to ensure the existence and functioning of civil society.

The basic features of the state of law are sketched out above. However, depending on each particular state of law, there are other particular and idiosyncratic signs and features. As historical analysis has shown, the idea of the state of law can stem from different socio-economic forms even if it is universally used and results in different interpretations and actualizations depending on social and class interests, national traditions, cultural level and other factors. A prominent division in reality has been the capitalist state of law and socialist state of law. The capitalist state of law is currently developed in most of the developed and developing capitalist nations. The socialist state of law is in the making in Vietnam, a nation that currently advances its society towards socialism. This stems from the fact that although the state of law itself is a universal idea, there is no absolute model for every state and nation. Rather, depending on its historical, political, socio-economic features and level of development, each state or nation develops its own state of law model and opts for a particular method of constructing and running its state of law. However, each particular state of law is supposed to hold universal features and worldwide values of the state of law, and at the same time reflect its particular attributes and the idiosyncrasies of its nation and people. For example, the socialist state of law not only has the said general features but also other particular attributes such as its socialist-based economic relations and its being led by a communist party. In contrast, the capitalist state of law is built on an economic basis formed by capitalist relations of production and is under the leadership of a capitalist party or a coalition of capitalist parties.

---

[30] Nguyen Duy Quy/Nguyen Tat Vien (2008), 62.

34

References

Dao Tri Uc (ed.) (2006): The Organization and Functioning of the Vietnamese Socialist State of Law (Mô hình tổ chức và hoạt động của Nhà nước pháp quyền xã hội chủ nghĩa Việt Nam). Hanoi.

Ellis, William (ed.) (1941): The Politics of Aristotle or A Treatise on Government. London.

Konrad-Adenauer-Stiftung (ed.) (2002): The State of Law. Hanoi.

Lã Trấn Vũ (1964): History of Chinese Political Ideas. Hanoi.

Luu Kien Thanh/Pham Hong Thai (eds.) (1993): History of the World Historical Theories (Lịch sử các học thuyết chính trị trên thế giới). Hanoi.

Nguyen Dang Dung (ed.) (2007): Vietnam National Assembly on the State of Law (Quốc hội Việt Nam trong Nhà nước pháp quyền). Hanoi.

Nguyen Duy Quy/Nguyen Tat Vien (eds.) (2008): The Socialist State of Law of Vietnam of the People, by the People, for the People – Theoretical and Practical issues (Nhà nước pháp quyền xã hội chủ nghĩa Việt Nam của dân, do dân, vì dân-lí luận và thực tiễn). Hanoi.

Nguyen Van Dong (1996): Theories on the State of Law – Historical and Contemporary Issues (Học thuyết về nhà nước pháp quyền-Lịch sử và hiện tại). Journal of Legal studies, issue no 4/1996. 21.

Nguyễn Văn Huyên (1996): Immanuel Kant Philosophy (1724–1804) (Triết học Imanuin Cantơ). Hanoi.

Pham Huy Chiem (ed.) (1971): The Prince by Machiavelli (Vietnamese Translation). Saigon.

Phan Ngoc (ed.) (2001): Han feizi of hanfei. Hanoi.

Montesquieu, Charles-Louis de Secondat de (1996): The Spirit of the Laws. Hanoi.

Thích Mãn Giác (1967): History of Indian philosophy. Saigon.

Truth Publisher (ed.) (1986): Karl Marx/Friedrich Engels. Collected Works. Third Volume (Vietnamese edition). Hanoi.

Vietnam Academy of Social Sciences (1991): The State of Law and Civil Society (Nhà nước pháp quyền và xã hội công dân). Hanoi.

VNU Press (ed.) (2009): The History of Political Theories (Giáo trình Lịch sử các học thuyết chính trị). Hanoi.

Thoughts and Policies on Governing the People under the Ly-Tran and the Early Le Dynasties: Experiences and Historical Lessons

Pham Duc Anh

Among the factors that constitute the power of a political system, popular participation and support always hold an important role. The Vietnamese monarchical political systems are no exception. A study by Vu Minh Gia showed that during the period of the 10th–19th centuries, the presence of decentralized feudalistic states was occasionally seen (most notably during the "disorder of the 12 warlords"), but in general the centralized system was the dominant form of government. This system always rested on three pillars: the economic power of the state, authoritarian sanctions and popular support.

In Vietnam, three forms of centralized systems existed, people-oriented, bureaucratic and authoritarian, which reached their peak corresponding with the Ly-Tran dynasties (11th–13th centuries), Early Le (15th century) and Nguyen dynasty (19th century). The similarity between these is a high degree of centralization, while their difference lies in the various sources from which the above pillars of power stem.[1] Being aware of this fact, after gaining independence from the domination of the Northern aggressors, the self-sufficient courts in Vietnam began to establish and continuously consolidate their centralized institutions, and simultaneously attempted to develop their social underpinnings based on popular support. This resulted from an awareness to ensure the survival of the imperial court and monarchy.

---

[1] Vu Minh Giang (2008), 43–61; Vu Minh Giang (2009), 139.

Within this scope, the article focuses on dissecting the main differences that make up the characteristics of two forms of governance in Vietnam during the 11th–14th centuries and the 15th century, as reflected in the political viewpoints, ideas and policies of each state towards its populace. The Ly and Tran dynasties put a particular emphasis on popular power, the construction of a centralized system based on a harmonious relationship between villages and nation, and the consolidation and support of the populace, all of which forged a prosperous and successful dynasty in every aspect, repeatedly defeating the invaders, and protecting national independence and sovereignty of the country. The Early Le dynasty, although being attentive to the role of the populace, due to its excessive consolidation of a centralized, pro-Confucius system and strengthening of the bureaucratic and legal system, gradually weakened its connection with the populace and lost its support. Two different political worldviews and management approaches led to differences in the relationship between the authorities and the masses, producing completely opposite results. The following presentations somewhat clarify this fact.

The "People-oriented" Ideas and Policies of the Ly and Tran Dynasties

Compared to the political institutions of the governments in the 10th century (Ngo, Dinh and former Le), it is obvious that the Ly and Tran dynasties made fundamental, even contrasting shifts in their viewpoints about the role of the populace, their ideas of governance, and their closeness to the populace and people-centric propensities.

Historical statistics show that the word "populace/people" (dân) was almost absent in various decrees, edicts or proclamations of the emperors prior to the Ly dynasty (1009–1225). Policies such as popular reassurance and consolation were never implemented, although military suppression happened quite frequently in this era. Historical records also prove that no tax exemption and reduction or food relief policies were introduced, although famines, poor harvests, natural disasters and foreign aggressions were quite common. The only amnesty scheme was released in 989, after Le Dai Hanh king changed the name of the era.[2] Normally, the emperors maintained a great distance from the populace. They made few policies to improve the wellbeing of the people, and even showed no outward tendency to get close to them, except for the ploughing (tịch điền) ritual which initially took place in 987 and continued during the former Le dynasty. By establishing a centralized system based on complicated military apparatuses and severe penalties, the Dinh and former Le dynasties set themselves against the majority of the population, heightening existing socio-political conflicts. The introduction of the Ly dynasty (in 1009) was the result of a relatively smooth campaign for political mobilization, receiving the support of various social forces, but was also due to the low popular confidence in former dynasties.

Meanwhile, words such as "populace/people" (dân) or "the under heaven" (thiên hạ)[3] used to refer to the masses, thus reflecting the "people-oriented" ideas and actions of the Ly and Tran dynasties, are regularly embedded in official historical records.

Before shifting the capital to Thang Long, King Ly Cong Uan issued the Edict on the Capital Rearrangement (Thiên đô chiếu). Apart from other notable values, this was the first political document composed by a dynasty which addressed issues pertaining to civil welfare and livelihood. In this edict, the founder of the Ly dynasty emphasized that the capital relocation was "the answer to heaven's imperative above and the people's will below", conveying his wish that "his people were prosperous" and "free from adversity". In addition, the edict was based on the consultation of nationwide mandarins and population. Such heedfulness of an emperor was unprecedented. In response, the the entire population answered: "Your Majesty has made a long-term strategy for the under heaven so as to ensure not only the great success of His royal career but also the prosperity and abundance of the population. No one dares to deny such a favorable deed".[4]

When attempting to form his royal court, Ly Thai To received sincere words from Dao Cam Moc which urged him to "answer heaven's imperative

---

[2] Social Science Publisher (1993a), Complete History of the Great Viet, 226.

[3] In the original Chinese version of Complete History of the Great Viet, the historians under the Later Le dynasty primarily used "dân" (民) and "thiên hạ" (天下) to refer to the population/people.

[4] Social Science Publisher (1993a), Complete History of the Great Viet, 241.

above and the people's will below" and words of wisdom from Monk Van Hanh which told him to "be tolerant and forgiving" to "win the people's hearts" and "direct the whole population".[5] Aside from the Edict on the Capital Rearrangement, the Ly dynasty issued several edicts to ask for straightforward opinions (in 1076, 1392), and edicts to ask for ingenious people (in 1182).

The decrees and edicts compiled by the kings might have retained some remnants of such ideas as "heaven's imperative", "emperor's authority" typical of Chinese Confucianism. On not a few occasions did the Ly kings emphasize their role as "ruler of the population", "superior to the populace", or the Tran kings proclaimed themselves as "father of the people" (dân chi phụ mẫu). Yet these notions were not baseless and dogmatic as the typical Confucian ideas, but were transformed into practical deeds and bore humanistic values. The emphasis on and familiarity with the people was a characteristic ruling philosophy and the essence of these political institutions.

In June lunar 1300, two months before his death, Tran Hung Dao (Tran Quoc Tuan) caught a serious illness. Tran Anh Tong king personally returned to Hung Dao's palace in Van Kiep. On Hung Dao's deathbed, the king sincerely inquired about his health and also asked about his ideas on national defense and protection. Tran Hung Dao summarized his experiences and historical lessons on the national struggle against foreign aggressors, in which he focused on clarifying that the victory of the Tran dynasty over the Yuan-Mongolian army was thanks to "consensus between the king and his servants, harmony between royal family members, and national solidarity". His testament was short yet full of meaning. It was not only a heartfelt and profound product of a senior statesman who had spent more than 70 years of his life serving the imperial court during its most desperate yet epic period; the amalgamation of professional military experiences of a grand general who three times took on the responsibility of leading his people in their national struggle against a foreign invasion; but it was by and large the political idea and guideline of the Tran dynasty. More importantly, Tran Hung Dao released his testament not only at the time when the victories were fading into the past, but also when the popular confidence and support for the imperial court was seemingly diminishing. It was a lesson on winning the popular confidence.

---

[5] Social Science Publisher (1993a), Complete History of the Great Viet, 238.

Table 1: "People-oriented" Policies and Actions of the Ly and Tran Dynasties

	Reign	Familiarity with the people	Popular assurance	Tax reduction, food relief	Amnesty, official pardon	Total
Ly dynasty (1009–1225)						
1.	Thai To (1009–1028)	2	2	4	1	9
2.	Thai Tong (1028–1054)	6	5	4	11	26
3.	Thanh Tong (1054–1072)	1	–	2	2	5
4.	Nhan Tong (1072–1127)	12	–	1	5	18
5.	Than Tong (1128–1138)	1	–	1	5	7
6.	Anh Tong (1138–1175)	2	–	–	2	4
7.	Cao Tong (1176–1210)	1	–	1	2	4
	Total:	25	7	13	28	73
Tran dynasty (1226–1400)						
1.	Thai Tong (1226–1258)	1	–	–	4	5
2.	Thanh Tong (1258–1278)	–	–	–	2	2
3.	Nhan Tong (1279–1293)	–	–	3	5	8
4.	Anh Tong (1293–1314)	–	2	1	2	5
5.	Minh Tong (1314–1329)	3	–	–	1	4
6.	Hien Tong (1329–1341)	–	–	–	2	2
7.	Du Tông (1341–1369)	–	–	5	3	8
8.	Nghe Tong (1370–1372)	1	1	–	1	3
9.	Due Tong (1373–1377)	–	–	–	1	1
10.	Phe de (1377–1388)	–	–	–	1	1
11.	Thuan Tong (1389–1398)	1	–	–	1	2
12.	Thieu De (1398–1400)	–	–	–	1	1
	Total:	6	3	9	24	42

Source: Based on statistics of the author in Complete History of the Great Viet

Indeed, even before Tran Hung Dao gave his advice to "wisely use the energy of the people as a sustainable strategy", the Tran dynasty had been well aware of the principle of "people as a central foundation". Since establishing his imperial court, Tran Thai Tong king was especially fond of the words expressed by monk Truc Lam: "He who is king must take the aspirations of his people as his own and take the heart of his people as his own". Therefore, a golden throne for a king "is nothing more than a rugged pair of shoes which can be disposed of whenever." Later generations of kings were all devoted to the people and respected the entire population. According to history, on an occasion, when the first national struggle against the Yuan-Mongolian army (1258) reached its climax, the king inquired of his people about the situation of the invaders: "Where is the Yuan army?" A fisherman named Hoang Cu Da, a former courtier who was sailing along the Red River, impudently answered: "I don't know, go ask those who eat mangos."[6] Responding to such contempt of Cu Da, the king not only tolerated him but blamed himself for having treated his subordinates unfairly.

Statistics from official records on the policies and actions that reflect the people-oriented governance of the Ly and Tran dynasties (table 1) show that the Ly and Tran kings made the most efforts to get close to their people. With their populist lifestyle, the Ly kings often left their imperial citadel or visited rural areas to watch such activities as fishing, wrestling, cock-fighting, ploughing or harvesting, and even personally engaged in ploughing, etc. There were in total 25 occasions in which the kings made these efforts, 12 of which happened in era of Ly Nhan Tong. Similar behaviors were rare under the previous and following dynasties. Right in the era of Ly Thai To, the king decided to build Long Duc palace (the East palace) outside the Imperial Citadel, wherein the Prince resided. His purpose was to let the one who would inherit his throne live among ordinary people and learn in the process about their life.[7] Tran Thai Tong once said: "I would like to go out to hear the people's voice and assess their opinions, learn about their difficulties".[8] On February lunar 1022, judging that the construction of an artificial mountain would be too difficult for the populace, king Ly Thai To suspended it.[9] In May 1371, King Tran Nghe Tong issued an edict to

"construct the palace in a simple and cost-effective way, and hire only royal family members and mandarins to build it without bothering the people".[10]

---

[6] The story goes: The king once offered mangos to his close servants but forgot about Hoang Cu Da. He then held a grudge against him and thus replied in such way. See Social Science Publisher (1993b), Complete History of the Great Viet, 28–29.

[7] Social Science Publisher (1993a), Complete History of the Great Viet, 243.

[8] Institute of Historical Studies (1981), 316.

[9] Social Science Publisher (1993a), Complete History of the Great Viet, 246.

[10] Social Science Publisher (1993a), Complete History of the Great Viet, 155.

Under the Ly and Tran dynasties, especially the early Ly dynasty and late Tran dynasty, military suppression occurred on a regular basis in many local areas, not to mention the aggressions for territorial expansion into the Champa kingdom in the 11th–14th centuries. However, unlike before, whenever the king launched an expedition, he issued a proclamation[11] clearly laying out his intent to pacify for the sake of peace. On their expedition, the soldiers were forbidden to get involved in robbing or harming the populace. After the campaign, the court made an edict to reassure and comfort the people. For example in 1028, when Ly Thai Tong personally led his army to pacify the Truong Yen Palace (now in Ninh Binh), as soon as he reached his destination, he ordered, "Whoever robs the villagers will be beheaded." The soldiers arduously listened to his order and dared not to transgress. Upon entering the palace, they were met by hundreds of people who paid tribute to them in the form of buffaloes and wine. The king issued a decree to comfort the people, creating a jubilant atmosphere.[12] In a similar vein, after having attacked Hoan district (1031), Ai district (1035), Phat The Citadel (1044), Nghe An (1371), or after having established Thuan and Hoa districts (1307), the Ly and Tran kings sent their emissaries to comfort and console the people.

The Ly and Tran dynasties emphasized the improvement of the population's wellbeing. As statistics show, the Ly dynasty introduced at least 4 tax reduction schemes (for half a year), 3 tax exemption schemes (for 1 to 3 years) and 6 food relief schemes for the poor; while the corresponding numbers of the Tran dynasty were 3, 1 and 5. Tax reduction and exemption and food relief schemes were implemented most frequently under the dynasties of Ly Thai To (4), Ly Thai Tong (4), Tran Nhan Tong (3) and Tran Du Tong (5). These policies were often carried out as soon as the new king ascended his throne or during Buddhist festivals. The king decided to issue tax exemptions not only when the people faced drought, a bad harvest and famine, but also when they achieved a good harvest (as in 1016). When a major cold spell came in 1055, King Ly Thanh Tong told his subordinates that:

"Even in the palace, basking near the fire made of bone char, wearing squirrel fabric, I am still cold, let alone the prisoners down in the dungeon who are miserably bound in

---

[11] For example the proclamation on the expedition to Ma Sa cave (Thảo Ma Sa động hịch), in 1119.

[12] Complete History of the Great Viet (1993a), 251.

42

chains. Whether they are guilty, they are nevertheless hungry, wearing only rugged cloth, being frozen to death, some even dying regretfully. How I pity them. I thereby order the warders to provide them with blankets and two meals a day".[13]

The Tran kings also introduced a new way of distributing relief food by involving the rich in this activity (The Edicts in 1358, 1362). Tolerant legislations clearly reflect the people-oriented guiding principle of the Ly and Tran dynasties. Although it was not regulated by any official document, amnesty was frequently granted and can be considered a consistent policy of these two dynasties. Amnesty was given as soon as the king ascended his throne, changed the name of the era or on the occasion of a Buddhist festival. Statistics show that, except for Ly Hue Tong and Ly Chieu Hoang, the other 7 kings under the Ly dynasty and 12 kings under the Tran dynasty issued at least 1 to 5 decrees (Ly Thai Tong) which provide for amnesty.[14] Contrary to terrifying tiger cages and cauldrons in front of the royal palaces in Hoa Lu capital under the Dinh and former Le dynasties, King Ly Thai Tong (1029) decided to build bell towers along the sidelines of Thien An royal hall (where he gave audiences) and ordered that: "Whenever a citizen would like to complain about a false charge against him, he should ring the bell".[15] Also to make it convenient for the people, in 1052 the king ordered the construction of a big bell at Long Tri palace. These kinds of cases, kings judged directly or handed over to crown princes to solve them. People coming to the royal palace where the kings gave audiences was a practice which only took place under the Ly and Tran dynasties. In a trial, King Thanh Tong pointed to princess Dong Thien next to him and told the warders:

"I devote as much affection to my daughter as I do to my people. I truly pity those who unwittingly commit their crimes, so from now on, let's alleviate their charges whether they are heavy or not".[16]

Brutal punishments imposed in former dynasties were no longer applicable. The trials were conducted justly, transparently and legally. From the Ly dynasty to the Tran dynasty, the "people-oriented" propensity was consistent and

---

[13] Social Science Publisher (1993a), Complete History of the Great Viet, 271.

[14] According to our statistics, the Ly dynasty issued totally 20 grand amnesty schemes in the following years, the Tran dynasty made 20.

[15] Social Science Publisher (1993a), Complete History of the Great Viet, 254.

[16] Social Science Publisher (1993a), Complete history of the Great Viet, 273.

lasting, but there were still a few shifts. It was the transition from a "people-centric, people-based" state under the Ly dynasty to a "people are the origin" state under the Tran dynasty.[17] In particular, since the middle of the 14th century, the increasing influence of Chinese Confucianism and the internal bureaucratization led to significant changes in the ideas and policies of the state.

In commenting and evaluating the "people-oriented" propensity of the Ly and Tran dynasties, historians in the Later Le dynasty argued that it was a rating scale that measures the quality and intellect of an emperor and the progressiveness of a dynasty. Several kings are valorized and remembered in historical records for this quality. In the Complete History of the Great Viet, the Confucian historians speak highly of such qualities as "easing people's energy", "love for the people" (by Ly Thai To), "nurturing the whole population" (Ly Thai Tong), "lenience", "true love for the people" (Ly Thanh Tong), "harmony, compassion and consolidating the people's hearts" (Tran Nhan Tong); so as to create a "wealthy and abundant population", "a peaceful land". Therefore, they are "loved by the people", "followed by the people", "supported by the people", and considered "good kings".

But the Ly and Tran kings are criticized for these very qualities from time to time. Two aspects that are discussed most frequently in the historical comments on the Ly and Tran dynasties are their overemphasis on Buddhism and excessive lenience in legal decisions. Ngo Si Lien commented on the lifting of the death penalty imposed on Grand Preceptor Le Van Thinh by Ly Nhan Tong (in 1096): "A servant (criminal) who murdered his own king is spared capital punishment; that is an error in criminal law, which stems from the king's belief in Buddhism."[18] Or the "(king) who avails of the occasion of a (Buddhist) festival to spare a criminal, does not act rightfully." "Meanwhile a king such as (Ly Nhan Tong) unwisely spares the life of many petty men (...) if all petty men are freed of their guilt by mere luck it is not good news for the gentlemen."[19] What matters here is the perspective. Perhaps the Confucian historians in the Le dynasty failed to acknowledge that the Buddhist tendency is only an outward manifestation of the characteristic ruling principles of Ly and Tran dynasties, which are harmony and "oneness with the people".

---

[17] Nguyen Phan Quang (1995), 194, Phan Dang Thanh 1995, 153.

[18] Social Science Publisher (1993a), Complete History of the Great Viet, 283.

[19] Social Science Publisher (1993a), Complete History of the Great Viet, 302.

Thanks to their practical guidelines and policies, the Ly and Tran dynasties successfully developed a strong unity between their authorities and their population, which acted as a source of power for the cause of national construction and development in every aspect and demonstrated its capacity most vividly during the struggles against foreign invaders for national salvation. Due to the distinctiveness of the political systems under these dynasties, especially under the Ly dynasty, their forms of governance are deemed by some foreign scholars as "not typically centralized enough", and "the political power of the Ly dynasty was based on traditional consensus and the independence of villages."[20] The viewpoints of international scholars are recognized by Vietnamese domestic historians as they reveal the transitional character of Vietnamese political systems during the 11th–14th centuries, which still bore characteristics resembling those of the typical Southeast Asian communal democracies and were insufficiently affected by the Chinese Confucian political model.[21] However, the total denial of a centralized power structure in these eras is not tenable and requires further investigation.[22]

Confucianism, Bureaucracy and Civil Policies of the Early Le Dynasty

The introduction of the Le dynasty (in 1428) was the result of a great war for national salvation, of the efforts and contributions of all the masses. More than anyone, the Le kings were deeply aware of the role of the people's confidence. Therefore, popular confidence is always regarded as a great strength and a constitutive element that helps to maintain the State's power. The Le dynasty is also one the most politically influential and prestigious eras for the population.

The viewpoints and guidelines of the Early Le dynasty (1428–1527) and their implementation were essentially people-oriented. Many policies were created to win the hearts of the people and improve every aspect of their life. This is reflected in our collected statistics (table 2). The Le kings, especially the five early ones (from the reign of Thai To to Hien Tong) released a large number of decrees and edicts (now commonly referred to as edicts) related to

---

[20] Taylor (1990), 139.

[21] Polyakov (1996); Momoki Shiro (2011).

[22] See Pham Duc Anh (2011).

the people. Among them at least 27 edicts were issued by Le Thanh Tong. In terms of the average number of edicts per year, King Thai Tong (1434–1442) produced 16 edicts within 8 years, which was the highest number (approximately 2 edicts annually). More importantly, this period was when the Le dynasty was in turbulence. It strived to strengthen its authority while at the same time seeking to secure a foothold among the people. Since the beginning of the 16th century (after the period of Le Hien Tong), previous constructive policies of the state towards its people had almost ceased.

Table 2: The Policies towards the People of the Early Le Dynasty

No.	Reign	Self-corrective and disciplining edicts	Tax reduction-food relief	Amnesty-Official pardon	Total
1.	Thai To (1428–1433)	2	2	3	7
2.	Thai Tong (1434–1442)	7	3	6	16
3.	Nhan Tong (1443–1459)	9	3	4	16
4.	Thanh Tong (1460–1497)	10	5	12	27
5.	Hien Tong (1498–1504)	4	1	3	8
6.	Tuc Tong (1504)	–	–	1	1
7.	Uy Muc (1505–1509)	–	–	1	1
8.	Tuong Duc (1510–1516)	–	–	2	2
9.	Chieu Tong (1516–1522)	–	–	3	3
10.	Cung Hoang (1522–1527)	1	–	2	3
Total:		33	14	37	84

Source: Based on statistics of the author in Complete History of the Great Viet

The civil policies established by the Early Le dynasty primarily focused on the practical demands such as tax exemption and reduction, food relief distribution for the poor and amnesty and official pardon. In April 1428, the state introduced two important policies: removing all taxes previously imposed on land plots, gold and silver, lagoons, berry plantations and reducing taxes imposed on the "locations plundered by invaders" (the Ming army).[23]

---

[23] Social Science Publisher (1993b), Complete History of the Great Viet, 239.

Later, tax exemption and reduction schemes were regularly set up as soon as a new king ascended the throne, especially when famine and bad harvests occurred. Apart from the general keywords such as "nationwide amnesty", "tax exemption", "tax cutback" or "tax reduction", official historical records also kept in-depth statistics on the tax reduction policies, including both land and head taxes, introduced by the imperial court. Accordingly, farmers who owned berry plantations in the army were granted 5 sào (1.800m^2) of cultivable lands and ordinary farmers were given 4 sào (1.440m^2) of berry farms to ensure their livelihood and were exempted from tax for their whole life. Male and female widows were provided with 3 sào (1.080m^2) of land and exempted from tax.[24] On 1488, the king issued an edict:

"From now on, the scholars who have been educated, know how to write, have good conduct, passed their exam or were exempted from it will be freed from half of the amount of tax and corvée."[25]

By 1501, the state had regularized the duration of corvée and the amount of head tax. The handicapped that were unable to work were exempted from both corvée and head tax, while those that could earn a livelihood were exempted from half of the amount of their head tax.[26] The food relief policy was maintained on a regular basis, especially when famine happened. Besides, in this era the state itself allowed its people to borrow paddy which had to be paid back when they successfully harvested their rice (the edicts issued in 1437, 1448, and 1497).[27]

The above statistics show that the decisions to provide for a "grand" amnesty and "amnesty" for the prisoners were frequently mentioned in official historical records, in which the density of these decisions was even higher than those during the Ly and Tran dynasties (37 decisions in total). In particular, under the Le Thanh Tong reign, at least 12 decisions were recorded. These decisions were made on such occasions as the coronation of a king and the changes of an era name, but unlike before no decision was made when natural disasters happened, and fewer decisions were made at the same time as the Buddhist festi-

---

[24] Social Science Publisher (1993b), Complete History of the Great Viet, 331.

[25] Social Science Publisher (1993b), Complete History of the Great Viet, 504.

[26] Social Science Publisher (1993c), Complete History of the Great Viet, 27.

[27] Social Science Publisher (1993b), Complete History of the Great Viet, 347, 362, 523.

vals.[28] The number of prisoners benefiting from each amnesty decision often amounted to a few hundreds.[29] As for the unsolved cases, the kings issued many edicts that provided for commutation and even acquittal.[30] It should be further noted that "grand" amnesties were maintained until the beginning of the 16th century. Subsequently, the policy possibly only retained a ceremonial significance and primarily served as a tool to legitimize the king's throne.

However, the ideas of the Early Le dynasties for their population and their practical manifestations were different from those held by the Ly and Tran dynasties. The differences are as follows.

The king "received his heavenly imperative" that asked him to care for and rule over the whole population. On the other hand, the root of royal power originates from within the people. In The Royal Poem about the way of the king (Ngự chế quân đạo thi), Le Thanh Tong stated that the "way of a king" is to "devote his love to the people and his respect to heaven." Or in an edict, it was declared that "A king is made by heaven to care for his people, and thus he is supposed to answer heaven's imperative by loving his people".[31] A Le king "cannot sleep well for he worries for his people/He dares not to postpone a task bestowed by heaven" (Personal statement-Tự thuật), and always wishes that "everyone lives in abundance and tranquillity towards a prosperous nation."[32] A devoted king first and foremost "creates a role model by improving his ethical conduct and improves agricultural productivity to ensure the people's livelihood."[33]

The masses and ordinary citizens therefore were responsible for honoring the king and adhering to his orders. It should be noted that the first edict given by the Le dynasty (dated January 1428)

---

[28] Except for one occasion in which Le Thanh Tong offer amnesty to 50 prisoners during the Vu lan Buddhist festival. Social Science Publisher (1993b), Complete History of the Great Viet, 318.

[29] In 1434, 225 prisoners were granted amnesty on one occasion. See Social Science Publisher (1993b), Complete History of the Great Viet, 315.

[30] Social Science Publisher (1993b), Complete History of the Great Viet, 362, 402.

[31] Social Science Publisher (1993c), Complete History of the Great Viet, 98.

[32] Social Science Publisher (1993b), Complete History of the Great Viet, 412.

[33] Social Science Publisher (1993b), Complete History of the Great Viet, 497.

48

"orders the ministries (...) to establish legislations to govern the army and the people, so that commanders know how to manage their army, officials at localities know how to govern their people, and the nation as a whole knows that the laws exist." Because "chaos will ensue if there are no laws", "the laws are established so that (...) the whole population knows what are good and bad behaviors. They should advocate good conduct while avoiding mischiefs and violating the laws."[34] A year after his coronation, in March 1461, Le Thanh Tong issued a decree: "In farming (...) every citizen should devote himself to increasing his livelihood and ensuring his basic needs, without resorting to shortcuts, petty businesses or hooliganism. Whoever owns lands but displays sluggishness will be given due punishment by the authorities."[35]

The mandarins– parents of the people – were required to love and care for the people as much as possible. Le Thai Tong once issued a decree: "To be a servant essentially requires two conditions. He must be respectful to his king and affectionate towards his people. With full loyalty he loves his king; with genuine faithfulness he loves his people."[36] On another occasion Le Nhan Tong propagated: "The mandarins, who are currently in service must motivate their people to work hard and conduct fair trials. In combating theft they must be resolute and shun irresponsibility and idleness."[37] Three requirements were introduced into the examination system for mandarins at local areas under the Le Thanh Tong dynasty: 1. they had to love their people, 2. they had to earn popular trust and affection, 3. they had to prevent the people from abandoning their local areas.[38] As for mandarins in remote and bordering areas, whoever "knows how to nurture his people and peacefully govern them while still managing to collect enough taxes, within 6 years, will be transferred to a better position", and if he failed, he would have to wait 6 years until re-examination.[39] In 1498, Le Hien Tong announced a decree: "(The mandarins) who abuse their power and are haughty to the people, who pursue their own

---

[34] Social Science Publisher (1993b), Complete History of the Great Viet, 291.

[35] Social Science Publisher (1993b), Complete History of the Great Viet, 393.

[36] Social Science Publisher (1993b), Complete History of the Great Viet, 310.

[37] Social Science Publisher (1993b), Complete History of the Great Viet, 381.

[38] Social Science Publisher (1993b), Complete History of the Great Viet, 447.

[39] Social Science Publisher (1993b), Complete History of the Great Viet, 433.

interests at the expense of people's wellbeing, whether they are caught red handed or not (...) shall be categorized as unqualified."[40]

Therefore, whenever political disorder or a natural disaster happened or the people suffered from bad harvests, the kings issued an edict in which he blamed himself and disciplined his servants (see table 2 above). He repeatedly questioned his conscience in the edicts:

"Am I possibly not devoted enough to receive heaven's blessing, or so insufficiently committed to the cause of my ancestors, so inadequately accommodating to the population that I end up in this situation? Am I so incapable of utilizing talented people or my servants are so incompetent that I end up being like this? Is it because bribery has become so widespread and concubines have abused their power so much that I end up in this situation? Or is it because I have mishandled public properties through overspending and extravagance? Or is it because the generals and vassals do not care about their people and have sunk into corrupting habits? Or because the generals at different levels only care about possessions without regard for their duty as public servants?"[41]

The nature of the relationship between the State and its population changed, mostly due to changes in the former. The main causes are the influence of Confucian ideology and the resulting bureaucratization and administratization within the political system.

For one thing, Confucianism absolutized the role and power of the king. Within the Eastern and Vietnamese monarchies, the emperor/king holds enormous authority. The king is the originator of the law. Every imperative from the king in the form of a decree or an edict has the highest legal value. The laws are compiled and distributed primarily according to the will of the king and first and foremost serve his rights. Only the king is permitted to amend or dispense the laws. The "king's order" itself is "national laws". The king is also head of the national administrative system, who directly leads the government. The king holds supreme rights in the appointment, evaluation or punishment of the entire system of mandarins. As far as private law is concerned, the king is held as the supreme judge, who makes the decisive judgments in all kinds of legal cases and unitarily changes the (even already made) rulings or offers amnesty. The emperor as well as everything that belongs to him is sacred and inviolable. Legislations made by the Le dynasty prohibited

[40] Social Science Publisher (1993c), Complete History of the Great Viet, 12.

[41] Social Science Publisher (1993b), Complete History of the Great Viet, 370.

50

any idea and action that might have damaged the emperor's reputation and status. Such crimes as profanity, blasphemy or sedition, and mutiny were deemed serious deserving the highest charges. Through different administrative layers, the emperor maintained his authority and deeply intervened into every segment from the political, socio-economic, and ideological to the cultural sector. [42]

The era when "As brothers, people from the four corners of the nation joined one another to hoist the bamboo flags/Soldiers of all ranks like fathers and sons drank mixed drinks from river water" (Proclamation of victory/ Bình Ngô đại cáo) began to recede into the past. Of the same fate was the image of 10 arduous years struggling against the Ming army when

"Upon entering the palace, the king and his army were met by hundreds of people who paid tribute to them in the form of buffaloes and wine (...) As the local people crowded the palace as if they had been going to public fairs, the king issued a decree to comfort them, creating a jubilant atmosphere." Instead, to take just one example: As soon as the king's envoy entered Lam Kinh (Thanh Hoa), the men and women started to perform rí ren singing at the gateway. In this custom, men and women formed two opposite lines and started singing, and occasionally they hooked their legs and necks together in the shape of flowers, which looked very ugly nevertheless. Counsellor Dong Hanh Phat told Field Marshal (Trinh) Kha that: "This is an irreverent custom, which aims to satirize the king's envoy". The custom was immediately banned by Kha."[43]

And the paradox showed itself. The more it claimed to care for the people and take them under its protection, the more the imperial court became bureaucratized and distant from them. Nguyen Trai's earlier sincere advice and also a warning: "May his Majesty care for his people so that no complaint can be heard at any commune or village" came to light.

From the court's viewpoint, the king's edicts revealed that power abuse and haughtiness and the oppression of the people became more and more persis-

---

[42] In the Criminal Codes of the National Imperial Court (Quốc triều hình luật), especially in the two chapters Protection of the imperial palace (Vệ cấm) and Forbidden behaviors (Vi chế) there are dozens of stipulations directly related to the king venerated and revered position (see stipulations 51, 52, 57, 63, 110, 111, 122, 123, 125, 127, 132).

[43] Social Science Publisher (1993b), Complete History of the Great Viet, 358–359.

tent.[44] From the people's perspective, though little was mentioned by historical records, in reality: "The people made complaints after complaints", "the people were distressed by delays in the legal procedures" (1465), "the people showed great resentment" (1481), "the people dared not to make any suspicious move" (1509), "the people became desperate due to magnified taxes and fees" (1522).

Though being quickly anticipated, bureaucratization and disconnection with the people not only persisted but increasingly became intensified. Such was a natural consequence and a side effect, or a "sickness" or "social evil" that originated from the very administrative system of this dynasty.

Some Concluding Remarks

State apparatuses under the Ly-Tran dynasties (11th–14th centuries) were established as soon as national independence had been firmly secured, resulting from the objective demands for centralized authority, territorial integrity and the adaptation of foreign ruling models. A prominent trait underpinning the

---

[44] This situation is reflected in the royal edicts (in the Complete History of the Great Viet). In 1429: "I (…) assign you (the officials) with important military and civil tasks. Yet you only sit idly and disregard your tasks, disappointing the trust put on you by the imperial court, and being apathetic towards your soldiers and people". In 1435: "Many officials ignore the royal regulations. Those in charge of the national treasury and imperial documents are ineffective or haughty, and willfully delay their decisions with regard to tax collection or exemption, causing distress for the people. Those in charge of military services have no compassion for the people as they borrow items from the people without showing proper care to them, blaming them for the broken or lost items that are otherwise useful. Those in charge of civil services only care for their self interest while ignoring the people, excuse the rich while arresting the poor, buy expensive limber to build houses, make unfair judgments, cause inner divisions, feed on bribery, show slackness while being gluttonous." In 1471: "Those of you, who are responsible for an entire area, have to dutifully take care of your people. (Yet) you are willfully ignorant of your humanistic task granted by the court which is to care for the people, and only show interest in such minor businesses as disciplining the people or arranging records." In 1481: "(Mandarins) dispose of their responsibilities, ignore the people's hardships, and sit lazily without devising any policy, thus leaving the people deprived."

political institution of these dynasties is the reliance of state power on popular support and on the harmonious and tight relationship between villages and nation. On the other hand, "people-oriented" had always been the crucial tenet of these reigns, which was actualized in their policies. These positive ruling ideas and policies constituted strong socio-political structures and firm political institutions, which helped the Ly and Tran dynasties persevere for four centuries and became the main reason why these dynasties were "celebrated for their civilization" and successfully united their military and civil policies as well as repeatedly defeated the invaders, protecting the national independence and sovereignty of the country. Under the Ly and Tran dynasties, the strength of the whole people was highly promoted because the interests of the monarchy were always tied to national sovereignty and the rights of citizens.

In establishing its monarchy after having emerged victorious from a great war for national liberation, which was achieved with the pains and blood of countless people, the Le dynasty became all the more aware of the profound lesson about the power of popular support. Also thanks to leading all the people to defeat the Ming army and regaining national independence, the Le dynasty had huge political prestige with its population. This allowed the Le reign to consolidate and strengthen the centralized institutions which brought no little success for the country. However, the Early Le dynasty only lasted for a century (1428–1527) and the heyday of centralized monarchical institutions actually only lasted about three decades under the reign of the talented king, Le Thanh Tong (1460–1497). Political institutions and the state apparatus of the Early Le dynasty revealed themselves as very restrictive and inadequate. More importantly, those institutions were not built on a solid social foundation. By prioritizing the consolidation of its centralized, pro-Confucius system and overly focusing on the development of its bureaucratic and legal system, the Early Le dynasty slowly disintegrated the strong cohesion between villages and nation and lost its credibility among the people. It was the consequence, the flipside or the cost incurred by a centralized and bureaucratic governance system.

Under centralized monarchies, there is almost no possibility of creating a democratic or egalitarian system. However, the fact remains that the Ly, Tran, Le and other Vietnamese feudal dynasties put a strong emphasis on the population and on constructing their foothold based on the confidence, backing and support of the people. It is basically a survival aspect of their sovereignty and system. The idea of "people as a central foundation", although changing in terms of its contents and outward manifestation, nevertheless retains an ever-lasting value. In other words, that is traditional political thought and a legacy of Vietnam. Since the construction of the Revolutionary government (in 1945), especially from Innovation (Đổi mới, 1986) to nowadays, "taking the people as the basis" as well as "promoting the people's self-mastery" has become a guiding principle and motto of the Vietnamese government – a government of, by and for the people. However, in view of the achievements and the challenges that lie ahead, especially in the context of the strong development of a market economy and international integration, Vietnam's government needs to seriously evaluate experiences and historical lessons. So the Vietnamese state must today represent the rights and interests of the people and highly promote the people's sovereignty. The basis of the rule of law is the establishment of a democracy which recognizes and ensures the implementation of the people's power in the most profound and intrinsic way.[45] By this, Vietnam could continue to promote the precious values and traditions of its nation as well as set up an important social platform for reforming and perfecting the political system and state apparatus of today.

References

Dao Tri Uc (2007): Model of Organization and Operation of the Rule of Law in Vietnam (Mô hình tổ chức và hoạt động của Nhà nước pháp quyền xã hội chủ nghĩa Việt Nam). Hanoi.

Institute of Historical Studies (ed.) (1981): Studying Society in Vietnam under the Ly and Tran Periods (Tìm hiểu xã hội Việt Nam thời Lý-Trần). Hanoi.

Momoki Shiro (2011): The Process of Formation and Transformation of the Great Viet State under the Feudal Period. Osaka.

Nguyen Phan Quang (ed.) (1995): Some Issues on the Management of the State and Strengthen the Rule of Law in Vietnamese History (Mấy vấn đề về quản lý đất nước và củng cố pháp quyền trong lịch sử Việt Nam). Hanoi.

---

[45] Dao Tri Uc (2007), 233.

Pham Duc Anh (2011): On the Nature of Centralized Political Institutions under Ly Dynasty (1009–1225) (Về tính chất tập quyền trong thiết chế chính trị triều Lý (1009–1225). In: Journal of Historical Studies, 10 (426). 7–22.

Phan Dang Thanh (ed.) (1995): History of Political Institutions and the Rule of Law in Vietnam (Vol.1) (Lịch sử các định chế chính trị và pháp quyền Việt Nam) (Tập 1). Hanoi.

Polyakov, A. B. (1996): The Restoration of the Great Viet State in the 10th to 15th Centuries (Sự phục hưng của nước Đại Việt thế kỷ X–XV). Hanoi.

Social Science Publisher (ed.) (1993a): Complete History of the Great Viet (Vol. 1) (Đại Việt sử ký toàn thư). Hanoi.

Social Science Publisher (ed.) (1993b): Complete History of the Great Viet (Vol. 2) (Đại Việt sử ký toàn thư). Hanoi.

Social Science Publisher (ed.) (1993c): Complete History of the Great Viet (Vol. 4) (Đại Việt sử ký toàn thư). Hanoi.

Taylor, K. W. (1990): Authority and Legitimacy in 11th Century Vietnam. In: Marr, David/Milner, A. C. (eds.): Southeast Asia in the 9th–14th Century. Singapore. 139–170.

The Justice Publisher (ed.) (1991): Criminal Codes of the National Imperial Court (Quốc triều hình luật). Hanoi.

Vu Minh Giang (2008): The Basic Characteristics of the Management Apparatus and Political System in Vietnam Before the Innovation Period (Những đặc trưng cơ bản của bộ máy quản lý đất nước và hệ thống chính trị nước ta trước thời kỳ đổi mới). Hanoi.

Vu Minh Giang (2009): Vietnamese History: Tradition and Modernity (Lịch sử Việt Nam truyền thống và hiện đại). Hanoi.

Some Signs of a State of Law in Vietnam in the Monarchical Time

Vu Thi Phung

Introduction

In recent years, researchers and managers have had long-running discussions about the issue of a state of law in Vietnam. Some argue that a state of law has never existed in Vietnam, thus one has to be built. Others hold that in Vietnam there has been a state of law already, but one that has not been fully developed. There is also an extreme opinion that "state of law" is an ideal model that only few countries can achieve, and therefore the fact that there is no state of law, or only an imperfect one, in Vietnam is understandable. In the academic debate on the history of states and laws in Vietnam, researchers have regularly discussed whether a state of law has ever existed in Vietnam. In this paper, on the basis of available sources, we would like to contribute some thoughts on the above issue. Due to the scarcity of materials, the scope of our study is limited to the monarchical period (from the 10th century to the mid-19th century). To help clarify the issue, we propose three basic questions based on the available literature and theoretical debates about state of law:

- During the monarchical time in Vietnam, did Vietnamese states recognise the importance of the law and did they actually compile and promulgate laws? How were laws established in this period?
- If Vietnamese states did pay attention to the law, how did laws in the monarchical time regulate the relationship between the state and citizens, and the issue of human rights?
- How were laws implemented in reality?

The Awareness of Monarchical States of the Law

Our research results show that, during Vietnam's feudal era, states already recognised the role of laws in governing and managing the country. Building on available materials, researchers today agree that before the Ly dynasty, in Vietnam there were no written laws, and laws only existed in the forms of conventions and customs. From the Ly dynasty onwards, one of the most important progresses of this time was that leaders of dynasties realized that in order to maintain social stability and order, to make people observe laws and regulations, and to punish those who violated the law, there had to be written laws. Therefore, monarchical states made several achievements in the field of legislation, especially in issuing written laws. First of all was Ly dynasty's Royal Code (Bo luat Hinh thu) (1042) and then Tran dynasty's Royal Code (Bo luat Hinh thu) (1341), Le dynasty's Royal Penal Code (Quoc trieu hinh luat) (also called Hong Duc Code – 1483), Nguyen dynasty's Hoang Viet Code (also called Gia Long Code – 1815) and thousands of legal documents in the forms of royal proclamations, decrees, ordinances, edicts, etc. The reason for the issuance of the Royal Code by the Ly dynasty was mentioned in Dai viet Su ky toan thu (Complete Annals of Dai Viet):

"Previously, the legal procedures for suing and trial in our country were complicated; the officials responsible for legal matters were too finicky about rules and too rigid and harsh in the implementation of laws to the extent that many people were mistreated and became victim of injustice. The king felt pity for them, thus he ordered the Head of the Cabinet office to adjust laws to keep up with the situation, to divide laws into sections and specific regulations and combine them all in a single text, the Royal Code, which is intelligible to everyone."[1]

The materials show that the Ly dynasty's emperors realized the necessity to have written laws in order for the people to know how to adjust behaviours, for the state to have the means to investigate and supervise officials. In the context of a period 1000 years ago, these thoughts on the importance of issuing written laws, as a basis for the enforcement of laws, was an important progress in legal thinking. Inheriting the above thoughts, succeeding dynasties highly valued and appreciated the role of laws. In 1428, when giving order to officials to compile laws to promulgate, Le Thai To points out clearly that:

---

[1] Social Sciences Publisher (1998), Dai Viet su ky toan thu, 263.

"from the past to present, the governing of the country has always relied on laws, or else the society has been in chaos. Therefore, we follow our precedents to issue laws to tell commanders, officials and the people what is right and wrong, what to do and what to avoid so as they will not violate the law."[2]

By the time of the Nguyen dynasty, in the preface of Hoang Viet Code, King Gia Long wrote:

"Everyone living in the society has infinite desires, and without laws to prevent their illegal conducts, it will be impossible to educate them so that they understand ethics. Therefore, as our ancestors have said, laws are the critical tools for good governance."[3]

In order for the code to be effectively implemented, King Gia Long stated that:

"Authorized officials have to follow these rules and consider them the guiding model about laws."[4]

These statements and declarations of Vietnamese emperors, the heads of state (as recorded by state historians in ancient historical works) show that laws had a certain role in Vietnamese society during the monarchical time. This was demonstrated through the fact that monarchical states compiled and issued many written codes and several other legal documents. However, another issue that needs to be taken into consideration is how monarchical states organized the compilation of laws. Based on the records in Dai Viet su ky toan thu, the compilation and issuance of Ly dynasty's Royal Code is described as follows:

"The king felt pity for them (those who suffered injustice), thus he ordered the Head of the Cabinet office to adjust laws to keep up with the situation, to divide laws into sections and specific regulations and combine them all in a single text, the Royal Code."[5]

The position of the Head of the Cabinet Office (Trung Thu) mentioned above might refer to the head of the organization that managed the entire adminis-trative matters of the court.[6]

---

[2] Social Sciences Publisher (1998), Dai Viet su ky toan thu, 263.

[3] Culture-Information Publisher (1994), Hoang viet luat le, 1, 3.

[4] Culture-Information Publisher (1994), Hoang viet luat le, 1, 3.

[5] Social Sciences Publisher (1998), Dai Viet su ky toan thu, 263.

[6] In the Nguyen and Ming dynasties (China), Trung Thu was a position that played an important role in the royal court, also referred to as the prime minister.

Also according to historical records, many basic legal documents of the Le dynasty stated clearly the name of law-drafting officials (for example: the Legal Code complied by Nguyen Trai (1440–1442); Royal Laws and Orders compiled by Phan Phu Tien (1440–1442); Thien Nam du ha tap compiled by Than Nhan Trung, Quach Dinh Bao, Do Nhuan, Dao Cu and Dam Van Le (1483). Only Hong Duc Code (during Le Thanh Tong's reign) did not state the name of law-drafting officials because this code was compiled based on legal regulations issued by previous kings. Hoang Viet Code (Nguyen dynasty) was compiled by Northern Citadel Governor Nguyen Van Thanh.

It can be seen that most monarchical states assigned the compilation of laws to officials holding important positions. These were knowledgeable and gifted people, thus they were entrusted with important duties by kings. However, based on the above documents, we did not find any record reflecting that ordinary people were involved in the compilation of laws at the time, nor did we find any materials about drafts of laws being sent to those affected by the laws for review and feedback. Therefore, it can be concluded that, laws in the monarchical time were mostly compiled by court officials following orders from kings, who were also the final reviewers of drafts of laws and the ones that gave approval for the laws to be promulgated. There was no involvement of the people in this process. Thus one question is whether this method of law-making was democratic and objective.

Some Notable Regulations in Laws in the Monarchical Time

An examination of the contents of laws in the monarchical time (in general codes and specific legal documents) shows that scales and types of issues governed and mentioned in these laws were massive, diverse and complex. For convenience, we would like to summarize the contents of legal normative regulations in the monarchical period based on the following issues.

Firstly, based on the current method of classification, the contents of laws in the monarchical time governed social relationships in fundamental legal fields namely: Administrative law, Criminal law, Civil law, and Marriage and Family law, Prosecution law. For example: both Quoc Trieu hinh luat (the Hong Duc laws-Le dynasty) and Hoang viet Luat le (The Gia Long laws – Nguyen dynasty) had regulations on the organization of state agencies and

officials' duties; types of crime, types of punishment and principles to determine crimes and sanctions; rights of ownership of land and property; rights of
inheritance; marriage and divorce, relationships between family members;
procedures and order of investigation processes, and rules about detaining and
interrogating, etc.[7]

Secondly, laws in the monarchical time also specified the power of the king,
the authorities and responsibilities of officials and the duties of the people. For
example: Among crimes, the ones considered most serious by monarchical
states were the Ten Crimes,[8] including ten most serious crimes that violated
the king's power, the existence and rule of the feudal state, the survival of the
nation, and the most important social relationships according to Confucian
ideals at the time (king-subject, father-child, husband-wife). Criminals were
sentenced to the toughest punishment (death). Even if they were among the
"Eight Cases of Remission", they were not granted remission and they could
not compensate for their crimes by money. In the chapter "Royal Guards", the
laws ruled that behaviors violating the royal citadel and palaces; violating the
king's life and property; violating national security and border (for example:
people without authorization were not allowed to be inside the royal palace out
of official working hours; not allowed to tease others, to be arrogant or to spontaneously talk to imperial maids; not allowed to sell territory and land to foreigners; not allowed to reveal national secrets, etc.). Those committing these
crimes were often sentenced to high punishments (penal servitude, banishment, and execution). Officials would be severely punished if they committed
crimes such as: taking bribes, contravening the king's orders intentionally,

---

[7] For particular regulations, see Vu Thi Phung (1990): History of Vietnamese States
and Laws. Reprinted 1993, 1998, 2003, 2008. Hanoi.

[8] Ten Crimes includes: Mưu phản (high treason, attempt to overthrow the sovereign
or harm the country and society); Mưu đại nghịch (destroy royal shrines, temples
and palaces); Mưu bạn (betrayal and cooperation with the enemy); Ác nghịch (kill
grandparents, parents and relatives); Bất đạo (kill many people at the same time),
Đại bất kính (steal ritual items in shrines and royal tombs, fake royal seals and do
harm to the king's health and prestige), Bất hiếu (denounce, insult grandparents and
parents, or refuse to mourn deceased grandparents and parents); Bất mục (kill relatives, wives beating or denouncing husbands); Bất nghĩa (ordinary people killing officials, students killing teachers) and Nội loạn (have sexual intercourse with relatives
and concubines of father and grandfather).

being irresponsible at work, using power to harass people, etc. (punishments for these crimes ranged from whipping, caning, to death depending on the seriousness of the crimes committed). As for the ordinary people, the crimes to be punished included: robbery; murder; fighting with and injuring others; insulting and calumniating others; cheating and faking papers, royal seals and job titles for personal benefit; adultery, rape; disseminating false rumors, engaging in superstitious activities, etc.

Thirdly, containing detailed and specific regulations covering many fields, laws during the monarchical era basically and firstly served the purpose of securing the power of the feudal state. Regulations in laws as well as in other documents focused on protecting the absolute ruling power of the feudal landlord class, of which the king was the highest representative (thus all behaviors violating the power, life and honor of the king were always sentenced to the most severe punishments). Laws also focused on safeguarding the privileges of the king and the royal family; of officials, patricians and the landlord class (politically and economically). Laws also protected the foundations for the state to exist and develop, including: the ideological foundation (mainly Confucianism); the economic foundation (laws protected the right of the state as the supreme owner of land and the only entity with the right to collect taxes; protected the private ownership of land and property, especially the private ownership of the landlord class; protected the means of production and the supply of labor); the social foundation (laws protected class order, the interests of upper classes and the inequality inside and outside the family). For example: both Hong Duc code and Gia Long code had regulations about the "Eight Cases of Remission".[9] According to this regulation, when people included in this system committed serious crimes (except for the Ten Crimes), judges could only identify their crimes and proposed their punishments to the king to decide; if the punishment was from banishment downwards, it would be decreased by one level. Besides, laws also specified the remission of the punishment of descendants of people with great contributions to the country, or wives of man-

---

[9] Eight Cases of Remission include: close relatives of the King and the Queen, the Queen mother (nghi than); people who serve the king for a long time or those who served previous kings (nghi co); people of great morality (nghi hien); people with great talent (nghi nang); people with great contributions to the country (nghi cong); officials from third rank upwards (nghi quy); industrious officials (nghi can); previous kings' descendants (nghi tan).

darins based on their husbands' official position, etc. Among the people who could redeem their guilt by money were relatives of the king and the queen.

Fourthly, although focusing on safeguarding privileges of the king, aristocrats and officials, laws in the monarchical era still had regulations about the rights of ordinary people. For example: Among the subjects that were granted privileges and allowed to redeem guilt by money, old people above 90 and children under 7 were cleared of charges even if they committed crimes that would lead to death sentence; old people above 70, children under 15 and disabled people were granted privileges and considered for less severe punishments. Laws also had regulations on the grant of exemption from legal proceedings or remission to people who committed minor crimes but had given themselves up; on the reward for people denouncing crimes or punishments for people covering up for criminals. There are some regulations that prevented officials and village nobles from exploiting and harassing the people. Especially, to a certain extent, Quoc trieu hinh luat had some regulations to protect women's rights (to inherit, to propose for divorce) and ethnic minorities (to deal with disputes in their communities based on their own laws, to use their own languages in trials), etc.

About Disseminating and Implementing Laws in the Monarchical Era

Disseminating Laws

In order for laws to be implemented, the most important issue is to disseminate and communicate the contents of laws to officials, who would implement laws, and the people. However, in feudal societies, this was not a simple task because at that time there was not the possibility to print and make copies of laws like today; and only a small proportion of the population was literate. In order to disseminate laws, feudal states applied the following methods:

Firstly, after issuing important legal documents, the state appointed court officials to make (by hand) three copies of any document (Giap copy, At copy, Binh copy).[10] Giap copy (also called the original copy) was stored at the king's

---

[10] Therefore, in Vietnam there is an idiom, "After three copies are made, the original will be lost" to indicate that in the past, it was impossible to avoid mistakes when copying documents.

archives; At copy (copied from the original) was sent to and stored at the relevant department (the central organization responsible for the implementation and monitoring of the implementation of that law); Binh copy (also a copy of the original) was sent to local regions to implement. However, that process of copying documents cost a lot of time and effort, and could not guarantee absolute accuracy in comparison with the original document. Therefore, laws disseminated in this way only reached a small portion of officials. In order to solve this problem, later dynasties (especially the Nguyen dynasty) engraved important documents on wood (so called wood blocks) then used the wood blocks to print on paper. This method also cost great efforts to engrave Sino scripts on wood blocks (each block was equivalent to a page). The advantage, however, was that the document could be printed into many copies and the accuracy could be guaranteed.[11]

Secondly, as for the ordinary people, in the situation that many people were illiterate, feudal governments also had some methods to disseminate laws which were quite effective and appropriate. Ancient historical works recorded methods to copy the king's orders or some particular regulations of the state and local government. These copied would then be put on public display at crowded places. When seeing those announcements, people usually gathered, literate people read and explained to illiterate ones, then they discussed with each other to clearly understand the regulations and to observe them willingly. However, this method had a limitation: the law in question could not reach all citizens because not everyone came to crowded places and when they listened to explanations, each person understood them in a different way. Therefore, in order to solve the above problem, feudal governments used the method of orally disseminating laws through "village criers".[12] However, this method made Vietnamese people passive in studying laws, which forced the government to "bring" laws to their home because they thought "no announcements, no wor-

---

[11] At the moment, the National Archives IV in Da Lat have stored thousands of wood blocks of this kind, including the important wood block collection used to print Hoang Viet code of the Nguyen dynasty.

[12] A village crier was a special civil servant serving village officials especially in the Northern delta region. Besides handling trivial chores such as making tea, cleaning the communal house, laying mats, carrying trays, when village officials gathered for discussion, the village crier had the duty to go to everyone's home to announce regulations of the central or local government for the people to know and implement.

ries". That mentality and habit have posed a difficulty to the disseminating, communicating and implementing of laws amongst a large part of the population nowadays.

Implementing Laws

As mentioned above, although feudal states used many methods to disseminate laws, the implementation of law did not meet the expectations of state authorities. In reality, for many reasons, the problems of corrupt officials and people disobeying the law were observed in all dynasties. In this situation, in order to guarantee the enforcement of laws, the main method of Vietnamese states was to stipulate sanctions and strictly implement them.

Regarding Officials

Having clarified officials' roles in implementing laws, the state issued and applied several methods to inspect and supervise officials' implementation of laws in places where they were in charge. According to ancient historical works, when seeing that officials lacked credibility and integrity, and misused laws to harm people, King Le Hien Tong (in 1449) straightforwardly criticized and expressed a tough attitude toward these corrupt acts through his words in the following royal ordinance:

"Our state uses the strength of people to determine the laws of the nation; the guards inside and outside the palace are responsible for implementing regulations, all kinds of services have to be considered for awards. It is clearly stated that corrupt officials should be punished and honest people should be rewarded. Sanctions are ready at all times to prevent briberies. Thus it is hard to understand why authorized officials do not follow state regulations. Few care more about the nation than their personal gain, while many ignore their responsibilities and duties. Many keep committing evils that we have tried to eliminate, such as letting the rich go and only arresting the poor and misappropriating state money. Some pursue their own benefit at the expense of others, some submerge themselves in wine and girls while ignoring their duties, some abuse their position to exploit others, some cover up for others and ignore state laws, some only think about conspiracies and torture without mercy for the poor (...) That is why I issue new regulations to eliminate these evil old habits. Those who observe these new rules will be forgiven; those who fail to do so will be strictly punished. Whether you will face disasters or fortune is up to you. Choose wisely."

In codes as well as other legal documents by the king, the following behaviors of officials were forbidden:

- Must not be greedy and plunder people's assets.
- Judges have to be fair and must not take bribes to make wrong judgements, which can lead to injustice.
- When travelling abroad, must not buy goods without reporting.
- Officials must not take bribes; if they do they will be punished, depending on the amount they take.
- Tax collectors must not misappropriate tax payment.
- Must not abuse public work for personal purpose.
- Must not take bribe or favor relatives to promote people without morality and talent.

All the officials committing the above behaviors were punished by laws. For example: taking bribes was considered the most typical act of corruption, which was regulated both in Hong Duc Laws and Gia Long Laws. In order to deal with this behavior, laws had regulations to punish those who accepted bribes (usually officials) and those who bribed (usually ordinary people and subordinates). The level of punishment depended on the amount of bribes.

During the monarchical time, regular examinations of officials was an effective method to prevent corrupt behaviors and enhance the enforcement of laws because through these examinations, the government collected a lot of information about officials and took timely actions to deal with corrupt officials. On the other hand, pressured by the investigations, officials had to adjust their behaviors to avoid making mistakes. This method, therefore, was a mechanism of active prevention of corruption.

Regarding the Masses

In order for the masses to observe laws, illegal behaviors were severely punished to set examples for others as well as to show the rigorousness of the law. This is shown through notes in ancient historical works, according to which any behavior that did not follow the orders of the king and the government was considered crimes of "violating majesty" or "internal upheaval". Once accused of these crimes, no one can avoid being punished, from light punishments such as the whip or cane, to more severe punishments namely banishment, decapitation, or extermination of three generations of kinship. These sanctions were considered effective because they made the people afraid and made them follow the laws. However, because people's intellectual standard at that time was low, punishments by the state were usually combined with punishments by village communities through regulations in village conventions (also known as village regulations).

Several Inequalities in Implementing Laws

Basically, feudal states' laws usually focused on protecting the interests of the governing, oppressing and exploiting classes. Therefore, although officials' illegal behaviors were strictly punished, in reality, there were many injustices in the enforcement of laws in the monarchical period. Ordinary people were punished more severely than officials for the same violations. Additionally, several officials exploited this discrimination to distort cases, to force people to admit crimes they did not commit, and to punish many people unjustly. This sparked anger amongst the people. For example: Dai Viet su ky toan thu recorded the case of Do Thien Thu (younger brother of Do Khac Chung – a high-ranking mandarin in the court), who was involved in a lawsuit with another. While he was absolutely wrong, local officials kept delaying the prosecution. Consequently, the other person intercepted the king's chariot to report the case. After the king ordered an investigation, it was concluded that Do Thien Thu was really wrong.

Therefore, in order to reduce people's dissatisfaction, some dynasties applied several methods for the people to report urgent matters to the king. Dai Viet su ky toan thu recorded two events:

- In March 1052, under the reign of King Ly Thai Tong, the king ordered the casting of a large bell, located in the Dragon Pond, and allowed people to ring it should they want to report any injustice they had suffered.
- In 1158, King Ly Anh Tong, following the model of the Song dynasty (China), put a bronze chest in the middle of royal palace, and anyone who had anything to report or denounce could put a letter into it.[13]

Conclusion

Through the above materials and research, we conclude that: Based on the criteria of a state of law, we can argue that in Vietnam in the monarchical peri-

---

[13] Some argue that nowadays state agencies also use this method in the form of suggestion boxes for people to express their needs and suggestions.

od some signs of a state of law already existed. Those included the fact that the state, upon recognition of the role of the law, organized the compilation and promulgation of general codes and other specific legal documents for the people to know and observe, and for officials to implement. Vietnamese feudal states also had many methods to disseminate and communicate laws to the subjects, using many different forms which were suitable to the specific context of different areas and the level of awareness of the masses. Vietnamese feudal states also strictly punished illegal behaviors. Those methods partly enabled the implementation of laws. Thanks to that, many dynasties were able to maintain social order, mobilize armed forces to fight against foreign invaders and maintain power for hundreds of years.

However, the above signs still have not provided sufficient evidence to affirm the existence of a state of law in the monarchical time because many basic and important factors were missing. Those included the process of compiling laws (without the people's involvement and discussion); laws were issued mostly for the king and the state to impose on and control the people, instead of being a "contract" between the state and citizens; laws still expressed inequality between officials and ordinary people; there were still many shortcomings in the implementation of laws, especially officials' abuse of power to violate regulations in laws; human and people's rights, although noticed, still received limited attention; punishments still depended on social hierarchy, corruption was still rampant, and the implementation of laws was still arbitrary. Those limits significantly undermined the legitimacy of many dynasties. Some dynasties even lost their power because of that reason.

Those were historical lessons for us to consider, finding and applying effective methods to build and improve the state of law in Vietnam at the moment and in the future.

References

Culture-Information Publisher (ed.) (1994): Hoang viet luat le. Hanoi.
Social Sciences Publisher (ed.) (1998): Dai Viet su ky toan thu. Hanoi.
Vu Thi Phung (1990: History of Vietnamese States and Laws. Reprinted 1993, 1998, 2003, 2008. Hanoi.

The French "État legale" in Vietnam. Between Legal Pluralism and Police State

Detlef Briesen

The following article examines the effects of the French "État legale" in its colonies in Southeast Asia. This question at least implicitly plays an important role in the other contributions collected here. Since French law is an integral part of the continental-European legal tradition, it is also being studied here with the respective categories. Obviously I am not pursuing a Euro-centric perspective, but I am primarily interesting in describing one of the starting points for the contemporary Vietnamese debate on the rule of law: the abolishment of the Confucian system of law and order by virtue, and its replacement by a rather arbitrary French "État légale" from 1858–1954. Other toeholds, which are not discussed in my article, are developments after 1945, 1954, and 1986 in particular.

France and the Law in its Colonial Empire

A constitutional state is a state in which constitutional powers are legally bound, which is particularly limited in its actions by law to secure the freedom of the individual. Judging from today's prevailing opinion in Germany the state of law (rule of law or more accurately "Rechtsstaat") includes other elements in addition to the rule of law:
- legal guarantee of fundamental human rights,
- legal guarantee of coexistence of the people in the same personal freedom,
- securing material justice,

- ensuring legal certainty (certitudo and securitas),
- institutional moderation of government activity by the separation of powers, the prohibition of excess and the principle of proportionality,
- laws binding all government activity by a primacy of law,
- salvo of a legal authorization for all incriminating state acts,
- verifiability of state acts through independent courts, in particular on whether government action which engages the rights of an individual, is legitimate and appropriate.[1]

In French law, there is today, under the influence of the German tradition, a similar schema of categories that indicate whether a country is to be regarded as a "Rechtsstaat" or not. This has led to the loan translation of the German term into "État de droit" in French. Originally, the term "État légale" was more common in France. It designated a state in which control had been completely taken over by a civil society and its expression of political will, the parliament. This found its expression in a common understanding that laws are the central tool for the control of the state by the parliament. Consequently, only by means of laws adopted by parliament was it possible to interfere legitimately in society, politics, economy etc. French legal thought focused originally on the creation and enforcement of laws.[2] The rule of law in an extended interpretation is in contrast a relatively recent historical achievement. In countries like France or Germany it was fully established only in the decades after World War II. When it comes to the specific character of the French rule in Vietnam 1858–1946, so far two factors must always be taken into account.

First: The enforcement of a fully developed "Rechtsstaat" beyond the mere binding of governmental activity to laws was also in France itself a protracted process. Much more was required than just the famous Declaration of the Rights of Man and of the Citizen ("Déclaration des droits de l'Homme et du Citoyen"), which was announced by the French National Assembly on 26 August 1789. During the 100 years of French colonial rule over Vietnam, the state of law had severe deficits, was controversial and even endangered in France itself. The Second Empire was an authoritarian state, during the Third Republic the state of law was seriously threatened by attempts of restoration, political justice, martial law, first and foremost during the World Wars, and

---

[1] Zippelius (1999), 296 ff.; Stern (1984), 781 ff.

[2] Ridder (2010), 179.

by another authoritarian government, the State of Vichy. Even the Fourth and Fifth Republic were shaken to their foundations by the anti-colonial liberation wars in Indochina and Algeria, and the associated substantial violations of human and civil rights.

Second: The fact that the rule of law was a contentious issue in France itself, was in addition to the strong anti-democratic forces caused by the dual character which the country had from the mid-19th to mid-20th century: France was from 1871 until 1940 one of the few democratic republics in Europe, but at the same time it possessed a colonial empire. The latter was actually the largest in the world but for the British, and provided France with resources to compete with the strongest power of continental Europe until 1945, Germany. To keep control over its empire was therefore the fundament of its status as a Great Power. This implied another iron necessity: All colonialized people in Asia, Africa, America and Oceania could not be provided with the same human and civil rights and particularly not with full legal equality and freedom as the French from the motherland.

The limited extend of the rule of law in the colonies therefore had a logic that was established on the one hand by the role of France in the system of Great Powers and its capabilities to conquer a country like Vietnam so easily. On the other hand, there were fiscal reasons. Colonization could cause political problems in France, so it had to be at least cost-neutral for the French taxpayer. To achieve this, the colonies and protectorates had in turn to be profitable, that is, they had to yield profits for France. This restricted certain forms of development, especially political participation and a full development of a "Rechtsstaat". The French empire overseas was therefore characterized by legal pluralism, and inevitably applied to political and economic oppression and exploitation.[3]

The Law in Vietnam before Colonization

To understand the French encroachment on Vietnam, it is essential to have an idea about the preceding Empire of Vietnam and its law. Seen from the perspective of European constitutional theory, the Empire of Vietnam was a state

---

[3] Brocheux/Hémery (2011), 71.

of law in the limited sense. Its constitutional structure was based on a complex network of multiple actors legitimized by written law, customs and rites. It consisted of the emperor and his mandarins, the village communities and the extended family groups.

The Emperor and his Mandarins

The reign of Emperor and his elite, the mandarins, was ritually-morally legitimized by a "heavenly mandate". The objective of the latter was to achieve an ideal society which guaranteed peace, order, harmony, social satisfaction and material prosperity. While such socio-political objectives are universal in principle, the means to achieve to them were of pure Confucian origin: "virtue", "knowledge", "righteous path", including the idea of "governing by virtue".[4] Virtue was also the central category of political theory, and it was nothing but an expression of a cosmological moral law called "Tao". It was the common regulator of cosmic and social order and thus extended to the subunits of the latter or the entire hierarchy of the cosmos, society, family and individual.

Law in the Empire of Vietnam had therefore a cosmological source, and in daily practice it was mainly a product of moral action. This raised the question of how the ruling classes could ensure order in society from their Confucian view, namely through harmonious moral action itself, also known as "Li".[5] It went far beyond the right ceremonial-ritual behavior and was a collective formula for harmonious action in the sense of equilibrium in all actions. Emperors and mandarins had thus to act as role models in moral action, in the hope that a positive impact on the people would arise therefrom. They also had to behave in accordance with the three basic social commitments and the five cardinal virtues, and were confronted with specific obligations arising from the respective social position too. Writers, farmers, artisans and merchants each had to follow specific ethical imperatives and to provide full dedication in the service of the community.[6]

At the top of this ethical-ritual-oriented system of rule of law or virtue was the emperor. French observers usually interpreted his role primarily as that of

---

[4] Vu The Quyen (1977), 44.

[5] Wilhelm (1967), Li Gi, 35 ff.

[6] Wilhelm (1967), Li Gi, 56.

an "idole sacrée",[7] who would formally remain in power in order not to unnecessarily provoke the population. However, the French missed a crucial component, because the sacral legitimation also implied a political mandate. An emperor who failed could be forced by his subjects to resign or even commit suicide. However, since this meant a considerable effort, it was enough, as a rule, when an Emperor kept the "imperial attitude" and operated its function as a "ritually-sacred object" without mistakes.[8] This became increasingly impossible under the conditions of the colonial state.

Below the Emperor there was a ruling class in pre-colonial Vietnam, the mandarins, whose authority was based on the success in the imperial examination system and thus acquired Confucian knowledge. Since mandarins lived among the illiterate population, the rise of an education contender to a higher degree was witnessed by the masses. Extensive ceremonies were also held to honor mandarins when reaching a new status.[9] Their training not only consisted of technical skills such as reading and writing and a general knowledge about Confucian theory, but of acquiring correct thinking as it was understood as a precondition for right action when in office.

The mandarin bureaucracy consisted only of a very limited number of men. Figures from the colonial era-until the 1930s when the mandarins remained under the protectorate treaties in office in Tonkin and Annam confirm such a view: In 1896, a total of 418 mandarins with 858 assistants administered the first and second class managed prefectures in Tonkin, not more than one administrator per 4,000 to 5,000 residents.[10] Mandarins were ordered by a hierarchy of ranks, of certain positions at the imperial court, which corresponded to the respective organizational level of provinces, sub-provinces and cantons.[11] Mandarins governed in principle by the ancient Chinese system of undivided state authority, particularly the administrators of lower units were in their prelacies in charge of "everything."[12] Nevertheless, there was a certain division of public tasks among them: revenue collection, public works, recruitment of

---

[7] Harmand (1885), 36.

[8] Vu The Quyen (1977), 27.

[9] Texier (1962), 349 ff.

[10] Brocheux/Hémery (2011), 88.

[11] Blazy (2012), 58.

[12] Brocheux/Hémery (2011), 88.

soldiers, monitoring of the population, and jurisdiction.[13] The latter was a main task of mandarins and differed significantly from judicature in contemporary European countries like France.

The entire law was characterized by the fact that the essential elements of contemporary European jurisdiction, especially the division between private, penal, and public law were non-existent as well as that codes of procedure were lacking. The Vietnamese judiciary was dominated by the Confucian principle of morality and harmony, court disputes were seen as an expression of the failure of the peaceful social order, even as immorality. One central attempt was, therefore, to engage as few persons as possible in a court hearing, which all in all rather resembled an administrative act: There was no litigation, no litigant, no lawyers etc. Only few persons were involved even in an important legal dispute, the mandarin, the defendant or his deputy, and sometimes witnesses. The only guarantee against arbitrary justice was the moral integrity of the mandarin judge who had to face severe penalties in case of failures or corruption.[14] In addition, there was no division into public, private and criminal law, because the underlying code, the Gia Long, was written exclusively as a moralizing criminal code. Some other sources of law were characterized by the same idea: the King, a collection of five books on metaphysics, history, ethics and literature, the Statutes of the Emperor, in which, inter alia, the administrative structures had been established, and finally the Lê Code. It retained some significance despite the Codification of Gia Long Code. The latter had been introduced in 1812 by the homonymous Emperor and was basically a copy of the penal code of the Chinese Qing Dynasty. Committed to the same legal thinking the Gia Long Code defined standards for criminal law (penalties, definition of crimes, exceptions for the privileged etc.) as well as other legal regulations including management of granaries, commercial law, civil status, sacred position of the Emperor, sacrifices, military, and public works.

Court cases were dealt with at the various stages of mandarins' hierarchy. It consisted of three stages. If a party to the conflict did not want to bow to the verdict of the notables, it could petition to a low-ranking mandarin. His decision was not based necessarily on a court hearing. In the case of a crime or offense mostly local notables who were responsible for law and order at the local

---

[13] Blazy (2012), 49 ff.

[14] Blazy (2012), 60.

level addressed directly to the mandarin. He had full authority over all forms of punishment. On the provincial level, there was a sort of Court of Appeal chaired by the provincial judge. It was the last resort for cases in which corporal punishment was imposed. The third stage of case-law was the Court of Appeal in imperial Hue. It was primarily responsible for severe cases of moral failure in which the highest forms of punishment, detention, exile and death penalty, had been imposed. In addition, at Hue special courts met for cases, which involved high-ranking mandarins, infamous rebels or similarly serious cases. Another court dealt with matters which concerned the imperial family. For the military, there was a different jurisdiction anyway.[15]

The Village Community

The village community was largely autonomous in imperial Vietnam, and its dual autonomy as an administrative and social unit was a result of a long historical process, which is not be reproduced in detail here. Originally the villages were supervised strictly by an imperial mandarin, who was also in charge of tax collection. Since the introduction of population and cadastral registers the payment of taxes came more and more under the control of the local Council of Elders.[16] With general revision of the civil register under the Emperor Le Thanh Tong, the amount to be paid by the respective village became dependent on the number of taxable inhabitants. Since then villages simply gave lower population figures to reduce their tax burden. The revision led consequently to a tedious and permanent conflict between the central government and municipalities about the real population figures. Since the tax reform by Le Huyen Tong (1662–1671) the villages had to apply only a fixed amount that was calculated on the basis of the last census.

This compromise had benefits for both sides; especially for the peasantry in the villages. The Council of the Elders now apportioned the lump-sum taxation for the entire municipality to the male patriarchs. This created a significant local autonomy with extensive executive powers. The withdrawal of the state on the issue of taxation was only the first step towards a far-reaching self-government of the municipalities in Vietnam. Finally, it included the independent organization of local government and the autonomous mobilization of

---

[15] Blazy (2012), 67.

[16] Nguyen Huu Khang (1946), 41 ff.

resources (taxes, fees and charges) for tackling common tasks. Municipalities had their own common law system which was partly oral, partly written down, and deeply influenced by traditional values and local experiences. Local common law was based on general ethical and moral principles and on codified conventions on administrative, judicial, fiscal, police and other matters.[17]

The community was nevertheless not completely autonomous, but integrated into the authoritarian and centralist imperial government which controlled military, justice and religion. In addition, village and imperial state were connected by the common, above-described culture of "social harmony". An important task of the village community was therefore to ensure peace and order internally and externally. This commandment was so strong that it could lead to collective punishment against entire communities in case of subordination.[18] Communities had therefore regulatory functions. They were responsible for protecting their members from external enemies, bandits and robbers. Internally they were supervised by a municipal police. The municipality was also responsible for fending off magical powers that could either produce harmful weather phenomena or bring disorder into the "social harmony" of the village community.[19] In addition villages were providers of mutual solidarity.[20] In order to meet the variety of tasks, the village council was also organized by function. There were lower dignitaries for archive, finance, public security, construction and dissemination of news, higher dignitaries for external contacts, and the interpretation of the imperial edicts.[21] A central position was occupied by the ly truong (mayor) of the village, but the entire political and social structure of it was far from being simply hierarchically organized.[22]

The Family

The third pillar of the Vietnamese society was the family. It was on one hand a social interaction system, which was structured by the idea of an "order" that

---

[17] Vu The Quyen (1977), 72.

[18] Nguyen Huu Khang (1946), 92 ff.

[19] Nguyen Tien Huu (1969), 12 ff.

[20] Nguyen Huu Khang (1946), 204 ff.

[21] Nguyen Huu Khang (1946), 96 ff.

[22] Papin (2002), 49–52.

produced family roles and a hierarchy of authority. Secondly, the family was based on the absolute nature of the paternal power, which was bound to the general authoritarian structure of the society, based on authority and order (Vu 1977, 110). The family hierarchy was formally determined by Confucian principles, the "three chains" of family role relationships, better subordination and the corresponding values: between father and son (piety), husband and wife (modesty), and older and younger brother (obedience) (Silvestre 1889, 124). Added to this was ritualized role behavior that was based on rules of conduct, which should guarantee the functioning of the role relationships and make them visible.

This family order was also viewed as a prerequisite for the harmonious society. Only those who knew how to perpetuate order in family life were suitable for a state office. At the same time the order inside of the family was not a private but a public affair. Violations of the fundamental value of filial piety, for example, were among the ten most serious crimes and punishable by death.[23] Here it becomes visible how tightly moral and ethical principles were linked to law.[24] However, law was only part of a comprehensive strategy to enforce morality within the entire society. Especially the educated men had to set good examples of right conduct, and the Confucian concept of virtue was also spread among the illiterate people by memorized poems and stories. The patriarch was held responsible for morality and order in his family, and in severe cases of misconduct even three generations of a wrongdoer faced execution. In order to fulfill this collective commitment, the family was equipped with great autonomy and substantial rights. The head of the family was allowed to take all major decisions, including the assets, he even had power over the lives of his family members as the kin's judge. Their main obligation was the submission to the paternal authority. Specifically violations of this duty were severely punished.

On the whole, the legislation in Vietnam's villages, families and in the entire country at the time prior to colonization was not designed to protect the rights of the individual; it was primarily a system to ensure harmony in family, village and society.[25]

---

[23] Deloustal (1908), 97 ff.

[24] Huard/Durand (1954), 13.

[25] Phan Thi Dac (1966), 47.

France and the Legal Tradition in Vietnam

Below we deal first with the question of which elements of Vietnam's traditional legal system were preserved or altered by the French. In another section, we try to determine which new forms of state power and societal organization were introduced through law by the colonial regime. Generally speaking, for the majority of the Vietnamese population, farmers in villages and family groups, colonial rule only changed their legal status slowly and slightly. In that perspective, the French rule was characterized by a legal pluralism not uncommon in the European overseas empires until their collapse during or as a result of World War II.[26] By contrast, the Vietnamese elites were ousted. The sacred position of Emperor became increasingly undermined, and the power of the mandarins was limited by the French administration, or better the mandarins were assimilated into the colonial power structure.

Village and Family Clan during the Colonial Period

Model for the persistence of the regulations for the mass of Vietnamese were those decisions that had been made already in 1864 for Cochinchina[27] and for Tonkin after 1890.[28] Thus, Annamite civil and commercial law was applied continuously during the colonial period, insofar as it concerned the relations of the Vietnamese among themselves or with other Asians. The French comments specified repeatedly the sources of colonial law for non-Europeans in Indochina, especially the Gia Long Code. In contrast not only the French but all Europeans were subject to France's law; so were the legal relations between them on the one hand and the "indigènes" on the other hand. From this principle, there were only few exceptions. The "code civile" for example could also be applied to cases which concerned "sujets" when French law as "raison écrite" helped to overcome the shortcomings of Annamite, traditional law. This was exercised in the case of legal innovations unknown to the traditional law, for example insurance contracts.[29]

---

[26] Benda-Beckmann (1992), 307 ff.

[27] Fourniau (2002), 161 ff.

[28] Fourniau (2002), 453 ff.

[29] Girault (1922 I), 541.

During the colonial period most regulations of striking importance for "indigènes" or "sujets" remained effective which were based on the traditions of family and municipality law, or on written law, the Gia Long Code in particular. These included the ancestral cult, marriage, adoption and inheritance law, and the provisions relating to that part of assets which were scheduled to maintain the ancestral cult. The enormous authority of the family's patriarch was only touched in so far, as that with a Précis of 1883 the "pouvoirs publiques" received a general permission to monitor it.[30] Primarily, even the provisions on land ownership, land and civil registers were left untouched, but beginning in Cochinchina in 1871 records were no longer kept in Chinese characters, but in French. A risk for the farmers, however, was the legally unclear situation of their land ownership. The cadastral was not performed correctly to colonization, as mentioned above. Property titles were often based on privileges or on claims to the communal land. As French citizens increasingly acquired land in the context of "mise en valeur" in what now is Vietnam, this led to ambiguity, arbitrary interpretation of law, and to considerable conflicts between colonial administrations, French colonists and natives.[31]

The most important changes in villages and family clans were of a fiscal nature. These reforms were introduced when Paul Doumer reorganized Indochina under the aim to make it finance its colonial status itself.[32] France had primarily taken over the Empire's tax system.[33] It was based on a poll tax for male adults, taxes on land ownership and an obligation to work-called Corvée. This system was, as shown above, inefficient because the registers used for this purpose had not been properly maintained since the 17th century. With the Decree of 1/2 June 1897 Doumer introduced a new form of taxation in Tonkin, which was transferred a year later to Annam. New civil registers and cadasters were its fundament.[34] Previously unregistered male adults were taxed by 0.40 piastres per year, registered by 2.5 per year. Two thirds of the Corvée now could be replaced by additional tax payments. Real estate tax was also reformed by introducing four types of rice fields and six different land classes. To

[30] Girault (1922 I), 545.

[31] Deroche (2004), 95 ff.

[32] See Doumer (1905).

[33] Eli (1967), 67 ff.

[34] Eli (1967), 69 ff.

fight tax fraud, a personal tax card was introduced in 1884 in Cochinchina, 1897 in Tonkin and 1913 in Annam. All male "sujets"were obliged to carry their tax cards permanently hence they also served as identity cards:

"The individual, in the modern sense of the term, appeared in Indochina in the form of a taxpayer."[35]

While one should not overestimate individualization on such a basis for the rural population, measures like these joined with other colonial transformations according to the model of "western" lifestyles, especially in the cities of Vietnam. Thus, traditional paternalism was called more and more into question at least in urban contexts, though the actual thrust of the modernization movement in Vietnam became the anti-colonial liberation struggle.[36]

The Disempowerment of Vietnamese Elites

The colonial rule made great use of the strict paternalism in Vietnam, especially since the French acted hardly less authoritarian than the traditional ruling classes. In recognition of the authoritarian structures only few interventions in the traditional law system took place during the colonial period. Added to this was the experience that the violation of religious feelings and moral values only provoked unnecessary problems (Girault 1922, 488). Therefore, for purposive-rational reasons, it seemed obvious to utilize the traditional authorities to administer the colony. The debate was mainly on what forms of traditional domination colonial rule should primarily rely on, and which of its components should be developed further to the benefit of the colonial power. Again the starting point was experience in Cochinchina. While replacing the old "mandarinat" by a group of French and French trained officials, the colonial administration encountered severe problems. These were to be avoided in Annam and Tonkin.

Since 1874 a treaty between France and the Empire of Vietnam regulated the status of both as French protectorates. The treaty text itself, however, did not include the term protectorate, but the non-binding "protection". The court in Hue stuck to its narrow interpretation to protect the country's remaining sovereignty (Vu 1977, 139). The French Government, however, had in 1880 laid the groundwork for a future policy in Vietnam. According to the Frey-

---

[35] Brocheux/Hémery (2011), 91.

[36] Vu The Quyen (1977), 127.

cinet-plan, the political goal was to subject it to the direct sovereignty of France. But France was initially hesitant when it came to an early realization of this goal by military intervention. This was less due to the military weakness of the government in Hue, but rather to two other factors: Firstly, until 1880 it was still unclear which value France could gain from colonies in Indochina. Secondly, France initially was not interested in a further military confrontation with China, which also had significant interests in Vietnam.

French policies in Indochina became clearer after the outbreak of the Franco-Chinese War, and a following series of rebellions in Vietnam. Harmand Convention (1883) and Patenôtre Treaty (1884) established three different legal statuses for Cochinchina (direct French possession), Tonkin (control by French resident) and Annam (relative independent administration).[37] Since the Patenôtre Treaty in particular France dealt more carefully with the existing institutions, and implemented a strategy which was based on the idea of an intermediate-term co-operation with the traditional elites in securing its colonial interests. In the long-term Emperors and mandarins were to be ousted.[38]

Colonial rule therefore led to a gradual degradation of imperial authority. France firstly reduced it through rigid interpretation of the protectorate's status, in a second step the Emperor was also damaged as a sacred symbol. Provisions of the Gia Long Code about imperial privileges were simply ignored, and its sanctions were at least mitigated.[39] The French were so successful in destroying the power and sacral function of the emperorthat already in 1920s that he served as a nation-wide symbol of collaboration, decay and corruption.

Since the Patenôtre Treaty the mandarins' position of power was curtailed systematically. In Annam the "Resident général" took over all functions that had previously been in the hands of the high mandarins: Secret State, Regency and Privy Council. Furthermore, he monitored the content of decrees and edicts, and controlled public works, finance, army and the various ministries.[40] The competencies of the "Resident supérieur" in Tonkin were even more extended because he also supervised common people and mandarins, and created his own system of indigenous office-holders. Later, under de Lanessan, France

---

[37] Vu The Quyen (1977), 148.

[38] Vu The Quyen (1977), 153.

[39] Vu The Quyen (1977), 162.

[40] Brötel (1971), 210 ff.

partly revised its strict control over the administration, and re-strengthened the position of the traditional mandarins in Tonkin.

Nevertheless, there was no going back to the old order any more, which was secured by a deep transformation of the educational system. Classical Confucian thought had been one of the quintessential fundaments of governance in countries like Vietnam, because its acquisition by imperial exams was directly linked with a career within the imperial mandarinat. The abolition of the traditional civil service exam, and its replacement by the governmental French "école" therefore formed a deep, not only educational incision, which was completed in the different parts of Vietnam at a different time. In Cochinchina, there had been no examinations since the withdrawal of the imperial mandarins in 1868; in Tonkin, the exams were abolished in 1906, and in Annam 1919. The transition from a Vietnamese-Chinese to a European-French education system was carried out slowly and in several stages until the 1930s. Especially in an initial stage France was primarily interested in teaching the French language to a limited number of local experts and translators. Educational reform grew in importance when France changed its colonial policies from "assimilation" to various forms of "association". Since then the French influence in education became even more ambivalent.

Vietnam under the Nguyen Dynasty had been decisively influenced by the model of the Qing dynasty and Chinese culture. Vietnamese was a language that was rarely written even in the Nom script. With the Latin letters of "Quoc Ngu" the French therefore presented a medium for the dissemination of the vernacular language, that was for both, the colonial administration and the Vietnamese population, on the one hand of great advantage. The Vietnamese language transformed from a spoken language to a written one. French officials at least could read written Vietnamese without being forced to learn hundreds of Chinese characters. On the other hand the proliferation of "Quoc Ngu" posed for the colonial power a serious disadvantage as it hampered the successful dissemination of the colonialists' language. The educational reform even promoted the emergence of a "national culture", in particular a literature in Vietnamese.[41] Even though France tried to improve its co-operation with the mandarins after 1890,[42] in total, the French law of education had adverse ef-

---

[41] Vu The Quyen (1977), 258 ff.

[42] De Lanessan (1895), 6.

fects. It produced new academic elite, with European knowledge and equipped with a new means of communication, Vietnamese as a written language.

The Creation of the Colonial State and Its Ambivalences

The starting point for the creation of the colonial state had been military conquest and force, but the latter was transformed more and more by non-military regulations until the end of the colonial era. Compared to the mother country a different law was effective in the French overseas empire, the so-called colonial law.[43] All possessions, colonies as well as protectorates, were French territories, and under the same French state power as was the motherland. As such, all the inhabitants of French overseas territories were French nationals. Legally, however, there were four classifications which determined their legal status. French law distinguished between full citizens, called "citoyens", "étrangers" from other European countries, "indigènes" or "sujets", indigenous persons from the respective colonies, and "étrangers assimilés à l'indigènes", in Indochina for example persons from other Asian countries. "Indigènes" or "sujets" had only limited legal rights. Only a "citoyen" was under the Code civile and had therefore full citizenship, particularly the "droits politiques", especially active and passive suffrage.[44] "Citoyens" took part in the French parliamentary elections, even if they resided in the colonies. A "sujet", however, was a citizen in the colonies, for whom not the Code civile but his "statut indigène" was effective.[45] If we consider the continuing validity of the local laws for the Vietnamese, this meant a serious discrimination for them. A "sujet" could ascend by four stages to "citoyen"; but this status could it be withdrawn again. Amongst other things France tried on the creation of the French Union to reform the personal law after the Second World War, but it was too late already, as the colonial empire disappeared in the following two decades.[46]

Metropolitan France knew four sources of law: the Constitution, laws, decrees and orders of the head of state ministers, prefects or mayors, decrees and

---

[43] See Kley (1920); Durand (2015).

[44] Girault (1923 II), 418 ff.

[45] Girault (1923 II), 483 ff.

[46] Urban (2010), 489 ff.

orders served for implementation of laws, and legislation on the basis of special authorization. In the colonies the entire legislation of the mother country was in force, if not opposed by other regulations (such as provisions of protectorate treaties). Once French authority had been implemented, laws from the motherland were only effective in the possessions if they were explicitly introduced by decree of the governor. This provided the colonial administration with an enormous power over its sujets. The latter was even increased by the peculiarities of French administrative law, which guided the proceedings of the "administration publique" in France and in its colonial empire. Even today French administrative law has a praetorian character as it is not codified, and is based on the jurisprudence of the "Conseil d'État",[47] and complex discussions about individual decisions. It is more about enabling the proper functioning of the administration in its principal activity of serving the public, rather than the control of the administration or even the protection of citizen's rights.[48] Particularly before World War II French administrative law caused considerable legal uncertainty that could be even arbitrary in a colonial context.[49]

The Colonial Ministry had precedence in the control of protectorates and colonies, and it also maintained a "Conseil coloniale" for advice on draft laws and decrees. However, the ministries of justice, home, postal, and foreign affairs possessed important competences too. For the entire colonial administration there was a General Inspectorate and (in 1920) inspections of Health, Public Works and information. The administration in the various French possessions was headed by a governor, whose field of responsibility was defined in the older colonies by a statute. In more recent acquisitionsthe governor was directly subordinated to the authority of the Minister of Colonial Affairs. The governor had extensive competences, which included the right to legislate, to manage the colonial administration, and to supervise jurisdiction. He could communicate diplomatically with neighboring countries. In addition, the governor had the supreme command of the French troops and the right of inspection. In some colonies, there were also colonial entities, such as the advisory "Conseil privé", and a "Conseil général", or a "Délégation financières" if

---

[47] See Weidenfeld (2010).

[48] Bell (2008), 168.

[49] Hübner/Constantinesco (1988), 57.

French from the motherland controlled the colonies' budget through elected or corporative assemblies.

The administrative organization for the control of Indochina was created in 1887 with the Union Indochinoise. It consisted originally of the colony Cochinchina and the protectorates Annam, Tonkin and the Kingdom of the Khmer. In 1893 Laos was incorporated, and in 1900, finally, Guangzhouwan in southern China. Union Indochinoise was a culturally and economically very inhomogeneous political union. However, the full establishment of an Indochinese state was the work of Paul Doumer.[50] Doumer reorganized French Indochina as a powerful political-administrative structure with a dual function: "to integrate all the Indochinese political structures into the French state-controlled system and to neutralize the former Vietnamese, Khmer, and Lao states, as well as the political structures of the montagnards, and to convert them into subordinate apparatuses that could be used to control the colonized populations."[51]

The political-administrative structures of the Indochinese Union were designed along the lines of British control in India. The concept of association replaced assimilation.[52] Union Indochinoise was headed by a "Gouverneur général" based in Hanoi,[53] but in practice, however, the different parts of the Union were controlled by various, rather independent sub-administrations – the Governor of Cochinchina, and High Residents in Tonkin, Laos, Annam and Cambodia. There was a Governor-General but no General-Government. Therefore, the colonial rule was not homogeneous, but marked by deep conflicts, such as between the Governor of Cochinchina on the one hand and the High Resident in Hanoi on the other. There were also conflicts that involved the motherland, as between the Indochinese merchants, French industrialists and Catholic missionaries. Perhaps precisely because the administration was lacking uniformity there was an enormous presence of French officers in Indochina, at least if we compare it with the model-giving British India. The num-

---

[50] Eli (1967), 25.

[51] Brocheux/Hémery (2011), 80.

[52] Betts (1961), 106 ff.

[53] Girault (1923 II), 261 ff.

bers of French made the administration of the Union and its parts a costly affair.[54]

The direct presence of the French in Vietnam contributed to a substantial disempowerment of the traditional ruling elites. We should avoid drawing too dark a picture of French Colonial rule in Indochina,[55] but we cannot overlook how limited France's attempts were until the 1930s to introduce reforms or even political participation. Several reasons can be cited. The French colonial administration stood from the beginning in the tradition of supposedly insurmountable Indochinese authoritarianism. From this point of view to compromise with the subjects was nothing but weakness in the eyes of the colonialized. The rigidity in which France exercised its power in Indochina was also caused by the enormous competences of the administration, which was not controlled by the colonial "sujets" but from the distant capital Paris, by the French parliament, ministries and the press. Their Indochina policy was not consistent, but mirrored complex political conflicts and constellations of interests that were negotiated by parties and business associations. Aside from these specific interests all the French who were involved in governing Vietnam were influenced by Orientalism: Political left as well as right idealized the Indochinese societies as traditionalist, immobile and dominated by small-scale social structures. Accordingly, the real "mission civilisatrice" of the French in Indochina was primarily to preserve its valuable traditions and cultural treasures,[56] and only secondly, if even at all, open it up to a cautious modernization.

The French Police State

Modernization mainly was limited to changes in the apparatus for surveillance and in penal law. France not only kept the significant authoritarian structures in Vietnam unchanged, but preserved them by a modernization of Vietnam's police units. A Garde indigène – in Cochinchina Garde civile – was founded and given the task to monitor the villages. Especially to combat the growing anti-colonial movement or other types of unrest since the outbreak of World War I, courthouses, and prisons were built, and police units were created to prevent and combat anti-colonial movements and revolts: the Sûreté générale

---

[54] Brocheux/Hémery (2011), 82 ff.

[55] Brocheux/Hémery (2011), 106 ff.

[56] See Larcher Gosha (2000).

Indochinoise was established in 1917, the Police spéciale de Sûreté in 1922.[57] In both cases the number of personnel was limited, but infamously effective due to the fact that colonial police forces in general were above the law. French rule in Vietnam was based on violence; brutality and electric torture during interrogations were on the agenda particularly since in the 1930s. During rebellions, squad teams traversed the riot areas and carried out summary executions. Because of colonial racism and the lack of an indigenous tradition of the prison sentence until 1954, no prison in Indochina served the concept to rehabilitate the inmates.[58] Under often terrible conditions political and "normal" prisoners were detained in provincial jails, penitentiaries and in total 9 penal colonies in Vietnam. Per capita, the rate of the prison population in Indochina was significantly higher than in France. Political prisoners were also deported to French Guyana. Forced labor, which was forbidden by law theoretically, was just as common as corporal punishment; mortality among the prisoners was high. In particular, the penal colonies were notorious for bloody revolts and violent attempts at liberation.

Political participation by elected provincial or municipal assemblies existed only in Cochinchina and in some major cities. Evidently French "citoyens" were overrepresented but even the expression of their political will was increasingly restricted by colonial administration after the turn of the century. At least the limited political participation of missionaries, officials, planters and businessmen could be compensated by a free press. This was not the case for the "indigenous" population of Vietnam: The French press law of 1881 only applied in Cochinchina and for publications in French. In December 1898 the Gouverneur général introduced by decree pre-censorship for publications in Vietnamese and Chinese. The censorship of the press was even tightened in the protectorates with the Decree of October 1927: Since then the editors of newspapers had to obtain a license, make a deposit, and to subject their products to pre-censorship. Only periodicals in French and issued by a "citoyen" were exempt from these provisions. Finally, the decree of August 30, 1930 abolished the obligation for press products both in Vietnamese and French to be censored before publication.[59]

---

[57] Morlat (1990), 71 ff.

[58] Zinoman (2001), 63.

[59] See Huynh Van Tong (1971).

The character of a French police state becomes more obvious if we take a closer look at criminal justice. During the conquest, martial law had been applied by the French army in Cochinchina. Thereafter, by the decree of July 1864, two different systems of penal law were established; "citoyens" and "sujets" were treated separately. For the former, the "Code pénale" was introduced, for latter the indigenous criminal code, Gia Long, was reinstated. It extended – with a few exceptions when sujets" had to appear before the French courts – in principle over all "indigènes" and other Asians in the colony.[60] The validity of indigenous law was abolished again by the decree of March 16, 1880. Since then, with few exceptions, the "code pénale" was in effect for Cochinchina, and French judges also conducted the proceedings of Annamites' and other Asians' cases according to it. .But some provisions of the criminal law of the Empire of Vietnam remained in force. For this, the Code pénale was supplemented by certain provisions and became a penal code particularly for Cochinchina. Since the 1880s, the entire organization of jurisdiction in the extreme south of Vietnam followed the model of the mother country. It established a court of appeal at Saigon and in total seven first-instance criminal courts in Cochinchina. While this system suffered from staff shortages, it nevertheless improved jurisdiction for the French "sujets", since many cases now were excluded from the traditional moralism and strict punitive approach of the Gia Long code. It also had provisions of criminal procedural law. Only since then was a due process guaranteed to all defendants in Cochinchina.[61]

The reforms in Cochinchina laid the fundament for a growing influence of the French criminal law and penal system in all three parts of Vietnam until 1954. French laws and prisons became the rule for French or other non-Asians in Indochina. This influence was slowly extended over the "sujets" and Asian nationals from Cochinchina over Tonkin to Annam. Penitentiaries, prisons, and juvenile detention centers under the supervision of the French authorities were established, where also for political reasons convicted "indigènes" did their time. The traditional penal system in Vietnam had known no prison sentences, but only lighter and heavier forms of corporal punishment, forced

---

[60] Girault (1922 I), 553 ff.

[61] Blazy (2012), 328.

labor, exile and various forms of capital punishment. Therefore imprisonment was an innovation in Vietnam.[62]

In Tonkin and Annam a tripartite judicial system had been created by an agreement from March 15, 1874. Originally cases in which only Europeans were involved were treated by the French High Residents, cases which concerned Europeans and Annamites were processed by common French and Annamite courts, acts which concerned only Vietnamese, only by the mandarins. Since that time, the jurisdiction was extended more and more by the French authorities.[63]

Labor Law

Thus, different legal areas show that France not only used law in a repressive way to defend its power in Indochina. Sometimes it also tried – but at the same time always in its own interest – to eliminate internationally indicted grievances. This was the case for labor law which was an important issue in all European colonies because it was directly linked with the problem whether a possession was profitable for the colonial power or not.[64] Theoretically in Vietnam a sufficient indigenous workforce was available for its "mise en valeur".[65] The general problem in Indochina was rather that those areas that should be developed economically for the benefit of the colonial power were not congruent with the traditional economic and settlement areas of the Vietnamese majority population.[66] While Kinh were predominantly farmers and lived mainly in the Tonkin Delta and on the coast of Annam, the colonial interests targeted rather the development/exploitation of the highlands of Tonkin, Cochinchina, Southern Annam and the southern Mekong Delta. The recruitment of workers in these areas faced mainly three difficulties: the work in mines and on plantations meant for the Kinh farmers a significant change. They were also linked with their farmland or their place of residence for religious and economic reasons. Only the locals could operate ancestor worship

---

[62] Girault (1922 I), 554 ff.

[63] Girault (1922 I), 555 ff.

[64] Chanock (1992), 293 ff.

[65] Girault (1923 II), 201.

[66] Nguyen Van Vinh (1961), 12 ff.

and had access to a share of the common lands.[67] The Kinh population had not without reason shunned the highlands and the Mekong Delta as settlement areas for centuries, because living there was in fact a substantial health risk. However, high morbidity and mortality were explained by the presence of evil supernatural causes. In fact, both were alarmingly high on the plantations and in the mines.[68]

All this meant that by the end of the 19th century only people from the rural underclasses volunteered to work on plantations and in coal mines. The recruitment was carried out by private companies, and for those who signed contracts with them significant protection by labor law existed. In order to prevent social unrest and problems (and to make taking up work for larger masses of Vietnamese more attractive), the colonial power passed two decrees in March 1910 and in November 1918. Since then labor contracts had to be registered with the authorities, the contract duration was set at maximum three years, working, living and conditions for returning home had to be determined by the contract. In theory, the colonial authorities had since that time the right to control whether the promised conditions had actually been complied with or not.[69] However, these tentative steps to regulate labor stood in conflict with a massive interest of the colonial power – the smooth operation of the plantations in particular. Therefore, in colonial Indochina even labor law remained penalized. Since 1899 breaching workers had to expect up to five days in prison and fines between 1 and 15 francs. These penalties were even increased in 1918. Since then absence from the workplace was punished with prison terms of between six days and three months, and fines between 16 and 20 francs.[70] Nevertheless, these measures proved inadequate; they protected neither the rights of workers, because the colonial administration did not succeed in actually enforcing its control rights, nor did it really satisfy the interests of the employers, as the high absence rate did not decrease significantly.[71]

Especially after the First World War a practice of recruiting labor spread that hardly could be called voluntary: Employment agencies negotiated direct-

---

[67] Nguyen Van Vinh (1961), 14.

[68] Nguyen Huu Khang (1946), 207.

[69] Bureau International du Travail (1937), 96 ff.

[70] Bureau International du Travail (1937), 19.

[71] Bureau International du Travail (1937), 3.

ly with the village councils. They were even bribed for an opportunity the recruitment agencies offered to them: to get rid of unwanted or poor community members, and send these "en masse" (Montaigut 1929, 40 ff.) to the plantations, and coal mines. Basically, this kind of "voluntary" recruitment hardly differed from forced labor. The option to work in the plantations and mining areas remained unattractive. Workers, who had been dismissed from the contracts and returned to their homeland, came back in a worse health condition and just as poor as before. When the abuses became increasingly evident, the French authorities undertook in 1927 a new attempt to ensure by legal measures occupational health and safety. This time, however, specific provisions were taken: "Inspection général du travail" was created, and rules for the recruitment of workers and their taxation adopted. Especially "pécule" was introduced, a system of compulsory saving by means of "Livret du travail" to which equally employees and employers had to contribute.[72] Nevertheless, the late 1920s saw such severe collective action that further (unsuccessful) reforms were introduced by the colonial authorities in 1929, 1930 and 1932.[73]

Summing up these decrees, it cannot be denied that the colonial administration's will existed to remedy the social ills and to abolish the de facto forced labor. In the 1930s, however, the differences between what the colonial administration was willing and able to realize and an emerging labor movement were already so large that the deficiencies created a powerful strike movement. It formed an important part of the anti-colonial resistance.[74]

Summary

It is possible to point out that the main character of France's colonial rule in Vietnam and other parts of Indochina was that of a "rule of law". Since the military subjugation of the Indochinese territories and the separation of military and civilian administration, the French apparatus had always tried to base its decrees, regulations and thus actions on law from the motherland. This rather formal interpretation must not obscure our view of how limited this

---

[72] Bureau International du Travail (1937), 53 ff.

[73] Bureau International du Travail (1937), 21 ff.

[74] Vu The Quyen (1977), 215 ff.

approach was, however, and how deeply it was linked with the deficiencies of the constitutional state in France itself, and with the general lack of political participation in the French colonial empire. We also have to take into account that the societal order prior to colonization was rather influenced by the concept of Confucian morality and not of Roman law.

Colonies are states in the making. The colonial power abolished an ancient law system, that of the Empire of Vietnam and attempted to replace it by the French one. The plan was to implement a political-legal system in Vietnam, which should meet the standards defined by France (and its interests). The main dispute among the colonialists was how long this process should take, and whether it was to be guided by the principles of assimilation or association. Anyhow, colonization was connected with a significant transformation of law, first and foremost the disempowerment and de-privileging of the ancient elites, the imperial family and the mandarins. To a far lesser extent the legal traditions of the Vietnamese village were severed. France applied a top-down approach to change the society of its possession. All intrusions were blatant breaches of law as it was understood in the Confucian interpretation: as a moral all-encompassing cosmological order. Vietnam therefore lost more than only a couple of legal regulations. By the abolishment of its moral-legal tradition it was deprived of its idea of a harmonious society, whatever it may have looked like in reality.

France replaced Confucian morality by a contemporary interpretation of the constitutional state, which, as mentioned above, was characterized by severe deficits and rather arbitrary. Though French rule in Indochina was liberal compared with other colonial regimes (in India for example neither the provisions of habeas corpus nor the freedom of the press were contemporarily secured) it was based primarily on military conquest and strict police control. France established a police state, which would not have been possible to such an extent in the mother country. Like in most other European colonies in general, central provisions of the constitutional state were not guaranteed to the majority of Vietnam's population, not in the present-day interpretation of "Rechtsstaat" but even not in the contemporary, rather progressive peculiarities of the French "État légale". Like other colonies the different parts of Indochina therefore were subjected to a hybrid legal framework, which in the view of the colonizers compromised with their backwardness. In addition, interventions in the originally existing legal-moral order were based on purpose. Colonies are not only states in the making but they are colonies, areas where the freedom of the individual is not always the most important dictum the state is acting on.

Regarding the overall balance of the French État de droit in Vietnam, it was mainly an uncompleted attempt at nation-building following the European model, and deeply influenced by French global ambitions of power and economic interests. This process changed the Vietnamese society greatly, but rather in terms of the destruction of an old order than in establishing a new legal order. The Confucian unity of morals, ethics, law and order was delegitimized especially at the top of society. Therefore the legal changes regarding the sacred position of the Emperor and the educational reforms were of utmost importance as the latter led to the gradual replacement of mandarins by new elites, which were westernized. Below this level, a colonial vacuum was created; the lower social strata were in theory at the colonial administration's disposition, though in practice the real impact of French governance was limited. The same was true for the substance of change France actually reached by 1954 in Indochina. France destroyed more than it created, and the main changes occurred in areas which were essential for the colonial regime to maintain its control over Vietnam: labor and educational law and criminal justice.

The outcome of the "État légale" in Vietnam, Indochina, and generally in the French overseas empire was modest at best, and deeply influenced by a legal pluralism which left written and unwritten law, customs, and moral-legal provisions of Vietnamese families and villages generally untouched. But the consequences for the development after 1954 must be seriously taken into consideration – combined with other central elements of historical development of rule of law since 1945, 1954, and 1986. Today Vietnam is confronted with the question whether to further develop its constitutional state following the European or German model of "Rechtsstaat". Another option of growing importance is the modernization of the Confucian tradition which is intensively debated on an international level today. Perhaps Vietnam like other South East and East Asian countries can reach similar success in further developing its rule of law by adopting concepts of moral virtue again.[75]

---

[75] See Bell/Chaibong (2003); Holz/Wegmann (2005).

References

Benda-Beckmann, Franz von (1992): Symbiosis of Indigenous and Western Law in Africa and Asia: An Essay on Legal Pluralism. In: Mommsen, Wolfgang J./de Moor, J.A. (eds.): European Expansion and Law. The Encounter of European and Indigenous Law in 19th- and 20th-Centuries Africa and Asia. Oxford. 307–325.

Bell, Daniel A./Chaibong, Hahm (2003): Confucianism for the Modern World. Cambridge.

Bell, John (2008): Administrative Law. In: Bell, John (et al.): Principles of French Law. Oxford. 168–200.

Betts, Raymond F. (1961): Assimilation and Association in French Colonial Theory 1890–1914. New York.

Brötel, Dieter (1971). Französischer Imperialismus in Vietnam. Die koloniale Expansion und die Errichtung des Protektorates Annam-Tongking. Zürich.

Bureau International du Travail (ed.) (1937): Problème de travail en Indochine. Genève.

Chanock, Martin (1992): The Law Market: The Legal Encounter in British East and Central Africa. In: Mommsen, Wolfgang J./de Moor, J.A. (eds.): European Expansion and Law. The Encounter of European and Indigenous Law in 19th- and 20th-Century Africa and Asia. Oxford. 279–305.

Deloustal, M.R. (1908): La justice dans l'ancien Annam: Code des Lê. In: Bulletin de l'Ecole Française d'Extrême-Orient 8, 177–220.

Deroche, Alexandre (2004): France coloniale et droit de propriété. Les concessions en Indochine. Paris.

Doumer, Paul (1905): L'Indo-Chine française (Souvenirs). Paris.

Durand, Bernard (2015): Introduction historique au droit colonial. Un ordre au gré des vents. Paris.

Eli, Barbara (1967): Paul Doumer in Indochina 1897–1902. Heidelberg.

Fourniau, Charles (2002): Vietnam. Domination coloniale et résistance nationale 1858–1914. Paris.

Gantès, G. de (1994): Coloniaux et gouverneurs en Indochine française 1902–1914. Paris.

Girault, Arthur (1922): Principes de colonisation et de législation coloniale. Les Colonies françaises depuis 1815 I. Paris.

Girault, Arthur (1923): Principes de colonisation et de législation coloniale. Les Colonies françaises depuis 1815 II. Paris.

Harmand, Jules (1885): Notes diverses sur quelques questions relatives à l'Indochine, Juin–Juillet, Note III: Du protectorat et de l'administration directe. Ministère des Affaires Etrangères. Mémoires et Documents. Asie 24, 58, 1884–1887.

Holz, Harald/Wegmann, Konrad (eds.) (2005): Rechtsdenken: Schnittpunkte West und Ost. Recht in den gesellschafts- und staatstragenden Institutionen Europas und Chinas. Münster.

Huard, Pierre/Durand, Maurice (1954): Connaissance du Vietnam. Paris.

Hübner, Ulrich/Constantinesco, Vlad (1988): Einführung in das französische Recht. München.

Huynh, Van Tong (1971): Histoire de la presse vietnamienne jusqu'en 1930. Paris.

Kley, Bruno (1920): Rechtsprinzipien der Verwaltung überseeischer Herrschaftsgebiete nach britischem und französischem Staats- und Kolonialrecht. Greifswald.

Lanessan, Jean L. de (1895): La colonisation française en Indochine. Paris.

Larcher-Goscha, Agathe (2000): La légitimation française en Indochine: Mythes et réalités de la collaboration franco-vietnamienne et du réformisme colonial (1905–1945). Paris.

Montaigut, Ferdinand de (1920): La colonisation française dans l'Est de la Cochinchine. Paris.

Morlat, Patrice (1990): La répression coloniale au Vietnam (1908–1940). Paris.

Nguyen, Anh Tuan (1967): Les forces politiques au Sud-Vietnam depuis les accords de Genève 1954. Löwen.

Nguyen Huu Khang (1946): La commune annamite. Etude historique, juridique et économique. Paris.

Nguyen Tien Huu (1969): Dörfliche Kulte im traditionellen Vietnam. München.

Nguyen Van Vinh (1961): Reformes agraires au Vietnam. Löwen.

Papin, Philippe (2002): Who Has Power in the Village? Political Process and Social Reality in Vietnam. In: Bousquet, Gisele/Brocheux, Pierre (eds.): Viet Nam Exposé. French Scholarship on Twentieth-Century Vietnamese Society. Ann Arbor. 21–60.

Pham Thi Ngoan (1973): Introduction au Nam-Phong (1917–1934). In: Bulletin de la Société des Etudes Indochinoise 2–3, 175–496.

Phan Thi Dac (1966): Situation de La Personne au Viet-Nam. Paris.

Ridder, Helmut (2010): Die soziale Ordnung des Grundgesetzes. Leitfaden zu den Grundrechten einer demokratischen Verfassung. In: Deiseroth, Dieter (ed.): Gesammelte Schriften. Baden-Baden. 7–190.

Silvestre, Jean (1889): L'empire d'annam et le peuple annamite. Paris.

Stern, Klaus (1984): Das Staatsrecht der Bundesrepublik Deutschland. Band I: Grundbegriffe und Grundlagen des Staatsrechts, Strukturprinzipien der Verfassung. München.

Urban, Yerri (2010): L'indigène dans le droit colonial français 1865–1955. Paris.

Vu The Quyen (1977): Die vietnamesische Gesellschaft im Wandel. Kolonialismus und gesellschaftliche Entwicklung in Vietnam. Köln.

Weber, Max (1963): Gesammelte Aufsätze zur Religionssoziologie, Bd. I. Tübingen.

Weidenfeld, Katia (2010): Histoire du droit administratif. Du XIVe siècle à nos jours. Paris.

Wilhelm, Richard (ed.): Li Gi (Das Buch der Sitte). Aus dem Chinesischen übertragen und erläutert. Düsseldorf.

Zinoman, Peter (2001): The Colonial Bastille: A History of Imprisonment in Vietnam, 1862–1940. Berkeley.

Zippelius, Reinhold (1999): Allgemeine Staatsrechtslehre. Politikwissenschaft. München.

II. Theoretical Reflections

Separation of Powers in Pre-modern Western Political Thought and the Building of the State of Law in Vietnam

Lai Quoc Khanh

Among the signs of a state of law, there is one that is widely recognized by researchers in the world, which is that the power of the government is operated according to the principle of separation of powers as an internal control method to avoid the abuse/manipulation of power. In the organization of governing systems in many countries, the separation of powers principle has been applied in different ways. The birth of the separation of powers principle and the fact that this concept is used widely in the political life of humankind is a proof of its value.

The Constitution of the Socialist Republic of Vietnam (amended in 2013)[1] states that the Vietnamese state is a socialist state of law, of the people, by the people and for the people. All the power of the state belongs to the people based on the alliance between the working class, the peasantry and the intellectuals. State power is united, and at the same time is entrusted to state agencies that collaborate with and monitor one another in the implementation of legislative, executive and judicial powers. Thus, technically, the Vietnamese state is not constructed based on the separation of powers principle. Nevertheless, it cannot be denied that the useful values of the separation of powers principle have been applied in organizing and exercising Vietnamese state power, thereby establishing the principle of "division, collaboration and mutual monitor-

---

[1] From now on Constitution of Vietnam.

ing amongst state agencies in implementing legislative, executive and judicial powers." This is a new point, a step forward in Vietnamese political and constitutional thinking, which overcomes the old thinking that rigidly regards the separation of powers principle as a distinctive feature of Western capitalist-ruled states.

In order to understand the values underlying the separation of powers principle, and through which to understand more clearly the values of the Vietnamese constitution (2013) and utilize these values more in the future, we started to research the separation of powers principle in pre-modern Western political thought by studying three representatives: John Locke, Charles-Louis de Secondat de Montesquieu and Jean-Jacques Rousseau.

During the Dark Middle Age, the progressive political thoughts that were established in the period of Ancient Greece including the separation of powers principle associated with the reputation of thinkers such as Solon (c. 638–558 B.C.), Cleisthenes (c. 570–508 B.C.), Ephialtes (5th century B.C.), Pericles (495–429 B.C.), etc., and especially Aristotle (384–322 B.C.), re-emerged and developed together with the establishment of the pre-modern mode of capitalist production and became ideological guidelines for Western European bourgeois revolutions. The separation of powers principle has been developed and improved by outstanding thinkers namely John Locke, Charles-Louis de Secondat de Montesquieu, and Jean-Jacques Rousseau and has become the theory underlying the organization and building of modern states.

Locke's Thoughts on the Separation of Powers

John Locke (1632–1704) is the author of a series of classic works in the history of philosophical and political thoughts of humankind such as "An Essay concerning Humane Understanding", "Two Treatises of Government", "A Letter Concerning Toleration", "Some Thoughts Concerning Education", etc.

If "The First Treatise of Government" was written with the purpose of criticizing the patriarchal perspective on government of authors at the time, then the "Second Treatise of Government" is the work by which Locke developed his view about the state. In this writing, Locke's thinking on the separation of powers was strongly expressed. Locke claimed that in a republic state there are three main types of powers: legislative, executive and federative. In these three types, the legislative power is the first and basic power of every nation state, so the legislative body holds supreme power. Locke wrote: "The legislative body holds not only the supreme power of a nation community, but also the sacred and non-transferable power once the community puts it into that position."[2] The law is only effective, supreme, and forces all members to follow it once it is approved by the legislative body. The "recognition" of the legislative body represents the "recognition" of the society. However, originating from the popular thoughts at his time, i.e. the thoughts on natural rights and the social contract, Locke pointed out that, as an authorized body, the legislative body is bound by the following principles:

- It does not and cannot hold arbitrary power, meaning that its power cannot be higher than that of the subject that has granted power to it – the citizens. In other words the "natural rights" that human beings receive when joining the community is the supreme power that controls everybody, including the legislators.
- The legislative agency has to act properly according to rules that are "transparent and approved" which reflect human beings' natural rights.
- These transparent and approved rules have to protect people's rights, especially property rights.
- The legislative body cannot transfer the power of law-making to anybody else because it is power assigned by the citizens.

However, because laws "can be made in a short period of time, it is unnecessary for the legislative agency to be present and to have tasks to perform at all times."[3] Simultaneously, to avoid the trend that legislators "monopolize power" to serve personal purposes, legislative power "has to be assigned to many people gathering at the right time (...) Upon finishing that duty, they will dismiss and themselves will be subject to the laws that they make."[4] In order to satisfy the demand of enforcing the law in the long run, "there must be a power that always is present to observe the enforcement of already-made laws by means of violence", so legislative and executive power have to be separated, and the executive body has to be present at all times.

---

[2] Locke (2007), 183.

[3] Locke (2007), 199.

[4] Locke (2007), 200

100

Beside legislative and executive powers, there is another power that can be considered natural, said Locke, which is federative power. Federative power means "the right to war and peace, to form union and alliance, to make other agreements, with individuals and communities outside the national community."[5] Executive and federative powers have to be distinctive; however they still have a close connection because they both "need the force of the society to be enforced."[6]

Not only contributing to specifying the factors that constitute state power, the distinction between key types of state power as well as the allocation of these powers to different official authorities, Locke also thoroughly discussed the relationship between the types of power and these agencies. Locke always argued that supreme power belongs to the people. At first, this point is true in the case of the organization with the supreme power, the legislative body. He wrote: "among the people lies a supreme power to terminate or change the legislative body, when they realize that the legislative body acts in ways that run counter to its assigned missions."[7] This is the "supreme power" of the people to "save themselves" when the authorized organization plots and acts in ways detrimental to their benefit. Regarding the relationship between the legislative and executive bodies, Locked argued that the legislative body holds the supreme state power, and other powers, held by any member or group in the society, have to originate from it and depend on it.

Executive and federative powers have to depend on legislative power. According to Locke, executive power cannot be put elsewhere rather than on a person that is also a member of the legislative body (the king), and because the legislative body assigns the right to implement laws that they make to executive officials, they still have the power to take it back if they see a reason to do so, even to punish any weak operation that contradicts the law. The same principle applies to federative power. The right to assemble and perform their activities are set by the constitution. They themselves have the power to postpone meetings and their own activities. Although dependent, executive power is independent in some way and can also influence legislative power. This influence is manifested through the mechanism of summoning and dissolving

---

[5] Locke (2007), 201.

[6] Locke (2007), 202.

[7] Locke (2007), 203.

the legislative body. Locke put the right to summon and dissolve the legislative body beyond constitutionally stipulated meetings into the hand of the legislative body, in situations when there is a need to hold a new election between two constitutionally stipulated meetings, when emergency cases of the society require amendments of existing laws or the issuance of new laws, etc. The act of assigning the power to assemble and dissolve the legislative body to the executive body is also a form of authorization by citizens. If legislators use this power to hinder legitimate activities this is a declaration of war against the people, and the people will use their supreme power to take back all the state's power, even by means of violence. The executive body also has another power over the legislative agency, which is the power to decide the number of representatives of the people in different regions and their privileges of action. Privileges of action as well as other rights of the executive body all originate from the principle of "Salus populi suprema lex" (the happiness of the people is the supreme power), and is very necessary because in reality, there are things that the law cannot or should not prescribe, and also due to the inability of the legislative body to be always present, as well as the "delay" of legislative activities in comparison with the rapid pace of social life. In order to prevent the privileges of action from doing harm to the people, it is necessary to understand that this is the power assigned by the people to executive officials, and therefore the citizens have the right to limit it, and executives cannot have so many privileges of action anyhow.

Therefore, it can be seen that Locke has made immense progress in the thinking about the separation of powers. His opinion of the division of power, the interdependence of different types of power and state agencies as mentioned above is the profoundly practical materialization of simple ideas about the separation of powers since the period of ancient Greece. The most special point in Locke's thought on the separation of powers is that he is consistent in the idea that the supreme power should always belong to the people, and all the methods to govern and operate state apparatuses are to be aimed at guaranteeing the people's benefit. However, it is obvious that Locke faced a difficulty in answering a practical question that he himself created: Who will judge whether an authorized power is used properly? His answer is that the people cannot find a secular judge and thus they have to "pray to heaven". This opinion expresses the incompleteness of Locke's thought on the separation of powers as he did not give enough attention to judicial power and "secular" judicial organizations.

Montesquieu's Thoughts on the Separation of Powers

Charles de Secondat Montesquieu (1689–1755) wrote a number of works including the three most popular ones namely "Persian Letters", "Considerations on the Causes of the Greatness of the Romans and their Decline" and "The Spirit of the Laws". The writing that made him one of the most preeminent political thinkers of humankind – "The Spirit of the Laws" – was published in 1784, after 20 years of diligent research as its author admitted. Setting up the research topic as "the spirit of the laws", Montesquieu proposed an opinion that the existence of the law is indispensable and universal:

"The law, in the broadest meaning, is indispensable relationships that are inherent in the nature of things or events. According to this meaning, everything has its own laws."[8]

Therefore, humankind has its own laws. He argued that, humankind has two main kinds of law, political and civil. "In a society, in order to maintain discipline, it is necessary to point out the relationship between the administrator and the administered. That is political law. The regulation of relationships between citizens is civil law."[9] Political and civil laws, according to Montesquieu, are the particular application of "human reasoning" in specific cases. Political laws create a governing system, and civil laws help maintaining it. Nevertheless, the reason for the existence of both political and civil laws is to guarantee people's political freedom. Montesquieu wrote:

"Political freedom (...) only exists if there is no abuse of power. However, the experience of all times point out that, those who are granted power tend to abuse that power and seek to maximize that power for their own use (...) In order to avoid this behavior, a natural necessity is that power has to be controlled by power. One government like that can be established if no one is forced to do things that the law does not oblige him to do, and no one is prevented from doing things that the law permits"[10]

---

[8] Montesquieu (1996), 39.

[9] Montesquieu (1996), 44.

[10] Montesquieu (1996), 75.

This is a really important quote from Montesquieu because it shows that he is more progressive than Locke and preceding thinkers on the separation of powers. It was not until Montesquieu's opinion that the core of the separation of powers principle, i.e. "power has to be hindered by power," was established. Before him, the main focus was just on the allocation of political power to different state organizations and the relationship between the powers and these organizations, without showing the nature of that relationship.

Discussing the types of state power, Montesquieu stated that in each nation there are three types of power: "Legislative power, executive power to implement rules that are compatible with international laws and executive power to implement civil law."[11] He explained further that the second type is "national executive power" and the third one is "judicial power".[12] It can be seen that Montesquieu clearly defined the division of political power into three types that are legislative power, executive power and judicial power. This is one of his contributions.

Montesquieu affirms clearly that the three types of power above have to be assigned to different governing organizations of the state. It is because:

"When legislative and executive powers are both assigned to one person or one Senate, there is no such thing as freedom; because there is a danger that the person himself or the Senate itself issues authoritarian laws to implement in an authoritarian way. There is no such thing as freedom if judicial power is not separated from legislative and executive powers. If judicial and legislative powers join together, the holder of these powers will dictate the right to live and freedom of the citizens; the judge will issue laws. If judicial power and executive power join together, the judge will have the power of a suppressor. If one person or an organization of officials or of aristocrats, or of the people holds all the above powers, then everything will vanish."[13]

Montesquieu took the examples of European, Turkish and Italian politics to justify the above opinion. His general comment after comparing those regimes was: If the three types of power join together, this will lead to autocracy.

Regarding judicial power, Montesquieu stated that it should not be assigned to a permanent senate, "but it should be assigned to the people elected by the citizens each time in a year, prescribed by laws, who set up a court and

---

[11] Montesquieu (1996), 100.

[12] Montesquieu (1996), 100.

[13] Montesquieu (1996), 100–101.

104

work as long as required."[14] In this way, the judges have the same position as the accused, so the accused will not think that he is in the hands of those that are able and willing to do harm to him. The purpose of the above mechanism is to reduce the permanent fear of the people towards judging power. Thus, Montesquieu held that judging power should not be assigned to an organization or a fixed position, but a judging "mechanism" should be created. Additionally, when the accused have a dispute with the law, they have to be able to choose their judges, or to decline the assigned judges. However, to avoid another extreme as well as to avoid rendering the people helpless before judging mechanisms, Montesquieu thought that the court should not be fixed, but sentences should be recorded, and laws should contain only particular articles (legal precedents).

About legislative and executive powers, Montesquieu argued that it is possible to "assign these types of power to permanent organizations and officials, because these powers should not be given to an individual. Legislative power expresses the collective will of a nation and executive power exercises that collective will."[15]

With the idea of a free state as a state where citizens control themselves, Montesquieu stated that the people "must have legislative power" and implementi this power by "assigning to the representatives all the tasks that individuals cannot do by themselves."[16] This idea shows that Montesquieu already paid attention to the techniques of legislative work rather than only discussing abstract democratic notions. He considered that the people are the supreme holder of power, but within political work, not every task can be done by everyone. According to Montesquieu, the people's representatives have to be elected by regions, not the whole country. The function of the legislative body is not solving particular problems, but "creating laws, and considering how these laws are implemented."[17] As to the structure of the legislative body, Montesquieu proposed a model with two sections: one includes representatives of aristocrats (Senate) and the other consists of people's representatives (House).

---

[14] Montesquieu (1996), 102.

[15] Montesquieu (1996), 102–103.

[16] Montesquieu (1996), 104.

[17] Montesquieu (1996), 105.

In order for the senate not to fall into the habit of focusing on their own interests without considering the people's will, he thought that there should be a supreme law stating that the senate should only have the function of preventing, not the function of making rules and regulations. According to Montesquieu, executive power should be assigned to a king, because executive power always requires immediate actions which should be conducted by one person rather than many.

Highlighting the importance of the separation of powers, Montesquieu opposed the idea that executive power should belong to some members or the whole parliament. He also agreed with Locke that the executive body should have the right to summon or set the date and time of parliamentary meetings. Moreover, the executive body also has the right to prevent the legislative body's plans, in order to reduce the risk that the legislative body becomes autocratic. Obviously, the executive body has limited power, which means it can only solve temporary issues and cannot be involved in legislative work, "cannot argue about works", "cannot propose petitions". The legislative body, although it does not hold the power of preventing executive power and judging executive officials, has the right to "consider how established laws have been implemented", which, in modern parlance, means it has supervisory power. Judicial power should not combine with any part of legislative power, but with three exceptions:

- Aristocrats are judged by a legislative body including aristocrats only, because "big men are often objects of envy".
- Laws are mechanical, sometimes even blind and severe; therefore the aristocrats in the legislative body should use their power, for the laws' benefit, to reduce the harshness when issuing a sentence.
- In order to prevent aristocrats from covering for each other, the people's legislative body has the right to report to the aristocrats in the legislative body.

State power is associated with violent instruments, thus in order to protect the people from being repressed, Montesquieu proposed that the army had to be close to the people and dependent on the executive body, not the legislative one.

Thus, after examining some basic opinions of Montesquieu about organizational forms and operational methods of state apparatuses, we can say that he made a great contribution to the establishment of the separation of powers principle. Montesquieu's thoughts on the separation of powers not only inherited but also developed previously incomplete ideas about the separation of powers. Furthermore, because he focused on summarizing practical experience and at the same time was influenced by experimental methods, Montesquieu's thoughts on the separation of powers are profoundly practical and have great potential to be applied.

Rousseau's Thoughts on the Separation of Powers

The writing that expresses Jean-Jacques Rousseau's (1712–1778) distinctive thoughts on the separation of powers and other political ideas is "The Social Contract, or Principles of Political Right", published in 1762. "The Social Contract" serves the purpose of "looking in the civil order to see whether there is any strong, reasonable rule that can treat human beings as human beings", and "whether there is any law that matches its true nature".

Rousseau wanted to use his work to "connect what the law allows to which interests that should be promoted, which prevents justice and interests from being separated."[18] In order to do this, Rousseau divided his book into four parts (four books), in which part 1 discussed the transition of human society from natural status to civil status, about common will, and about the establishment of "social conventions"; part 2 mainly discussed legislative issues; part 3 focused on executive issues and part 4 discussed judicial issues and other guarantees of democracy.It is essential to pay attention to the core argument in part 1 of Rousseau's book:

"No one naturally has power on others. And strength alone does not create power; therefore only conventions can be the base for all reasonable power between people."[19]

The establishment of conventions marks the transition of humankind from natural to civil status. With conventions, people lose the natural freedom and the limited rights to do what they want; but on the other hand people regain civil liberty and the right to own things that they have. With this transition, people give up the freedom that is limited by the individual's ability in exchange for much more freedom defined by the community's common will.

---

[18] Rousseau (1992), 28.

[19] Rousseau (1992), 35.

When all members of society join the conventions, common will and public power are established. The state is the manifestation of that common will and power.

Public power is formed because the people join the conventions, thus the people are the holders of public power and public power cannot be divided either mechanically or casually like magic tricks. The people's common will also needs to be guaranteed; and when a common will is the true common will, then it is always good.[20] Rousseau wrote: "If the people are informed properly, when they discuss problems, although there is no private interaction, or they have many minor differences in their opinions, the discussion still leads to the common will, the result is always good." He argued that all the plots of private individuals to turn private will into common will, even if that was able to cover everything, in reality still destroy the common will. However, only conventions and common will are not enough. Rousseau thought that:

"With social conventions, we make the political body exist and give it a life. We have to use the legislative activity to give the political body movement and will."[21]

But what are laws? According to Rousseau, laws are regulations of the common will and the citizens who follow laws have to be the ones who make the laws. That is the common principle, but in order to have harmony between the common and the private, between the body and the parts, there is a need for lawmakers. The law is the manifestation of the common will, so "legislation is the pinnacle of the perfection that collective strength can achieve", and legislators, in all aspects, have to be "the outstanding persons in the country."[22] Rousseau discussed the characteristics of lawmakers among which knowledge is of great importance, and the knowledge of lawmakers has to be outstanding, "to see clearly people's desires without giving preference to a certain desire."[23] Rousseau also indicated that the purpose of the legal system is freedom and equality. He also distinguished four types of law,; "political law" that governs the relationship between the common and the private, "civil law" that governs the relationship among individuals, "criminal law" that governs the relationship between the citizens and the law, and "customary law" or "people's opin-

---

[20] Rousseau (1992), 58.

[21] Rousseau (1992), 67.

[22] Rousseau (1992), 72.

[23] Rousseau (1992), 71.

ions" that are not engraved on rocks or bronze but in people's minds, and which creates the nation's true constitution.

In part 2 Rousseau discusses the government or the executive body. If the legislative body is the highest organ of state power, then the government, according to Rousseau, is the intermediary body between the people and that highest organ. The legislative power belongs to the people, and can belong to it alone, while the executive power cannot belong to the generality. Members of the executive body cannot be involved in legislation. The function of the executive body is to implement tasks assigned by the legislative body, and the legislative body is able to take back, edit, and limit the power of the executive body. The existence of the executive body is essential, because if the legislative agency wants to perform an executive function, or the people do not follow the law (because there is no executive authority and the legislative body does not have an executive function), the country will be in chaos. Rousseau argued that there are three forms of government,

- democratic (the legislative body assigns the duty of managing the government to the people or the majority of people),
- aristocratic (the government is controlled by a small group), and
- monarchical (there is only one supreme judge).

There is also the mixedtype of government. Each form of government suits a specific type of nation. There is no absolutely good form or government. A good government is the government that educates the population, and vice versa. In order to prevent the government from seizing absolute power, the officials are only civil servants. The people are able to promote or dismiss them, and they have no choice but to follow. The people implement the above power through the people's conference (or congress).

Regarding the judicial body, Rousseau thought that this is a special organization which is not part of any other section; it "puts each section in the right position, serves as the connection and intermediary factor between the government and the people, or between the government and the highest organ of state power, or between all those three parties when necessary."[24] It is "the most sacred organization" and most highly appreciated because it protects the law. The function of the judicial court is to announce public opinion, not to judge public opinion. "If the court deviates from that function, all of its deci-

---

[24] Rousseau (1992), 174.

sions will become absurd and will have no effect."[25] The judicial body has to be separated from other organs of state power. "The judicial body will exceed its authority once it takes possession of executive power, which it is supposed to monitor. The judicial body also misuses its power if it issues laws, which it supposes to protect."[26] In order to prevent the judicial body from being corrupted, there is a need to determine a proper duration for it. This duration should not be too long so that the abuse of judicial power cannot take shape.

With the above opinions, Rousseau made distinctive contributions to the thoughts on the separation of powers. While Locke focused on the sovereignty of the people without discussing enough about the structure or the state system based on the spirit of separation of powers, and Montesquieu discussed in depth the structure of the state system without really focusing on the matter that the supreme holder of power is the people; Rousseau broke through both of the above limits by interpreting strength, right, power, conventions, and the manifestation of the position of the people as the holder of power in the structure of separation of powers. Rousseau's thinking on the separation of powers is profoundly dialectical. He himself did make the separation of powers concept a comprehensive theory.

Conclusion

It can be seen that the thoughts on the separation of powers of John Locke, Charles-Louis de Secondat de Montesquieu and Jean-Jacques Rousseau – three outstanding representatives of modern Western political thinkers – contain many profound values. Pervading all their thoughts is a noble goal: to protect human rights, to protect the supreme sovereignty of the people. That goal is manifested differently in the works of each of these thinkers, in rules to organize the state system and principles to operate state power. In this aspect, the common spirit that emerges – which is also a value that needs to be researched and applied – is to guarantee that the state system and state power are truly the people's tools to prevent the abuse of state power, or to prevent one part of state power from gaining the ability to control and govern other powers unrea-

---

[25] Rousseau (1992), 181.

[26] Rousseau (1992), 175.

110

sonably. All of those do harm to the people and prevent them from being the supreme holder of all power in the society. It is evident that this is the opinion of using power to control power – the principle to internally control state power. Obviously, there are historical limits in these thinkers' opinions, and especially if we approach from the standpoint of Marxist politics, the inability to realize relations of interests, especially class interests, a key form of interest that plays a basic role in all political relationships, the substantiality and feasibility of the separation of powers principle is lacking a solid base, both in theoretical and practical terms.

References

Academy of Journalism and Communication, Faculty of Politics (ed.) (2005): Political Institutions in the World Today. Hanoi.

Chu Duong (2005): State Institutions in Different Countries in the World. Hanoi.

Ellis, William (ed.) (1985): The Politics of Aristotle or a Treatise on Government. London.

Ho Van Thong (1998): The Political Systems of Developed Capitalist Countries Today. Hanoi.

Locke, John (2007): The Second Treatise on Government. Hanoi.

Montesquieu, Charles-Louis de Secondat de (1996): The Spirit of the Laws (Vietnamese translation). Hanoi.

Nguyen Canh Binh (2013): How the Constitution of the USA was Made. Hanoi.

Nguyen Thi Hoi (2005): The Principle of Separation of Powers and the Organization of State Systems in Several Countries. Hanoi.

Nguyen Van Huyen (ed.) (2007): Political Systems of England, France, the USA. Hanoi.

Rousseau, Jean-Jacques (1992): The Social Contract. Ho Chi Minh City.

The Institute of Legal Science (ed.) (2005): Political Institutions and State Systems of Several Countries in the World. Hanoi.

Vu Hong Anh (1997): Organization and Operation of the Governments of Several Countries in the World. Hanoi.

Rousseau's Thoughts on the Division and Control of State Power. A Comparison with Montesquieu's Model

Nguyen Thi Chau Loan

Rousseau's thoughts on the methods to organize, divide and control state power are not only the core of his conception of the state of law but also an indispensable part of Rousseau's political philosophy. This paper focuses on analyzing methods to organize and divide different types of state power such as legislative, executive and judicial powers based on Rousseau's state of law model which aims at the effective implementation of the common will, supreme sovereignty and social contract of the people in order to guarantee human beings' natural rights. In particular this paper interprets the similarities and differences between two models to control and divide power: Rousseau's model and Montesquieu's separation of powers model to avoid and prevent the threat of misusing state power. I argue that Rousseau's thoughts have more potential to be applied in establishing the state of law of the people, by the people and for the people in Vietnam today.

According to Rousseau, supreme power is united and cannot be split. However, in order for supreme power to be implemented effectively and coherently, it has to be distributed via its three indispensable constituents. They are legislative, executive and judicial powers.

Methods to Organize and Divide State Power

Legislative Power

According to Rousseau, legislative power is the basic part of supreme power. Indeed, legislative power is the ability to compose, approve and issue laws and codes based on social contracts which reflect the common will of all citizens. The question is: Who will be the legislators in a nation? Who will compose and create common codes relevant to everyone?

First of all, according to Rousseau, neither the masses nor individuals are able to be legislators with the ability to compose, approve and issue laws. The masses always have desires, but they cannot realize these desires all the time. On the contrary, even if individuals realize these benefits in principle, they tend to deny them. Rousseau thought that, in all relationships, the legislators in a nation are outstanding persons.

Secondly, in the fields of legislation and laws, there are numerous abstract thoughts which are unable to be explained in ordinary language to ordinary people; especially there are issues which are too general and surpass "the level of knowledge of ordinary people who are only interested in issues relating to their own immediate benefits and have difficulty in realizing benefits that the right rules bring about by revoking their personal rights."[1] Therefore, the language of legislators, according to Rousseau, is not the ordinary language that can be understood by normal people.[2]

Legislators have a "supreme" and special position and hold a kind of power which is different from normal power. By answering the question "Who is the legislator in the nation?" Rousseau concluded: "Legislators, in all aspects are outstanding persons in the nation; because of not only their innate talent but also the way their talent is used."[3]

Duty and means of legislators: Legislators have to perform duties that exceed the ability of an ordinary human being. Meanwhile, legislators have no necessary power to accomplish that task, because legislative power only belongs to the people. The only means that legislators can use is persuasion.[4]

---

[1] Rousseau (2004), 102.

[2] Fetscher (1989), 146–151.

[3] Rousseau (2004), 101.

[4] Fetscher (1989), 146–151.

The legislative body: The legislative body is the supreme organ of state power which performs its mission and exercises its authority through laws. Rousseau wrote: "the supreme organ of state power has no power but legislative power so it only operated by laws. Laws are the proper behavior of common will; so supreme power can have an impact only when citizens gather."[5] He said that there should be regular and extraordinary meetings. The best choice is meetings that include all of the people to determine the common will and desires of each nation. Rousseau also raised another method, which is to "let the government set up headquarters at one city after another and respectively reunite the citizens to study around that city."[6] However, we think that this ideal choice and similar methods in reality are infeasible and create difficulty for the legislative body. Nevertheless, this thought of Rousseau laid the basis for the idea of direct democracy already.

According to Rousseau, the duty of the legislative body is to issue a constitution and a legal system and codes for the nation. The legislative body will propose the establishment of a government to implement executive function. He thought that because legislative power only belongs to the people, the people themselves have the right to solve problems about the form of government. At the same time, the legislative body has the duty to propose methods to select judges, and court officials for judicial organizations. Therefore, Rousseau put legislative power in the highest position which controls other types of power, because legislative power is the most direct expression of people's will – the supreme power. People's sovereignty is expressed through people's legislative power. In his dialogue with Montesquieu, Rousseau stated thatpolitical freedom only emerges in a country where the people have direct legislative power. He said that freedom is expressed in the way the citizens are protected by laws and can approve and issue laws on their own. He wrote:

"All laws that are not directly approved by the people are valueless and cannot be called laws."[7]

Engaging in politics is not only the citizens' right but the citizen's obligation. Legislative authority has the responsibility to reflect people's common will,

---

[5] Rousseau (2004), 170.

[6] Rousseau (2004), 173.

[7] Rousseau (2004), 179.

114

and not the personal opinions of parliament members or of the people's representatives.

Executive Power

Rousseau defined executive power as:

"The true name of executive power according to law is government or the supreme governing body. The person or organization that is assigned that governing duty is called head of state or the supreme judge."[8]

Rousseau distinguished clearly between legislative and executive powers. While legislative power belongs and only belongs to the people, executive power cannot belong to the common folk like legislative power or supreme power:

"Executive power only relates to particular clauses, does not belong to the authority of basic law or the highest organ of state power; and all of its conducts have to be laws."[9]

Rousseau defined and analyzed the government as the executive body. He thought that "the government is an intermediary mechanism between citizens and the highest organ of state power in order for two parties to be correlative, to implement laws, to maintain civil as well as political freedom. Members of this structure are called supreme judges or kings which mean governors. This whole intermediary body is named government".[10] Therefore, the government plays an intermediary role; it functions as a medium between the highest organ of state power and the citizens; it can be defined as the tool of people's legislative and supreme power. Rousseau analyzed the triangle of the relationship between three levels, between the highest organ of state power, the government and the people and stated that the relationship is not created by accident but is rather the indispensable outcome of the nature of the political body. Each part of that triangle has its own function. The function of the highest organ of state power, the legislative body, is to legislate and enact laws. The function of the government is to execute the law and govern directly. The function of the people or citizens is to follow the law. Those functions are defined clearly. The unclear definition or improper implementation of functions runs the risks of autocracy or anarchy. Rousseau wrote:

[8] Rousseau (2004), 123.

[9] Rousseau (2004), 122.

[10] Rousseau (2004), 123.

"If the highest organ of state power (that naturally performs the legislative function) wants to govern directly; or the supreme judge (that naturally performs the executive function) wants to issue laws; or citizens do not want to follow, the state will be in chaos immediately; strength and will do not interact harmoniously; the nation will be in the situations of either autocracy or anarchy."[11]

Rousseau anticipated and warned about the possibility of conflict between parts of that triangle of relationship. The strongest will of the government has to be the common will and has to be the law, the foundation of the government's public strength. However, if the government acts autocratically with its own will which is stronger than the will of the highest organ of state power by using the force it controls, there will be a huge threat: at that moment, in a nation there are "two highest organs of state power, one in law and one in reality".[12] The result is that "social union will collapse, the political body will die."[13]

In case of conflict between executive and legislative bodies, Rousseau's solution is "to be always prepared to sacrifice the government for the people, not to sacrifice the people for the government."[14] The executive body is established on the basis of law, not contract. The government established by the legislative body has the duty to follow and implement laws. The people assigned with executive power are not owners of the people but servants. The people and the highest organ of state power are able to promote or dismiss them. The legislative or the highest organ of state power can issue, edit government election law as well as change the executive system at any time.[15] However, Rousseau warned that each time the form of the government is changed, there will be dangers and it should only be changed once it cannot be harmonious with common benefit. He emphasized the relative freedom of the government as the executive body in comparison with the legislative body.

"Although the government is established for a specific purpose, it still has a certain independence, depending on its establishment method."[16]

---

[11] Rousseau (2004), 124.

[12] Rousseau (2004), 127.

[13] Rousseau (2004), 127.

[14] Rousseau (2004), 128.

[15] Fetscher (1989), 151–170.

[16] Rousseau (2004), 128.

The principles for constructing and classifying types of government: One of the most basic principles in establishing government structure proposed by Rousseau is: "The more officials, the weaker the government". Interpreting this principle, he analyzed three different kinds of will in an official's mind:

"The first one is his personal will aiming for his own benefits. The second one is all officials' will relating to the government's success: it can be considered to be the collective will of the government as well as the private will of one section (the government) in the whole nation. The third one is the nation's will or supreme will which is the common will of a nation as a whole and of the government as a part."[17]

However, according to Rousseau, in arranging the order of priority of those three kinds of will, there is a difference between natural order and the demand of social order. According to natural order, "each government official first of all is himself, then an official and finally a citizen."[18] In other words, according to natural order, each official normally prioritizes personal will, then government's will and lastly common will. It is vice versa in the case of social order. In the best legislative regime, personal will has to be zero; collective will of the government has to depend strongly on the supreme common will as the standard for all other types of will. Therefore, if the government is controlled by one person, personal and government's will are totally identical and of a very high intensity, thus the most active government according to Rousseau is that of one person.

Rousseau affirmed the necessity of forming a compact government, mostly in the case of a big country in order for the number of supreme officials to be inversely proportional to the number of the population. "The ratio between officials and government has to be inversely proportional to the ratio between citizens and the highest organ of state power, so the bigger the nation, the stricter and more compact the government, or the more the people, the less the governors."

Judicial Power

Judicial power is the power to judge based on law in order to punish and prevent illegal behaviors, protect the laws and the legislative power. The judicial body is a special, independent body that "does not involve in the work of any

---

[17] Rousseau (2004), 129–130.

[18] Rousseau (2004), 130.

other body", and has the duty to implement judicial power, and protect people's common will. According to Rousseau, the judicial body

"puts each section into its right position, serves as the connection and intermediary factor between the government and the people or between the government and the highest organ of state power, or between all those three parties when necessary."[19]

The function of the judicial body is to protect the law and the legislative power. There are times when the judicial body protects supreme power – the legislative body in the relationship with the government, there are other times when it protects the government in the relationship with the people, but it can also maintain the balance among the above parties.[20] According to Rousseau, the judicial body

"must not have even a little bit of legislative or executive power. But because of this, the judicial body has the highest power because it does nothing but can prevent everything. It is the holiest and most highly appreciated organization because it protects the law" and *"law is issued by the highest organ of state power and approved by the government."[21]*

An independent, cleverly harmonized judicial body will be a strong basis for a healthy political body. This is the basic principle of a state of law, which has important suggestive value to the structuring of a state of law in Vietnam in general and to the judicial reform in Vietnam at the moment. Rousseau also distinguished clearly between judicial, legislative and executive functions. He also mentioned the ability of the judicial body to abuse power and its immeasurable consequence.

"The judicial body will abuse power once it controls executive power which it is supposed to monitor. The judicial body will also misuse power if it issues laws which it is supposed to protect."[22]

In order to avoid the usurpation by the judicial body, according to Rousseau, the only way is to prevent it from holding a permanent position and its duration has to be fixed by law. The duration should be enough, not too long for the abuse of power to take shape. This method is effective because a new judi-

---

[19] Rousseau (2004), 128.

[20] Rousseau (2004), 128.

[21] Rousseau (2004), 129.

[22] Rousseau (2004), 219.

118

cial official elected based on law has to work based on law, not on his precedents.

When discussing the judicial body's function, Rousseau argued thatlaws manifest the people's common will, and judicial official positions express public judgment. Public opinions are a kind of law that the judicial body has to follow. He thought that a judicial court is not the one judging public opinion, but in reality is the one manifesting public opinion. If a court deviates from that function, all of its judgement will be partial and will have no effect. The ability of judicial officials is expressed in the ability to anticipate and control public opinion: "Who can anticipate public opinion can anticipate honor. Who can anticipate honor can control the rule of public opinion."[23] Additionally, judicial officials have to maintain tradition and prevent public opinion from corrupting, maintain straightforwardness and uprightness by smart methods. Even when necessary, they guide public opinion if it is not appropriate.

One of the most important things that Rousseau wanted to emphasize in his political philosophy is the indispensability of distinguishing clearly between different types of political powers in a nation: legislative, executive and judicial powers. The consideration of these types of power is an important part of his political thought to which he paid particular attention.

The Differentiation and Control of State Power

The Similarities and Differences between Rousseau's and Montesquieu's Opinions about Power Separation

Rousseau's and Montesquieu's political philosophy theories had a profound impact on the development of modern states especially through the works "Social Contracts" and "The Spirit of the Laws". These theories later strongly influenced different models of the state of law that are opposed to one another. The comparison of the similarities and differences of these two power separation models is necessary and has suggestive values to the structuring of the state of law in Vietnam at the moment.

We can see the basic similarities between Rousseau's theory about supreme sovereignty or people's sovereignty and Montesquieu's theory about the bal-

---

[23] Rousseau (2004), 126–227.

ance among different types of power. These two thinkers have similar views about the nature of state power: that the state is obliged to guarantee citizens' political freedom by differentiating types of constitutional power such as the legislative, executive and judicial. At the same time, we can also perceive differences between Rousseau and Montesquieu especially relating to how these legislative, executive and judicial components of power should be separated.

First of all, Rousseau's and Montesquieu's political philosophy derive from very different philosophical and anthropological traditions. The fundament of Rousseau's political philosophy is the strong belief in the righteousness of the people's common will; the people's voice is "the voice of the God" on earth. If the people's voice is regularly heard and disseminated more directly and freely, and if governors and citizens follow it, then the state is structured well, and political freedom is secured.. In contrast, due to his skeptical view of human nature, Montesquieu's political philosophy is designed to control the representatives of power, the ones who are considered to have the tendency to misuse it and thereby limit citizens' freedom.[24]

Secondly, Rousseau and Montesquieu built on different principles in dividing supreme power. According to Rousseau, all of the supreme power in a state belongs to the people; the people implement their power directly or indirectly through their "public servants"; people's sovereignty is associated with legislative power and the legislative body; this body's power is directly limited by certain rules that have to be followed. According to Montesquieu, there is no part in a state that is associated with supreme sovereignty and power like that, but there are some parts assigned with different functions of supreme power, so as to ensure that no part or body can have limitless power, and the power of each part (each body) is the restraining, limiting and controlling factor of the power of other parts (bodies). Montesquieu wrote:

"A governing authority that implements laws and at the same time considers itself to be the legislator can destroy the nation by their wrong assumption of the common will. And if they hold the judging power, they can crush each citizen at will."[25]

While Rousseau, believing in the people's common will, stated that guaranteeing the people's unlimited power in the state means guaranteeing the supremacy of the codes that are fair and stable, Montesquieu considered unlimited

---

[24] Fetscher (1989), 146–151.

[25] Montesquieu (2006), 107.

120

power, no matter to whom it belongs , always has the potential to create unacceptable evil even in a well-ordered state. The advantage of state organization, according to Montesquieu, does not depend on who the power belongs to, but on the practicalities of the conditions controlling and limiting that power. However, both Montesquieu and Rousseau distinguished between legislative and executive powers and assigned those types of power to different sections or bodies.[26]

Thirdly, Rousseau and Montesquieu have different opinions on the position of legislative and executive powers. Considering the absolute supremacy of the people's common will to be the origin of codes, Rousseau held that the legislative power that belongs to the people and is associated with the parliament or congress is the supreme power. He thought that executive power associated with the government only has the function to depend on or follow legislative power. The implementation of that function, he said, is assigned to organizations based on laws established by the people's sovereignty. These organizations acquire their authority from the people's sovereignty and implement it under the supervision of this sovereignty. In contrast, Montesquieu stated that supreme power is expressed not only in legislative power but also in executive power, that both legislative and executive powers are equal. He thought that legislative and executive powers are implemented freely and independently of each other. Legislative and executive powers control as well as limit each other by their authority. With Montesquieu, executive power associated with the government does not have the function to depend on or follow legislative power which is discharged by the legislative body.[27]

Fourthly, Montesquieu and Rousseau have different ideas about the paradigm of the nature and the organization of legislative and executive power and their relationship. In Rousseau's state model, executive power is assigned to executive agencies, subordinates are selected by the people from their representatives for a certain duration; these executive organizations, whether they are rulers, or a minority of aristocrats, or the democratic majority in any form, in reality, are just considered people's public servants who exercise their power based on people's desires. These organizations have to follow the people's common will and implement their authority as long as they still follow the

---

[26] Fetscher (1989), 146–151.

[27] Fetscher (1989), 146–151.

people's will. As to the people themselves, they can change governors and even the mode of governance if governors do not follow people's common will. In Montesquieu's state model, supreme executive power is discharged by an independent organization that is more than only an executive agency of the supreme legislative. In a constitutional monarchy for example, monarchs do not receive their authority from a legislative assembly but govern as an independent constitutional body. While Rousseau acknowledged that a government is only legal if it is is selected by the people through their parliamentary representatives, Montesquieu stated that the selection of executive officials from legislators (parliament) violates the basic requirement of state structure which requires power separation in order to guarantee citizens' political freedom. If executive and legislative powers unite, they are not separated, which therefore threatens citizens' political freedom.[28] Thus, in Montesquieu state model, the people who join the government and implement executive power are not allowed to be parliament members.

Fifthly, Montesquieu and Rousseau have different concepts of power control. According to Rousseau, legislative power does not need to be controlled; it cannot endanger political freedom because as the manifestation of common will that judges things based on common benefit, the legislative power always guarantees fairness. According to Rousseau, threats to political freedom come mostly from executive power. Its representatives tend to misuse power for their personal benefit and can do harm to common benefit. Therefore, it is essential to restrict executive power by a series of regulations to ensure its compliance with the law.

According to Montesquieu, any types of powers, even legislative and executive powers, can pose a threat to political freedom, thus it is essential to restrict both types of power. He thought that basically the executive power is restricted while legislative power is left uncontrolled, thus the latter needs to be restricted more. Regarding the relationship between the legislative and executive powers, unlike Rousseau who stated that, the legislator is the owner who holds the higher authority while the executor is just a person that implements, i.e. a people's public servant, Montesquieu stated that legislative and executive powers are the same and equal, that supreme power is expressed through both types of power at the same level. Unlike Rousseau who set criteria to force

---

[28] Montesquieu (2006), 117.

122

executive power to follow legislative power, Montesquieu put those types of power together, on the one hand to guarantee independence and self-control, and on the other hand to maintain the ability of the two to restrict and limit each other. Montesquieu wrote:

"If one person or an organization of officials, or aristocrats, or the people hold all the above types of power, everything will be gone."[29]

The Differentiation of Types of Political Power and the Prevention of Power Abuse by Legislative and Executive Bodies

It can be said that Rousseau inherited several basic concepts of Montesquieu's thinking on power separation. For example, when discussing the necessity to separate legislative and executive powers, Montesquieu wrote:

"Executive power has to use its preventing function to participate in legislative activity, or else its preponderance will be withdrawn. On the contrary, if legislators participate in executive activities, executive power will be terminated."[30]

Similarly, Rousseau emphasized the necessity to separate legislative, executive and judicial which cannot be assigned to one person or organization. He warned about the risk of losing everything if all those powers are held by one person or organization, whether aristocrats or common people. However, unlike Montesquieu, Rousseau did not consider privileges for prosperous or famous persons. He did not discuss the establishment of a first chamber of parliament for these groups (for example a senate), but focused on a single-chamber system consisting of a house of representatives only.[31] Discussing the relationship between legislators, executive and judicial officials, Rousseau made a simple comparison:

"A legislator is the inventor of a machine; the king is the mechanic who sets up and operates the machine (...) A legislator cannot be a supreme judge or a king."[32] *The king or emperor defined by Rousseau is just an executive official, not an autocratic king who holds all legislative, executive and judicial powers. A legislator or a parliament member cannot simultaneously be the king who directly governs as well as the judicial official who directly judges at trials. Similar to Montesquieu, Rousseau did not*

---

[29] Montesquieu (2006), 106.

[30] Montesquieu (2006), 117.

[31] Rousseau (2004), 250–251.

[32] Rousseau (2004), 100–101.

accept the situation of a soccer player who is also the referee and the one who randomly changes soccer rules.[33]

Among legislative, executive and judicial powers, Rousseau considered "legislative power the supreme form of perfection that collective strength can achieve."[34] When discussing the legislative power, Rousseau considered it "a special and noble function which does not resemble a particular person's function"[35] and stated that the employment of legislators means the establishment of a republic. The differentiation of legislative, executive and judicial powers, according to Rousseau, is essential. Explaining the reason for this differentiation, he wrote:

"Because those who give orders to humans cannot give orders to law. And who give orders to law should not give order to humans. Otherwise, the law which is the tool to control desires will be the tool to maintain inequality and the situation that personal opinions undermine the pureness of the work will be unavoidable."[36]

The differentiation between legislative, executive and judicial powers is a useful tool to avoid the influence of subjective factors and personal benefits in the name of the common will on the implementation and protection of the law.[37] According to Rousseau, executive officials or those who implement laws "should not have legislative power and the people, even if they want, cannot assign legislative authority to executive officials."[38] But the important thing is: "They never believe that personal will itself matches common will. They can only believe so after putting personal will into a free vote of the people."[39] This can be considered a valuable contribution by Rousseau to the idea of direct democracy. Considering legislative, executive and judicial powers to be the core of of the state structure, Rousseau always puts people's power as the supreme power in the highest position which controls other powers. No one stands higher than this power. Legislative power is the most direct expression

---

[33] Fetscher (1989), 151–159.

[34] Rousseau (2004), 100.

[35] Rousseau (2004), 101.

[36] Rousseau (2004), 101.

[37] Fetscher (1989), 151–158.

[38] Rousseau (2004), 102.

[39] Rousseau (2004), 102.

of the people's will and the supreme power. People's sovereignty is expressed in the people's legislative power. This is Rousseau's contribution to the establishment and development of a model of the state of law, which is also fundamental for the Constitution of the Democratic Republic of Vietnam from 1946.

The legislative body has the responsibility to reflect the people's common will, not the personal will of parliament members or people's representatives. Similar to the executive body the legislative body answers to the people, the true holder of a nation's supreme power. In particular, Rousseau analyzed the necessity to dismiss the government in two cases. The first case is when the head of the government does not govern based on law, but infringes on the power of the highest organ of state power and destroys social contracts. In this case, the people are confronted by a master and dictator; and therefore the people can revert to their natural free right. The second case is when cabinet members usurp the power separately, thus every supreme judge becomes a prime minister; the government and the nation are divided and disintegrated. Rousseau considered the situation of a disintegrating nation as well as of a government abusing power to be anarchical.[40] In order to prevent the abuse and usurpation of power by the government, it is essential to hold people's conference (congress) periodically. Two problems must be discussed then:

"Are the people satisfied with the current government? (...) Are the people satisfied with the administration work performed by the assigned people?"[41]

Rousseau considered the institution of a periodical people's conference as an essential tool to control political mechanisms, and government – and a time of real fear for cabinet ministers and secretaries. It can be said that this is a progressive, democratic thought which strongly influenced the political development in revolutionary France. The idea was later institutionalized in many Western constitutions by the mechanism of the vote of no confidence. This vote of no confidence can be organized to express collective distrust in the government as a whole or in a particular member of it. Reasons for distrust, according to Rousseau, may be violations of laws or power abuse by the government or its inefficient work.[42]

---

[40] Rousseau (2004), 165–166.

[41] Rousseau (2004), 189.

[42] Rousseau (2004), 189.

Summary

Rousseau proposed a type of a state of law as an institution that guarantees the natural rights of human beings by organizing, dividing, demarcating and controlling state powers into three branches, legislative, executive and judicial. In this model, Rousseau was guided by the principle that in a state the power must belong to the citizens, rather than being defined by "the law of the strong". He thought that legislative power is the main factor ruling all other powers such as the executive and judicial. Rousseau affirmed the indispensability of having a clear differentiation between legislation, executive and judiciary. Executive power only has the function to follow legislative power. The judicial power has the function to judge and protect the law and the legislative power. Rousseau proposed solutions to prevent the possibility of power abuse by executive and judicial bodies, especially the possibility that the government abuses or seizes power and does not follow common will, supreme power and social contracts of the entire people.

Rousseau's thoughts about the methods of organizing, dividing and controlling state power have important value in the structuring of the socialist state of law of the people, by the people and for the people in Vietnam at the moment, especially in the the fight against corruption, sectoral interests and moral degradation in a large number of party members, based on the spirit of the Resolution of Plenum IV and V of the Vietnamese Communist Party's Central Executive Committee.

References

Fetscher, Iring (1989): Rousseaus politische Philosophie. Frankfurt.

Montesquieu, Charles-Louis de Secondat de (2006): The Spirit of the Laws. Translated by Hoang Thanh Dam. Hanoi.

Rousseau, Jean-Jacques (2004): The Social Contract. Translated by Hoang Thanh Dam. Hanoi.

Ruling with Law. On the Significance of Rules of Organization and Procedure

Julian Krüper

Terminology first[1]

Legal work is linguistic work; legal problems are therefore more often than not terminological in nature. This is true not only for the detailed norms and provisions of criminal law, tax law or civil law, but for public law too. Among the various sources and forms of public law – federal, state and local, constitution, statutes and ordinances – constitutional law naturally reigns supreme. Its supreme nature does not protect the constitution from terminological ambivalence though, in fact, the opposite is true. In order to perform its functions as the paramount law of the land, the constitution necessarily ought to strive for a certain amount of linguistic flexibility and vagueness. Of course, this leaves any analysis or application of constitutional law with the somewhat ominous task of interpreting and inferencing the actual wording of constitutional provisions. Among the many ambivalences of constitutional vagueness is what in Anglo-American constitutional thought is referred to as the "rule of law". Although rich in philosophical, historical and legal overtones, pinpointing its

---

[1] This contribution remains in the form of my original lecture. I therefore make scarce use of references, mostly where they serve to verify quotations. Important input stems from the works of the German scholar Eberhard Schmidt-Aßmann on constitutional and particularly administrative law. Arguments drawing upon democratic and constitutional theory are inspired by works of the German constitutional scholar Martin Morlok.

essence is challenging. The same is true for the German term Rechtsstaat (Art. 20 § 1, 28 § 1 of the German constitution (GG), which – in a literal translation – reads "state of law". It has literal siblings in French (État de droit) and Italian (stato di diritto) that basically lean on the legal tradition of the German term, that in essence stems from 19th century constitutional thought.[2] Among many others, Immanuel Kant and Wilhelm von Humboldt contributed ground-breaking philosophical thoughts, Lorenz von Stein and Robert von Mohl contributed legal explications of the concept. How to distinguish the Anglo-American concept of rule of law from the continental tradition of Rechtsstaat is, in the words of Gustavo Gozzi, "una disputa senza fine".[3]

In this contribution, I will therefore not focus on that particular debate with its at times rather subtle differentiations. Instead I would like to address some broader aspects of the matter, therein applying a more generalized concept of Rechtsstaat. It aims at outlining some fundamental aspects, some of which I think are overlooked in their significance for a political system that aims to be constitutional and "lawful" in nature. Therefore I will somewhat arbitrarily use Rechtsstaat and rule of law synonymously.

Key Aspects of Rule of Law and Rechtsstaat

Both concepts obviously showcase "law" as the central aspect of the political and maybe even the social system they are applied to. Law in both concepts serves different purposes. It serves as binding mechanism for any yielding of public authority. In this sense law constitutes and apportions competencies and capacities to public institutions and organizations. For example: Lately, disputes on what intelligence agencies may or may not do nationally or internationally have been on the agenda in the United States, Great Britain, Germany and France. May the American National Security Agency (NSA) spy on government officials of allied states (or do they even reciprocate?). Obviously, the constitutional super-subject of separation of powers heavily relies on legal provisions either of constitutional or statutory nature.

---

[2] See Alemann in this volume.

[3] Gozzi (2003), 260.

But of course, there is more to law. At the same time it serves as a means of orientation for public action of any nature. This is particularly true for constitutional provisions that influence the application of statutory law, be it public or private. In this context, fundamental rights and freedoms are of utmost importance because not only do they guide and limit the legislative branch, but the executive and judicial branch as well.

Both rule of law and Rechtsstaat in their traditional sense come with a twist that on a terminological level is all but obvious. "Law" in both contexts claims a somewhat exclusive position. Not only does it bind public authority by forbidding any arbitrariness in yielding its power. It also limits ideological usurpation of the law, be it of religious, political or other nature. It therefore does not come as a surprise that for example the former socialist German Democratic Republic (GDR) strongly kept its constitutional scholars from drawing upon the bourgeois concept of Rechtsstaat. Instead, they came up with what became known as "sozialistische Gesetzlichkeit" (socialist lawfulness).[4] Public authority was not only to abide by the laws but also by the will of the party and its officials. Deviating from the law and its basic values in order to fulfil political requirements was expected of everyone applying the law.

In the Neighborhood: Constitutional Affinities of the Rule of Law

The anti-ideological bias of the traditional concepts of rule of law and Rechtsstaat of course reveal their own ideological roots. They are, as constitutional concepts, not neutral in the sense that they can be used to describe any system that runs along the lines of written legal provisions. Instead, they are constitutional concepts of liberal political systems which dominate the western hemisphere. At the core of those systems lies an unwavering, almost radical belief in the individual and his freedoms, in his prerogative of choice how to conduct his life, how sociable or introvert his acts, which beliefs are held and which purpose of life is chosen. We find that idea enshrined in various constitutional and quasi-constitutional provisions, among them the American Declaration of Independence and the German constitution. The American Declaration of Independence dates from 1776 and famously declares: "We hold these

---

[4] Mollnau (1999), 59 ff.; Stolleis (2009).

truths to be self-evident, that all men are created equal, that they are endowed by their Creator with certain unalienable Rights, that among these are Life, Liberty and the pursuit of Happiness". In a simpler, more legalistic way, Art. 1 § 1 GG prescribes:

"Die Würde des Menschen ist unantastbar. Sie zu achten und zu schützen ist Verpflichtung aller staatlichen Gewalt (Human dignity shall be inviolable. To respect and protect it shall be the duty of all state authority)."

Western constitutionalism therefore puts emphasis on the constitutional rank of human rights. Interpretation of human rights-provisions is a chief concern of constitutional scholarship and constitutional practice alike. It is therefore hardly surprising that public debates of Rechtsstaat and rule of law often concentrate on human rights, their legal guarantees and their efficacy in day-to-day state practice. And of course, human rights are at the core of any political system that considers itself a Rechtsstaat. The individualistic approach is often related to the constitutional concept of democracy, basically claiming that violations of human rights are in essence undemocratic. The conceptual background of the assumption is rather exacting and is rarely made explicit in public debates. It basically relies on the philosophical concept of constitutional contractualism according to which the guarantee and efficacy of human rights are a prerequisite of one's entering into the social contract. Whereas this assumption is equally true for any form of government that draws upon the contractual motive, it is particularly important to a democracy. It serves to prevent – as John Stuart Mill in his reflections "On Liberty" put it – a "tyranny of the majority". That is to say, that any true democratic form of government needs to put in effect a working means of protecting the individual's freedoms or it cannot be called democratic.[5]

It becomes clear that democracy and the rule of law are intimately intertwined in terms of the guarantee of human rights. Yet, their specific perspectives differ. The significance of human rights in respect to the democratic idea is of a more institutional nature whereas the perspective of rule of law is more of an individual nature, focusing on the actual efficacy of human rights-guarantees. To put it differently: Whereas the democratic approach asks if human rights are guaranteed, the Rechtsstaat-approach asks how they are guaranteed. This brings us back to the fundamental assumptions of the rule of

---

[5] Morlok/Michael (2015), 136.

law and to its conceptual presuppositions. From German constitutional scholarship stems the distinction of two dimensions of a Rechtsstaat, one being
more formal and the other being more substantive or – in German – "materiell" (the term "materiell" refers to the content, the essence, the subject matter
of a norm, to what the rule is about).

In it is reflected a development of legal thought that occurred between the
19th and 20th century: The dominating perspective of legal thought in the 19th
and the early 20th century was legal positivism. Positivism did not very much
care about the objectives of a legal system, of what the law was used to achieve.
In positivistic thinking, law was legitimate as long as it originated from the
power constitutionally authorized to make law (i.e. the monarch or parliament). All public authority, namely the executive and the judicial branch, had
to do was to enact the will of the legislator. This of course raises the question
of how to provide for means and measures for those branches to effectively
enact the legislative program. Given the case of Germany, the experience of the
formally legal Nazi Dictatorship, but also other historical events of the 20th
century led to a decline in positivistic thinking. Substantive perspectives
gained ground – and for good reasons. The international scope and depth of
the human rights-debates is only comprehensible against the back-drop of the
historic experiences of the 20th century.

Yet, along with the popularity of more substantive views goes an undeniable neglect of the more formal aspects of the rule of law, which are particularly
interesting for countries in transition to a system of rule of law. So, what needs
to be kept in mind is that running a state by the rule of law has to distinguish
between the outcome of public decision making (i.e. in the form of laws, executive orders or judicial decisions) and the way the decision was made. Whereas
the outcome-perspective raises substantive questions i.e. on how individual
rights are affected, the formal perspective focuses on aspects of the decision
making. Now, what are those formal aspects?

Dull but Decisive? Organization and Procedure

Three Aspects to Consider

When concentrating on the more formal aspects of a Rechtsstaat, three aspects
come into sight, in descending levels of abstraction: questions of legitimacy of

law (as dealt with above regarding positivism), the distinction between constitutional and statutory law and the means of organization and procedure.

The positivist approach basically provides a scheme of legal legitimacy: Not what the law is about matters, but whether or not it was given by the legitimate body. And although we have since come further in our idea of legal legitimacy, the initial idea of positivism is of course still correct. Therefore, what can be said today is that law is legitimate as far as it originates from a constitutionally authorized legislator (often, though by far not exclusively, parliament) and stays within the constitutional limits (mostly, but not exclusively human rights as granted by the constitution in question).

This scheme works well as long as we operate on the basis of a highly simplistic understanding of what law is. When we perceive laws as rules void of linguistic ambivalence and discretionary elements, we need not worry about their proper application. Yet, any law is full of both, voluntarily and involuntarily. This makes the application of law a treacherous business, full of possibilities to undermine the will of the legislator (or the will of the law itself, depending on one's methodological perspective) or even consciously deviating from it. This affects a fundamental objective of law in general that lies within the idea of law's generality: Equality of application. Law as we understand it is only legitimate if its application fulfils standards of equality. The law itself must provide that those standards are met.

Another aspect needs to be considered: Simply put, we like public action to be right. That is to say that we expect a certain level of rationality in whatever the state decides to do. The sources of rationality are twofold: They comprise the law itself as the normative standard of rationality; the law says what's right and what's not. Yet, the law's normative claim is not independent, it does not exist in itself, but naturally relates and relies on certain facts, which have to be considered, which are sometimes contested and ultimately need to be proven by the parties involved, be they private or public.

All this shifts the general focus away from the provisions of the constitution because its provisions conventionally do not deal with details of public power-yielding. Instead, what comes into sight are statutory rules made by parliament as the key legislator. Those statutory rules of course have to address an abundance of different forms and contexts in which public power is yielded. They have to address both administrative as well as judicial action. They need to be adequate in the sense that they need to meet the above mentioned standards. At the same time, they need to provide for a sufficient level of effectiveness of public actions. Of course, our desire is to achieve just and factually adequate decisions, but in due time and form.

Altogether, questions arise as to how to organize public authority and how to equip public authority with procedures and forms of public action that provide for the meeting of those standards. This, of course, is a highly demanding task to complete and confronts any legislator with challenges that might seem insurmountable. Given the example of Germany, legal scholarship and legal practice have worked decades to develop a somewhat coherent system of rules of organization and procedure. And yet, debates on how to reform and develop namely administrative law have been on the agenda for over twenty years now. European unification puts additional pressure on the structures and institutions developed. I will for reasons of efficiency concentrate on aspects of executive administrative law.

Specialization as an Organizational Principle

A key aspect of public authority in a Rechtsstaat is the fashion in which it is organized. Organization in this sense pertains to executive structures along the lines of specialization and hierarchy. If rationality is a desirable aspect of public decision making, specialization obviously serves this purpose: By limiting an agency's competencies to certain areas of the law (for example education, welfare, and public safety) public officials can develop expertise not only in respect to the laws to be applied, but a factual expertise, too. The importance of a proper assessment of facts can hardly be overestimated in the application of any law. Experienced judges or agency officials often can assess the legal gravitas of a case based on the way and which facts are presented by the parties.

In addition, specialization in the sense of exclusive administrative competencies furthers the cause of separation of powers within the executive branch of government because it limits the access of public officials to a closely defined area of the law. At the same time, expertise not only heightens the standards of rationality, but also serves the purpose of equal application of the law, because a smaller number of people deal with certain fields of law. Sub-legal standards and guidelines of interpretation and application of legal provisions can develop, practically "legalizing" informal expertise gathered by public officials in a certain field of law.

Hierarchy and Oversight as Organizational Principles

Another important feature of organizing public authority is different hierarchic levels. In Germany, administrative structure on the level of the federal states usually is threefold. Many of the executive branch's tasks are fulfilled on the local level or the "county"-level (the so called Kreise). The highest level is usually a minister (secretary) of the state government. The intermediary level, mostly called Bezirksregierungen (which loosely translates to district government) mostly serves as a secondary administrative level, in some cases though as the primary administrative agency.

Closely tied to the idea of hierarchic organizational patterns are of course mechanisms of review and supervision/oversight. Seemingly similar, the difference is that review is instigated by the private individual raising objections for example against a license permitting the erection and operation of an industrial plant (so called Widerspruchsverfahren). Although measures of administrative review have in recent years been abolished in some German federal states in favor of immediate judicial review, administrative review remains a vital part of the German administrative system. Supervision/oversight (Aufsicht), in contrast, is not (formally) initiated by the private individual, but by the superior administrative level.[6] German administrative law differentiates two forms of supervision, depending on different levels of intensity. Legal supervision (Rechtsaufsicht) is limited to merely rebuke violations of the law but needs to refrain from rebuking aspects of expediency of an administrative decision. In contrast, the so called Fachaufsicht (technical supervision) is free to act also upon its own ideas of expediency.

Independent Agencies

Exceptions to the rule of review and supervision are independent agencies that do not answer to a superior administrative level. The German national bank (Bundesbank) is an example of a (constitutionally) independent body (Art. 88 GG). The same is true for the European Central Bank. Two motives for independent administrative bodies, lately advanced by European Union law,[7] arise. The more prone administrative functions are to political interference, the more important are mechanisms securing the administrative process. Secondly, the

---

[6] Kahl (2000); Pieper (2006).

[7] Kröger/Pilniok (2016).

closer an administrative body serves the usage and expression of fundamental freedoms, the more independent its actions need to be (such as: broadcasting institutions, data protection agencies). Yet, independent agencies need to be the exception to the rule of effective administrative supervision. Not only do they raise questions in terms of the rule of law, but the democratic legitimacy of independent agencies is at stake, too.[8]

Rules of Procedure

Organizational aspects aside, rules of procedure play a prominent part safeguarding administrative decision making. "Rules of procedure" in this context serve as an umbrella-term. It includes all rules pertaining to administrative procedure in particular, to the parties involved and to administrative forms of action.

Legitimacy by Procedure

Rules of procedure are of utmost importance to any administrative system under the rule of law. Procedural provisions mainly serve to produce legitimacy of administrative decisions.[9] Often, administrative law does not determine legal consequences in detail but instead establishes discretionary decisions to be made by the respective administrative body. This results in legal uncertainty. Given the situation of several options available, procedural measures (for example of inclusion of parties affected by the decision) help to raise acceptance of a decision even if the outcome is not favorable for the affected party. Procedure therefore serves to change a situation of uncertainty into a situation of acceptable certainty.

Types and Objectives of Procedural Rules

Administrative procedures are structured and measured actions to obtain and process information.[10] Depending on the scope and the impact of the respective administrative decision (for example: licensing an industrial plant vs. issuing a driver's license), the preceding procedure needs to be adjusted accordingly: Whereas issuing a driver's license usually depends on fairly simple and easy-to-

---

[8] Hoffmann-Riem (2010).

[9] Luhmann (2005).

[10] Schmidt-Aßmann (2006), 305.

prove prerequisites, licensing an industrial plant is by far more complex. This of course must lead to more complex procedures involving various stakeholders and the interests they represent. Also, the complexity of matters regulated rises and shapes the decision to be made.

Generally speaking, different types of administrative procedures can be distinguished:[11]

- Procedures serving purposes of (quasi-judicial) review of administrative decisions (supervision/oversight).
- Procedures enabling administrative decision-making in individual cases (any form of licensing private actions, granting subsidies or ordering an individual to fulfil certain legal duties, for example).
- Procedures of a more complex nature, spatial planning for example. Namely the latter pose taxing objectives because usually complex nettings of different interests need to be examined and evaluated. Not only does that require comprehensive obtaining of information but also normative standards on how to process the information. Therefore, representation of interest, evaluation of interests and due processing of interests are the core objectives of any administrative procedure.

Depending on the complexity of the matter at hand, procedural provisions can be more or less strict, granting or restricting the administration's leeway in determining the necessary steps to be taken. Generally speaking, a high degree of formality is to be attained with any significant increase in the number of persons involved, the number and rank of legally protected interests and, generally speaking, the more complex the subject matter is. Complicated matters, for example, ask for mandatory hearings, documentation and probably publication of assertions made, deadlines for participatory actions need to be set and administrative decision-making needs to be coordinated with measures of judicial review. Of course, procedure is not a means in itself but serves to enable binding administrative decisions; procedure has therefore to be related to specific forms of administrative action (Handlungsformen).

Forms of Action

Each branch of government acts in particular forms. The legislative branch passes laws, the judicial branch hands down verdicts (procedural actions such

---

[11] Schmidt-Aßmann (2006), 148 ff.

as subpoenas or interlocutory judgements aside). The executive branch is pre-occupied with applying the law in numerous fields. The executive licenses businesses, it issues driver's licenses, it sets up development plans for cities, counties or entire countries, it supervises schools and universities, and it runs museums and public transportation and engages in other businesses. It takes action in individual cases (driver's license, licensing a business) as well as regulating a plurality of cases, for example in passing ordinances. Those forms of actions the executive branch takes differ in scope and impact.

It is a key objective of administrative law to supply the executive branch with adequate forms of action. Not only to fulfil the executive's tasks, but to secure that any form of action recognizes and respects different legal interests involved. Administrative forms of action are therefore inextricably linked to procedural law; they form the decisive part of the administrative process. Administrative law-making therefore needs to identify typical administrative decisions, frame them legally and set up a procedural framework they are linked with. Legally framing procedure and forms of action serves the purpose of rationalizing administrative action. If recurring decisions take the same form and are reached by same or similar procedural actions, they enable the administrative bodies to find solutions to the problems at hand. At the same time, they become easier to control, either by means of supervision or judicial review.

Rules and Procedure in Transitioning Countries

As could be seen, rules of organization and procedure are a worthwhile topic of any state following the idea of rule of law. Rules of organization and procedure serve very important purposes not only in terms of legitimacy and rationality of public action, but also in terms of its efficiency. For countries transitioning to the rule of law, rules of organization and procedure are essential and – from a political point of view – the foremost task to concentrate on.

Conclusion

Although the rationale of legitimacy by procedure is not entirely free of ideological overtones, it comes relatively free of the highly individualistic ideals the western concept of human rights abides by. Rules of organization and procedure aim at rational public decision making under complex circumstances, they are chiefly instrumental to the aims and objectives of substantive law (materielles Recht). At the same time, they are essential to any system of law that aims to fight despotism and arbitrariness in day-to-day legal work. Therefore, calling for a systematic development of rational procedures is – within reason – compatible with different ideological outlooks on law and its functions. Rules of organization and procedure can help to improve public decision making, largely, though not entirely independent of the contents of those decisions. Besides, the logics of modern bureaucratic states might not differ that much on the local, hands-on level, even if the ideological presumptions of the political system at large are different: Acceptability, reasonability and finally feasibility of administrative decision making are wished for anywhere in the world. At the same time, fighting for a broad guarantee of classical human rights serves little to no purpose if the administrative (and judicial!) structures to effectively implement those rights are not in place.

References

Gozzi, Gustavo (2003): Stato di diritto e diritti soggettivi nella storia costituzionale tedesca. In: Costa, Pietro/Zolo,Danilo (eds.): Lo stato di diritto. 2nd ed. Milano. 260.

Hoffmann-Riem, Wolfgang (2010): Eigenständigkeit der Verwaltung. In: Hofmann-Riem, Wolfgang (ed.): Grundlagen des Verwaltungsrechts. Bd. 1, 2nd Ed. Tübingen. § 10 Rn. 54.

Kahl, Wolfgang (2000): Die Staatsaufsicht. Entstehung, Wandel und Neubestimmung unter besonderer Berücksichtigung der Aufsicht über die Gemeinden. Tübingen.

Kröger, Malte/Pilniok, Arne (eds.) (2016): Unabhängiges Verwalten in der Europäischen Union. Tübingen.

Luhmann, Niklas (2005): Legitimation durch Verfahren, 6th Ed. Frankfurt.

Mollnau, Karl A. (1999): Sozialistische Gesetzlichkeit in der DDR: Theoretische Grundlagen und Praxis. In: Bender, Gerd/Falk,Ulrich (eds.): Sozialistische Gesetzlichkeit. 59–159.

Morlok, Martin/Michael, Lothar (2015): Staatsorganisationsrecht, 2. Aufl. Baden-Baden. 136.

Pieper, Stefan Ulrich (2006): Aufsicht. Verfassungs- und verwaltungsrechtliche Strukturanalyse. München.

Schmidt-Aßmann, Eberhard (2006): Das allgemeine Verwaltungsrecht als Ordnungsidee: Grundlagen und Aufgaben der verwaltungsrechtlichen Systembildung. Berlin.

Stolleis, Michael (2009): Sozialistische Gesetzlichkeit. Staats- und Verwaltungswissenschaft in der DDR. München.

III. Global Trends and Challenges

The Rule of Law and the Emergence of Market Exchange: A New Institutional Economic Perspective

Justus Haucap

Markets, where buyers and sellers can exchange goods and services, are key to the division of labor, specialisation, the realisation of economies of scale and scope and, therefore, economic prosperity, growth and development. The better markets work the easier it is to reap the benefits of specialisation and the gains from trade and voluntary exchange. For the emergence of market exchange, in turn, stable and secure property rights are crucial. These rights should be defined as clearly as possible and be as stable and secure as possible, in order to foster investment and to incentivize the careful and diligent treatment of assets. Hence, the rule of law and secure property rights go hand in hand with the emergence of markets, gains from trade and economic growth and prosperity.

Introduction

The emergence of modern law has been a prerequisite for the development of modern markets, in which buyers and sellers can trade on a more or less anonymous basis, without taking undue advantage of one another. While historically trade has often been organized through non-market forms, as Karl Polanyi (1944) has famously pointed-out, we have seen a development from (1) ceremonial gift exchange over (2) simple barter trade to (3) personalized trading relationships and (4) anonymous markets.[1] This development has not only been facilitated by technological progress, but – to a large degree – by institutional change, i.e. the development of law and property rights. As Douglass North has pointed out in his discussion of Karl Polanyi:

"An essential pre-condition for price-making markets is the existence of well-defined and enforced property rights over the good or service to be exchanged (...) The costs of defining and enforcing property rights – transaction costs – lead to non-price allocation of many goods and services today."[2]

In his theory of institutional change, North (1981) has analyzed how markets develop, depending on the size of societies and the costs of transport (which allows trade over long distances). More precisely, North (1981) has argued that exchange can take place without formal institutions such as property rights, as long as societies are of small size (families, tribes, villages...). In these societies, trade is guided and structured by informal rules. If, however, trade occurs over longer distances, institutions must be found to protect against what economists call opportunism, i.e. fraud and deceit. Institutions such as norms, measures and weights as well as money as a medium of exchange have basically developed in order to lower the costs of market exchange. Finally, urbanization and globalization require further institutional developments to facilitate trade (protection of property rights, international arbitration, diverse screening and signaling mechanisms). Coase has argued in a similar fashion:

"When the facilities are scattered and owned by a vast number of people with very different interests (...) the establishment of a private legal system would be very difficult. Those operating in these markets have to depend, therefore, on the legal system of the State."[3]

In this paper, we elaborate on the interdependence between property rights, the rule of law and the development of market-based exchange that facilitates the division of labor and according productivity gains which, in turn, foster economic growth and prosperity. For that purpose, we first elaborate on the role of markets in the economics literature in section 2. As we will see, economic theory has only perfunctorily dealt with the question of how markets emerge and how they are organised, even though markets play a major role in

---

[1] See Salisbury (1968), 122.

[2] North (1977), 710.

[3] Coase (1988a), 10.

most economic systems. In section 3, the historical development how trade was organized over time is outlined in a very brief manner, before section 4 analyzes the institutional and informational requirements for modern markets to work. Section 5 then explains how the rule of law facilitates market exchange, before section 6 summarises and concludes.

Markets in the Economics Literature

In neoclassical economics exchange is simply assumed to take place if there are benefits from trade to be realised. The question of how markets are actually organised has usually been neglected. Instead, two fictions have, by and large, been used to model the exchange process in the simple world of zero transaction costs. Either a (costlessly working) Walrasian auctioneer is supposed to postulate prices until demand equals supply, or individuals bargain about how to split the gains from trade and exchange goods along a so-called contract curve in an Edgeworth box.

However, as Ronald Coase has made clear, an "elaborate analysis of individuals exchanging nuts for apples on the edge of the forest"[4] is inappropriate to approach real world markets, since it completely ignores the social institutions facilitating exchange. While traditional, neoclassical economics basically determines the gains from trade and their distribution, it fails to show how much trade there is of which goods. The preconditions that facilitate trade are completely neglected. Put differently, the market is just assumed to be "there". In contrast to neoclassical economics, the New Institutional Economics (NIE) does not take an economy's institutional structure for granted, but aims at explaining why certain institutions such as a particular market exist.

Drawing upon the analysis of Coase (1937), a major focus of the NIE has been placed on the so called theory of the firm which explains under which conditions transactions are organised within firms, or more generally, within hierarchies and not carried out as price intermediated market transactions. The primary focus of Transaction Cost Economics (TCE) as developed by Oliver Williamson (1975, 1985, 1996) has been on the explanation of hierarchies within markets in terms of relative efficiency. From a transaction cost perspec-

---

[4] Coase (1988a), 8.

146

tive markets and hierarchies can be simply viewed as alternative governance structures to organise economic transactions.

Markets and hierarchies are not only seen as alternative governance modes though, but markets are typically viewed as the "natural" form of economic organization. Only if the costs of using the price mechanism exceed the costs of internal organization, transactions are moved from the market to the firm. In these cases, "market failure" can be overcome by other explicit or implicit contractual arrangements. As Oliver Williamson has admitted, "only as market-mediated contracts break down are the transactions in question removed from markets and organized internally. The presumption that 'in the beginning there were markets' informs this perspective."[5] Similarly, Coase found that in the absence of transaction costs "the firm has no purpose".[6]

Accounting for the fact that carrying out and organising transactions is a costly activity in itself, neither the use of markets nor the organisation of firms is costless. In general, to facilitate transactions three kinds of transaction costs are involved:
- information and search costs such as advertising costs or the cost of comparing prices,
- bargaining and contract negotiation costs, and
- monitoring and contract enforcement costs.[7]

One of the main hypotheses of the NIE, and the TCE framework in particular, is that in competitive environments transactions are organised in the most efficient way that minimises the transaction costs for a given transaction. Put differently, competition will lead to the emergence of the most efficient mode of organisation for every transaction. From this perspective, the crucial difference between markets and hierarchies consists in the way transactions are governed: Within firms the residual decision rights have been transferred to the firm's owner or manager, so that transactions are based on authority and command, whereas on markets property rights are voluntarily transferred, and transactions are price intermediated. Again, from a transaction cost perspective markets and hierarchies are basically viewed as different governance structures to solve the same problem – how to organise exchange.

---

[5] Williamson (1985), 87.

[6] Coase (1988b), 34.

[7] See Williamson (1989).

In addition to these two polar governance structures there exists a wide range of hybrid modes of organisations as, for example, franchise contracts.[8] Moreover, reasonably complex forms of governance, such as networks of relational contracts, may evolve to overcome coordination and cooperation problems. Ostrom (2010) has spoken about "polycentric governance of complex economic systems". In this context, a major hypothesis of institutional economic analysis is that because of "the filter of competition" only those contractual arrangements prevail that economise on transaction costs,[9] or, as Oliver Williamson has put it, "the economic institutions of capitalism have the main purpose and effect of economising on transaction costs."[10] In this sense Coase has explained that "markets are institutions to facilitate exchange, that is, they exist in order to reduce the cost of carrying out exchange transactions."[11]

From an anthropological or historical perspective, however, the view that markets are the "natural" mode of economic organization is rather flawed. In primitive societies exchange has been organized in network structures, if not hierarchies, and exchange relations have been highly personalized.[12] Impersonal spot markets, on the contrary, are a rather recent phenomenon.[13] One of the few economists who acknowledges this fact is Douglass North who wrote: "All of the modern neoclassical literature discusses the firm as a substitute for the market. For the economic historian this perspective is useful; its usefulness is limited, however, because it ignores a crucial fact of history: Hierarchical organization forms and contractual arrangements in exchange predate the price-making market."[14]

In contrast to Williamson one might therefore say that "in the beginning there were hierarchies" and, with respect to Coase, that in the absence of positive transaction costs the market has no purpose. Nevertheless, in economic theory the evolution of markets has not caught much attention: While the

---

[8] See Klein (1980), Dnes (1996) and Menard (1995).

[9] See Alchian (1950).

[10] Williamson (1985), 17.

[11] Coase (1988a), 7.

[12] See Landa (1994).

[13] Salisbury (1968).

[14] North (1981), 41.

institutional economics literature claims to analyse the emergence of different institutions and their relative efficiency, surprisingly little attention has been paid to the development of markets and the conditions that enable markets to evolve.[15] After all, one can hardly disagree with Coase who notes that "in modern economic theory the market itself has an even more shadowy role than the firm".[16] Similarly, Spulber noted that

"firms establish and operate most markets by setting prices, carrying out transactions, forming and monitoring contracts, and producing and distributing information. Firms create and manage markets by acting as intermediaries between buyers and sellers."[17] And furthermore, "just as producing and services consumes resources, so does the establishment and operation of markets to allocate those goods and services. (...) The market institutions that provide intermediation have not been given the attention they deserve."

In fact, the rise of many online platforms vividly demonstrates this fact: Firms organize and manage markets, markets are not simply "there".

The tendency to neglect market emergence and development in economic theory might be partially due to the influential work of Hayek who used the market as the standard example for a spontaneously emerging order (Hayek, 1944, 1960). From an anthropological or historical point of view, however, this perspective is misleading, and quite the opposite seems to be true. Neither do markets arise spontaneously nor are they simply "there". To explain their emergence is part of the challenge posed by Karl Polanyi (1944, 1957) as expressed by North (1977). How can the emergence of market-based exchange by explained and how can other forms of exchange such as reciprocity and distribution be explained by economic theory?

A very, very brief History of Trade

In fact, price-making markets in which the identity of the trading partners is irrelevant are a rather modern phenomenon. In early human history as well as in primitive societies exchange usually first took the form of ceremonial gift

---

[15] See North (1994).

[16] Coase (1988a), 7; also see North (1977).

[17] Spulber (1996), 135–136.

giving. As Polanyi noted, "over millennia trade between empires was carried out as gift trade."[18] Publicly presented gifts constituted trade in so far as the gifts were expected to be reciprocated. In his famous Essai sur le don, Marcel Mauss (1925/1967) has stressed the reciprocal nature of gifts. In primitive societies virtually every exchange and contract took the form of a gift, which is, according to Mauss, only voluntary in theory, but obligatory in practice.[19] By the presentation of a gift an obligation to return a countergift was created. As Mauss furthermore explained, although the presentations commonly take the form of generous gifts, the transactions were "based on obligation and economic self-interest."[20] What is also quite interesting to notice, is that exchange in primitive societies hardly ever occurred on an individual basis, but almost always between collective groups such as tribes, clans or families.

In this context, the institution that has probably caught the most widespread attention among economic anthropologists is the Kula Ring of Papua New Guinea. Since its detailed description by Malinowski it serves as the classical example of ceremonial gift exchange in the anthropological literature. The Kula Ring is a system of gift exchanges between several tribal societies that live on the different islands in the Western Pacific. Malinowski describes the trading system between these "stateless" societies as follows:

"The Kula trade consists in a series of ... periodic overseas expeditions which link together the various islands groups, and annually bring back big quantities of vaygu'a and of subsidiary trade from one district to another. The trade is used up, but the vaygu'a - the armshells and the necklaces - go round and round the ring."[21]

The so-called vaygu'a are two different valuable goods, necklaces and armbands, that permanently circulate in opposite directions. Their exchange is highly ceremonial and strictly regulated by a detailed set of rules. The basic purpose of the Kula exchange is not the ceremonial gift giving per se, but rather to facilitate peaceful commercial trade of useful commodities. Aside from the ceremonial gift exchange commercial goods are exchanged by members of different tribes through a chain of intermediaries. Each Kula partner is not only involved in the ceremonial gift exchange, but also in commercial

---

[18] Polanyi (1957), 262.

[19] Mauss (1925/1967), 1.

[20] Mauss (1925/1967), 1.

[21] Malinowski (1922/1953), 103.

trade with local residents and even with strangers "with whom an indirect exchange is carried on through the intermediation of the local men."[22] The Kula trade does not take place in the form of spot transactions, but is based on the principle of delayed reciprocity. As Landa has explained:

"No Kula valuables are carried on overseas Kula expeditions; the visiting Kula partner visits his host to receive gifts and not to give them."[23]

Similarly, Mauss argued:

"The rule is to set out with nothing to exchange or even to give in return for food (...) On these visits one is recipient only, and it is when the visiting tribes the following year become the hosts that gifts are repaid with interest."[24] *The fact that the gifts received are usually even returned with interest payments, lead Mauss to the conclusion that "economic evolution has not gone from barter to sale and from cash to credit. Barter arose from the system of gifts given and received on credit (...) Likewise purchase and sale - both direct sale and credit sale - and the loan, derive from the same source."*[25]

After all, the Kula exchange is not an anonymous exchange between atomized agents as it appears in neoclassical economics. Rather trading partners have to be member of the Kula ring, entry to which is strictly limited. As Belshaw explained

"to enter the Kula ring a man must have the knowledge of the appropriate etiquette (...) Knowledge of the etiquette is attained through general socialization, but much of the magic is idiosyncratic and must be learned specifically (...) The exchanges are accompanied by forms of words and ceremonial acts all of which reinforce the notions of honorable gift-giving and mutual dependence between persons who, in most instances, would be strangers in other circumstances."[26]

The ritual aspects of the Kula exchange can be seen as "institutional ways of establishing individual and group identity in a world characterized by uncertainty and high information costs".[27] Moreover, the ring structure of the Kula system as well as the fact that two different ceremonial goods flow in different

---

[22] Malinowski (1922/1953), 363.

[23] Landa (1994), 148.

[24] Mauss (1925/1967), 20.

[25] Mauss (1954), 35.

[26] Belshaw (1965), 12.

[27] Landa (1994), 144.

directions can also be explained by transaction cost considerations. As Landa argued, "the Kula Ring is an institutional arrangement that emerged primarily in order to economize on transaction costs of intertribal commercial exchange in stateless societies. (...) In a society that lacks that institutions for protecting life, property, and contracts, an institution like the Kula Ring may be interpreted as a club-like arrangement for economizing on costs of transacting across tribal boundaries."[28] In a similar way, Ziegler (1990) traced the structure of the Kula system back to advantages of peaceful commercial trade. According to his analysis, the ceremonial gift exchange acts as an efficient and reliable signalling mechanism to facilitate commercial trade and to maintain the social order.[29]

One might think that the Kula Ring is a rather singular phenomenon. However, quite on the contrary trade via mutual gift exchange has been the rule rather than the exception in primitive societies. To give another example, let us follow Mauss:

"A relationship analogous to the Kula is that of the Wasi. This sets up regular and obligatory exchanges between partners, between agricultural tribes on the one hand and maritime tribes on the other. The agricultural partner places produce in front of the house of his fisherman associate. The latter, after a great fishing expedition, makes return with interest, giving his partner in the agricultural village the product of his catch."[30]

It is quite obvious that these mutual gifts are based on gains from specialization and differences in availability. There exist a broad range of other exchange facilitating institutions such as the Kwakiutl Potlatch in the American Northwest, the Manus of the Great Admiralty Islands, the Tolowa-Tututni of California, or the Pokot of Kenya to name only a few. Descriptions and analyses of these exchange facilitating gift ceremonies can be found in Mauss (1925/1967), Polanyi, Arensberg & Pearson (1957), Belshaw (1965) or Sahlins (1965). All these institutions share some common features as Belshaw demonstrated:

"Although the details vary considerably from culture to culture, the main variables are remarkably constant. These include emphasis on relationships between individuals

---

[28] Landa (1994), 143.

[29] See also Posner (1980).

[30] Mauss (1925/1967), 27.

152

which are also seen as relationships between groups. (...) A very high proportion of social contacts between adults is accompanied by gift-giving."[31]

To summarize, in early human history and in archaic societies trade has usually taken the form of gift exchange and was based on the principle of delayed reciprocity. Exchange relations in these societies have been highly personalized and very stable. As Malinowski (1922/1953) reports, Kula relations were even passed on to heirs, so the reputation of a so called "Big Man" in the Kula Ring did not die with him. That way the last period problem of finite games is avoided, and the Kula gift exchange becomes an infinitely often repeated game. Furthermore, as Ziegler (1990) pointed out, trust played an essential role in Kula relations.

In a similar way, Geertz (1978, 1979) has analysed the institutional structure of the Moroccan bazaar economy. At a first glance, the bazaar might appear to come close to the classic spot transaction of the ideal market. However, as Geertz points out even on the bazaar continuing relations build the dominant pattern. Posner (1980), therefore, compared the bazaar economy directly to primitive societies as he argued: "In primitive societies if you trade repeatedly with the same man he becomes your blood brother and you owe him the same duty of generous and fair dealing that you would owe a kinsman. This 'barter friendship' resembles the pairing of buyers and sellers in bazaars that Geertz noted. It is a way of bringing reciprocity into the exchange process and thereby increasing the likelihood that promises will be honoured despite the absence of a public enforcement authority."

Fafchamps (2002) made a similar observation referring to empirical evidence of manufacturing and trading firms from Ghana, Kenya, and Zimbabwe. Personalized exchange is the rule in markets based on trust and reputation; commercial relationships between economic agents are long lasting. As Fafchamps (2002) has explained, trust and reputation basically replace court based enforcement mechanisms in these societies. Therefore, as in the case of the Kula Ring, trade cannot be anonymous, but is based on mutual trust and the sharing of information among traders. The identity of the trading partners is of major importance. However, if screening devices are costly, some agents are

---

[31] Belshaw (1965), 35.

excluded from the market, and the "business then becomes monopolized by a social network, possibly sharing the same ethnic or religious affiliation".[32]

Quite interestingly, the role of labels and identities for building trust has been also stressed by Landa (1994) to explain the dramatic success of ethnically homogeneous trading groups in many developing countries today, especially in South East Asia. She argued that ethnically homogeneous groups of middlemen are "a low cost clublike institutional arrangements (...) which emerged to economize on contract enforcement and information costs in an environment where the legal infrastructure was not well developed." These networks serve as an alternative to contract law or hierarchical structures. In these societies, ethnicity serves as a labelling device to signal credibility and to shape one's expectations.[33]

Furthermore, as Greif (1994) has shown, cultural beliefs may have a significant impact on the overall economic outcome. In his comparative study of the Maghribi traders of the eleventh century and the Genoese traders of the twelfth century, Greif argues that the "collectivistic culture" of the Maghribi traders is an impediment to economic development while the individualistic culture of the Genoese fosters the development of markets and thereby also economic development. In a similar way, economists as Kuran (1997) and anthropologists as Ensminger (1997) have pointed to the labelling value of Islam in Africa. Membership of a certain religion shapes trading partners' expectation about each other's behavior, or to put it differently, certain religious beliefs are connected with certain ethical codes of conduct, so traders know what to expect. As Kuran (1997) has argued, mutual trust between traders of the same religion is higher since they both have subscribed to the same religious beliefs. Hence, fewer safeguards are required and, accordingly, transaction costs are lower.

Viewed from this angle, it is not very surprising that in history trade has often been in the hands of specific ethnic groups or even families such as the Lombard and Genoese merchants in medieval Europe, Jews in the Mediterranean, Armenian in the Middle East, or Chinese in Singapore today, Asians in East Africa, Lebanese in West Africa.[34] After all, ethnicity and religion might

---

[32] Fafchamps (2002), 4.

[33] Landa (1994).

[34] See Fafchamps (2000).

play a more important role for the emergence of markets and economic development than has been recognized so far.

However, market conditions have changed in the course of world history as the population has increased, products have become more complex and communication and transport easier. As Salisbury argued, in this course trade can be characterized by a "sequence of ceremonial gifts, intercommunity barter, trading partnerships, and market place trade."[35] In a similar way, Belshaw (1965) distinguished between "traditional exchange" and "modern markets." While market exchange is rather connected with standardized spot transactions and legal enforcement mechanisms, traditional exchange is based on principle of reciprocity and mutual trust. This view is certainly influenced by Polanyi (1944), The Great Transformation, in which he understands economic and cultural development as a shift from an economy embedded in social relations to one of impersonal markets.

The historical sequence from ceremonial gift exchange over simple barter trade to personalized trading relationships to anonymous markets, as characterized by Salisbury (1968), has partly been explained by Coase as follows:

"When the facilities are scattered and owned by a vast number of people with very different interests (...) the establishment of a private legal system would be very difficult. Those operating in these markets have to depend, therefore, on the legal system of the State."[36]

Moreover, North (1981) in his theory of institutional change outlined the following sequence:

- As long as societies are of small size (families, tribes, villages...) exchange can take place without formal institutions such as property rights, trade is guided and structured by informal rules,
- If trade occurs over longer distances, institutions must be found to protect against opportunism (such as norms, measures and weights as well as money as a medium of exchange),
- Urbanization and globalization require further institutional developments to facilitate trade (protection of property rights, international arbitration, diverse screening and signaling mechanisms).

---

[35] Salisbury (1968), 122.

[36] Coase (1988a), 10.

The underlying principle behind this mechanism might be explained as follows: As the population size increases and transportation becomes easier, it becomes more difficult to keep track of every member of a society. The probability to meet the same trader again decreases, so that incentives for opportunistic behavior increase. Therefore, over the course of history different enforcement mechanisms and exchange facilitating institutions arose. As Coase noted, in the medieval ages the provision of markets became an entrepreneurial activity: "In the medieval period in England, fairs and markets were organized by individuals under a franchise from the King. They not only provided the physical facilities for the fair or market but were also responsible for security (important in such unsettled times with a relatively weak government) and administered a court for settling disputes (the court of piepowder)."[37] These market institutions, which usually consist of physical facilities such as the market place and an enforcement mechanism that might be called the market order, have to be built and maintained.

Exactly in this sense, Milgrom, North and Weingast (1990) have discussed the institution of the medieval law merchant the role of whom was to provide information to make self-enforcing agreements feasible. Similarly, Greif, Milgrom and Weingast (1994) have analyzed medieval merchant guilds as exchange facilitating institutions that economize on transaction costs under conditions of legal uncertainty. As Gambetta (1993) has argued, from a historical point of view even the rise of the Sicilian Mafia can be explained on transaction cost grounds. According to Gambetta (1993), the Mafia historically basically provided an enforcement mechanism to facilitate trade.

Fafchamps in his paper on "spontaneous" market emergence has summarized all this nicely as follows:

"To simplify a bit, early markets can be described as a two-tier system, with a core of sophisticated firms and traders and a fringe of small enterprises. Fringe agents operate on a purely cash-and-carry basis, largely in an anonymous fashion, and leave no room to breach of contract.[38]

---

[37] Coase (1988a), 8.

[38] Fafchamps (2002); see Fafchamps/Minten (2001); for Vietnam in particular: McMillan/Woodruff (1999a), (1999b).

Core agents are in long-term relationships with each other. They offer supplier credit and warranty and place orders.[39] The widespread existence of long term relationships between manufacturers and their suppliers and clients has, for instance, been noted in developed and developing economies alike.[40] Research by anthropologists, sociologists, historians, political scientists, and economists has shown that reliance on interpersonal relations at early stages of market development is nearly universal.[41]

Hence, the emergence of markets and market economies does not necessarily require efficient and costlessly working court based enforcement mechanisms as is often suggested or assumed in economic theory. In the absence of a state that enforces property rights with coercive power other institutions might arise to facilitate exchange. It is important to notice, however, that in the absence of court based enforcement systems, markets cannot function as anonymous gatherings, but identity of the trading partners becomes highly relevant. As Coleman (1991) explained, social mechanisms such as gossip might serve a valuable function in these markets.

Having now documented that markets can even work in the absence of well-defined property rights and the rule of law (as also black markets vividly demonstrate), it is also clear that well-defined property rights and the rule of law greatly simplify trade and market exchange, thereby simplifying both further specialization and credit-based relationships. In fact, the emergence of many platform markets in the digital economy is rather similar to the organization of historical markets in the medieval age. The provision of standard laws and enforcement mechanisms has greatly simplified exchange so that more transactions can actually take place and resources that were used to safeguard transactions can be saved.

---

[39] See Fafchamps (1997).

[40] E.g. Lorenz (1988); Aoki (1988); Dore (1987); Fukuyama (1995); Stone/Levy/ Paredes (1992).

[41] E.g. Hopkins (1973); Greif (1993); North (1990); Meillassoux (1971); Amselle (1977); Jones (1959); Bauer (1954); Sahlins (1972).

Modern Markets and their Institutional and Informational Requirements

In modern societies, business relations are usually based on explicit contracts which can be enforced by the state. With the development of the legal system and court based enforcement mechanisms trade in large, anonymous markets has become possible in principle.[42] Indeed, standard economic theory normally assumes that in modern societies all trade takes the form of spot transactions and impersonal exchange. Examples often used to illustrate the point are commodity and stock exchanges. It is important to notice, however, that anonymous price-making markets demand strong institutional and informational requirements.

The Role of the Institutional Environment

Regarding institutional requirements, only the development of the modern legal system has made possible the wide-spread emergence of price-making markets. Key to the emergence of modern markets are well-defined, stable and secure property rights, which are protected either by private order or by the Government or the state. According to the economic property rights theory, a property right in an asset consists of:
- the right to use the asset,
- the right to change its form and substance,
- the right to appropriate the returns from the asset, and
- the right to transfer (sell) all rights in the asset.[43]

Exchange can most easily occur if it is clearly defined who holds the property right in an asset in the above sense.[44] If there are no clearly defined property rights (including the right to use and to transfer an asset), markets are not likely to come into existence. Lack of clearly defined property rights does not

---

[42] One may therefore argue that traditional (private) enforcement mechanisms, trust and reciprocity have become less important in modern markets when compared to traditional forms of exchange (see Belshaw, 1965). This is quite different in less developed peasant societies though. See Ensminger (1992); and Fafchamps (2000), (2001), for further description and analysis.

[43] See Furubotn/Pejovich (1972).

[44] See Coase (1960).

necessarily mean that markets will not emerge at all (see black markets), but it is much more difficult to create them and to ensure they work properly.

Since it is costly to invest into the creation of a market, understood as the market facilities plus a market order and its enforcement, it is important that property rights are stable and secure and can be enforced through the courts or some other institution. If property rights are not stable and can be redefined relatively easily through other means (from theft or outright expropriation to Government regulation, which usually limits the right to use and/or change an asset), people will be less interested in trading these assets under uncertain conditions. Put differently, if people do not know what exactly it is they buy they will be less inclined to buy that particular asset. Also, it may be easier for them to lobby the Government to redefine property rights rather than buying the asset themselves and than change its use or form. If it is less costly for individuals to get the Government to redefine property rights rather than buying the asset themselves, it is risky to invest into the creation of a market.

Hence, for markets to work best, property rights should be defined as clearly as possible and be as stable and secure as possible. For the latter point, a judgement has to be made about how likely it is that the Government will intervene and redefine property rights. This in turn is dependent on a number of factors. First of all, one can ask whether private property rights are protected through a jurisdiction's constitution as it is the case in the US or Germany or through other legal means or not at all. The question is: How easy is it for the Government or other parties to limit or restrict private property rights?

Secondly, property rights are less likely to be guaranteed and stable if a given property rights allocation is not socially sustainable and acceptable for a majority of society. In this case, if a property rights allocation is not socially acceptable for a majority of voters, it is unlikely that this particular property rights allocation is politically sustainable either. Instead, the Government will have every incentive to redefine property rights through political/legal means. For example, the extent and type of taxation will typically also depend on demographic features of the electorate.[45]

Similar problems often occur with environmental issues when property rights in nature/natural resources are involved. While for example a market for water abstraction rights cannot exist without well defined property rights in

---

[45] See, Scheuer/Wolitzky (2016).

the respective water resource, a market for water rights may not be acceptable for a majority of voters and therefore not politically viable even though economic theory would predict a market for water rights to be an efficient mode of organisation. Another case are school vouchers where a market solution is predicted to be efficient from an economic perspective, but does not appear to be politically acceptable in many parts of the world. Hence, part from economic efficiency the political sustainability of any allocation of property rights needs to be considered.[46]

Information and Transaction Costs

While stable and well defined property rights are key to the creation and smooth working of markets, they alone do not suffice to make markets work best (as opposed to other mechanisms of exchange such as social networks or hierarchies). Put differently, the existence of secure property rights is only a necessary, but not a sufficient condition for markets to come into existence. In fact, price-making markets not only require well-defined and enforceable property rights, but in addition "it must be possible to measure the dimensions of a good or service" (North 1981, 42).

Information Issues

For purely price intermediated trade to take place it is not sufficient that property rights are well defined, but there are also strong informational requirements for the functioning of the price mechanism. Already Stigler (1961) in his seminal article on the economics of information has pointed out that information is not for free and that potential buyers have to invest in gathering information to find out where they can buy what at which price. Similarly, sellers have to find out what it is that buyers actually demand. This information gathering and processing takes up time and other resources. Price-making markets can only work smoothly if this information is easily and widely accessible for both potential buyers and potential sellers.[47]

---

[46] See Dixit (1996); Williamson (1996); Acemoglu/Robinson (2013).

[47] A more formal model which looks at buyers' and sellers' incentives to invest into information gathering has been provided by Gould (1980).

Quality Uncertainty

What is as crucial for the working of a market as information about a product's price and place etc is, in many cases, information about product quality, which can be much more difficult to convey. George Akerlof has demonstrated this quite plastically in his seminal paper on the "Market for Lemons" (Akerlof, 1970), where he shows that trading on the market for used cars may break down because buyers have inferior information about the quality of a used car than sellers. If buyers lack trust in sellers' promises, markets are very difficult to establish. This is because with lack of trust buyers will "deduct" a risk premium from the price they are willing to pay. Knowing this, owners of used cars will be less inclined to put a "good" used car on the market, which again leads to a deterioration of the average quality of used cars traded on the market which again confirms' buyers' suspicions that only "lemons" are offered.

For many products price is only one among many factors that buyers consider before making their purchase decision. Apart from the price, a product's quality (in the broadest sense of the word) and associated services are often as important as the product's price. However, for many goods and services buyers cannot evaluate the product's true quality ex ante, or it is rather costly for them to do so. Here the economics literature distinguishes between search qualities, experience qualities and credence qualities.[48]

Search qualities are those characteristics of a good that buyers can easily determine before purchase such as colour or size. In contrast, experience qualities are characteristics that buyers only learn after purchase, e.g. a good's durability or actual taste. That is, these qualities can only be determined though experience, but not through simple inspection. Credence qualities are finally those qualities which are even costly to determine after purchase. Examples are the quality of a car repair or medical services where most buyers do not know even after purchase whether they received the quality and extent of treatment that was best for them. Hence, information problems are severest for goods where credence qualities are important while informational aspects are the least important for search goods where most information can be gained through simple inspection.

---

[48] The distinction between search and experience qualities has been introduced by Nelson (1970). Darby/Karni (1973) later added the credence good category.

For credence and experience goods trust between buyers and sellers is decisive for a successful trading relationship. Hence, it is much more difficult to establish anonymous markets for experience or credence goods where sellers and buyers remain anonymous. In fact, most organised markets concentrate in the trade of highly standardised search goods where buyers and sellers have high degrees of certainty about the goods' quality.

Information and measurement costs can be reduced, however, through standardisation and classification procedures.[49] Through means of standardisation and classification experience qualities can be transformed into search qualities, at least to some degree. Reference standards make it easier to "measure" product quality, thereby reducing information costs. Also, if the numbers of traders is relatively small, training buyers and sellers may help overcoming the informational problems associated with quality uncertainty if training enables market participants to judge quality more accurately before purchase.

In general, however, it is least complicated to establish markets for search goods where quality is easy to determine and to describe. For experience goods, other trust building mechanisms have to be used such as guarantees, investment in branding,[50] or external reference systems (such as the reputation and information exchange systems on most online platforms where buyers and sellers can exchange information about their experience with other buyers and sellers).

When do Markets Work Best?

According to economic theory transactions are, all other things equal, organised in a way to minimise the sum of transaction and production costs. Hence, anonymous markets are usually replaced by other contractual arrangements as the contractual hazards that arise from asset specificity, uncertainty and low frequency of transaction increase. This is reflected in the work of North who writes: "Small numbers involved in exchange, the possibility of opportunism, and uncertainty as a result of a lack of well-defined property rights or an inability to forecast changes in conditions over the life of an exchange agreement all result in alternative contractual arrangements designed to reduce the at-

---

[49] See Barzel (1982), (1985).

[50] See Klein/Leffler (1981).

162

tendant transaction or production costs."[51] However, given that it is costly to organise markets, the perspective can also be turned around: Price-making markets (using standardised contracts) do not evolve as long as the strong institutional and informational requirements are not met. Highly personalised exchange relations will prevail instead.

Not surprisingly, the strong informational and institutional conditions necessary for impersonal exchange are almost only met in highly organised markets such as stock or commodity exchanges or some auctions. As Telser/Higinbotham explain, "in an organised market the participants trade a standardised contract such that each unit of the contract is a perfect substitute for any other unit. The identities of the parties in any mutually agreeable transaction do not affect the terms of exchange. The organised market itself or some other institution deliberately creates a homogeneous good that can be traded anonymously by the participants or their agents."[52]

Stock or commodity exchanges as well as auctions are usually explicitly organised by a club of traders or a firm which usually owns the physical facilities within which trade takes place. Moreover, the dimensions of the transactions such as the trading place and time are usually regulated by an underlying market constitution. Goods as well as traders have to be admitted to the exchange, and entry to the market is limited. Through these measures measurement costs and credibility problems can be reduced. A high degree of product standardisation and classification allows traders to use standardised contracts and procedures and reduces measurement and bargaining costs. Hence, key for anonymous, impersonal exchange is a high degree of product standardisation or classification which allows the use of highly standardised contracts. In organised markets, traders usually also have to pay a fee to use the market facilities. Since entry is limited and traders pay for the use of the market, organised markets can also be regarded as clubs. The exclusion of traders from the stock market serves to prevent free riding on the information costly generated in the market.[53]

As long as there are relatively few traders the market can still be explicitly and centrally organised as, for example, the New York Diamond Dealers' Club

---

[51] North (1981), 42.

[52] Telser/Higinbotham (1977), 997.

[53] For a further analysis see Telser & Higinbotham (1977) and Telser (1981).

the organisation of which has been analysed by Bernstein (1992, 1996). According to her analysis the sophisticated rules and codes of conduct of the diamond industry guarantee that trade is organised in a transaction cost efficient manner. Disputes are hardly ever settled by courts, but rather by market arbitration. Furthermore, reputation plays an enormous role in the diamond industry and serves as a bond to guarantee contractual performance. However, as Coase explains,

"when the facilities are scattered and owned by a vast number of people with very different interests (...) the establishment of a private legal system would be very difficult. Those operating in these markets have to depend, therefore, on the legal system of the State."[54]

Unfortunately, there is no clear indicator or rule of thumb what constitutes large numbers and small numbers or high and low transaction costs. One of the few academic economists who have specialised in the analysis of organised markets, Dennis Carlton, points out in his analysis of organised futures markets, that while it is possible

"to identify some important characteristics that make a commodity suitable for a futures market, it is extremely difficult to predict which futures markets will succeed."[55]

Finally, even in markets for highly standardised and measurable goods relationships between traders seem to play an important role. As Baker (1984) reports in his empirical study of floor trading of stock options, price volatility strongly increased with the number of trading groups. Granovetter (1992) explains these findings on grounds of the number of relations the average trader can sustain, relatively to the total number of traders. With a growing number of traders the market becomes more fragmented, the information flow becomes slower, and convergence to a single equilibrium more problematic.

---

[54] See Coase (1988a), 10. Nevertheless, court enforcement of contracts is rather an exception than the rule as Macaulay (1963) has observed. In a similar way, Bernstein (1996) argues that explicit contracts rather serve as a benchmark for the case that a relationship breaks down than as an agreement of how to proceed while the contractual relationship is still continuing.

[55] Carlton (1981), 244.

The Rule of Law Facilitates Market Exchange

As mentioned above, when property rights are well-defined, safe and secure, modern markets can most easily emerge. The extent of a given property right depends on (a) the contracts that have been concluded, and (b) the institutional environment that is in place. The institutional environment encompasses the definition and enforcement of property rights, which determine the transactions costs of and the gains from doing business.

A fundamental problem with the definition and enforcement of property rights is what has been called the "paradox of the strong state" by Barry Weingast (1995):

"The fundamental political dilemma of an economic system is this: A government strong enough to protect property rights and enforce contracts is also strong enough to confiscate the wealth of its citizens."

The problem, then, is how to empower government to subdue predators without letting it become an instrument of predation itself. How can one design an institutional environment that gives government the power to protect property rights while at the same time prevents government from using this power to curb property rights? How is it possible to simultaneously empower and constrain government? How can this paradox be solved?

Given that government has the ability to do good (enforce property rights) and bad (destroy property rights), how do we give government agents the incentive to do good and avoid bad? One solution proposed by constitutional political economists are constitutional constraints. Federalism, separation of powers, and the rule of law can structure government power in such a way as to limit how that power can be used. Another option can lie in the signature of international treaties and entry into international organizations such as the World Trade Organization (WTO), which implies a commitment to free trade.

More generally speaking, the law and regulations surrounding business activities should pursue, broad speaking, two objectives. On the one hand, consumers need protection against any producers' market power, but on the other hand investors also need to be protected against expropriation (hold-up) through the Government. Accordingly, regulation may be interpreted as an implicit contract between producers and consumers, which is administered by an (impartial) regulatory authority.[56] Every regulatory system is – necessarily – compromised with two types or errors, though. Firstly, regulation or government intervention can occur even though it is not necessary or beneficial (type-I- error), while, secondly, regulation or government intervention may not be in place even though it would have been beneficial (type-II-error). To find the optimal balance between these two errors is the difficult task of designing good regulatory systems to govern market exchange.

An optimal regulatory system should aim at achieving a balance between the following five objectives: (1) preventing the abuse of market power (allocative efficiency), (2) ensuring cost minimising production (productive efficiency), (3) facilitating optimal investment over time (dynamic efficiency), (4) inducing minimal transactions costs (transactions costs efficiency), and (5) providing minimal incentives for lobbying and unproductive rent-seeking (political efficiency). Of course, trade-offs are unavoidable, and in addition there are different political objectives for different industries. In order to facilitate investment, however, investor protection is necessary. The problem is especially difficult to solve if (i) investments are highly location specific, and (ii) investors are foreigners (who do not vote) and are easier to expropriate from a political-economy perspective.

Potential solutions include the international rule of law, the signature of international investment protection treaties and accepting "global governance" mechanisms. After all, the division of labor (which is responsible for our economic well-being) is limited by the extent of the market, as Adam Smith has said long ago, but the extent of the market is also limited by the extent of the law, as George Stigler has added. Hence, the extent of the law also affects economic growth and prosperity.

Summary and Conclusion

Summarising the analysis above, whether markets work better than other forms of exchange depends on the institutional environment, informational aspects and the dimensions of the transaction. In general, an organised market can only flourish if the transaction costs of exchange are lower on the market

---

[56] See Goldberg (1976).

than they would be under any other mode of organisation. If transactions costs are lower within a different mode of organisation, e.g. within long-term bilateral contracts, the market is unlikely to survive.

First of all, for markets to emerge property rights in the asset to be traded have to be well defined and should be as stable and secure as possible. How stable property rights are is not only a strictly legal question (whether property rights are legally protected and enforceable), but usually also a political question. If a property rights allocation is not acceptable to larger parts of society for whatever reason, the Government faces incentives to restrict or redefine property rights. The risk of (creeping) expropriation makes it more difficult to set up and operate organised markets. For example, before investing into the establishment of a market for tradable water rights, there needs to be some degree of certainty that these property rights will not be redefined and the market shut. Whether the creation of a market for some good or service is socially acceptable and therefore politically viable obviously depends on the particular circumstances. The key questions are whether property rights are well defined and expected to remain stable and whether the establishment of a market for the good or service is likely to be politically viable.

A fundamental problem with the definition and enforcement of property rights is what has been called the "paradox of the strong state" (Weingast, 1995):

"The fundamental political dilemma of an economic system is this: A government strong enough to protect property rights and enforce contracts is also strong enough to confiscate the wealth of its citizens."

The problem, then, is how to empower government to subdue predators without letting it become an instrument of predation itself. How can one design an institutional environment that gives government the power to protect property rights while at the same time prevents government from using this power to curb property rights? Given that government has the ability to do good (enforce property rights) and bad (destroy property rights), how do we give government agents the incentive to do good and avoid bad?

One solution proposed by constitutional political economists are constitutional constraints. Federalism, separation of powers, and the rule of law can structure government power in such a way as to limit how that power can be used. Another option can lie in the signature of international treaties and entry into international organizations such as the World Trade Organization (WTO), which implies a commitment to free trade.

More generally speaking, the law and regulations surrounding business activities should pursue, broad speaking, two objectives. On the one hand, consumers need protection against any producers' market power, but on the other hand investors also need to be protected against expropriation (hold-up) through the Government. Accordingly, regulation may be interpreted as an implicit contract between producers and consumers, which is administered by an (impartial) regulatory authority.[57] Every regulatory system is – necessarily – compromised with two types or errors, though. Firstly, regulation or government intervention can occur even though it is not necessary or beneficial (type-I- error), while, secondly, regulation or government intervention may not be in place even though it would have been beneficial (type-II-error). To find the optimal balance between these two errors is the difficult task of designing good regulatory systems to govern market exchange.

An optimal regulatory system should aim at achieving a balance between the following five objectives:
- preventing the abuse of market power (allocative efficiency),
- ensuring cost minimising production (productive efficiency),
- facilitating optimal investment over time (dynamic efficiency),
- inducing minimal transactions costs (transactions costs efficiency), and
- providing minimal incentives for lobbying and unproductive rent-seeking (political efficiency).

Of course, trade-offs are unavoidable, and in addition there are different political objectives for different industries.

References

Acemoglu, D./Robinson, J.A. (2013): Economics versus Politics: Pitfalls of Policy Advice. In: Journal of Economic Perspectives, 27 (2). 173–192.
Akerlof, G.A. (1970): The Market for 'Lemons': Quality Uncertainty and the Market Mechanism. In: Quarterly Journal of Economics, 84, 488–500.

---

[57] See Goldberg (1976).

Alchian, A.A. (1950): Uncertainty, Evolution, and Economic Theory. In: Journal of Political Economy, 58, 211–221.

Amselle, J.-L. (1977): Les Négociants de la Savanne. Paris.

Aoki, M. (1988): Information, Incentives and Bargaining in the Japanese Economy. Cambridge.

Baker, W. (1984): The Social Structure of a National Securities Market. In: American Journal of Sociology, 89, 775–811.

Barzel, Y. (1982): Measurement Cost and the Organization of Markets. In: Journal of Law and Economics, 25, 47–48.

Barzel, Y. (1985): Transaction Costs: Are They Just Costs? In: Journal of Institutional and Theoretical Economics, 141, 4–16.

Bauer, P. T. (1954): West African Trade: A Study of Competition, Oligopoly and Monopoly in a Changing Economy. Cambridge.

Belshaw, C.S. (1965): Traditional Exchange and Modern Markets. Englewood Cliffs.

Ben-Porath, Y. (1980): The F-Connection: Families, Friends, and Firms and the Organization of Exchange. In: Population and Development Review, 6, 1–30.

Bernstein, L. (1992): Opting out of the Legal System: Extralegal Contractual Relations in the Diamond Industry. In: Journal of Legal Studies, 21, 115–157.

Bernstein, L. (1996): Merchant Law in a Merchant Court: Rethinking the Code's Search for Immanent Business Norms. In: University of Pennsylvania Law Review, 144, 1765–1821.

Carlton, D.W. (1981): Futures Markets: Their Purpose, Their History, Their Growth, Their Successes and Failures. In: Journal of Futures Markets, 4, 237–271.

Chandler, A.D. (1977): The Visible Hand: The Managerial Revolution in American Business. Cambridge.

Coase, R.H. (1937): The Nature of the Firm. In: Economica, 4, 386–405.

Coase, R.H. (1960): The Problem of Social Costs. In: Journal of Law and Economics, 3, 1–44.

Coase, R.H. (1988a): The Firm, the Market, and the Law, Chicago.

Coase, R.H. (1988b): The Nature of the Firm: Influence. In: Journal of Law, Economics, and Organization, 4, 33–47.

Coleman, J. S. (1991): Constructed Organizations: First Principles. In: Journal of Law, Economics, and Organization, 7, Special Issue, 7–23.

Darby, M.R./Karni, E. (1973): Free Competition and the Optimal Amount of Fraud. In: Journal of Law and Economics, 16, 67–88.

Dixit, A. (1996): The Making of Economic Policy: A Transaction-Cost Politics Perspective. Cambridge.

Dnes, A. (1996): The Economic Analysis of Franchise Contracts. In: Journal of Institutional and Theoretical Economics (JITE), 152, 297–324.

Dore, R. (1987): Taking Japan Seriously: A Confucian Perspective on Leading Economic Issues. Stanford.

Eggertson, T. (1990): Economic Behaviour and Institutions. Cambridge.

Ensminger, J. 1992. Making a Market: The Institutional Transformation of an African Society. Cambridge.

Ensminger, J. (1997): Transaction Costs and Islam: Explaining Conversion in Africa. In: Journal of Institutional and Theoretical Economics (JITE), 153, 4–29.

Fafchamps, M. (1997): Trade Credit in Zimbabwean Manufacturing. In: World Development, 25, 795–815.

Fafchamps, M. (2000): Ethnicity and Credit in African Manufacturing. In: Journal of Development Economics, 61, 205–235.

Fafchamps, M. (2002): Spontaneous Market Emergence. In: B.E. Journal of Theoretical Economics, 2(1), Article 2.

Fafchamps, M./Minten, B. (2001): Property Rights in a Flea Market Economy. In: Economic Development and Cultural Change, 49, 229–268.

Fukuyama, F. (1995): Trust: The Social Virtues and the Creation of Prosperity. New York.

Furubotn, E.G./Pejovich, S. (1972): Property Rights and Economic Theory: A Survey of Recent Literature. In: Journal of Economic Literature, 57, 347–359.

Gambetta, D. (1993): The Sicilian Mafia: The Business of Private Protection, Cambridge.

Geertz, C. (1978): The Bazaar Economy: Information and Search in Peasant Marketing. In: American Economic Review Papers & Proceedings, 68, 28–32.

Geertz, C. (1979): The Moroccan Bazaar. In: Geertz, C./Geertz, H./Rosen, L. (eds.): Meaning and Order in Moroccan Society: Three Essays in Cultural Analysis. Cambridge.

Goldberg, V. P. (1976): Regulation and Administered Contracts. In: Bell Journal of Economics, 7, 426–448.

Gould, J.P. (1980): The Economics of Markets: A Simple Model of the Market-Making Process. In: Journal of Business, 53, 167–187.

Granovetter, M. (1992): Problems of Explanation in Economic Sociology. In: Nohria,N./Eccles, R.G. (eds.): Networks and Organizations: Structure, Form, and Action. Cambridge. 25–56

Greif, A. (1993): Contract Enforceability and Economic Institutions in Early Trade: The Maghribi Traders' Coalition. In: American Economic Review, 83, 525–548.

Greif, A. (1994): Cultural Beliefs and the Organization of Society: A Historical and Theoretical Reflection on Collectivist and Individualist Societies. In: Journal of Political Economy, 102, 912–950.

Greif, A./Milgrom, P./Weingast, B.R. (1994): Coordination, Commitment, and Enforcement: The Case of the Merchant Guild. In: Journal of Political Economy, 102, 745–776.

Haugland, S.A./Grønhaug, K. (1996): Cooperative Relationships in Competitive Markets. In: Journal of Socio-Economics, 25, 359–371.

Hayek, F.A. (1944): The Road to Serfdom, Chicago.

Hayek, F.A. (1960): The Constitution of Liberty, Chicago.

Hopkins, A. G. (1973): An Economic History of West Africa. London.

Jones, W.O. (1959): Manioc in Africa. Stanford.

Klein, B. (1980): Transaction Cost Determinants of 'Unfair' Contractual Arrangements. In: American Economic Review Papers & Proceedings, 70, 356–362.

Klein, B./Leffler, K. (1981): The Role of Market Forces in Assuring Contractual Performance. In: Journal of Political Economy, 89, 615–641.

Kuran, T. (1997): Islam and Underdevelopment: An Old Puzzle Revisited. In: Journal of Institutional and Theoretical Economics (JITE), 153, 41–71.

Landa, J. (1994): Trust, Ethnicity, and Identity: Beyond the New Institutional Economics of Ethnic Trading Networks, Contract Law, and Gift-Exchange. Ann Arbor.

Lorenz, E.H. (1988): Neither Friends nor Strangers: Informal Networks of Subcontracting in French Industry. In: Gambetta, D. (ed.): Trust: Making and Breaking Cooperative Relations. New York.

Macaulay, S. (1963): Non-Contractual Relations in Business: A Preliminary Study. In: American Sociological Review, 28, 55–67.

Macneil, I.R. (1974): The Many Futures of Contract. In: Southern California Law Review, 47, 691–816.

Malinowski, B. (1922/1953): Argonauts of the Western Pacific, London.

Mauss, M. (1925/1967): The Gift: Forms and Functions of Exchange in Archaic Societies, translated by I. Cunnison. New York.

McMillan, J. & Woodruff, C. (1999a): Dispute Prevention without Courts in Vietnam. In: Journal of Law, Economics, and Organization, 15, 637–658.

McMillan, J./Woodruff, C. (1999b): Interfirm Relationships and Informal Credit in Vietnam. In: Quarterly Journal of Economics, 114, 1285–1320.

Meillassoux, C. (1971): The Development of Indigenous Trade and Markets in West Africa. Oxford.

Ménard, C. (1995): "Markets as Institutions versus Organizations as Markets? Dis-entangling Some Fundamental Concepts. In: Journal of Economic Behavior and Organization, 28, 161–182.

Milgrom, P.R./North, D.C./Weingast, B.R. (1990): The Role of Institutions in the Revival of Trade: The Law Merchant, Private Judges, and the Champagne Fairs. In: Economics and Politics, 2, 1–23.

Nelson, P. (1970): Information and Consumer Behavior. In: Journal of Political Economy, 78, 311–329.

North, D.C. (1977): Markets and Other Allocation Systems in History: The Challenge of Karl Polanyi. In: Journal of European Economic History, 6, 703–716.

North, D.C. (1981): Structure and Change in Economic History. New York.

North, D.C. (1990): Institutions, Institutional Change, and Economic Performance. Cambridge.

North, D.C. (1994): Economic Performance through Time. In: American Economic Review, 84, 359–368.

Ostrom, E. (2010): Beyond Markets and States: Polycentric Governance of Complex Economic Systems. In: American Economic Review, 100, 641–672.

Polanyi, K. (1944): The Great Transformation. New York.

Polanyi, K. (1957): The Economy as Instituted Process. In: Polanyi, K./Arensberg, C.M./Pearson, H.W. (eds.): Trade and Market in the Early Empires, Glencoe, IL. 243–270.

Polanyi, K./Arensberg, C.M./Pearson, H.W. (eds.) (1957): Trade and Market in the Early Empires, Glencoe, IL.

Posner, R.A. (1980): A Theory of Primitive Societies with Special Reference to Primitive Law. In: Journal of Law and Economics, 23, 1–53.

Sahlins, M.D. (1965): On the Sociology of Primitive Exchange. In: Banton, M. (ed.): The Relevance of Models for Social Anthropology. Tavistock: Association of Social Anthropologists. 139–236.

Sahlins, M. (1972): Stone Age Economics. Chicago.

Salisbury, R. F. (1968): Trade and Markets. In: Sills, D. (ed.): International Encyclopedia of the Social Sciences, Vol. 16, New York. 118–122.

Scheuer, F./Wolitzky, A. (2016): Capital Taxation under Political Constraints. In: American Economic Review, 106, 2304–2328.

Spulber, D.F. (1996): Market Microstructure and Intermediation. In: Journal of Economic Perspectives, 10 (3), 135–152.

Stigler, G.J. (1961): The Economics of Information. In: Journal of Political Economy, 69, 213–225.

Telser, L.G. (1981): Why Are There Organized Futures Markets? In: Journal of Law and Economics, 24, 1–22.

Telser, L.G./Higinbotham, H.N. (1977): Organized Futures Markets: Costs and Benefits. In: Journal of Political Economy, 85, 969–1000.

Weingast, B. R. (1995): The Economic Role of Political Institutions: Market-Preserving Federalism and Economic Development. In: Journal of Law, Economics, and Organization, 11, 1–31.

Williamson, O.E. (1975): Markets and Hierarchies. New York.

Williamson, O.E. (1985): The Economic Institutions of Capitalism. New York.

Williamson, O.E. (1989): Transaction Cost Economics. In: Schmalensee,R./Willig, R. (eds.): Handbook of Industrial Organization, Vol. 1, Amsterdam. 135–182.

Williamson, O. E. (1996): The Mechanisms of Governance, Oxford.

Ziegler, R. (1990): The Kula: Social Order, Barter, and Ceremonial Exchange. In: Hechter, M./ Opp, K.-D./Wippler, R. (eds.): Social Institutions: Their Emergence, Maintenance and Effects. Berlin. 141–168.

The Rule of Law in the Global Development of Constitutionalism

Thomas Schmitz

Introduction: a Heterogeneous Legal Terminology

The legal terminology applicable to our topic is heterogeneous. The German law uses the term "Rechtsstaat" [state based on the rule of law] for a concept with a long tradition that nowadays emanates from the Constitution.[1] The French doctrine has adopted the corresponding term "État de droit" for a rather new concept, which is based, however, on long-known unwritten "general principles of law".[2] European Union law uses the analogous term "communauté de droit".[3] Meanwhile, in the Common Law tradition, the term "rule of law" is prevalent. It also prevails in the international and comparative legal discourse. This term is preferable in our context because it describes more accurately what is meant. However, the rule of law in the more vague and open sense of the international discourse should not be confused with the well-defined concept of rule of law in English or American law.

The fundamental idea of the rule of law is to overcome arbitrariness by moderating public power and reliably adjusting it to legal rules. "Rechtsstaat" or "rule of law" basically means that the law governs all activities in the state.

---

[1] Schmidt-Aßmann (2004), § 26 no. 10 ff.

[2] Chevallier (2014); Schmitz (1989), 27 ff. (in particular 37 ff.).

[3] European Court of Justice, case 294/83, Les Verts, no. 23 (German translation: "Rechtsgemeinschaft"; English translation: "community based on the rule of law").

Everyone, including every institution and power in the state is subject to the law. No one stands above the law; no cause is more important than the law. Thus, the rule of law is an antithesis to totalitarianism.

Originally, the concept was limited to this formal understanding. However, in the second half of the 20th century, it evolved from the narrow formal to a comprehensive material concept that includes numerous material (substantial) principles of law.[4] All these principles serve the implementation of the rule of law and ensure a fair balancing of conflicting interests within the law.

The rule of law is only one of several basic elements of the model of the "freiheitlich-demokratischer Rechtsstaat" [free and democratic state based on the rule of law], which is the prevalent model in contemporary Europe. It must not be confused with other basic elements, such as democracy and the protection of human rights, which are not part of it but complementing it. They are interlinked and mutually reinforcing but still separate principles. Unfortunately, in Hanoi this is not always the case, even not within the German-Vietnamese Rule of Law Dialogue. This sometimes causes misunderstandings.

Different Manifestations of the Same Fundamental Idea in Europe

"Rechtsstaat", "État de droit" and "rule of law" are different manifestations of the same fundamental idea. The German concept emerged in the 18th and 19th centuries as a liberal antonym to the absolutist concept of the "Polizeistaat" [police state] but also roots in the pre-liberal German public law doctrine. It was accomplished under the rule of the Basic Law after 1949.[5] In France, the term "État de droit" was not regularly employed until the eighties of the 20th century but many elements were developed since the 19th century in the form of unwritten "general principles of law" discovered in a long tradition of jurisprudence by the French Conseil d'État.[6] Some of them had already influenced the development of German administrative law via the famous scholar Otto

---

[4] See, for illustration, my overview on the many elements of the "Rechtsstaatsprinzip" in German constitutional law, www.thomas-schmitz-hanoi.vn/Downloads/Schmitz-_Rechtsstaatsprinzip-en.pdf.

[5] See on the development of this concept Tiedemann (2014), 171 ff.

[6] Schmitz (1989), 29 ff.

Mayer[7] at the end of the 19th century. In the late 20th century, the German concept was more developed and more comprehensive. However, this was partly because corresponding elements existing in the French law were not always linked to the concept of "État de droit". Concerning the "rule of law" in English law, there was a more substantial difference. The English concept focused on formal aspects and procedural fairness and was more reluctant to recognize material (substantial) principles, which would lead to a judicial review not just of the making but also of the contents of the decisions of public authorities.

Under the influence of the emerging European Community/Union law, which had its own, autonomous concept of "communauté de droit", and with the feedback from new modern constitutional states which had adopted and merged the three different concepts, these concepts converged. This is one aspect of the so-called "Europeanisation of law". EU law enjoys primacy over national law. Whenever implementing or applying EU law or encroaching on the rights of EU citizen, the member states must comply with the rule of law requirements of this legal order. Thus, the law of all member states came under pressure to conform with the numerous "general principles of European Union law", which have been discovered and developed by the European Court of Justice in Luxembourg in many decades of evaluative comparison of laws ["wertende Rechtsvergleichung"]. These principles are the most up-to-date incarnation of the rule of law in the 21st century.[8] They also represent the common legal heritage of the rule of law in Europe. The development of these principles and the harmonization of the different rule of law concepts in the European countries have also been stimulated by the jurisprudence of the European Court of Human Rights in Strasbourg when enforcing the European Convention of Human Rights.

---

[7] See in particular Mayer (1886); Mayer (1895). Both publications transferring elements from French administrative law to German administrative law doctrine.

[8] For a comprehensive presentation and analysis see Tridimas (2007); see also Lenaerts/van Nuffel (2012), marginal numbers 22–039 ff.

176

The Triumph of the Rule of Law in Europe

The triumph of the rule of law started in the seventies when Greece, Portugal and Spain put an end to dictatorship and enacted free and democratic constitutions that stressed the commitment to the rule of law.[9] Portugal and Spain also established constitutional courts that developed the constitutional concept of "Estado de direito"/"Estado de Derecho" by the way of constitutional interpretation. A strong cooperation with West-European, in particular German constitutionalists facilitated this development.

The triumph of the rule of law was as its zenith in the nineties, when most East European states, after the end of Soviet rule, established and developed their up-to-date free, democratic and rule of law based constitutional orders. This process was one of the greatest success stories in modern constitutionalism, since these states changed from law-negating totalitarianism to state of the art rule of law and constitutionalism within a decade. 15 years after the fall of the Berlin Wall, eight East European states, three of them former Soviet Republics, were able to join the European Union, which requires its member states to meet the most modern standards of the rule of law. This process was encouraged and promoted by the Council of Europe via a high-profile expert commission, the Venice Commission (European Commission for Democracy through Law).

One of the purposes of the Council of Europe is to promote the rule of law. The Venice Commission was established in 1990. It is supported by the member states of the Council of Europe and a number of other interested states. It consists of university professors of constitutional and public international law, judges of supreme and constitutional courts, experienced members of parliaments and some civil servants. Its members are designated for four years by the states, but act in their individual capacity. The Commission has a permanent secretariat in Strasbourg and is holding plenary sessions four times a year in Venice (Italy).[10]

---

[9] See Art. 25 of the Constitution of Greece of 1975, Art. 2 of the Constitution of the Portuguese Republic of 1976, Art. 1 of the Spanish Constitution of 1978.

[10] See on the contribution of the Venice Commission to the development of constitutionalism in East Europe Rülke (2003); Hoffmann-Riem (2014). For detailed information www.venice.coe.int/webforms/events. See also the list of articles on the Commission, www.venice.coe.int/WebForms/pages/?p=01_01_Articles.

The Venice Commission is the Council of Europe's advisory body and the most prominent think tank on constitutional matters in Europe. It shares and promotes the standards and best practices adopted within the member states of the Council of Europe. In 500 expert opinions on issues in more than 50 countries, 80 scientific studies and reports on topical issues, 250 seminars and conferences with dozens of courts and universities and the training of 3.000 civil servants in human rights and administrative law, the Commission has provided an impressive amount of sophisticated advice and training to its member states. In particular, it cooperates with the national constitutional courts. The European Court of Human Rights in Strasbourg has referred to Venice Commission opinions in more than 50 cases.[11] The Venice Commission also cooperates with interested non-European partners, for example within the EU-Central Asia Rule of Law Initiative.[12]

A second factor contributing to the triumph of the rule of law was the introduction of constitutional courts in the new East European constitutional states. Most states adopted the German model of a separate and independent constitutional court with the status of a constitutional institution and the jurisdiction of constitutional review.[13] This model had been invented in Austria but first realized with great success in Germany. As before in Germany, Portugal and Spain, the constitutional courts in East Europe developed the national constitutional law by interpreting the new constitutions and their clauses on the rule of law. Often it would need a whole book to describe what the constitutional court extracted by the way of interpretation from a small number of short constitutional clauses with some indefinite constitutional terms. Supported by the work of the Venice Commission, they kept in mind the achievements of constitutional jurisprudence and theory in the most developed constitutional states. They often adopted – but sometimes also criticized – the doctrines developed by the German Federal Constitutional Court. In some cases, a minority of judges would criticize the majority of judges in a dissenting vote for misunderstanding some inspiring ideas of the German Court.

---

[11] All data provided by the Venice Commission on its website, www.venice.coe.int/-WebForms/pages/?p=01_Presentation.

[12] See for details the website of the Venice Commission, www.venice.coe.int/WebForms/pages/?p=03_CARoLInitiative.

[13] See for details Starck (2007).

Without independent constitutional courts or supreme courts exercising their function, the rule of law can hardly be ensured in practice in a state, since without authoritative constitutional interpretation the constitutional dogmatic of the rule of law cannot unfold and there is a lack of orientation for the legislator and the ordinary courts. This is even more evident in the field of public international law where the rule of law is a binding principle too but usually cannot be enforced in practice. The current case of Russia, which has turned back to reject the rule of law in domestic as in international affairs, illustrates this problem. There are fears that China may follow this example. The idea of a "global constitutionalism"[14] is unrealistic as long as conflicts like in Ukraine or the Eastern Sea are not solved by legal experts in courts or arbitration panels but by the way of violence or confrontation.

The Spreading of the Idea of Rule of Law in the Wake of Globalization and Development

In the wake of globalization and development, the general idea of the rule of law has become popular in many countries with emerging economies.[15] In particular intellectuals and the emerging new middle classes but also government think tanks and highly qualified superior officials looking for a way to secure a sustainable development, are open-minded about it. A long-term sustainable growth of the national economy is impossible without the legal security and certainty provided by the rule of law – in particular in times of international economic integration.[16] The WTO necessarily promotes the rule of law because it is depending on it. The ambitious project of the ASEAN Economic Community cannot be realized without the rule of law. Furthermore, the contribution of the civil society to a sound development of the country, which is more and more accepted and appreciated by responsible governments, requires certain reliable legal conditions. Finally, the rule of law is essential for

---

[14] Peters (2009) with further references.

[15] For an overview see Konrad-Adenauer-Stiftung (2009): See in particular the analysis of Grote, 174 ff.

[16] See the special lecture on this topic at this conference. See also Ewing-Chow/Losari/Slade (2014).

an effective protection of human rights. At the same time it is helpful for the rebutting of unjustified allegations of human rights violations utilized as means of anti-government propaganda. Following strictly the rule of law may lead to a higher degree of rationality in the political process.

Thus, like many other countries in the world,[15] some East and Southeast Asian countries have anchored their commitment to the rule of law in their national constitutions (see Art. 1 (3) of the Constitution of the Republic of Indonesia of 1945, Art. 78 (6) of the Constitution of the Kingdom of Thailand of 2007, Art. 5 of the Constitution of the People's Republic of China of 1982). Some countries refer to certain elements of the rule of law in their constitution (see, for example, Art. 6 and 10 of the Constitution of the Lao People's Democratic Republic of 2003). Others have adopted the rule of law as an important concept of legal policy. They are supported by the United Nations Development Programme, NGOs, the EU and Western governments. Strengthening the rule of law is an integral element of modern development cooperation. For example, German institutions and NGOs are involved in a "Rule of Law Dialogue" with Vietnam.

ASEAN, as an international organization, is also committed to the rule of law. The ASEAN Charter defines the strengthening of the rule of law as one of the purposes of ASEAN (Art. 1 no. 7). It obliges not only the organization but also its member states to act in accordance with the principle of adherence to the rule of law (Art. 2 (2) lit. h). The ASEAN Secretariat even describes the rule of law as a fundamental feature of ASEAN on its website.[17]

However, the adoption of the fundamental idea of the rule of law has also brought misunderstandings and distortions.[18] There is no common sense or awareness of the various formal and material requirements of the rule of law. Continental and Common Law doctrines are mingled. Furthermore, the mixing-up with complementing and interacting but separate elements of the modern constitutional state such as separation of powers, democracy and human rights threatens to dilute its contours and to relativize it. Therefore, it would be helpful to have a second, global "Venice Commission" in order to facilitate orientation, work out a clear distinction between the Western model of a "free and democratic constitutional state" and other types of constitutional states

[17] ASEAN Sectretariat (2013).

[18] See the country reports at the wiki of the Freie Universität Berlin (2013).

and to provide sophisticated advice to developing constitutional states that may want to adopt some but not all doctrines of European constitutionalism. In ASEAN, the judicial development of law by an ASEAN geo-regional court would be helpful to build up an ASEAN rule of law doctrine.

The Rule of Law in the Constitution of the Socialist Republic of Vietnam of 2013

The Constitution of the Socialist Republic of Vietnam of 2013 emphasizes in several articles the primacy of the Constitution and the law. Art. 2 (1) defines Vietnam as a "state ruled by law" or "law-governed state" ["nhà nước pháp quyền"]. According to Art. 8 (1), it shall be "organized and operate in accordance with the Constitution and law" and "manage society by the Constitution and law." This can be understood as a general commitment to constitutionalism (unlike in the Soviet Union, other former European socialist states and perhaps China, the constitution is taken seriously) and to the rule of law. This commitment is underlined when Art. 4 (3) emphasizes that even the "organizations and members of the Communist Party of Vietnam shall operate within the framework of the Constitution and the law." So even the Communist Party, although it is the "force leading the state and society" (Art. 4 (1) does not stand above the law. This was a very important issue in the broad public constitutional reform debate in 2013. Finally, Art. 14 stresses that the human and citizens' rights shall be respected and protected in accordance with the law and only subject to limitations prescribed by a law.

However, Art. 2 (1) defines Vietnam more precisely as a "socialist state ruled by law" ["nhà nước pháp quyền xã hội chủ nghĩa"]. This does not refer to the ancient communist principle of socialist legality, which limited the law to the function to serve the building-up of socialism[19] and is incompatible with the rule of law. However, it neither refers to the classical, European concepts of the rule of law. The Vietnamese constitution of 2013 is not a free and democratic constitution in the sense of European constitutional theory but a modern example of the socialist type of constitution. Its commitment to the rule of law must be understood in this sense. For example, with regard to the fundamental

---

[19] Kühn (2011), 118 ff. with further references.

constitutional principle of democratic centralism (Art. 8 (1), separation of powers cannot be part of the rule of law in Vietnam. Consequently, Art. 2 (3) provides that the state agencies "coordinate and control one another" but does not refer to the concept of separation of powers and instead stipulates that the "state power is unified."

It will be the task and challenge for the Vietnamese scholars of constitutional law, the courts and the lawmakers to elaborate the special "socialist" features of the Vietnamese "socialist rule of law" without compromising or diluting the general idea. For example, there may be a greater focus on social justice, social coherence and public interests, some limited differences in the protection of legitimate interests and a stronger acceptance of the state exercising influence on the society. There may also be some special material (substantial) principles of law. With regard to Art. 2 (3) a specific system of checks and balances must be developed, which ensures that the state institutions control one another effectively but which does not yet amount to a real separation of powers. Thus, the global development of constitutionalism may lead to the emergence of a new variant of the concept of the rule of law. We, the European constitutionalists, are looking forward to studying it.

References

ASEAN Secretariat (ed.) (2013): The Rule of Law – a Fundamental Feature of ASEAN since Its Inception. http://asean.org/the-rule-of-law-a-fundamental-feature-of-asean-since-its-inception/.
Chevallier, Jacques (2014): L'État de droit. 5. edition. Paris.
Ewing-Chow, Michael/Losari, Junianto James/Slade, Melania Vilarasau (2014): The facilitation of trade by the rule of law: the cases of Singapore and ASEAN. http://www.wto.org/english/res_e/booksp_e/cmark_chap9_e.pdf
Frändberg, Åke (2014): From Rechtsstaat to Universal Law-State. An Essay in Philosophical Jurisprudence. Cham.
Freie Universität Berlin (ed.) (2013): Wiki Understandings of the Rule of Law in Various Legal Orders of the World. Last updated 2013. http://wikis.fu-berlin.de/display/SBprojectrol/Home.

Freie Universität Berlin (ed.): Understandings of the Rule of Law in Various Legal Orders of the World, http://wikis.fu-berlin.de/display/SBproject-rol/Home.

Grote, Rainer (1999): Rule of Law, Rechtsstaat and Etat de droit. Starck, Christian (ed.): Constitutionalism, Universalism and Democracy. A Comparative Analysis. Baden-Baden. 269–306.

Hoffmann-Riem, Wolfgang (2014): The Venice Commission of the European Council-Standards and Impact. In: European Journal of International Law 25. 579–597.

Konrad-Adenauer-Stiftung (ed.) (2009): Demokratie- und Rechtsstaatsförderung in der Entwicklungszusammenarbeit. Einschätzungen aus den Empfängerländern in Afrika, Asien, Lateinamerika und Südosteuropa. www.kas.de/wf/de/ 33.15679.

Kühn, Zdenik (2011): The Judiciary in Central and Eastern Europe. Mechanical Jurisprudence in Transformation? Leiden.

Lenaerts, Koenraad/van Nuffel, Piet (2012): European Union Law. Third edition. London.

Luchterhandt, Otto/Starck, Christian (2007): Verfassungsgerichtsbarkeit in Mittel- und Osteuropa. Vol. 1. Baden-Baden.

Mayer, Otto (1886): Theorie des Französischen Verwaltungsrechts. Straßburg.

Mayer, Otto (1886): Theorie des Französischen Verwaltungsrechts. Straßburg.

Mayer, Otto (1895): Deutsches Verwaltungsrecht. Vol. 1. München.

Mayer, Otto (1895): Deutsches Verwaltungsrecht. Vol. 1. München.

Peters, Anne (2009): The Merits of Global Constitutionalism. In: Indiana Journal of Global Legal Studies 16, no. 2. www.repository.law.indiana.edu/ijgls/vol16/iss2/2.

Rülke, Steffen (2003): Venedig-Kommission und Verfassungsgerichtsbarkeit. Eine Untersuchung über den Beitrag des Europarates zur Verfassungsentwicklung in Mittel- und Osteuropa. Köln.

Schmidt-Aßmann, Eberhard (2004): Der Rechtsstaat. In: Isensee, Josef/Kirchhof, Paul (eds.): Handbuch des Staatsrechts. Der Verfassungsstaat. Vol. II, Third edition. § 26.

Schmitz, Thomas (1989): Rechtsstaat und Grundrechtsschutz im französischen Polizeirecht. Baden-Baden.

Schmitz, Thomas (2013): The Rechtsstaatsprinzip (Principle of the Rule of Law) in German Constitutional Law. www.thomas-schmitz-hanoi.vn/-Downloads/Schmitz_Rechtsstaatsprinzip-en.pdf.

Sellers, Mortimer/Tomaszewski, Tadeusz (eds.) (2010): The Rule of Law in Comparative Perspective. Dordrecht.

Silkenat, James R./Hickey, James E./Barenboim, Peter D. (eds.) (2014): The Legal Doctrines of the Rule of Law and the Legal State (Rechtsstaat). Cham.

Tridimas, Takis (2007): The General Principles of EU Law. Second edition. Oxford.

Rule of Law and Global Governance

Ulrich von Alemann

History of the "Rechtsstaat"

The idea of the "Rechtsstaat" is very old. It was a common topic of debate in 19th century Germany. It is linked to statehood and is primarily supposed to control the administrative actions of the state with proper legislation – rule of law versus arbitrary rule of feudal authority.[1] Especially in Germany the normative doctrine of "Rechtsstaat" is older than the idea of democracy itself; in fact, it is older than the constitutional monarchies in, for example, Great Britain, France, or Scandinavia. In the absolute monarchy of France at the beginning of the 17th century King Louis XIV proclaimed: "L'État, c'est moi!" The Prussian King Frederick II the Great, on the other hand, saw himself as an enlightened monarch and designated himself: "Ich bin der erste Diener des Staates! (I am the first servant of the state!)"

This fits a wide spread story whose validity is questionable but which tells us a lot about the "Rechtsstaat". Frederick the Great, in his castle in Potsdam near Berlin, had been annoyed by the rattling of a mill and had someone inform the miller about this. The miller then answered that "there are still judges in Berlin." The story tells us: even the King of Prussia was subject to law. Until today, this has been a common saying in Germany. At around the same time, the Prussian-German philosopher Immanuel Kant had demanded a law of nations in his 1795 publication "Perpetual Peace: A Philosophical Sketch",

---

[1] Dose (1999).

which was built upon the idea of a "universally peaceful alliance of nations"[2]. The Ideals of Kant stated that all human actions, including the actions of the state, should ultimately be subject to legal principles. Today, in spite of a lot of progress, we are still a long way away from this vision.

But even more than 150 years earlier an international "rule of law" had German roots. This originated in the "Peace of Westphalia" of 1648. It ended the Thirty Years' War between the two Christian denominations, namely Catholic and Protestant. It was the first international congress ever in which all of the big European powers were represented. They arrived at a peace treaty and basically founded the preface to the law of nations in this process. It was a long way and took some 300 years to the "The Hague Conventions" at the end of the 19th century, when a legal containment of war and neutrality were codified. This effort was continued in the League of Nations of 1919 but ultimately failed during the 1930ies. It was not until the foundation of the United Nations in 1945 that a basic ground for international regimes was established. This encompassed not only organizations aimed at security and peace but also organizations concerned with health (WHO), labor (ILO) or culture (UNESCO) and many more.

The Concepts of "Rule of Law", "Law of Nations" and "Global Governance"

Originally the term "Rechtsstaat" defined a characteristic of the German "Sonderweg (unique path)" in the development of a democratic constitutional state. Rule of law binds every governmental authority to constitution, legislation, and law. The sovereign does not stand above the law. Initially, this was seen in a way that the law was often only perceived formally. It was essential that a law existed, even if the content and goal of this law might have been dubious. This view has since been abolished in Germany after the misuse by National Socialism. The fascists during the 1930s actually presented themselves in part as guarantors of a "Rechtsstaat", which itself passed race laws (Nuremberg laws) that can only be considered violations of human rights. These laws were used to implement inhuman governance. Nowadays, the rule of law is seen everywhere as a concept that enforces natural justice regarding, for example, inalienable human dignity and human rights.

---

[2] Hoeffe (1995).

Authority entails, especially in a democratic rule of law, a monopoly on the use of force. This means that only the state is authorized to use force internally (police, courts, legal system) and externally (military), which has to be subject to judicial examination. The state's monopoly on the use of force can only be justified by the effective comprehension of the constitutions in liberal democracies if the state exercises force lawfully and legitimately. These aspects point to the extraordinary role of the constitutional foundation of democratic authority and the normative expectation towards the state, to continuously gain the acceptance of its subjects. This German concept of "Rechtsstaat" was initially hardly comparable to the English definition of "rule of law". Today, the two concepts have become closer in meaning. In this respect, rule of law is a key to worldwide modern political theory, also in the development and foundation of young democracies.

The general law of nations encompassed all laws that governed the relationships of nations. Initially these nations were seen as international legal personalities that could not suffer any external authority over themselves. Noninterference in the internal politics of each nation was seen as a golden rule of classical diplomacy and law of nations. The world of states was anarchic and only voluntary contractual agreements were acknowledged. During a long historical process, which led to the foundation of the United Nations, this anarchy has been converted into a highly complicated legal framework. Today, we are still in the midst of this process. There is a change from the traditional law of nations to modern international law.

The players of the classical law of nations were the states and their representatives, namely the diplomats. This also changed some time ago. In today's United-Nations' conferences diplomats have been reduced to a minority since representatives of international organizations, corporations, unions, NGOs, scientists etc. make up the majority of delegates. This process has changed government to governance, even global governance and has advanced far. We will come back to this later.

Dimensions of the Rule of Law

So what is the rule of law? What are its criteria and scale? Can the rule of law be measured? There are an exceedingly large amount of criteria and scales for the rule of law historically and in the present days. We will focus on the present day. To do this I can extract four frameworks from recent publications which indicate definitions of the rule of law.

Table 3: Four Frameworks for the Rule of Law

	World Justice Report (2010)	Freedom House (2010)	Map of freedom in the world (2009)	Deficiencies of rule of law in failing states (2011)
1	*The government and its officials and agents are accountable under law*	*Independent judiciary*	*Is there an independent judiciary?*	*No real political participation of the electorate*
2	*The laws are clear, publicized, stable and fair, and protect fundamental rights, including the security of persons and property*	*Primacy of rule of law in civil and criminal matters*	*Does the rule of law prevail in civil and criminal matters? Are police under direct "civilian control"*	*No existence and guarantee of human rights*
3	*The process by which the laws are enacted, administered and enforced is accessible, fair and efficient*	*Accountability of security forces and military to civilian authorities*	*Is there protection from political terror, unjustified imprisonment, exile, or torture, whether by groups that support or oppose the system? Is there freedom from war and insurgencies?*	*No independence of the judiciary and frequent vigilantism*
4	*Access to justice is provided by competent, independent, and ethical adjudicators, attorneys or representatives, and judicial officers who are of sufficient number, have adequate resources, and reflect the makeup of communities they serve*	*Protection of property rights*	*Do laws, policies, and practices guarantee equal treatment of various segments of the population?*	*Notorious and widespread corruption and clientelism*

Source: Schulze-Fielitz (2011), 10.

This already is highly elaborate and does not need any further differentiation. The table points out the diversity of definitions. This is not a deficit, but rather the nature of the issue: There cannot be a universally binding definition of rule of law, for all time periods, regions and issues. Sometimes only a dichotomy exists between a weak rule of law, which especially emphasizes contractual security in international legal relations and a strong version, which particularly includes human rights. In general, the debate about rule of law is a dynamic and continuously differentiating process, which I will discuss in the next part of this text.

Dynamics of the Rule of Law

The classical old law of nations was applied, as we have seen, from the Peace of Westphalia in 1648 until the Vienna Congress in 1815. The sovereign states were the only players, public agents were non-existent. It was a soft law since no regulating instance stood above the nations. It was an anarchic law in which the strong could usurp the ius ad bellum, the right to war. Since the end of the 19th century, a rapid and dynamic advancement has been taking place from the conventions of The Hague and Geneva to the League of Nations in 1919 up to the United Nations in 1945. And since then advancements have picked up in speed. In light of the general globalization, international jurisdiction has increased exponentially. This has led to an increase in the amount of contracts based on the law of nations by a factor of four.[3] Nevertheless, this also is connected to an isolation of the source of the law, jurisdiction. In the past, this has always been the nations themselves through internal jurisdiction or externally through inter-country contracts. Nowadays, jurisdiction has become independent of individual nations. International organizations create laws in a way never before witnessed.

"The increasing development of international organizations and international law and its forms of implementation has raised the significance of the law of nations to a new level never before seen in human history."[4]

---

[3] Schulze-Fielitz (2011), 10.
[4] Schulze-Fielitz (2011), 10.

In this respect, we are witnesses to a new process of international rule of law. Not only has the number of contracts increased but also the number of judicial instances. There is now a "judicalization" of the law of nations which leads to an increase in politically independent international courts and arbitration instances. By now there are supposed to be a total of 125 such instances.

At the moment, a big German research project at Humboldt University Berlin is investigating "The International Rule of Law – Rise or Decline?" The research agenda is as following:

"The Research Group examines the role of international law in a changing global order. Can we, under the current significantly changing conditions, still observe an increasing juridification of international relations based on a universal understanding of values, or are we, to the contrary, rather facing a tendency towards an informalization or a reformalization of international law, or even an erosion of international legal norms? Would it be appropriate to revisit classical elements of international law in order to react to structural changes, which may give rise to a more polycentric or non-polar world order? Or are we simply observing a slump in the development towards an international rule of law based on a universal understanding of values?"[5]

We can thus come to an intermediary conclusion: The internationalization of law is increasing more and more dynamically with respect to the amount of international contracts and the amount of international dispute settlement institutions. Let us now look at the regional level in Europe.

European Experience of the Rule of Law

Europe is the world's leading region when it comes to integration and networking of international law. This is the case in two distinct but mutually overlapping institutions: The European Union and the Council of Europe.

The Council of Europe is far less known worldwide and is often confused with the European Union; despite it is a completely independent and self-contained institution. The Council of Europe was founded on May 5th, 1949 with the contract of London and today encompasses 47 European nations which represent 820 Million citizens. The Council of Europe is not a state-like structure, like the European Union, but rather a European international organization, a forum for debate and general questions concerning Europe. The

---

[5]http://www.jura.fu-berlin.de/fachbereich/einrichtungen/oeffentliches-recht/lehrende/-kriegerh/KFG/index.html, 21.02.2016

Council of Europe far surpasses the core of Europe, the Western- and Central-European area, and encompasses Russia and the former soviet states.

The most important treaty brought forth by the Council of Europe is the European Convention on Human Rights of 1950. This has led to the European Court of Human Rights being its most important institution. Every person in Europe can call upon the European Court of Human Rights and claim that his rights were violated according to the European Convention on Human Rights. Since its reform in 1998 the European Court of Human Rights has grown in influence and has passed multiple judgments that have impacted the legal order of individual nations. These court judgments can in fact not be enforced by any European executive authority, but they have considerable political and lasting effects.

Subject to the rule of law to an even higher degree is the European Union, founded with the Treaties of Rome in 1957, with initially five member nations, but which has continuously expanded and deepened through various treaties. At the moment the Treaty of Lisbon, signed in 2007, is in effect. Since the Treaty of Amsterdam in 1997, the rule of law is an explicitly accentuated foundation of the Union (Art. 6 Abs. 1, now Art. 2 EUV):

"The Union is founded on the values of respect for human dignity, freedom, democracy, equality, the rule of law and respect for human rights, including the rights of persons belonging to minorities. These values are common to the Member States in a society in which pluralism, non-discrimination, tolerance, justice, solidarity and equality between women and men prevail" (Art. 2 EU-Treaty).

The rule of law is also an explicit condition for entry into the EU. Even though the Treaty of Lisbon does not further differentiate the principles of the rule of law, multiple rules of the European Community Law include fundamentals of the rule of law. This is the case in, for example:
- the legality of administration,
- legal principles based on basic rights,
- the right to effective legal protection,
- the right to a fair trial based on the rule of law, public liability for legislative injustice,
- or in the sense of general elementary laws, like the elementary law of commensurability, legal certainty, legitimate expectation, the legal principle that measures should not have retroactive effects, or the prohibition of double jeopardy.

The ascertainment of all these principles is guarded by the European Court of Justice in Luxembourg, which has grown into a mighty guardian of the European treaties. But more core elements of the rule of law can be identified:

- the existence of basic- and human rights,
- the separation of powers,
- the independence of courts,
- the binding of all state authority in the constitution (Normenhierarchie),
- reservation of the law.

All these principles show a mutual learning process which is aimed at making rule of law a central benchmark in the European constitutional discourse.[6] In spite of all this general juridification and standardization of the rule of law in Europe, distinct differences in the ways that the rule of law is individually accentuated are evident. Thus different traditions in the rule of law are still continuing to grow, like the British Common Law in contrast to the continental codified law. This difference in the rule of law partly refers to important basic principles, whether a constitutional jurisdiction exists in the nation or not. In Germany the Federal Constitutional Court (Bundesverfassungsgericht) is viewed as the "summit of the rule of law" (Klaus Stern). This is not the case in other countries. All in all, the principle of the rule of law plays a smaller part in European Law in contrast to its paramount importance in the German constitution ("Grundgesetz") and in German law in general.

Global Governance

The function of the rule of law as a central benchmark for the existence and function of statehood in an international comparison becomes even more heterogeneous than in Europe. Rule of law is not constitutionalized on a global level, not even in the UN-Charter. In addition to that, no international definition or even term for it can be expected in an international linguistic usage. Nevertheless, a "grand coalition" of World Bank, human rights organizations and national and international security experts exists which all "sing the praises of the rule of law together".[7] The UN puts its emphasis on the rule of law particularly on the obligation to the law, separation of powers, effective legal protection through independent courts, and the protection of human rights.

---

[6] Schulze-Fielitz (2011), 3.

[7] Schuppert cited by Schulze-Fielitz (2011), 4.

The current globalization processes imply an increase and compression of cross-border interactions which involve almost all social classes, nations, organizations, group of players, and individuals in a complex system of mutual dependencies. The scope of actions of individuals, the scope of national politics, "Lebenswelten" (lifeworlds), social classification patterns, and deep structures of societies are undergoing lasting changes.[8] Local, regional, and national global spheres are constantly shrinking and connecting to each other in new ways. The process of globalization poses problems which far surpass classical foreign politics. In addition to that, it poses new requirements for national politics. Thus the development of a global rule of law and an international culture of cooperation is now needed more than ever.

The idea of rule of law is one of the great achievements of modern democracies. Global governance is only possible with a strong global rule of law. The long-term stability of global societies, democracy, freedom, and solidarity can only be sustained through a cooperation-encouraging set of rules, in other words, institutional and legal containment of power is needed. The formation of global rules has to incorporate the differing effects of globalization and combine them with generally accepted principles, norms, and rules with special provisions for specific groups of nations. The founders of the UN already pursued the goal of a worldwide rule of law but could only achieve it in incipient stages. For example they created the International Court of Justice in The Hague in 1945. However, nations could decide if they wanted to adhere to the court's rulings (Germany declared its submission in 2008). In 2002 the International Criminal Court was also established in The Hague. It has, however, not been recognized by some nations to this day (e.g. USA, China, India, Russia, Israel and Turkey). Vietnam, however, has joined.

Conclusion: Cultural Diversities of the Rule of Law?

Today, the rule of law has become a dynamic process which far surpasses the UN Charter and the UN-sub-organizations. For instance, it encompasses maritime law, diplomatic- and consulate law, space law, and trade law (WTO). Initially, the law of nations was only applied between sovereign nations. To-

---

[8] Messner/Gu/Humphrey (2008).

day, multiple networks of interconnected agents exist: Diplomats of nations, international organizations, corporations and civil society. This new situation is called "global governance". However, this process also experiences a lot of set-backs, contradictions, and inconsistencies. It is evident regularly in regional and global conflicts, even today. Thus, enforcement of international rule of law still constitutes a big challenge.

There are two understandings of the rule of law which vary in sophistication: Weaker doctrines (weak law: without connections to notions of democracy and justice, more commonly accepted in international law) and stronger doctrines (strong law: e.g. validity of human rights, more commonly accepted in the western hemisphere). The ASEAN-States have incorporated a strengthening of the rule of law since 20.11.2007 onwards (ASEAN-Charter). In Islamic constitutions the concept of rule of law has not prevailed and is sometimes even rejected completely. Most nations, however, are convinced that democracy cannot exist without the rule of law, but that the rule of law can exist without democracy. It is disputed whether the basis of the rule of a constitutional democracy has to be a market-based system with decentralized policymakers. But surely it is true that a market-based economy cannot exist without a fundamental rule of law, especially with regards to the freedom of contract and law of contract.

Finally, we can sum up by saying that the increasing development of international organizations and of international law and its forms of implementation has elevated the meaning of the law of nations to a level never seen before in human history. The juridification in the process of globalization, however, is subject to a multitude of set-backs, contradictions, and inconsistencies. There is a dramatic increase in juridification but no standardization.

Many questions thus remain unanswered: Do all involved nations understand the juridified rules in the same way? Does a hegemonic claim of European judicial values through the suppression of deviating traditions exist? In how far is legal thinking dependent on culture? Is there another rule of law, apart from the one coined by western culture? These are all questions that are still open and should be discussed further in a global forum.

References

Dose, Nicolai (1999): Der deutsche Rechtsstaat. In: Ellwein, Thomas/ Holtmann, Everhard (eds.): 50 Jahre Bundesrepublik Deutschland. Sonderheft der Politischen Vierteljahresschrift Vol. 30. Opladen. 118–134.

Hoeffe, Otfried (ed.) (1995): Immanuel Kant. Zum ewigen Frieden. Berlin.

http://www.jura.fu-berlin.de/fachbereich/einrichtungen/oeffentliches-recht/lehrende/kriegerh/KFG/index.html, 21.02.2016

Messner, Dirk/Jing Gu/Humphrey, John (2008): Global Governance and Developing Countries. The Implications of the Rise of China. In: World Development, Vol. 36. 274–292.

Schulze-Fielitz, Helmuth (2011): Zur Geltung des Rechtsstaates: Zwischen Kulturangemessenheit und universellem Anspruch. In: Zeitschrift für Vergleichende Politikwissenschaft 2011. 1–23.

IV. Contemporary Debates

State Reformation and Improvement – towards a Vietnamese State of Law

Bui Xuan Duc

Awareness and Improvement towards a Vietnamese State of Law

Adjusted awareness of the position and role of the state and of the Vietnamese Socialist state of law under new conditions is especially important. Our understanding of the state of law and of its development was made clear by the Party at the 2nd Plenum of the 7th Executive Committee (November 1991), and then was mentioned in successive speeches by the General Secretary of the Executive Committee Do Muoi at the 11th Plenum of the 8th National Assembly and the National Congress of judicial officials (August 10th 1992) in which he stated: "The development of a state of law is one of the central tasks in reforming the political system".[1] The statement was officially confirmed at the 8th National Congress of the Party (under article 3 on state construction and improvement):

"state construction and improvement must be performed on the basis of these points: (…) – Consolidate the legal system and develop a Vietnamese Socialist state of law."[2]

The construction of a socialist state of law in our country is also proposed and made clear. Document of the 3rd Plenum of the 8th Executive Committee (June 1997) confirms:

---

[1] Do Muoi (1993), 143–149.

[2] Vietnamese Communist Party (1996), 44–45.

200

"Construction of a socialist state of law is a new mission (...) there are various tasks and experiences to be gained. But we are slowly developing our viewpoints and principles on the construction of a socialist state of law."[3]

Up to now, the Party Documents have proposed three main features of a Vietnamese socialist state of law:

- The state of law must ensure all civil rights. Its legislature, executive and judiciary must be of the people.
- Close supervision between the branches of power must be ensured to avoid abuse and exploitation of civil power.
- Human rights must be protected; the state is to serve popular sovereignty.
- The state of law must foster and generate substantive legal awareness among all public organs, organizations and individuals so that they abide by the constitution and law.

These viewpoints on the construction of a state of law are in conjunction with the general criteria in the world now. First of all, it is necessary to develop a strong mechanism that serves popular power, sufficient task allocation between power branches to ensure efficiency and effectiveness; and close supervision of state authorities to avoid abuse and exploitation of state power.[4] Democratic centralism must be followed and socialist legislation must be consolidated. Also, society must be regulated by the law and moral education must be promoted. According to legal theory and practice, a state of law has four main features:

- (1) The state of law upholds and is regulated by the law and has appropriate mechanisms to ensure the supremacy of law.

---

[3] In many countries, a state of law is said to consist of the following elements: the state is legally bound, performs and ensures individual rights and freedom, applies the separation of powers and devise mechanisms to control power enforcement among different power branches.

[4] See the first documents such as: Document of the 2nd Congress of the 7th Central Executive Committee (November 1991); speech by General Secretary of the Central Executive Committee at the 11th Plenum of the 8th National Assembly and in the National congress of judicial officials (August 10th 1992); Document of the 8th National People's Congress of the Party (1997), Document of the 9th National People's Congress of the Party (2001).

The first basic feature of a state of law is the supremacy of the law. Law is the basis for the organization and implementation of public power, which means that every policy and "command" of the state must be based on and serve the law, and all state-individual relations are also maintained by it. The state of law carries out its activities primarily on the basis of legislation and strictly follows it. This state makes clear and acknowledges that all state organs and public officials are bounded by the law, which means that their activities are based on their authorities and responsibilities as regulated by the law.

- (2) The state of law ensures individual freedom and makes sure that the state and its citizens are equal in terms of their rights and responsibilities. Freedom, democracy and human legitimate interests must be protected by the state through legal measures.

The state of law must facilitate the protection of individual rights and freedom against the abuse of public authority. In civilized societies, the state is primarily and of necessity concerned with protecting human interests and rights. A state of law seeks to protect human freedom and respect the law and human rights. In legal terms, it means civil and public liberty is recognized and state interventions are minimized, and the state is subject to the law and thus has to adhere to it.

In a state of law, personal liberty, rights, interests, honor and dignity are protected, ensured and infrangible. Also, reciprocity between the state as the holder of political power and individuals who partake in its execution is emphasized. This reciprocity is based on the following principles:

- Individuals have the upper hand in their reciprocal relations with the state. This means that a state of law is supposed to serve individual interests. Its goal is to serve social and individual rights. State organs hold responsibilities (obligations) in relation to the people. They cannot ask the people to beg for these rights.
- Civil rights and liberties must be applied in realistic conditions.
- The supremacy of the law must be respected in the regulation of state-individual relations, and random, harmful or arbitrary decisions in policy-making and law enforcement must be minimized. Binding regulations are created to govern these relations.
- Administrative procedures to ensure civil rights are simplified.
- The state is supposed to serve the individual.

- The state and its organs are liable for their violation of the law. To this end, judicial bodies and independence must be respected. Only courts can make decisions on legal disputes.
- (3) In a state of law, state power is properly managed, the separation of powers between the legislature, executive and judiciary is clearly demarcated based on a checks and balances system to stabilize state power as a whole and produce popular power.

In the past, outdated thinking led Vietnam to disregard the separation of powers in favor of a centralized power, in which the National Assembly was endowed with absolute power. Other organs were not independent but were only part of the National Assembly and tasked with fulfilling its ongoing work, and at the same time were put under its supervision and management. The past showed that this method of organization was highly deficient. Since the 1992 Constitution, separation of powers has been included and introduced as a principle to ensure power coordination and distribution among the legislature, executive and judiciary.

- (4) The state of law must ensure efficient review of the constitutionality and legality of public organs through such institutions as constitutional and administrative courts.

The state of law creates a review system to check the constitutionality of legal documents made by the legislature and the legality of decisions and documents made by the executive. This system is responsible for monitoring all three power branches, namely the legislature, executive and judiciary. The constitutional bodies (constitutional council, constitutional court) are even superior to the legislature. Constitutional review is highly developed and functional in countries where the state of law is taken as a basis for development goals. In general, the basic features of a state of law are supremacy of the law, the assurance and protection of human rights and the separation and balance of powers and responsibilities.

Before the Renovation Policy (1986), our Party never used the concept "state of law", but the features and requirements of such a state had been recognized and clarified in its documents such as the 1946 Constitution, 1959 Constitution and 1980 Constitution and other specific legal documents. Since the introduction of the Renovation Policy (1986), Vietnam has commenced the construction of a state of law by specifying its requirements and features, studying and investigating vital institutions that enforce the state to obey the law and respect democracy, that promote social administration based on the law, which eventually leads to a state of law of the people, by the people and for the people. Especially after the 5th Party Congress, ideas on the state of law have been regularly included in the Party's documents,[5] reflecting an ever more inclusive, rational and complete understanding of the state of law in human history and Marxist-Leninist and Ho Chi Minh's viewpoints on the construction of a socialist state of law under the Party's leadership.

The construction of a socialist state of law in our country is also proposed and made clear in various documents. The document of the 3rd Plenum of the 8th Executive Committee (June 1997) confirms:

"Construction of a socialist state of law is a new mission (...) there are various tasks and experiences have to be gained. But we are slowly developing our viewpoints and principles on the construction of a socialist state of law."

Up to now, the Party Documents have proposed three main features of a Vietnamese socialist state of law:

- The state of law must ensure all the civil rights. Its legislature, executive and judiciary must be of the people.
- Close supervision between the branches of power must be ensured to avoid abuse and exploitation of civil power.
- Human rights must be protected; the state is to serve popular sovereignty.
- The state of law must foster and generate substantive legal awareness among all public organs, organizations and individuals so that they abide by the Constitution and law.

These viewpoints on the construction of a state of law are in conjunction with the general criteria in the world now. First of all, it is necessary to develop a strong mechanism that serves popular power, sufficient task allocation between power branches to ensure efficiency and effectiveness; and close supervision of state authorities to avoid abuse and exploitation of state power.[6] Democratic centralism must be followed and socialist legislation must be consolidated. Also, society should be regulated by the law and moral education should be promoted.

---

[5] See National Politics Publisher (1997), 36–40.

[6] Vietnamese Communist Party (2006), 127.

State Reforms towards a Socialist State of Law in Recent Years

The State's Position and Role in the Political System

The amended constitution 2013 defines the role and position of our state as follows:

"The state guarantees and promotes the people's right to mastery; facilitates the goal of prosperous people and a strong, democratic, just and civilized country, in which all people enjoy an abundant, free and happy life and are given conditions for their comprehensive development; and severely punish any act that goes against the interests of the motherland and its people" (Article 3). The role of our state is twofold: an instrument to promote the people's mastery and lead them to a free, abundant and happy life and a guardian of the country that protects it against any act that infringes on the fatherland and people's interests. This is a democratic and socialist state of law. It serves the working class along with workers and nations in the world. The state creates democracy among the people but is also vigilant of their enemies and any force that may threaten the fatherland."

Utilization of the Separation and Balance of Powers in Managing State Power

In developing a state of law, in recent years our country has been conducting state reforms based on the criteria of state of law, including the principle:

"The state power is unified and delegated to state agencies which coordinate with and control one another in the exercise of the legislative, executive and judicial powers" (Document of the 11th Congress, 2011).

Since 1986, driven by the goal of constructing a Vietnamese socialist state of law, the organization and performance of state apparatus have seen fundamental changes in both quality and quantity. The organization and performance of each state body is consolidated and improved to fulfill the requirements and demands of comprehensive national renovation and international integration. The state is organized in accordance with the development of a socialist market economy and state of law under the Party's leadership. The separation and coordination between state powers become more and more systematic, specific and consistent. The National Assembly is regarded as the highest state body which is given constitutional and legislative powers, decides on important issues for the country, and conducts the supreme oversight over the activities of the state. Its organization is perfected while its activities are improved and renewed. The government is the highest administrative body of the Socialist

Republic of Vietnam, and is the executive body of the National Assembly. The government manages the overall performance of political, economic, cultural, social, security tasks and foreign affairs of the state. Its organization and apparatus are gradually arranged and amended towards a more simple and effective performance by a focus on inclusive and important issues of the country. The judiciary and its court system are also enhanced. The organization and performance of judicial bodies see positive changes. Local authorities are also reformed to become less bureaucratic and formal to adapt to local circumstances at different levels. Most of the public servants and cadres are trained and improved in both political consciousness and professional skills so that they are able to complete their assignments; some of them have become mature enough to handle challenges and difficulties in the process of state reforms; their activeness and dutifulness have increased; most of them uphold political standards and become intimate with the masses; and they are conscious about following the law and general principles.

It can be said that the separation, coordination and control of state power in Vietnam in recent years have contributed to effective state's activities; improved the quality of supervision and self-supervision of administrative bodies, the control of the supreme procuration and supervision of state organs by National Assembly and people's councils and regular assessments of state organs, public servants and state employees by subsidiary bodies of the Fatherland's Front and the people.

Reforms of the State Organizational Structure

The position of National Assembly as the highest representative body of the people and the highest state body of the Socialist Republic of Vietnam is emphasized. The principles of people-based state power, democratic leadership and people's creative power are adhered to. State power is unified and delegated to state agencies which coordinate with and control one another in the exercise of the legislative, executive and judicial powers. The organization of the National Assembly is increasingly reformed for better performance. Its permanent members increase and their quality also improves. The Ethnic Council and Committees are upgraded. The National Assembly's Party and Unions have improved their leadership. The legislative has increased in both quality and quantity. Legislative procedures are increasingly revamped towards more efficiency, better and faster law-making, more unity and synchronicity to better adapt to the state of law.

The administrative system and bodies are organized and divided more thoroughly than other state organs. The role and functions of government, ministries and people's committees in the whole administrative system are redefined; and administrative bodies are rearranged to ensure more efficiency, simplicity and less bureaucracy. The organizational structure and membership of the government are also reformed. Ministries with similar functions are combined into multi-sector and multi-area departments. State agencies are reorganized so that no agency has to be involved in state management. In 1992, the government consisted of 23 ministries, ministerial-level agencies and 25 government-attached agencies with one prime minister, five deputy prime ministers, 25 Ministers; in 2002 there were 26 ministries and ministerial-level agencies and 13 government-attached agencies with one prime minister, three deputy prime ministers, 26 ministers and heads of ministerial-level agencies. Ministries' tasks are relocated. Local authorities have been restructured according to administrative units by removing the people's councils at some levels and reducing the number of departments, offices, committees and people's committees at different levels (from 40 to 25 at the provincial level and from 20 to 10 at the district level). Responsibilities of individuals and groups working for administrative bodies are clearly defined on a collegial basis. Public services and public officials are retrained to be more specialized.

The organizational structure of the people's court, people's public procuration and public auditing groups are gradually improved and consolidated according to judicial requirements and their performance also increases. The quantity and quality of cadres, public officials and employees in the political system increases and they are better trained for state management and public services. Other policies such as wages, retirement benefits, insurance and privileges are regularly changed.

Shortcomings, Weaknesses and Remaining Problems

An important requirement in state reforms at central level (National Assembly, President, Government and judicial organs) is to follow the new principle of "unity of power" as demonstrated in the 11th National Congress of the Party Resolution: "state power is unified and delegated to state agencies which coordinate with and control one another in the exercise of the legislative, executive and judicial powers" and as included in the mission of constructing a state of law. However, even after changes were added to the Amended Constitution 2013, the coordination, delegation and control between state agencies in the exercise of the legislative, executive and judicial powers are still limited without necessary "radical" changes to realize the above principle; in particular, mutual control, checking and supervision between power branches are not sufficient to help avoid power abuse. The unity of state power is currently limited to the National Assembly and People's Councils, while the power of other agencies is not significant and mutual control between different agencies is inadequate (if not absent). The organizational structure of local authorities is still generic and stereotypical without specific partition according to administrative units (rural, urban, basic, intermediary levels) and self-governing and self-responsible authorities are not clearly defined.

The functions and organizational structure of the National Assembly's agencies and government-attached ministries and departments are not clearly marked so that they can fulfil their role and power. The functions and responsibilities of judicial bodies, especially the People's Public Procuration, are not fully made clear. The organization and membership of people's court and people's procuration are not relevant to judicial reforms. Urban and rural authorities are not clearly differentiated. A number of cadres and public officials and employees are not responsible and enthusiastic enough. The shrinking of political, ideological and moral standards among a large number of cadres and party members is serious and unsettling.

Many agencies still retain excess and overload personnel with too many nodes and intermediaries. The goal of personnel reduction is underperformed. Many cadres, public officials and employees are not ready to complete their new missions, especially in assessing theoretical and practical events based on which to give recommendation and feedback to central organs on strategic issues in socio-economy, security, politics and foreign affairs.

Administrative and judicial reforms drag on yet produce limited results, especially judicial reforms. Many cadres and public officials today are limited and deficient in many ways: their professional skills are not sufficient, especially foreign languages and IT skills, as well as knowledge of science and technology; their pro-activeness, receptiveness, and self-discipline are still low; their management and governing skills are not ample; some of them are even involved in corruption, misappropriation and embezzlement, and display biased and irresponsible attitudes in performing public services, causing indignation among the people.

The relations between party and state are blurred. Therefore, it is necessary to identify the influence of the ruling party on state organs and emphasize the supremacy of the law to avoid arbitrary intervention of the Party into the affairs of state organs, overlapping responsibilities and disrespect for the law.

The construction and perfection of the legal system still lacks legal consciousness. Although various reforms in the legislature have been made after 30 years of renovation, the Vietnamese legal system is currently outdated and falls short of itself. Thus, it is necessary to change our legal thinking to cope with such issues as defining a proper legal model; studying and synthesizing domestic and foreign experiences in the construction and execution of legal institutions to gain valuable experiences of our own; amend legal procedures; and change our thinking on law-making by focusing more on regulations of smaller governing scope.

Although party and state have promulgated useful measures to combat corruption and abuse of power, these problems remain serious and relatively widespread. From an objective viewpoint, this reality results from the negative aspects of the market economy. On the other hand, the Party and State themselves are partly responsible for it by not being aware of the flipside of a socialist-driven market economy, and by not providing cadres and party members with necessary ideological training to respond to this situation. It is also caused by irresolute personnel management and slow realization of effective punitive measures, policies and mechanisms against officials who commit corruption. A number of public officers, including managers and leaders, are not committed to self-improvement on a regular and conscious basis, distance themselves from the masses and fail to rally other members in the political system and society into anti-corruption and anti-extravagance efforts.

Continue to Reform and Improve the State Apparatus and Develop a Vietnamese Socialist State of Law

The Conclusion no 64-KL/TW (February 28th 2013) of the 7th Congress of 11th Central Committee on some issues such as reforming and improving the political system from central to grassroots levels stated that: the reformation and improvement of political system must go hand in hand with improving the party's leadership towards efficient and effective state management, and promoting the people's mastery. Political and social stability must be maintained to serve national development in a new era. Political organizations must be renewed and improved in accordance with economic restructuring. In addition, this has to go in line with the renewal of the party's leadership in a single-party system, the construction of a socialist state of law, a socialist-oriented market economy and international integration. State reformation and improvement must be associated with improving the functionality and professional skills of public officials and cadres. The relationship between collective leadership and individual responsibility must be identified, and power must go hand in hand with responsibility.

The development of a socialist state of the people, by the people, for the people is crucial to modernizing the state and fundamental to promoting the people's mastery and ensuring that power belongs to them. The development of a Vietnamese state of law is the continuation of developing a Socialist State under new circumstances. The Vietnamese state of law is a state of the people, by the people and for the people led by the Communist Party. State power belongs to the people and rests on the coalition between working class, farmers and intellectuals. The state of Vietnam helps foster a happy life and comprehensive and free development of human, protects human legitimate rights and interests, and commits to international treaties on human rights to which Vietnam is a member.

The role of the state is emphasized under the new political system. To effectively perform its role within the new political system, the state has to be necessarily revamped in every aspect. This urgent renovation is driven by many factors, both subjective and objective, and most basic among which is the need for a simple yet dynamic state apparatus that is able to quickly respond to external events and social requirements, and ensure that development goals are rightly and aptly pursued. More importantly, under the current situation of Vietnam's revolutionary path, an appropriate state model must be found so that: one the one hand, such a state is a useful and pertinent instrument that not only fulfils its assigned tasks and functions but also strengthens state order and organization; on the other hand, it can ensure a democratic and energetic society – in which freedom, equality, fraternity and human rights become actualized. The more society is democratic, the more social relations, especially political and power relations, become more complicated and less apparent, thus requiring strong organization and management and strict order imposed by the state. Freedom and democracy must be realized, respected and protected, and once their safety (security) is ascertained, no one (individuals or state organs) will dare to violate and threaten them.

The execution of state power must be fixed and direct democracy extended. The organization and enforcement of state power have to be performed in a democratic way, so that the state apparatus can be flexible, dynamic and relevant to everyday activities of civil society. Currently, the abuse of power and bureaucratization are not resolutely combated. In addition, irresponsible management, disregard for the law and state power, provincialism, sectarianism, petty individualism, disorganization and partisan "democracy" are immanent and likely to emerge given the right conditions.

To stabilize state-civil relations, necessary legal safeguards must be established so that citizens are not left out of (marginalized) state power relations. To this end, we must make sure that the state as represented by state organs is established on the basis of free will, through rational election of state officials in a democratic and objective manner. With regards to the state of law and civil society, liberal election is one of the most important instruments in making sure that the people's will is embedded in state power. Elections (especially self-nomination and nomination – liberal, direct and public election contest) must bring voters and candidates closer. Mutual understanding between the voters and candidates empowers the former to make their right choice and encourage the latter to fulfill their responsibilities, obligations and expectations in relation to voters. What is required now is to reform the current election system so that election becomes an important political occasion, where citizens are aware of their mastery to choose rightful candidates, and where capable nominees engage in fair competition.

State reforms must abide by the principle of unity of power, in which state power is delegated to state agencies which coordinate with and control one another in the exercise of the legislative, executive and judicial powers. The organization of central state apparatus must be improved so that the position, functions, tasks and rights of each agency is properly and attentively assigned according to the principle of unity of power, in which state power is delegated to state agencies which coordinate with and control one another in the exercise of the legislative, executive and judicial powers as designated by the Document of the 11th National Congress. The boundaries between the legislature, executive and judiciary must be clearly defined and so are their direct equivalents: National Assembly – the legislature, government – the executive, courts – the judiciary. The president is the head of state that links all three branches of power which coordinate and control one another at the same time. Regulations on the position and role of the National Assembly and the Government of Vietnam should be reworked.

Power control between state organs must be established and conducted more efficiently through specialized constitutional review. In constructing a state of law, to ensure that the state and society function within legal boundaries, the Constitution should be regarded as a vital document based on which the constitutionality of all other acts and legal documents is judged. In addition, the constitution should have a direct impact on the regulation of social relations, which means that it should be directly cited to establish civil rights and responsibilities. It has been often said that legal documents are the realization of the Constitution of Vietnam and sub-legal documents are the actualization of the laws. But the question remains: does the actualization of the constitution and the laws commit to constitutionality and legality? Similarly, do executive and judicial agencies enforce the law according to the constitution and the law? To make sure that the state does not fall into formalism, one of the important requirements is to protect the constitution and review the constitutionality of state agencies from the National Assembly to lower organs. This can be done through specialized constitutional review as stated in the "Resolution of the 10th Party Congress" (2006):

"The establishment of a system to address unconstitutional acts within the legislature, executive and judiciary."[7]

State reforms should focus on the following goals:
- (1) The role of National Assembly should be promoted and reformed. As the highest representative organ of the people, the highest state power organ, and fully responsible for constitutional making and legislation, the National Assembly should focus on the following three functions: legislation, deciding on important issues of the country, particularly on the basic principles of state organization and activities (including the appointment

---

[7] Vietnam Communist Party (2006), 127.

and dismissal of heads of senior state agencies), and supreme oversight over the activities of the state.

- (2) How to help other state organs maintain power control over the National Assembly which has been long defined as the "highest state power body" is what concerns us both theoretically and practically. Power control (primarily manifested in constitutional review) over not only the executive or judiciary as in the current Vietnamese political system, but also over the legislature and eventually all three power branches, must be carried out within constitutional boundaries.

- (3) However, the National Assembly's activities, first and foremost law – making, while not entirely constitutional (if not highly likely to be unconstitutional), are not put under the supervision of any state organ but are self-regulated by itself, thus are probably not objective and appropriate. But to assign the supervision of any organ over the National Assembly would derail its position as "the highest state power body". This is precisely the obstacle to the recent ideas of establishing constitutional bodies (such as Constitutional Council, Constitutional Court) for constitutional review of the National Assembly. If the constitution is emphasized and its protection is highlighted through constitutional review, it will be imperative to resolve this dilemma, namely the position of the National Assembly in relation to other state organs. As long as the National Assembly is still the highest state power organ that can intervene into constitutional, legislative, executive, judicial and supervisory activities, mutual power control and genuine constitutional review are still wishful thinking.

- (4) The judiciary must be given more independence so that it is less dependent on administrative bodies and more relevant to the law. A developed and efficient judicial system indicates a civilized and democratic state. This is one of the essential conditions for the protection of human rights and civil liberty and interests. A strong judiciary also contributes to a stable legal order and state control. As a component of the state of law and according to the principle of "mutual delegation, coordination and control between state organs" introduced by the Communist Party, the People's Court must become a truly independent, neutral and impartial institution in protecting the rights of relevant parties. The court should assume all judicial responsibilities previously performed by other institutions in a trial-and-error manner (such as providing administrative sanctions and duties;

interpreting the law or legal documents to be handled to it), and extend its scope of jurisdiction. It must be an efficient mechanism that controls and restricts the legislative and executive through constitutional and legal initiatives. If this is realized, the one-sided supervision over judicial activities and organs by state power bodies as of now will be replaced by "mutual control" and management through public litigation and trials.

- (5) The People's Public Procuration, from a body that "oversees legal observance by all organs of the Council of Ministers, state authorities at local level, employees of public organs and citizens" (Constitution 1959) to a body that "oversees legal observance by ministries and other organs of the Council of Ministers, local authorities, social organizations and people's armed services, public employees and citizens, and launches public prosecution" (Constitution 1980) to one that "exercises prosecution right and supervises judicial activities" (amended and revised Constitution 1992), will be transformed into a Public Prosecution Office and given more responsibilities in the mentioned areas. This is a great step that reflects our Communist Party's new thinking in political and state reconstruction in general and in judicial renovation in particular, driven by socio-economic objectives in a new context such as the state of law, international integration and more efficient and effective state's performance. This is a rational and positive move in the long run. First, it liberates the public procuration from administrative functions (as supervisor of legal compliance and initiator of uniform and consistent legal observance) and helps it focus more on prosecution – which currently needs more improvement and attention. Second, this step is a requirement for state reformation and the state of law according to the principle of mutual control and coordination between legislative, executive and judicial powers. And finally, experiences of countries around the world, especially developed countries, show that such a transition is inevitable.

- (6) Local authorities need reforming to become more diversified, more self-governing and autonomous. The trial removal of people's councils at district and provincial levels must be completed as soon as possible. The institutionalization of local agencies (People's Council, People's Committee, Administrative Committee, Mayor (if any) at all levels, especially at communal, ward and town levels must be implemented in conjunction with new requirements, situation and tasks. Anti-corruption and the prevention of abuse of power to purify the state apparatus are decisive in improving the effect and efficiency of state management.

References

Do Muoi (1993): Speech at the National Congress of Judicial Officials (August 10th 1992). In: Đẩy mạnh sự nghiệp đổi mới vì chủ nghĩa xã hội (Promoting the cause of renovation for socialism). Hanoi. 143–149.

Vietnamese Communist Party (ed.) (1996): Document of the 8th National People's Congress. Hanoi. 44–45.

National Politics Publisher (1997): Document of the 3rd Congress of the 8th Central Executive Committee. Hanoi. 36–40.

Vietnamese Communist Party (ed.) (2006): Document of the 10th National People's Congress. Hanoi.

The Issue of the Rule of Law in Vietnam in the Constitution of 2013

Dinh Xuan Ly

The Vietnamese Constitution of 2013[1] is the basic law with the highest legal value of contemporary Vietnam. As a political-legal document it contains the following provisions: legal provisions on socio-political systems; state regime and the fundamental principles of organization and operation of the state apparatus; the legal status of the people, the fundamental rights and duties of citizens, economics and, culture as well as the relations between Vietnam and the international community.

The basis and objectives of Constitution formulation, implementation and protection of the Constitution of 2013 were recorded in the Preamble: "Institutionalizing the Platform for national construction during the transition to socialism and inheriting the Constitution of 1946, the Constitution of 1959, the Constitution of 1980 and 1992, the People of Vietnam have drafted, implemented and protected this Constitution for the sake of the well-being of the people, a strong country, democracy, equality and civilization."[2] Therefore, to thoroughly understand the rule of law issues in Vietnam in the Constitution of 2013, it is necessary to learn the viewpoints and policies of the Communist

---

[1] Constitution of the Socialist Republic of Vietnam (SRV) in 2013 (hereafter referred to as the Constitution of 2013) ratified by the National Assembly of the SRV of XIII, 6th session on 28 November 2013; and President of the SRV signed the announcement order on 08 December 2013.

[2] National Political Publishing House (2014), 8.

Party of Vietnam (CPV), since the Constitution of 1946 is directly related to the rule of law in Vietnam.[3]

The Rule of Law's Provisions in the Constitution of 2013

Regarding the State Regime

Clause 1, Article 2 of the Constitution of 2013, stipulates that

"the State of the Socialist Republic of Vietnam is a state of the People, by the People and for the People."[4]

This provision has clearly defined the nature of the rule of law in Vietnam to be a state of socialist rule of law, with government of the People, by the People, for the People.

Looking back at the history of Vietnam's Constitution since the August Revolution in 1945, the process of mobilization of state institutions in Vietnam was as follows: the Constitution of The Democratic Republic of Vietnam in 1946 stipulated that the country of Vietnam was a "democratic republic" (Article 1); the Constitution of the Democratic Republic of Vietnam in 1959 defined it as a "democratic state of the People" (Article 2); the Constitution of the SRV in 1980 stipulated, the "dictatorship of the proletariat" (Article 2); the Constitution of the SRV in 1992 stipulated the "State of the people, by the people, for the people" (Article 2); In 2001, Article 2 of the Constitu-

---

[3] From 1946 to the present (2014), Vietnam has promulgated five constitutions and named the Constitution of The Democratic Republic of Vietnam in 1946 (hereafter referred to as the Constitution of 1946); Constitution of the Democratic Republic of Vietnam in 1959 (hereafter referred to as the Constitution of 1959); Constitution of the Socialist Republic of Vietnam in 1980 (referred to as the 1980 Constitution); Constitution of the Socialist Republic of Vietnam in 1992 (referred to as the 1992 Constitution); and in 2001, the 1992 Constitution was amended and supplemented, but not renamed the Constitution (referred to as the amended Constitution in 2001); and Constitution of the Socialist Republic of Vietnam in 2013 (referred to as the Constitution of 2013)

[4] National Political Publishing House (2014), 8.

tion of 1992, amended and supplemented by the provisions, "SRV is the socialist rule of law state of the people, by the people, for the people."[5]

From the above study, it is shown that: In legal terms, the rule of law in Vietnam was stipulated in the Constitution of 1992 (already amended and supplemented by Resolution No. 51/2001/QH 10 dated 25 December 2001 of the National Assembly). And this provision is repeated in Clause 1, Article 2 of the Constitution of 2013.

When discussing the perception of rule of law of the CPV, some have opined that until the Convention of National Representatives in midterm VII (1994), the CPV "mainly considered the rule of law as a product of capitalism and acquired and inherited this perception."[6] But the fact is that a month after the Seventh Convention of the National Congress Party, the issue of building the rule of law was officially mentioned by the General Secretary of the CPV, Do Muoi in his speech at the 9th session of the National Assembly term VIII (dated 27 July1991) as follows:

"The National Congress should have focused on the implementation of two basic requirements: Firstly, building the rule of law, the state has the capacity to formulate a synchronous legal system to meet the new requirements of socio-economic development and manage all aspects of social civilization and progress; the legal system is the basis of ensuring the guidelines and policies of the Party and State that are implemented effectively, is a key factor in making the social relations become healthier and stronger. Secondly, to ensure the practical power and effectiveness of the National Congress that is defined by Constitutional provisions."[7]

More than two years later, at the midterm VII Convention of National Delegates (January 1994), CPV proposed the policy of "continuing to build and gradually perfect the rule of law in Vietnam. That is the state of the people, by the people, for the people, managing all aspects of social life by the law."[8] Therefore, it can be said that the issue of building the rule of law in Vietnam

[5] All quotations are taken from the paragraph: the Declaration of Independence in 1945 and the Constitution of Vietnam (1946, 1959, 1980, and 1992), National Political Publishing House (2006), 12, 31, 69, 125, 199.

[6] VNU. University of Social Sciences and Humanities. Faculty of Philosophy (2012), 536.

[7] Vietnam Communist Party (1994), 56.

[8] Vietnam Communist Party (2007), 340.

has been formally laid out and directed by the CPV, as the ruling political party, since the second half of 1991.

The issue of building a socialist rule of law state in Vietnam continued to be thoroughly implemented through the National Congress Conventions of CPV and the Convention of the Party Central Committee. The policy of the Ninth National Congress Convention (April 2001) was to "build the socialist rule of law under the leadership of the Party".[9] The Tenth National Congress Convention (April 2006) advocated "continuing to build and perfect the socialist rule of law state."[10] By the Eleventh Party Congress Convention (January 2011), the Party urged to "continue to promote constructing and completing the socialist rule of law."[11] And, the program for national construction in the transition to socialism (Supplement, developed in 2011), defined: "our country is the state socialism of the People, by the People, for the People."[12] Construction of state socialism of the people, by the people, for the people is one of the eight basic guidelines to build Vietnam to become a modern industrial country under socialist orientation.[13] The view of the supplement program, developed in 2011 and the Eleventh Party Congress Convention has been thoroughly defined and institutionalized in the Constitution of 2013.

Regarding the Subjectivity of State Power

Clause 2, Article 2 of the Constitution of 2013, stipulates that:

"the SRV is owned by the people; all state power belongs to the people but the foundation is the alliance between the working class and the peasantry and the intelli gentsia."[14]

Stipulating that "all state power belongs to the people" reflects the political-legal status of people of Vietnam as the subject of state power in state socialist rule of law in Vietnam. The Constitution of 2013 stipulates that people perform state power by direct democracy, representative democracy through the

---

[9] Communist Party of Vietnam (2001), 131.

[10] Communist Party of Vietnam (2006), 126.

[11] Communist Party of Vietnam (2001), 246.

[12] Communist Party of Vietnam (2011), 85.

[13] Communist Party of Vietnam (2011), 72.

[14] National Political Publishing House (2014), 8.

National Assembly, People's Councils and through other agencies of the state (Article 6). Among them, "the state guarantees and promote ownership rights of the people; recognizes, respects, protects and guarantees human rights, citizenship rights; implements the objectives of prosperous people, a strong country, democracy, justice, civilization, and all people have an abundant life, liberty, happiness and favorable conditions for a comprehensive development (Article 3)"; "The state agencies, officials and public servants have to respect the people, devotedly serve the people, in close contact with people, listen to their opinions and be subject to the supervision of the people; We struggle against corruption, wastefulness and all manifestations of bureaucracy, arrogance, authoritarianism" (Clause 2, Article 8); Vietnam Fatherland Front is considered as representative to protect the legitimate rights and interests, the legitimacy of the people (Article 9). The above provisions create the constitutional basis for the continuation of institutionalizing the relevant laws of the state power belonging to the people.

In fact, although under different interpretations, the Constitution of Vietnam since the August Revolution of 1945, specified "all state power belongs to the people", for instance; the Constitution of 1946 stipulates that "All authority in the country of Vietnam belongs to the people, regardless of race, sex, wealth, class, religion" (Article 1); "People have the right to approve the Constitution and the relations to the destiny of the country" (Article 21); Constitution of 1959, stipulates that "All power in the State of Vietnam Democratic Republic belongs to the people" (Article 4); Constitution of 1980, stipulates that "All power belongs to the people" (Article 6); The Constitution of 1992 stipulates "the State of the Socialist Republic of Vietnam is a State of the people, by the people and for the people. All State power belongs to the people that the foundation is working class allied with the peasantry and intellectual classes" (Article 2).[15] However, to the Constitution in 2013, has specified new mechanisms for people to exercise their state power.

In the reform era (since 1986), the viewpoint of the CPV on the subjectivity of state power belonging to the people and associated with the policy of building a law-governed state socialism in Vietnam has been proposed since

---

[15] All quotations are taken from the paragraph: the Declaration of Independence in 1945 and the Constitution of Vietnam (1946, 1959, 1980, and 1992). National Political Publishing House (2006), 12, 31, 70, 125.

the beginning of the 1990s , with the requirement "to secure power and effectiveness in the practice of Congress, regulated by Constitutional provisions". The actual power of the Parliament is the indirect power of people through national members of parliament who are elected. The Ninth Party Congress affirmed "our country is the main tool for the implementation of the people's sovereignty, the rule of law of the people, by the people, for the people";[16] the Tenth Party Congress (April /2006), which set out requirements "to develop operational mechanisms of socialist rule of law, ensuring the principles of all state power belonging to the people";[17] the Eleventh Party Congress (1/2011) emphasized the policy of building and perfecting state socialist rule of law, ensuring our State is of the people, by the people and for the people.[18] Supplementary Program developed in 2011, determined "all State power belongs to the people that its foundation is the alliance between the working class and the peasantry and the intelligentsia led by the CPV."[19] The view of the CPV on the subjectivity of state power in legitimate state socialism in Vietnam has been institutionalized by the 2013 Constitution.

The Issue of Decentralization among State Authorities

Clause 3, Article 2 of the Constitution of 2013 stipulates

"State power is unified with the assignment, coordination and control among state agencies in the implementing of the legislative, executive and justice rights."[20]

Earlier, the Constitution of the SRV in 1992 (Amended and supplemented in 2001), has stipulated "state power is unified with the assignment and coordination among state agencies in the implementing of the legislative, executive and judiciary rights" (Article 2).[21] In Clause 3, Article 2, of the Constitution of 2013, the word "control" has been added which means "controlling the power". The stipulation of the principle of "controlling the power" in the Consti-

---

[16] Communist Party of Vietnam (2001), 131.

[17] Communist Party of Vietnam (2006), 126.

[18] Communist Party of Vietnam (2011), 246.

[19] Communist Party of Vietnam (2011), 85.

[20] National Political Publishing House (2014), 9.

[21] Declaration of Independence of 1945 and the Constitution of Vietnam (1946, 1959, 1980, 1992), National Political Publishing House (2006), 199.

tution is progress in the constitutional history of Vietnam, this is the first time "controlling the power" has become a constitutional principle of the rule of law, the mechanism for the legislature, executive, and judiciary to enforce the effective, efficient functions, duties and powers under the Constitution and laws, avoiding misuse and abusing of power. The Constitution of 2013, specifies the competence of the power branches, the rule of law in socialism in Vietnam, such as the National Assembly exercises the constitutional functions, and decides important issues of the country, and exercises supreme control over the activities of the state (Article 69); the government is the supreme state administration agency of the SRV performing executive power, the executive agency of the National Assembly (Article 94); People's Court is the judicial agency of the SRV implementing judicial right (Article 102). Thus, the Constitution of 2013 had the clear assignment (decentralization) between the power branches of the state socialist rule of law in Vietnam:

"It is an important basis for relevant agencies to work together more rhythmically. Also, a power control mechanism has been identified, in which people's rights as owner of all state power is enhanced; the forms of democracy are expanding. The oversight role and social criticism of the Vietnam Fatherland Front and its member organizations are confirmed."[22]

The fact is that the views of the CPV on assignment (decentralization) between the power branches of the socialist rule of law are recorded in the Party Program of 1991. The Vietnamese State unified three rights: legislative, executive and judicial rights with clear assignment of these rights; the viewpoint of the Eighth Party Congress was: state power is unified with the assignment and coordination among government agencies in the implementation of legislative, executive and judiciary rights.[23] This is also the viewpoint of decentralization of the Ninth Party Congress. The Tenth Party Congress (April 2006) also continued to advocate the policy of "state power is unified with the assignment and coordination among agencies in exercising the legislative, executive and judiciary right." The Eleventh Party Congress stipulates that the "principle of state power is unified, with the assignment, coordination and control among agencies in the implementation of legislative, executive and judiciary rights."[24]

---

[22] Hoang The Lien (2014).

[23] Communist Party of Vietnam (1996), 45.

[24] Communist Party of Vietnam (2011), 247.

The Supplementary Program developed in 2011, determined that: "state power is unified; with the assignment, coordination and control among relevant agencies in the implementation of the legislative, executive and judiciary rights."[25] The viewpoint of the Party on decentralization among the power branches in the rule of law in Vietnam in the Supplementary Program, developed in 2011, has been institutionalized in the Constitution of 2013.

Regarding the Position of the Law toward Vietnamese State and Society

Clause 1, Article 8 of the Constitution of 2013, stipulates that: "the State is organized and operated under the Constitution and law, social management defined by the Constitution and laws, implemented the principle of democratic centralization"; Clause 3, Article 9, stipulates "Vietnam Fatherland Front and its member organizations and other civil societies operate in the framework of the Constitution and law". In relations with the world community, Article 12 stipulates that the SRV comply with the United Nations Charter and international treaties in which the SRV is a member; contribute to the cause of peace, national independence, democracy and social progress in the world.[26] Earlier, the Constitution of the SRV in 1980 had stipulated: State

---

[25] Communist Party of Vietnam (2011), 85.

[26] The Constitution of 1946 does not contain provisions on relations of Vietnam with the international community; Constitution of 1959 did not also set out specific rules, but the Preamble has written that: strengthening solidarity with the socialist faction and the peace-loving people in the world; the Constitution of 1980 stipulates that: Strengthen friendship and cooperation in all aspects with the socialist countries on the basis of Marxism-Leninism and proletarian internationalism; friendly relations with neighboring countries, with peoples struggling for national independence and social progress; policy implementation peaceful coexistence between countries with different socio-political systems; actively support and contribute to the struggle against imperialism, colonialism, hegemony, neo-racism, for peace, national independence, democracy and socialism (Article 14); the Constitution of 1992, which regulates the relations of Vietnam with the international community, essentially the same as the 1980 Constitution, but in which there are noteworthy changes, such as: 1) emphasizing the implementation of a policy of peace, friendship, expand exchanges and cooperation with all countries in the world, irrespective of the political regime and different societies; 2) not directly mentioning imperialism, colonialism, hegemony etc.; 3) not declaring socialism as a common and global target. In 2001, the Constitution kept the above mentioned content.

management in accordance with law and unceasingly strengthening socialist legality. All State agencies, social organizations, government employees, staff of social organizations and all citizens must strictly abide by the Constitution and laws, to resolutely prevent and fight against the crime, violation of the constitution and the law (Article 12). The basic contents above were inherited in the 1992 Constitution.

In comparison with the 1980 Constitution and the 1992 Constitution, it shows that the provisions of the Constitution in 2013 strongly reflected the high appreciation of the legal system, and legislation became the basic characteristic of the rule of law in Vietnam. This can be considered a development of political thought.

State Legislative Jurisdiction in the Constitution of 2013

Since 2013, the Communist Party Congress of Vietnam term VI (December 1986), has set out the policy: "heightening the position and role of National Assembly and people's Councils at all levels, enabling the elected bodies to comply with the functions, duties and powers under the Constitution's stipulation. Strengthen the socialist legal and social management by law;"[27] the Seventh Party Congress (June 1991) states guiding viewpoints: "the important condition for promoting democracy is to build and complete a system of laws and strengthen socialist legislation, improve the intellectual level, the level of legal understanding and awareness of law-abiding of the people;"[28] the 8th Party Congress (June 1996) advocated "strengthening socialist legislation, building the rule of law in Vietnam, society managed by law, and emphasis on education, improve morality;"[29] the 9th Party Congress: "State managing the society by law. All agencies, organizations, officials, public servants and all citizens are obliged to abide by the constitution and the law;"[30] the 10th Party Congress (April 2006), proposed the policy of "perfecting the legal system, increasing specificity, feasibility of the provisions in the legislation documents. Preparing, compiling the checking mechanism, monitoring the constitutional-

---

[27] Communist Party of Vietnam (1987), 226.

[28] Communist Party of Vietnam (1987), 90–91.

[29] Communist Party of Vietnam (1996), 129.

[30] Communist Party of Vietnam (2001), 132.

ity and legality of the activities and decisions of public authorities;"[31] the Eleventh Party Congress (February 2011), which proposed the requirements on "improving the capacity management and administration of the State under the law, to strengthen socialist legality and discipline;"[32] the supplementary program, developed in 2011, determines: "the State shall enact laws; organize and manage the society by law and constantly strengthen the socialist legality."[33] Thus, in the period of innovation, strengthening of the legal issues and the management of the State under the constitution and laws, were deeply concerned by CPV with the policies strongly reaffirmed their determination to implement the "organization and management of society by law."

On the Issue of Human and Civil Rights

Clause 1, Article 14 stipulates that: In the RSV, human rights, the political, civil, economic, cultural, social rights of citizens have been recognized, respected, protected and guaranteed by the Constitution and laws; everyone is equal before the law. No one is discriminated in political, civil, economic, cultural and social life (Clause 1, Clause 2, and Article 16).

In addition, the 2013 Constitution also specified the human rights and civil rights in specific areas, such as the right to life, human life is protected by law (Article 19); everyone has the right to inviolability of the body and protected by law on the health, honor and dignity (Article 20); the right to inviolability of private life (Article 21); citizens have the right to have a legal residence (Article 22); everyone has the right to freedom of belief and religion, to follow or not follow a religion (Article 24; citizens have freedom of speech, freedom of the press, access right to information, assembly, association and demonstration (Article 25); men and women are equal in all aspects (Article 26); citizens have the right to participate in managing state and society (Article 28);); everyone has ownership right of lawful income (Article 32); right to guarantee social security (Article 34); citizens have the right to work, to choose care, employment and workplace (Article 35); the right to marry and divorce (Article 36); rights to enjoy and access to cultural values, rights to participate

---

[31] Communist Party of Vietnam (2006), 126–127.

[32] Communist Party of Vietnam (2011), 247.

[33] Communist Party of Vietnam (2011), 85.

in cultural life, to use cultural facilities (Article 41), right to determine the ethnicity (Article 42), the right to live in healthy environment (Article 43).

Overall, the Constitution of 2013 has amended and supplemented provisions on human rights, fundamental rights and duties of citizens; confirmed and clarified the principles of human rights; clarified the content of human rights, fundamental rights and duties of citizens in political, civil, economic, social, cultural affairs and the responsibility of the state and society in respecting, guaranteeing and protecting human rights; presented more clearly as the responsibility of the State in ensuring the implementation of human rights and civil rights. The provisions of human rights is consistent with international treaties to which Vietnam is a member, expressed the clearer awareness of human rights and affirmed a strong commitment of Vietnam in implementing human rights.

Some Emerging Issues

The Concept of the Rule of Law and the Socialist Rule of Law

It is a fact that there are many different interpretations of the rule of law. The report titled "Organizational structure and operation of socialist rule law state of the People, by the People, for the People in Vietnam in the period of industrialization and modernization", code KX04-02, provides comments: "The concept of "the rule of law" is used very differently. We can say for sure that documents such as the US Constitution, the French Declaration on human and civil rights, the American Declaration of Human Rights do not use the concept of the rule of law. The Germans have the concept "Rechtsstaat" and the French use the term "État de Droit", the Russians "Pravavoe gosudarstvo". All these three concepts of the Europeans can be generalized as "The government must be bound by law."[34]

Meanwhile, researchers in Vietnam launched various conceptions of the rule of law according to the following three trends. The first tendency, the rule of law concept is a model of a state. This trend considered the rule of law state as

"a type of state that is built on the basis of democratic opposition to the authoritarian state (...) The rule of law state does not just mean that the state is ruled by law. Many

---

[34] Nguyen Dang Dung (2007), 34–35.

totalitarian states in history were ruled by law (...) If the principle of dictatorship and of a tyranny state is that the people have to obey the state then the principle of the rule of law is a state that is obedient to the citizens. The first condition of the rule of law is to guarantee the rights and freedoms of citizens by the clear provisions of the law. In the rule of law state, the law is the measure (norm) of freedom (...) This includes two sides closely related to each other: the law guarantees the rights and freedoms of citizens – every state organ and citizen has to obey the law. The rule of law, therefore, is built on the principles of democracy. The bodies of state power (legislative, executive and judicial) are elected freely with direct participation of all citizens to be able to adequately represent their will. Historical experience shows how these powers should be organized so that each power has real independence. All those appointed to bodies of state power must bear full responsibility before the citizens. The rule of law is the state model most likely to combat a monopolistic and bureaucratic power apparatus.[35]

The second trend is based on the perception of the rule of law state as a method to organize and operate the society on the basis of these rights.

"These rights are assigned and organized so that abuses cannot occur and the democratic freedoms of the people are protected. The Constitution is the most important tool to define and delimit the rights. The Constitution is regarded as the soul of the rule of law."[36]

The third trend, the perception of the rule of law not as a state model but as common values, and the expression of a democratic development level. This trend sees the rule of law state as an organization of democracy; a state and social organizations based on democracy. The rule of law as a method of organizing and implementing a state regime and society is built not only in capitalism, but also in a socialist regime.[37]

---

[35] Nguyen Khac Vien (1994), 207–208.

[36] Nguyen Dang Dung (2007), 28.

[37] This opinion expresses that: The common values of the rule of law are presented in different forms and depend on the political-legal standpoint, academic viewpoint of each person, but in reality, emphasize the following values: 1) the rule of law is the fundamental pattern of democracy. Accordingly, democracy is both the essence and prerequisite for building the rule of law; 2) a legitimate state apparatus is organized and operated on the basis of the principles of organization of power in a democratic manner; 3) a judicial regime is truly democratic; judicial authorities only comply with the law with a public procedural regime and democracy. See also Nguyen Duy Quy (2007).

Thus, in fact there are two different perspectives on the rule of law among Vietnamese researchers:

- Firstly, the viewpoint that the rule of law is a state model (a state); with this perspective, it is understandable that there is only one state model the rule of law in the world.
- Secondly, the perspective that the rule of law is the common value, the expression of a democratic development level; with this view, it is claimed that there is a bourgeois rule of law and a socialist rule of law.

Some Issues of a Socialist Rule of Law State in Vietnam

Constitutional amendments in 2001 and then the Constitution of 2013 stipulate that the State of Vietnam is a socialist rule of law state of the people, by the people and for the people. This provision marks the process of the CPV's innovative thinking about state politics. This is regarded as a theoretical achievement of innovation marking the transition in the perception of the ruling party "the rule of law is not something separated from capitalism. Socialism must practice the rule of law.[38]

Through researching some concepts, perspectives and the reality of the rule of law, at a certain level the fundamental characteristics of the rule of law can be proposed as such: 1) the law holds supremacy in the state and society; 2) the people are the source of state power; 3) human rights, citizenship rights are confirmed and guaranteed; 4) there is a clear separation of powers among the legislative, executive and judicial; 5) the rule of law has capable most of countering the monopolistic trend of power and bureaucratic tendency of a power apparatus.[39]

By the Constitution of 2013, the socialist rule of law state model in Vietnam can be visualized based on the following fundamental features:

- On the nature of the rule of law in Vietnam – a legitimate state socialism; the government of the People, by the People, for the People.

---

[38] Communist Party of Vietnam (2005), 143.

[39] It was also suggested that the rule of law has some typical features such as: 1) the supremacy of the constitution; 2) the objective of ensuring the freedom and equality of human beings, as opposed to state violence or an authoritarian state; 3) a state against the abuse of power and organized on the principle of decentralization. See also: Nguyen Dang Dung (2007), 63–67.

- Regarding the fundamental characteristic of the socialist rule of law – all State power belongs to the people; the foundation is the alliance between working class, the peasantry and intelligentsia.
- Regarding the operational mechanisms of the bodies of state power – state power is unified with the assignment, coordination and control among state agencies in the implementation of the legislative, executive and judiciary rights.
- Regarding the position of law in the state and society – the State of Vietnam is organized and operating under the Constitution and law, social management by the Constitution and laws implement the principle of democratic concentration; theVietnam Fatherland Front and its member organizations and other civil society organizations operate in the framework of the Constitution and the law.
- Human rights, and the rights of citizens in political, civil, economic, cultural, social affairs are recognized, respected, protected and guaranteed by the Constitution and law; all persons are equal before the law.

In comparison with the fundamental characteristics of the rule of law in general, the socialist rule of law state in Vietnam has the following characteristics.

In the Preamble, an important foundation for the construction of the Constitution of 2013, is the "Institutionalization of the Programme for national construction in transition to socialism" and Article 4 of the Constitution in 2013, stipulates that the CPV is the leading force of the State and society. Since then it is shown that the socialist rule of law in Vietnam is essentially characterized as the organization and operation under the leadership of the CPV. Therefore, the question is to scientifically determine the relationship between the leadership of the CPV and the socialist rule of law as to how to ensure the effective and efficient operation of the State of the socialist rule of law in Vietnam.

One of the fundamental features of the rule of law is the clear separation of powers between the legislative, executive and judicial. The Constitution of 2013, the provisions in the socialist rule of law state in Vietnam is that the National Assembly shall exercise the constitutional, legislative power (Article 69); the Government implement executive powers (Article 94); People's courts implement judicial power (Article 102). The delimitation of such powers is quite clear, however, and Article 100 stipulates "The government, the Prime Minister, ministers, heads of ministerial-level agencies enact laws to implement tasks and their powers, supervise the implementation of those documents and handle unlawful documents as prescribed by law."[40] Thus it is understandable that apart from Parliament, the "Government, Prime Minister, ministers; heads of ministerial-level agencies" are also empowered by people to "enact law documents". Before, the Constitution of 1992 stipulated that "the National Assembly is the only body with constitutional and legislative rights (Article 83)."[41]

Summary

In summary, and under a legal perspective, the socialist rule of law of Vietnam officially was initially enacted in the Constitution of the SRV in 1992 (already amended and supplemented by Resolution No. 51/2001/QH 10 dated 25 December 2001 of the National Assembly). In the Constitution of 2013, new provisions have been added "on the organization and operation of the state apparatus in accordance with the rule of law and the excellent organizing principle of state power in Article 2 of the Constitution."[42]

References

Communist Party of Vietnam (ed.) (1987): Documents of the Sixth National Congress. Hanoi.

Communist Party of Vietnam (ed.) (1996): Documents of the Eighth National Congress. Hanoi.

Communist Party of Vietnam (ed.) (2001): Documents of the Ninth National Congress. Hanoi.

Communist Party of Vietnam (ed.) (2005): Report on Some Theoretical-Reality Issues over 20 Years of Reform (1986–2006). Hanoi.

---

[40] National Political Publishing House (2014), 54.

[41] Declaration of Independence of 1945 and the Constitution of Vietnam (1946, 1959, 1980, 1992). National Political Publishing House (2006), 150.

[42] Hoang The Lien (2014).

Communist Party of Vietnam (ed.) (2006): Documents of the Tenth National Congress. Hanoi.

Communist Party of Vietnam (ed.) (2011): Documents of the Eleventh National Congress. Hanoi.

Hoang The Lien (2014): The New Points of the Constitution (amended) of the Government http://www.nhandan.com.vn/chinhtri/tuyentruyenhienphap-/item/22697502-nhung-diem-moi-cua-hien-phap-sua-doi-ve-chinh-phu.-html.

National Political Publishing House (ed.) (2006): Declaration of Independence of 1945 and the Constitution of Vietnam (1946, 1959, 1980, 1992). Hanoi.

National Political Publishing House (ed.) (2014): Constitution of the Socialist Republic of Vietnam. Hanoi.

Nguyen Dang Dung (ed.) (2007): National Assembly of Vietnam in the Rule of Law. Hanoi.

Nguyen Duy Quy (2007): Construction and Finishing Legitimate Socialist State of Vietnam. In: Journal of Philosophy 11 (198).

Nguyen Khac Vien (ed.) (1994): Dictionary of Sociology. Hanoi.

Vietnam Communist Party (ed.) (1994): Document of National Representatives Convention. Midterm VII, Internal Circulation, May 1/1994.

Vietnam Communist Party (ed.) (2007): Party Documentation Vol. 51. Hanoi.

VNU. University of Social Sciences and Humanities. Faculty of Philosophy (ed.) (2012): The Rule of Law: some Theoretical and Practical Issues. Proceedings of the International Scientific Conference. Hanoi.

The State of Law and the Creation of a Human Rights Culture

Hoang Thi Kim Que

The Development of the State of Law as an Idea and a Doctrine

The state of law as an idea, doctrine, theory and reality has been through a long process of creation and development in the history of mankind.[1] Today, theories about the state of law have been adjusted, amended and improved to be more adaptable to the current political, legal and social reality of the world. In both theory and practice, the state of law is witnessing a development combined with inheritance, addition and amendment. This all the more confirms the universal and particular values of the state of law on a global scale.

In ancient times only the fundamental components of the state of law were discussed such as the supremacy of the law, the power of the law over individuals, moral institutions and issues and to some extent even the separation of powers. In in early-modern times, the idea and doctrine of the state of law took a greater and further leap into the dialectics between the different elements of political systems, such as the state of law, civil society, human rights and legal measures to defend them, the separation of powers. Later, constitutionalism, legal procedures and legal systems are formed with the aim of protecting personal rights, freedom, and social security.

---

[1] Nguyen Xuan Tung (2016), Đẩy mạnh xây dựng Nhà nước pháp quyền XHCN Việt Nam dưới ánh sáng đại hội Đảng lần thứ XI. http://moj.gov.vn/ct/tintuc/Pages/-nghien-cuu-trao-doi.aspx?ItemID=4376.

The theory as well as practice of the state of law in recent decades has been adjusted and become more and more extensive in terms of its contents, such as the state policies and responsibilities in protecting the security and safety of every individual in economic, political, social and cultural areas. A quick look at the constitutions throughout the history of mankind and especially at contemporary ones indicates this tendency, as coeval constitutions have extended their regulations on human rights and various socio-economic policies pursued by the nations. There are many similarities and differences between the ideas about the state of law from nation to nation and region and region, and this situation is best reflected in the reality of the state of law today. The realities of societies are introducing more issues to be studied and explained from the angle of state of law theory. There are more and more challenges to be coped with by nations, regions and the entire human race, such as human rights and national sovereignty, the role of civil society in developing policies and law; the interrelation between national and international laws; anti-terrorism; law and justice, morality, etc. These are emergent issues in reality but in theory they need further investigations.

The origins of the state of law as an idea and doctrine date back to ancient history, and since then both have been constantly enhanced and improved. The state of law as a social value shows its relevance in ideas, theories and reality. When the democratic revolutions in capitalist countries break out, these important values, especially in the West, are inherited from ancient states of law and transformed into a doctrine of state of law. The state of law's core elements are manifested in political and legal doctrines of various Westerns thinkers throughout history from antiquity to the modern period. Most notable among these doctrines are the ideas of separation and management of state power, human intrinsic rights and the relations between state of law and civil society. The doctrine of the state of law is diverse in its contents and applied at different levels and scales in countries around the world, in which genuine doctrines are diverse. As mankind's history is constantly on the move, social theories in general and state of law theories in particular have to be adjusted and reformed. Inheritance and improvement of previous versions are basic features of the idea, doctrine and reality of the state of law around the world.

In terms of its ideological basis, the context that gives rise to the idea of the state of law in the West is different from that in the East, as Greek and Roman democracies are to some extent more sophisticated because they are based on philosophical thinking and the pursuit of an objective and rational mindset, and are at relatively higher stages of development. Thus Western ideas are different from their Eastern counterparts, according to which the law is not only a ruling instrument but a social value which regulates social relations and a common principle to be adhered to by the state. Many fundamental issues of state of law are thoroughly dissected in the works of prominent ancient Greek and Roman thinkers, especially the ideas on innate human rights and the state's responsibility to protect these.

In Western ancient conceptions as a whole, the law has an important value and position and is the art of the good and the equitable "Jus est ars boni et aegui". This idea also points to the connection between the law and morality, i.e. moral basis, functions and values of the law and, vice versa, the law as an instrument to protect and ensure social morality. In his Philosophy of Right, Hegel also considered legal issues in relation to moral and ethical issues.

Ancient Western ideas on the state of law include such basic elements as the role of the law in protecting human intrinsic rights, settlement of civil disputes, supremacy of the law, adherence to the law as a responsibility of every individual; the correlation between human law and natural law, ethics and justice; and the proper organization of a government that allows for the avoidance of abuse and autocracy. Basic ideas on the state of law are articulated in such works of prominent and well-known thinkers as Aristotle, Plato, Solon, Socrates and Cicero. Most notable of which is the state of law idea of the great ancient thinker Aristotle that emphasizes the domination of the law and separation of powers. According to Cicero, Socrates and Plato, it is necessary to legitimize the power of the law over individuals, even over the state, and to respect and observe the law is to respect rationality, justice and universal intellect, without going astray.[2]

Ancient ideas on the state of law are inherited and promoted by bourgeois thinkers. The introduction of the state of law doctrine is associated with the names of great thinkers such as John Locke, Montesquieu, Rousseau, Kant and Hegel, etc. The bourgeois doctrine of the state of law include such basic components as the protection of human rights and freedom by the law, the supremacy of the law as a general principle regulating state affairs, equality be-

---

[2] Le Doan Ta (1994), 55.

tween the state and individuals, civil sovereignty, and the separation and control of state power, etc.

The renowned French thinker Montesquieu in his work "The Spirit of the Law" introduces the theory of separation and control of state power – one of the basic conditions to protect human intrinsic rights and freedom. In philosophical terms, German thinkers have developed more profound ideas of the state of law and civil society. According to Immanuel Kant, the state consists of law-abiding and legally-conscious citizens, and the state itself has to abide by the law. Any slight departure from the separation of powers would lead to an authoritarian state. Hegel in his Philosophy of Right defines the structure of a state of law as composed by civil society and a state of law legal order.

Components of a state of law are also indicated in Marxist-Leninist thinking on state and law. On freedom and the state's role and duty in protecting and ensuring human liberty, Karl Marx writes: "the development of individual liberty precedes the development of communal liberty."[3] Marx wrote to American President Abraham Lincoln in which he highly appreciated the American Declaration of Independence, valorizing human rights and the role of republican and democratic governments in protecting these rights.

The question has arisen: is the state of law present in Eastern ideas, and what are the similarities and differences between Eastern and Western ideas and doctrines on the state of law? In recent decades when the human race has witnessed a more comprehensive understanding of the state of law and especially of its reality, a common assumption is being formed that the state of law also exists in various schools of thought, policies and legal systems of Eastern states. In particular, moral and humanistic values are among the core components of Eastern states of law.

Looking back at the Eastern political-legal thinking, the concept of the state of law exists for example in different viewpoints on the law, state and morality of ethical and legal principles. Basic as they are, elements of the state of law are manifested in the works of Chinese thinkers such as Confucius, Mencius, Xun Kuang, Han Fei and Vietnamese feudal politicians and thinkers such as Nguyen Trai and Le Thanh Tong. We also recognize many similarities in moral and legal conceptions of both Eastern and Western thinkers such as Confucius, Mencius, Han Fei, Aristotle, Montesquieu, Hegel and Kant.

---

[3] Marx/Engels (1980), 569.

Mutual recognition between Eastern and Western values and ideas in the construction of the state of law can also be regarded as one of the dynamics in the theory and practice of contemporary political and legal systems. Confucian ideas on morality, though still limited and far from being legal ethics if judged from the perspective of human rights and liberty, contain many values. Confucian legal ideas are based on humanistic tenets and compassion. Similar ideas are prevalent in contemporary constitutional theory. Confucius' anthropological ideas on the law are clearly embedded in his doctrine of the people and doctrine of the mean, which reflects his humanistic principles.[4]

A common juncture of all Eastern and Western schools of thought throughout history is the desire for an ideal and virtuous state and society in which everyone enjoys happiness and social stability and justice. Whether from a Western or Eastern perspective, the state of law has to cope with such legal and moral issues, especially in contemporary society, as capital punishment, the application of biological and medical technologies, and criminalization and decriminalization, etc.

The individual plays an important role throughout Eastern ideas and doctrines but is viewed divergently depending on the human's role in community, family, society and state. Therefore, the character of relations such as those between the individual and the state and the society are interpreted differently in Eastern and Western ideas during the ancient, medieval and early-modern periods. Today, in the context of globalization and the worldwide development towards a state of law and market economy, in legal and social theories and realities there have been fundamental changes in the relations between the state and individuals, the state and society, and between individuals and collective institutions, including the sphere of family. The state of law has broad implications, but its core principles are the protection and promotion of human rights, freedom, interests and an all-rounded development based on moral and legal values. This is the main similarity between Eastern and Western ideas on the state of law.

The similarity between Eastern and Western conceptions of an ideal state, commonly known as the "state of law", is nothing but respect for people themselves and is agreed by politicians and scholars. Here I would like to cite the

---

[4] Du Vinh Căn (2008), 335.

236

words of the British Secretary of State for Justice during his visit to our university on September 11th 2008:

"Let me quote one of the teachers from Asian ancient history. To the question, 'Is there one word that can serve as a principle of conduct for life?' Confucius replied, 'It is the word shu – reciprocity. Do not impose on others what you yourself do not desire (Doctrine of the Mean). Whether your tradition is eastern or western, ancient or modern, shu is an important principle for us all. The state of law can give effect to it and make it the foundation of a peaceful, prosperous and just society."[5]

In Vietnam, before long President Ho Chi Minh introduced the idea of the state of law, especially as a part of the constitution, which includes important components such as the spirit of the law, independent jurisdiction, and relations between law and morality, between law and democracy and social justice. His ideas were realized in the Declaration of Independence dated September 2nd 1945, the first Constitution of Vietnam. Ho Chi Minh adopted the ideas of human rights by citing the statement of Thomas Jefferson – a renowned statesman who participated in the American struggle for independence:

"All men are created equal. They are endowed by their Creator with certain inalienable rights; among them are Life, Liberty, and the pursuit of Happiness." And he further added: "In a broader sense, this means: All the peoples on the earth are equal from birth, all the peoples have a right to live, to be happy and free."[6]

The 2013 Constitution inherits Ho Chi Minh's basic points on the state of law, including the idea of human rights, civil sovereignty and state's responsibilities with respect to its people.

Similarities and Differences, Universality and Particularity and the Current Development of the State of Law Around the World

Conception of the State of Law

This issue is no longer new but needs further discussions, as the ideas, theories and practical affairs of different nations and regions regarding the state of law

---

[5] Speech by British Secretary of State of Justice Jack Straw at the Department of Law, Vietnam National University, Hanoi, 2008. http://www.justice.gov.uk/news/sp-120908a.htm

[6] Hồ Chí Minh (1995), 1.

share both similarities and differences, expressing both universal and particular aspects of the state of law. This is especially the case in state policies and legal regulations and in citizens' awareness and behaviors. For example, the viewpoints and policies on social security and state responsibilities vary quite regularly from country to country in the world.

On the Concept of the State of Law in the World

The widely used term in the world is currently "state of law" or "Rechtsstaat". The state of law has quite a long history but was officially introduced in the 19th century and became an increasingly popular term in the second half of the 20th and early 21st century.[7] It originally came into being in Germany (Rechtsstaat) and later spread to France (État de droit) and other European countries and other continents and is now widely referred to in English as "state of law". In my opinion, this issue needs further discussions as it is not merely a concept but reflects similar and different viewpoints on the state of law across nations and regions.

In the German term "Rechtsstaat". Recht means law while Staat means State. In French there is "État de droit" and English there is "state of law". The United States used to retain a corresponding concept "due process of law" which was introduced by the 14th Amendment (1868). This term expanded to include not only the government's responsibility to maintain procedural due process, such as organizing proper court cases, but also substantive due process.

Today, the term "state of law" in English is generally favored. Sometimes, to adapt to other interpretations of nations of "state of law", other usages have to be included such as "the state governed by the state of law" and "the law-governed state".[8] Even in Vietnamese, nhà nước pháp quyền (state of law) is actually opted for instead of nhà nước pháp luật (legal state) and nhà nước pháp trị (state by law). An interesting point that can be drawn from this is that in another version of the Anglo-American interpretation, "the state of law" indicates "state of law" without referring to the word "state", whereas in European and Russian terms the "state" is included. Despite different interpretations and angles pursued by these concepts, they share a common point of view that "state of law" implies the supremacy of the law by which the state has to

---

[7] See Thai Vinh Thang (2009), 63–74.

[8] See Nguyen Si Dung (2004).

abide (i.e. state power is limited), as it is in charge of protecting human rights and freedom; and everyone is equal before the law.

"The state of law" encompasses a broader meaning which goes beyond "the state". Of course, what leads to the usage of "the state of law" instead of other German, French and Russian terms is not yet fully answered and results from the different social, cultural, political and moral systems of aforementioned countries in both the past and present. The state of law is necessarily associated with "the state of law" instead of "the rule by law". This is one of the basic and important principles in the making and implementation of policies and laws and in interpersonal relations. This is especially true for countries witnessing a transition from a top-down management system to a more civilized system based on the principles of equality, justice, transparence and legal and constitutional supremacy.

The term "pháp quyền" in Vietnamese also has important and relevant associations with the humanistic nature of state of law. It is closely related to Western and human conceptions of "pháp luật" – "right" today. Pháp luật means "droit" in French, "right/law" in English, "Recht" in German, "dirito" in Italian and generally refers to the proper conduct, fairness, justice, impartiality, precision, truth, appropriateness and also rights. The original term "jus" springs from "justitia" – judgments, jurisdiction, justice, as law is a science and art of what is good and just and is always justice and goodness – the law is expected, rational and meaningful. Justice has long been considered an advanced legal aspect of human society as said by the ancient Latin maxim: Jus est ars boni aequi: law is the art of benevolence and justice.

In Search of a Definition of State of Law

The concept of the state of law contains a broad range of meanings and its components and basic features are qualitatively different from that of non-states of law. Thus, there are various definitions of this term, which share both similarities and differences. What distinguishes these definitions from one another is that each tends to focus on its preferred and prioritized aspects of the state of law. Accordingly, while some relate state of law to human rights, others concentrate on the separation and control of power and the limitation of state power; supremacy of the law, democracy, and independent jurisdiction, etc. Each definition is both relevant and important in the clarification of the state of law.

According to Roman Herzog, "state of law implies a state that does not interfere with the affairs of individuals and only exists to benefit its citizens."[9] Renowned English lawyer, A.V. Dicey, in his Introduction to the Study of the Law of the Constitution (1915) explicates the state of law by using three characteristics: the law is supreme and the state is not allowed to abuse it in any case; everyone is equal before the law; and the state of law means constitutional law.[10] German legal and political scholars in their monograph on the state of law evaluate and introduce this concept by elucidating its main features: the state of law is established and run on the basis of moral values, justice and integrity, and state power is limited by the law; the state of law ensures human rights; the core essence of a state of law is that the state functions to benefit its citizens, etc.[11] By studying and referencing theoretical and practical examples, we attempt to define state of law as follows:

State of law is a political system that is organized and maintained on the separation and control of state power, limiting state power by means of laws as the ultimate power according to justice, integrity and the assurance of human interests; the state is responsible for respecting and devising necessary legal measures to safeguard and defend human rights and freedom from any violation, and for democratizing social activities, and its relations with citizens are based on equality and mutual accountability. Regarding its basic and notable features (or principles), there are differences in the theorizing the state of law. These features also indicate the level of development of each state of law and civil society. Generally speaking, the state of law can be said to possess the following features/principles that also contribute to its identification.

The state of law is responsible for ensuring the supreme position of the Constitution and law in social and state affairs. It is the law that dominates a state of law and not individuals. This is ensured by the fact that the power of the law is created, respected and followed. When the law is supreme, regulations are legitimate, legally and constitutionally created. It is not only the state law that is supreme but also justice, because the law serves humanity and justice, revealing its moral aspects. According the German author Josef Thesing,

---

[9] Thesing (1997), 36–47.

[10] See Dicey (1915), 120.

[11] Thesing (1997); and ibid essays of Robber, 48–85; Beson/Jasper, 180–200; Martin/Kriele, 223–250; Herzog/Thesing, 9–17.

the state of law has to base on "the supremacy of the law and ethical concepts of justice."[12]

The state of law is responsible for respecting, protecting and ensuring the rights and freedom of humans and citizens. By and large: "human rights imply the intrinsic, natural and objective demands and interests of humans which are recognized and inscribed in national laws and international legal treaties".[13] Former UN General Secretary Kofi Annan once declared:

"Human rights are common to every culture and a friend of every nation."[14]

Human and civil rights are the basis and purpose and also criteria for the evaluation of all state bodies and public servants. The state is charged with protecting and ensuring the rights and freedom of humans and citizens, identifying and providing necessary conditions in political, economic, cultural, social and technological fields to maintain these rights in practice. The state is obliged to abide by constitutional principles on the rights and freedom of humans and citizens, and is prohibited from abusing and misusing the law to restrict, distort and manipulate the nature of these rights.

The state is organized and maintained on the separation of state power between the legislative, executive and judicial branches which are clearly defined in the Constitution and law. Compliance with the law is required of all individuals and organizations, including the state. The state is responsible for compensating material and spiritual loss of its citizens and organizations caused by unconstitutional decisions and acts. Judiciary bodies have to be independent and capable of protecting the rights, freedom and legitimate interests of individuals and citizens, and have to decide on and resolve disputes according to the law, integrity and justice.

Democracy, Civil Society and Sustainable Development

The state of law is a democratic state, and all of its policies and operations are transparent and public so that citizens and social organizations can contribute their opinion and feedback. The state of law can only function and exist in conjunction with a well-developed civil society. In return, civil society and its

[12] Thesing (1997), 55.

[13] Nguyen Dang Long/Vu Cong Giao/La Khanh Tung (2009), 209.

[14] Statement of UN General Secretary Kofi Annan on International Human rights day in 1977, paragraph 3.

members can only exist and function when a state of law is ensured. The law within a state of law must ensure such qualities as justice, humanity, equality, the protection of human freedom and interests, harmony of interest between individuals, state, community and society, and compatibility between national law and international law. What distinguishes contemporary conceptions of state of law is the increasing expansion of its contents instead of a mere focus on forms as in previous interpretations. In the past the state of law is primarily understood and explained in terms of its forms, i.e. compliance with the law, binding regulations towards the state, limited state power, and even power control, although they are its basic, prominent and innate characteristics. In contemporary society, the contents of state of law become more vital, namely the responsibility of states in protecting, ensuring and promoting human rights, freedom and interests, maintaining justice and democracy, and promoting the economy, culture, social security and welfare and living conditions. The state of law has a new role as a social servant and its permanent responsibility as a modern state is to "facilitate the authentic life of everyone as a human being."[15]

Creation of a Human Rights Culture and Human Rights Education. A Prerequisite for the Construction of a State of Law

Human rights culture is one of the cultural forms in general and at the same time the foundation of every other cultural form in contemporary life. The category of culture has a broad range of meanings and is not easy to define.[16] Currently there are around 400–500 definitions of culture. This concept encompasses material and spiritual values formed and created by human activities, which are transferred back and forth between generations and communities, creating particular national identities along with universal elements.

Legal culture is the system of material and spiritual values within the hemisphere of the law and manifests in human consciousness, ideas, conventions, legal principles and behaviors. The most culturally relevant aspect of juridical acts is reflected in legitimate judgments that are based on prudence and justice

---

[15] Ysumirrô/Takahara/Bikishimoto (1994), 30.
[16] See Central Committee for Ideology and Culture (2001), 222.

and the protection of human rights, freedom and legitimate interests.[17] Humanity is the core element of culture. Human rights culture refers to the understanding and respect, recognition, protection, assurance and promotion of human rights; human rights and freedom are the highest values protected and guaranteed by the system of social, political and legal institutions. Human rights culture is the center of political-legal-moral aspects of modern society. Human rights today have become universal values and are said to constitute part of human culture. Without human rights, it is impossible to make full evaluation of the complicated formulation of political, social, economic, legal and cultural relations.

Authentic culture always takes humans as its purpose, objective and ultimate aim. The state is thus responsible for acknowledging and respecting human rights and its citizens' rights, freedom and legitimate interests. Humanity is served by the state and is never mechanically understood as just a tool. Culture goes hand in hand with sacred values of the spiritual life which together make up a human being. State of law is constitutional, legitimate, reasonable and effective, a state that is organized and maintained based on moral principles, a fair State with its ultimate aim to ensure safety and development for all.

The creation of a human rights culture is prerequisite for the foundation of a state of law. Human rights culture is reflected in the policies and laws, in the operation of public organs and services and in interpersonal conduct. In particular, it is expressed in the collection and making of legal documents and law enforcement; in the system of protective measures to guard human rights. The most relevant manifestation of human rights culture is in the spirit and principles of a democratic constitution, in which the state of law is recognized, respected, protected, ensured and cited by first of all public sectors and officials who are most likely to make unconstitutional acts.[18]

Human rights culture is a multi-dimensional category and a complex formulation consisting of different components, layers and degrees of manifestation. Overall, it is a combination of basic elements such as knowledge and understanding of human rights, protective measures for human rights, respect for human rights and recognition of moral norms and values; and skills in protecting human rights and the supremacy of law and constitution. The na-

---

[17] See Hoang Thi Kim Que/Ngo Huy Cuong (2011).

[18] Nguyen Dang Dung (2012), 5.

ture of human rights culture is marked by this formula: knowledge-respect-practice (recognition, compliance, use) of human rights and freedom. This is especially true for public servants, who have a higher probability of violating the constitution compared to other individuals and citizens. The indicators of a developed human rights culture and a constitutional culture are acknowledgment, admiration, protection and assurance of the rights and freedom of citizens in both attitudes and behavior.

Human Rights Education

There are both long-term and immediate tasks to in order to create a human rights culture. First of all, it is necessary to establish effective human rights education for the entire society, especially for public staff who are making legal decisions that affect these rights. The human rights education is a common statement of this era:

"the more a human is cognizant of his own rights, the more he respects the rights of others and further contributes to peaceful coexistence. Only when the people are educated about human rights can we hope to prevent their violation and reduce conflicts."[19]

The human rights education is aimed at providing everyone since his childhood with necessary knowledge on human rights according to national and international law and on important values such as democracy, equality, justice, freedom, responsibility, tolerance and accountability to oneself and to others. Compassion, lenience and care for others are traditional ethical values that need to be retained and given their right position in the new system of moral values.

At the international level, since 1994 the United Nations has been proposing the decade of human rights education on a global scale. The sacred mission and spirit of the Global Strategy on Human Rights Education are manifested in the acquisition of necessary knowledge and understanding of human rights so that each individual is aware of and practice their own rights while respecting and protecting the rights of others. In this way human beings become closer and more tolerant towards each other regardless of any distance and are more likely to live in peaceful development.

---

[19] Statement of UN General Secretary Kofi Annan on International Human rights day, December 10th 2000; UN Press release, 10 February 2000.

Human rights education is a purposeful and oriented task that aims to provide citizens and public officials with necessary know-how on human rights and defensive methods so that they can practice and protect their own rights while valuing others' according to national and international laws on human rights.[20]

Human and civil rights have become basic indicators of the development of each state in terms of its social system, respect for humanity, democracy and civilization. Human rights education needs to be widely applied. "Prioritized" targets of this activity are public staff and servants and especially law enforcers who are endowed with legal authority and at the same time responsibility to ensure the maintenance of human and civil rights.

Humanity holds the highest values, and any discussion about humanity and human rights necessarily has to relate to a humanistic aspect, namely morality. Thus, human rights education can be only be efficient and genuine in combination with moral education. Moral education, human rights education and legal education have to be in line with economic and cultural education, and the training of living skills and law application. Without basic economic and cultural conditions and proper cultural conduct, it is impossible to maintain and protect human rights, except in mere slogans. Human rights education should constitute an important part in developing a just society in which basic human rights are valorized and respected.

Human rights education and legal education not only prevent the violation of the law but also promote in everyone a sense of respect for human values, for the rights and freedom of oneself and everyone else. The teaching of human rights must take in account the dissection of basic human values and the importance of respect for human rights; the awareness of human values, respect for others' rights and interests, and understanding of justice, freedom and personal responsibility towards one's community and society.

The idea of human rights in connection with freedom and national independence has been most vividly indicated and inscribed in Vietnam's constitutions up to now, especially the 2013 Constitution. Vietnam has made great achievements in the protection and assurance of human rights. The construction of a human rights culture and human rights education are especially important in realizing the 2013 Constitution by introducing constitutional prin-

---

[20] Hoang Thi Kim Que (2006).

ciples into daily life, in particular by actualizing regulations on human rights and the basic civil rights and duties.

References

Central Committee for Ideology and Culture. Ministry of Culture and Information (ed.) (2001): Culture and Business. Hanoi.

Dicey, Albert Venn (1915): Introduction to the Study of the Law of the Constitution. London.

Du Vinh Căn (2008): Confucius Legal Ideas (Tư tưởng pháp luật Nho gia). Hanoi.

Hồ Chí Minh (1995): Collected works. Volume Four. Hanoi.

Hoang Thi Kim Que (2006): Human Rights and Human Rights Education in Vietnam Today (Quyền con người và giáo dục quyền con người ở Việt Nam hiện nay). In: Journal of Science, VNU, Special Issue on Economics-Law, issue 3/2006.

Hoang Thi Kim Que/Ngo Huy Cuong (eds.) (2011): Legal Culture – the Basic Theoretical and Applied Issues (Văn hóa pháp luật – những vấn đề lý luận cơ bản và ứng dụng chuyên ngành). Hanoi.

Le Doan Ta (ed.) (1994): Essays on Historical Philosophy. Second volume. Hanoi.

Marx, Karl/Engels, Friedrich (1980): Selected Works. Volume 1. Truth Publisher. Hanoi.

Nguyen Dang Dung (2012): The Violation of the Constitution and Forms of Unconstitutional Behaviors (Vi phạm Hiến pháp và các loại hình vi phạm Hiến pháp). In: Journal of Legislative Studies, 9 (216).

Nguyen Dang Long/Vu Cong Giao/La Khanh Tung (eds.) (2009): Textbook on Human Rights Theory and Law (Giáo trình Lý luận và pháp luật về quyền con người). Hanoi.

Nguyen Si Dung (2004): The Origin of Rule of Law (Cội nguồn pháp quyền). Tia sang magazine, 2004, 7, and Youth newspaper dated 16 August 2004.

Nguyen Xuan Tung (2016): Promote the Construction of Vietnamese Socialist Rule of Law under the Orientation of the 11th Party Congress (Đẩy mạnh xây dựng Nhà nước pháp quyền XHCN Việt Nam dưới ánh sáng đại hội

Đảng lần thứ XI). http://moj.gov.vn/ct/tintuc/Pages/nghien-cuu-trao-doi.aspx?ItemID=4376.

Speech by British Secretary of State of Justice Jack Straw at the Department of Law, Vietnam National University, Hanoi, 2008. http://www.-justice.gov.uk/news/sp120908a.htm.

Statement of UN General Secretary Kofi Annan on International Human rights day in 1977, paragraph 3.

Statement of UN General Secretary Kofi Annan on International Human rights day, 10 December 2000; UN Press release, 10 February 2000.

Thai Vinh Thang (2009): Reformation and Amendment of the 1992 Constitution towards the Development of a Socialist State of Law and International Integration (Sửa đổi, bổ sung hiến pháp năm 1992 đáp ứng yêu cầu xây dựng nhà nước pháp quyền xã hội chủ nghĩa và hội nhập quốc tế). Essay from Hanoi Law University. The Vietnamese Laws in the Process of International Integration and Sustainable Development (Pháp luật Việt Nam trong tiến trình hội nhập quốc tế và phát triển bền vững). Hanoi.

Thesing, Josef (ed.) (1997): The Rule of Law. Sankt Augustin.

Ysumirrô, O./Takahara, M./Bikishimoto, S. (1994): Japan's Politics and Economy (Chính trị và kinh tế Nhật Bản). Hanoi.

The Development of the Civil Society and the Socialist Law-based State in Vietnam

Duong Xuan Ngoc

In the era of globalization and international integration, building the state of law has become an objective trend for every country. Vietnam, a democratic country, is not out of this general trajectory. However, from the perspective of theory and practice, the construction and perfecting of the socialist state of law in Vietnam are bringing many problems that need to be studied and resolved. This article does not intend to carry out a comprehensive study on the rule of law in Vietnam; instead, this paper tries to approach the issue from the perspective of the construction and development of civil society, an indispensable aspect reflecting the degree of completion of the state of law. It is time to be fully aware of the position and role of civil society in social development, in building and perfecting the socialist state of law.

The concept of the state of law has a long history. Nevertheless, to date, different views on the definition of the state of law are still debated. At the Berlin International Conference (September 1991) in which over 40 countries participated, a general definition was given: "The state of law is a political regime in which the state and individual have to obey the law and everyone's obligations are legally recognized and protected; all legal processes and rules are ensured by an independent court system. The state of law is obliged to respect the highest values of humanity and ensure that citizens have the ability and conditions to resist against the arbitrariness of law as well as the activities of the state apparatus. The state of law must ensure that citizens are not required to do what is out of constitution and regulations. Within the legal system, the constitution is supreme and must be built on the basis of freedoms and rights of citizens."

In Vietnam, the awareness of the requirements of building the state of law was first officially launched by the communist party of Vietnam in the 7th National Party Congress:

"The National Assembly should focus on the implementation of two basic tasks: First, building the state of law, the state has the capacity to establish a synchronous legal system meeting the new requirements of social economic development and control all aspects of a civilized society; that legal system is the basis to ensure that the guidelines and policies of the party and state will be implemented effectively and is a key factor in making social relations become stronger. Second: ensuring the real power and effectiveness of the National Assembly guaranteed by the constitution."[1]

In so far, after more than 20 years, the Vietnam Communist Party has positively realized and resolved the requirements of building and perfecting the socialist state of law. This is shown as follows:

- The objective necessity of the socialist state of law in Vietnam has been recognized and the requirements of building it have been gradually realized.
- The thinking about the socialist state of law has become deeper and changed from qualitative to quantitative. If the 7th National Party Congress only raised the awareness of the requirements of building the state of law in Vietnam, then the nature of the socialist state of law was developed in the 8th National Party Congress; the 10th and the 11th National Party Congress, the essence of the socialist state of law in Vietnam had been confirmed, i.e., the state of the people, by the people and for the people. All state power belongs to the people. Naturally, the state has no rights but authorized by the people. The state was established, not to be served by the people, but to serve the people.
- The operational mechanism of the state organs has gradually been realized, state power is unified with the assignment, coordination and control among state agencies in the implementation of the legislative, executive and judiciary. The 10th National Party Congress confirms: "to build the operational mechanism of the socialist state of law and to ensure the principles of all state power belong to the people and state power is unified with the as-

---

[1] National Political Publishing House (2007), 340.

signment and coordination among the bodies in the implementation of the legislative, executive and judicial; to perfect the legal system, increase the concreteness and feasibility of the provisions in legal documents; to construct, and complete checking mechanisms, monitor the constitutionality and legality of the activities and decisions of public authorities."[2]

- Missions and principles of organization and operation of the state have been recognized and realized, i.e., the state is organized and operated under the constitution and law, the state manages the society by the constitution and law, democratic centralism is applied. The state shall respect and protect human rights and civil rights; care for happiness, the free development of the individual. The rights and obligations of citizens are stipulated by the constitution and law. People perform state power through direct democracy and representative democracy via the National Assembly, People's Council and other state agencies. The state shall respect and fully implement the international treaties in which the Socialist Republic of Vietnam is a member. The state implements the foreign policy of openness, multilateralism and diversification of international relations; Vietnam has signed and joined many international treaties and become a member of many regional and international organizations.

- The enforcement of the party's leadership of the state in the process of developing and perfecting the socialist state of law in Vietnam has been acknowledged and guaranteed.

The achievements in the perception and realization of the demands and content of building the socialist state of law in Vietnam are not in doubt. But so far, particularly in terms of theory, there are still unclear questions that need to be answered: What are the nature and characteristics of the socialist state of law in Vietnam? Is Vietnam a socialist state of law or a socialist-oriented state of law? How to understand "state power is unified"? What are the acknowledgments of assignment, coordination and control in executing state power? What are the relations between party and state within the mechanism of party leadership, state's governance and the people's mastery? What kind of mechanism is in place to ensure control and supervision rights of the people, of the Fatherland Front, the political social organizations for the activities of the state? What is the legal thinking behind building and perfecting the legal

---

[2] Communist Party of Vietnam (2006), 126.

system? In particular, what is the relationship between the state of law and civil society? These concerns not only require the work of scientists but also depend on the will, capacity and commitment of all levels of the entire society.

In fact, in Vietnam, up to now, civil society has been still considered a sensitive issue and has not been formally mentioned in the party's documents. Nevertheless, from both a theoretical and a practical perspective, civil society has become a mirror and an effective measure of the degree of perfection of the socialist state of law in Vietnam. It has been a long time since the launch of the country's fundamental reform and its shift to a socialist-oriented market economy, and civil society has become a real entity confirmed and promoted in the fields of economic development, social democratization and national defense.

The development of the socialist-oriented market economy (now seen as a modern socialist-oriented and internationally integration-oriented market economy) has created an environment and conditions for the economic development of private sectors and democratization of social life. The economic actors are given more autonomy and self-responsibility as required by the market economy and law.

They are provided with more possibilities and conditions to improve their capacity to grasp development opportunities compared to the previous centralized, bureaucratic and state-subsidized economy. Thus, the socialist-oriented market economy not only creates a solid basis for the development of social organizations but also provides mechanisms to liberate resources including human resources. People are free to develop in accordance with the law and ethics and, as a result, this leads to the more active and self-confident involvement of citizens in social organizations to meet the demands and interests of individuals and thecommunity as a whole. The socialist-oriented market economy also provides more conditions for the formation and development of the civil society, i.e., the material facilities and the freedom of liberated people.

Naturally, accompanying the development of a socialist-oriented market economy is the process of building and perfecting the socialist state of law. There is a dialectical relationship between the development of a socialist-oriented market economy and the building of the socialist state of law. Without the development of the socialist-oriented market economy, the requests for and the creation of material facilities to complete the socialist state of law will not be fulfilled. Vice versa, there will be no legal environment for the development of a socialist-oriented market economy without building and perfecting the socialist state of law. Only when a socialist-oriented market economy and a socialist state of law are developed and promoted in reality, will human rights be respected and furthered, will the civil society be formed and developed on the basis of material facilities, law and social environment. In fact, there is no perfect socialist state of law without the development of the market economy and civil society.

It can be assumed that the state of law and the civil society are two sides of the same coin. The formation and development of the state of law stem from social demands and vice versa, civil society is formed and developed on the basis of social demands and the requirements of perfecting the state of law. A socialist-oriented market economy and a socialist state of law, of the people, by the people and for the people in parallel with civil society constitute the necessary and sufficient conditions for the construction and development of the democratic society in Vietnam. The 10th National Party Congress affirms: "to build a democratic society in which cadres, party members and civil servants should really be servants of the people; to identify the organizational forms and mechanisms for the people to exercise democratic rights in economic, political, cultural and social fields."[3]

In Vietnam, social organizations have been increasingly formed. Their activities are based on the principles of self-determination, voluntariness, democracy and autonomy in funding; those organizations are playing a vital role in implementing the millennium development goals: poverty reduction and social welfare. The members of civil society help each other to reduce poverty and hunger as well as participate in charitable activities and effectively fight against social evils. These organizations share responsibilities with the state and support the state in responding to the growing demands and diversity of the members of the society while the state cannot solve or can solve, but not efficiently.

More importantly, civil organizations are also involved in monitoring and criticizing the state apparatus and the economic institutions and party organizations. At the same time, civil organizations are forums which gather opinions and demands of the people of the party and state; they also are bridges between people and party, people and the state, ensuring the democratic

---

[3] Communist Party of Vietnam (2006), 125.

mechanisms of the society, e.g., "party's leadership, state's governance and the people's mastery". As a matter of fact, it is necessary to mention here that civil society is a sensitive issue; any sensitive issue may be abused and distorted which causes incalculable harm. There is no reason to avoid facing the civil society as it is an objective necessity and condition for building and perfecting the state of law as well as the socialist-oriented market economy. Therefore, simultaneously with the active construction and development of civil society, we need to struggle against the abuse and the so-called "administrative disease" in the organizations and operations of civil society.

Additionally, creatively building and developing Vietnam's civil society is seen as a revolutionary attitude that reflects an objective tendency on the one hand, and requirements of the society in creating a democratic environment for the renovation and development of the country on the other hand. Within the present context, to build and develop civil society in Vietnam to meet the requirements of an environment ensuring democratic freedoms for the people in economic development and democratic exercise, it is necessary to solve the following tasks.

Positive attitudes toward civil society should be raised, particularly, it is necessary to see civil society is not a "restricted zone" because of its sensitiveness. The success of almost 30 years of innovation has led our country to enter a new development period: economic progress, political stability, physical and spiritual life of the people has been constantly improved; the position of Vietnam on the international scene was confirmed. Therefore, to further develop the success of the innovation process requires us to bravely face all the problems posed both in terms of theory and practice whether they are still a sensitive issue or not. Moreover, civil society has been existing as an entity already in our country, in the spirit of looking straight at the truth, we should have a scientific attitude towards civil society. Then, we should do research to get a better perception of civil society in terms of: its nature, characteristics, role, objective requirements and the "barrier" to building a civil society in Vietnam. Currently, the perception of a large number of Vietnamese people in general and civil servants in particular are basically limited; therefore, to raise awareness in society about civil society is a necessary and objective requirement.

The state should soon enact laws on association and other legal documents related to civil society in order to create a favorable environment for the socialist-oriented development of civil society. To build and develop civil society, we need to actively create the institutional system of law and compatible related systems followed by suitable mechanisms and policies for organizations and members of civil society to act in accordance with the law and that must be consistent with community interests. That means we should soon complete a legal environment for directing, managing, monitoring and adjusting the formation and operation of civil society. Like it or not, in fact, many social organizations have been created and are operating, many of which are performing very effectively and are recognized by society. However, some of them are acting less successfully and even some organizations are being exploited, consequently, the image of the civil society and the stability of the entire community are also influenced. It is now the right time to take the initiative to create a legal environment for the development of civil society; it is also needed to manage and to limit the negative issues of civil society based on strong institutions with the compatible legal system. Moreover, the promulgation of the law on associations will contribute to preventing the abuse of the sensitiveness of civil society to undermine the country's political and social stability.

It is necessary to diversify the forms of aggregation of funds for the performance of the organizations of civil society. Unlike other political organizations serving the benefit of the ruling class and financially secured by it, civil society organizations are created by their members and financed by them, the civil society should diversify the forms of aggregation and mobilization of funds for the operation. This, on the one hand, creates the material conditions for the activities of civil society organizations, and contributes to preventing the administration disease of political and social organizations on the other hand.

Party and State should have plans to train specialized staff and professionals for civil society organizations. Staff had always played a decisive role in defining success or failure of the revolution. The formation process of social and career organizations in our country in past years has been mainly spontaneous and partial. As a matter of fact, the staff of these organizations has not been trained yet; therefore, the key task now is to foster professional qualifications in order to further improve the quality of the existing staff so that they really have the ability and enthusiasm to undertake key positions in associations and unions. In the long term, to promote the role of civil society organizations, party and state should offer basic and professional training plans for managers to assure that they could serve for the long term in social organizations. By doing so, the active role of civil society can be promoted, particularly in implementing democracy, and assure the close relations between the party and the people as well as between the state and the people.

National strength must be promoted to continue pushing the renewal process, political stability and sustainable development. During the revolution, especially in the renovation period, the party has firmly seen "people as the root", "the masses who make history"; innovation must rely on the people and serve the interests of the people and be in accordance with the practice and always creative. Therefore, our party always focuses on building and strengthening the national unity bloc based on the alliance of the working class with the peasantry and the intelligentsia under the leadership of the party. Building and strengthening national unity is the revolutionary strategy of Vietnam; it is also the power source and the important factor promoting economic development and maintaining the social and political stability of the country and ensuring the success of the renewal process.

After almost 30 years of conducting the renovation, it has been reaffirmed that building and promoting the strength of the nation is always a tremendous momentum of the innovation. However, in terms of socialist-oriented economic and international integration, the foundation to build and strengthen national unity is not only in the unified target including prosperous people, a strong country, social justice, democracy, and civilization. But more important is that the party and the state must implement a national policy with these principles: ensure a fair and equal society, bring practical and legal benefits to the people; harmonize individual, collective and social interests; exercise a democracy associated with maintaining social discipline and struggle against bureaucracy, corruption and waste; constantly nurture and enhance the spirit of patriotism, the sense of national independence and territorial integrity, and the spirit of self-reliance in building the country.

In particular, it is necessary to strongly promote the role of state and government at all levels in performing the function of serving the people; constantly improve the mechanism of both direct and representative democracy; continue to improve and implement the Ordinance on Grassroots Democracy to practice the motto "People know, people discuss, people do and people check" in all types of organizations and units based on all levels and sectors, including in the party, state, Fatherland Front and mass organizations; rectify all signs of democratic violations. The promotion of democracy must be entwined with upholding the law and other social disciplines.

The state should coordinate with the Fatherland Front and ensure necessary conditions for it and other mass organizations to have the true right to reflect thoughts and aspirations of the social strata; actively participate in developing guidelines, policies and laws; gather and mobilize people to successfully implement these policies and tasks of the state; simultaneously, monitor effectively the operations of state agencies, elected representatives, officials and civil servants in order to build and protect a clean and strong government.

Of course, at the beginning of the innovation process, based on the practice of domestic and international situation, we identified the following principles: the maintaining of socio-political stability is considered a prerequisite for any change; innovation is the method and development is the goal. And, thanks to the proper awareness and creative practice of those principles, the socio-political situation of the country has always been stable, the economy has developed, physical and spiritual life of the people have been significantly improved, international integration has increasingly deepened. So, in order to build and develop civil society in Vietnam, in addition to overcoming the barriers of perception and the low level of economic development that limit personal liberation and prevent building favorable conditions for the construction and development of the civil society, we should apply synchronous solutions among which a renewed perception of civil society can be seen as a key solution. More than ever before, we need to understand and act timely in the construction and development of civil society in Vietnam to pave the way for it to promote its inherent strength in the renewal period for socialism and for the happiness of the people; at the same time, we should draft strategic and specific plans for managing the activities of civil society organizations in accordance with the law in order to motivate and ensure the correct orientation for the construction and development of civil society in Vietnam.

References

Bùi Ngọc Sơn (2004): Xây dựng nhà nước pháp quyền trong bối cảnh văn hoá Việt Nam, Nxb Tư pháp. Hanoi.

Bùi Việt Hương (2006): Quan niệm về xã hội công dân trong tư tưởng chính trịphương Tây, T/C Lý luận chính trị, số 4.

Communist Party of Vietnam (ed.) (2006): Documents of the 10th National Party Congress. Hanoi.

Đào Trí Úc (2009): Xây dựng nhà nước pháp quyền xã hội chủ nghĩa Việt Nam trong giai đoạn hiện nay: Một số vấn đề lý luận và thực tiễn, Nxb Từ điển bách khoa. Hanoi.

Đỗ Văn Thắng (2006): Vấn đề xây dựng xã hội công dân ở nước ta, T/C Lý luận chính trị, số 9.

Dương Xuân Ngọc (chủ biên) (2009): Xây dựng xã hội dân sự ở Việt Nam – một số vấn đề lý luận và thực tiễn, Nxb CT-HC. Hanoi. (Duong Xuan Ngoc (ed.) (2009): Constructing the Civil Society in Vietnam – Some Theoretical and Practical Issues. Hanoi.).

National Political Publishing House (ed.) (2007): Complete Documents of the Party. Vol. 51. Hanoi.

Nguyễn Am Hiểu (2006): Xã hội dân sự nhìn từ góc độ luật học, T/C Nhà nước vàpháp luật, số 12. (Nguyen Am Hieu (2006): Civil Society under the Perspective of Legal Science, Journal of State and Law, vol. 12).

Nguyễn Duy Quý (2008): Nhà nước pháp quyền xã hội chủ nghĩa Việt Nam của dân, do dân, vì dân-lý luận và thực tiễn, Nxb Chính trị quốc gia. Hanoi. (Nguyen Duy Quy (2008): The Vietnam's Socialist State of Law of the People, by the People and for the People – Theory and Practice, National Political Publishing House. Hanoi).

Nguyễn Minh Phương (2006): Vai trò của xã hội dân sự ở Việt Nam hiện nay, T/C Triết học, số 2. (Nguyen Minh Phuong (2006): The Role of the Civil Society in Vietnam Nowadays, Journal of Philosophy, vol. 2).

Trần Thành (2009): Một số vấn đề xây dựng nhà nước pháp quyền xã hội chủnghĩa ở nước ta, Nxb Chính trị quốc gia. Hanoi. (Tran Thanh (2009): Some Issues on the Construction of the Socialist State of Law in Our Country, National Political Publishing House. Hanoi.).

Vũ Duy Phú (Chủ biên) (2008): Xã hội dân sự – một số vấn đề chọn lọc, Nxb Tri thức, Hanoi. (Vu Duy Phu (ed.) (2008): The Civil Society – Some Selected Issues, Knowledge Publishing House. Hanoi).

Anti-Corruption from the Perspective of Ho Chi Minh's Ideology: Towards a Vietnamese Rule of Law

Lai Quoc Khanh/Nguyen Ngoc Anh

According to the UN Convention against corruption in 2003, "corruption is the abuse of state power for personal interests." Section 1 of Article 2 in the Vietnam anti-corruption law in 2005 states that: "Corruption is the behavior of an official who abuses his/her rights and position for personal gains." The Dictionary of Law indicates:

"Corruption is the exploitation of one's position and rights to gain illegitimate interests, which causes damage to the properties of State, organization, individuals and infringes on the activities of public authorities."[1]

Despite its different interpretations, corruption is commonly understood on a global level as the abuse of one's position and rights for personal interests through illegal behaviors, in other words, the dishonest use or appropriation of public power or collective resources. During feudalism in Vietnam, corruption was reflected in the custom of donating, bribing and giving presents to mandarins and colonial officials. Through time, it became a social evil and a bad custom that denigrated the social structure to its core.

Recognizing anti-corruption as an insidious and long-term problem of the country, since the August Revolution 1945, apart from encouraging diligence, frugality, integrity and righteousness (Cần, kiệm, liêm, chính) among party members and the people, party, state, government and President Ho Chi Minh were particularly concerned about the struggle against corruption, misappropriation and abuse of power. Corruption, misappropriation and abuse of power

---

[1] General Vietnamese Dictionary (1998), 695.

have a broad range of meaning under the framework of Ho Chi Minh's ideology. In this paper we would like to shed light on the issue of corruption according to Ho Chi Minh and relate it to the development of a Vietnamese socialist rule of law.

Ho Chi Minh's Ideas on Corruption and Anti-corruption

Definition and Concept of Corruption under Ho Chi Minh's Ideas

Ho Chi Minh's anti-corruption ideas constitute an important part of his ideology. The main features and contents of his ideas on anti-corruption have been adopted by party, state and Vietnamese population as a whole in the battle against corruption today.

President Ho Chi Minh is an excellent leader and warrior in Vietnam's liberation movements in the 20th century, and is also a pioneer and director in anti-corruption efforts – a global issue. Ho Chi Minh is one the few leaders who relentlessly and resolutely committed himself to battling corruption during his revolutionary career. Ho Chi Minh continuously maintains a critical standpoint towards corruption in former colonial and imperial systems and also their new counterparts.

His synchronicity between words and deeds through resolute anti-corruption acts and being an example of "diligence, frugality, integrity and righteousness" constitute the exceptionality of Ho Chi Minh's ideology and his ideas on anti-corruption in particular. Ho Chi Minh clarifies the role of mitigating corruption, misappropriation and abuse of power, considering it an important task for Party's members and the people:

"Corruption, misappropriation and abuse of power are social evils. They must be erased in the pursuit of diligence, frugality, integrity and righteousness, to encourage production and an economical lifestyle, to lead our national salvation to victory and success, and to nourish ethical practices among the entire population. This is an important task of every one of us."[2]

---

[2] Collection of Ho Chi Minh works (2000), 534.

The battle against corruption, misappropriation and abuse of power is a permanent and great concern of Ho Chi Minh, who considers them "most debasing and appalling behaviors."[3] The nature of misappropriation is "To steal from the public, which is equivalent to deception and greed", and is "no less than robbery". President Ho Chi Minh produces a conceptualization of misappropriation:

"Concerning public servants, misappropriation (tham ô) means to steal from the public; to starve the people; to rob from the army. He who misappropriates secretly misuses public funds, and also appropriates the State's properties to enrich his own division and local area. Concerning the people, misappropriation means to steal from the public, to lie and avoid tax."[4]

Ho Chi Minh considers the nature of misappropriation as "to steal from the public" – i.e. to steal public properties contributed by the people not in order to fulfill collective tasks but to enrich oneself or even one's inner circle. Any misuse of "public properties" as "private properties" is considered by Ho Chi Minh an act of misappropriation. This is its general meaning. In this sense, the parties involved in misappropriation include not only public servants, who hold certain power in the political system, but also ordinary citizens who "embezzle, lie and avoid tax". More importantly, Ho Chi Minh reveals a more subtle and sophisticated kind of misappropriation, namely indirect misappropriation. He provides an example of this practice:

"any public official or citizen who receives a monthly wage yet is irresponsible, greedy, sluggish, and wasteful of the time of the Government and others."[5]

This is a special kind of misappropriation. Though not liable to cause serious damage as direct misappropriation, this kind happens on a regular, daily basis and proves to be devastating to the efficiency of public authorities and state management, which greatly threatens the national revolutionary project. Similar to misappropriation, extravagance is considered by Ho Chi Minh as misconduct in the eyes of the population. Extravagance is caused by public servants, military servicemen, factories and citizens who irresponsibly waste or misuse time, wealth and labor. He makes clear:

---

[3] Collection of Ho Chi Minh works (2000), 110.

[4] Collection of Ho Chi Minh works (2000), 488

[5] Collection of Ho Chi Minh works (2000), 436.

"Some say that extravagance is not as bad a conduct as misappropriation. In fact, they are two different acts, but both deplete the resources of the Government and the people."[6]

Ho Chi Minh even states that extravagance is more threatening than misappropriation, because "it is more common." He indicates three kinds of extravagance: "extravagance of labor", "extravagance of time", and "extravagance of wealth". While each has its own forms and different manifestations, they all lead to consequences which "maybe even more serious than caused by misappropriation", damaging the properties of Government, people and disrupting the national liberation and construction as a whole.

Both misappropriation and extravagance are dangerous illnesses. To effectively combat these, it is necessary to understand their causes and origins. Ho Chi Minh says: "Misappropriation and extravagance both result from the abuse of power."[7] He makes clear that abuse of power (quan liêu) directly leads to and accelerates the two former. He insists that whenever abuses of power show up, there are misappropriation and extravagance and vice versa. President Ho Chi Minh thoroughly analyzes the nature, causes and symptoms of abuse of power. According to him, it takes the form of

"unnecessary bureaucratic rules and red tape, detachment from and mistreatment of the masses, and disobedience of the policies set out by the Party and Political Organizations."[8]

Abuse of power can mean willful ignorance of one's own tasks, failing to acknowledge general affairs, and providing insufficient and obscure instructions. It can also mean alienation towards the masses, lack of knowledge of subordinates' performance, denial of feedback, and avoidance of criticism and self-criticism. The overall manner of an abuser of power is undemocratic and disrespectful of the principle of "collective leadership-individual duty" (lãnh đạo tập thể, phân công phụ trách). Ho Chi Minh characterizes it as

"to focus on the formalities of every task without going into its substance, and to only report, instruct and inform on the surface without making thorough and sufficient investigations."[9]

---

[6] Collection of Ho Chi Minh works (2000), 436.

[7] Collection of Ho Chi Minh works (2000), 394.

[8] Collection of Ho Chi Minh works (2000), 394.

[9] Collection of Ho Chi Minh works (2000), 489.

In performing his own duty or delegating tasks to subordinates, without proper supervision, it is not possible for an official to instruct and oversee his subordinates; and by failing to make timely correction of wrongdoings, he causes the loss of wealth and resources of the state and people. Ho Chi Minh writes:

"Abuse of power can mean that public authorities at different levels and sectors fail to oversee themselves, their subordinates and the masses. It is the seed of misappropriation and extravagance. Therefore, to combat misappropriation and extravagance, we must prevent abuse of power. But this has to be done with enough preparation, planning and clear objectives. In every sector and every area, public officials, people and servicemen must be informed about these bad practices."[10]

According to Ho Chi Minh, public servants and authorities who abuse their power are so blind and numb that they fail to maintain overall regulations and self-discipline. As a result, they become wrongdoers who drown themselves in misappropriation and extravagance. This leads to a consequence in which not only these officials practice misappropriation and extravagance for their own interests, they fail to maintain overall management and administration and inspire corrupting behaviors among their own subordinates, causing loss and damage to the resources and time of the State and the people.

Ho Chi Minh deems these bad practices "allies of the colonists and feudalists", and "enemies of the people, army and Government."[11] For these practices are disrupting. First and foremost, they drain public properties. Many officials are in charge of public properties donated by the State, the people and foreign partners, which are used to serve revolutionary efforts and improve living conditions. Due to their egoism and desire for personal gains, these officials take from the public and misuse common possessions of the State, threatening the cause of national construction and diminishing overall living standards. By abusing power and neglecting responsibilities, they exhaust the wealth, time and resources of the State and people. While not directly leading to robbery and embezzlement, extravagance happens on a regular basis and in different forms and cause just as much damage as misappropriation.

Misappropriation and extravagance debase and corrupt the moral consciousness of an official and diminish his lucidity and enthusiasm, causing popular skepticism towards party and state. Ho Chi Minh affirms that most of

---

[10] Collection of Ho Chi Minh works (2000), 436.

[11] Collection of Ho Chi Minh works (2000), 490.

Vietnamese party members, union members, public servants and staff are clean and devoted, commit to the revolutionary spirit and practice diligence, frugality, integrity and righteousness. They are willing to endure hardship and sacrifice for revolutionary efforts and popular aspirations. However, among them there are still a number who practice misappropriation, abuse of power and extravagance for their own sake, thereby corrupting and alienating themselves from moral principles. This discourages the Party, spoils the reputation of party and state and threatens revolutionary efforts. Ho Chi Minh makes clear: "the battle against misappropriation, extravagance and abuse of power must rely on the masses to be successful."[12] The participation of the masses determines its accomplishment. The more they actively contribute to it, the more it is likely to succeed. Ho Chi Minh confirms that "the more people participate, the more its victory is complete and timely."[13]

The prevention of misappropriation and extravagance is extremely important and must be regularly addressed at all levels and by different sectors. Like in other areas, to be successful in the area of anti-misappropriation and anti-extravagance; we must be aware of the instructions that lead us in this struggle. Ho Chi Minh emphasizes: "it is necessary to be prepared by making plans, and thus leadership, organization and loyalty are needed."[14]

Causes, Origins and Conditions of Corruption

At the objective level, Ho Chi Minh considers misappropriation and extravagance "serious diseases" of any state. Whether in feudal, capitalist or socialist state, without thorough education and if state activities are conducted without the supervision and control of the people, it is not difficult for these two practices to occur: Those who hold authority, whether influential or not, are likely to be corrupt. Ho Chi Minh makes clear:

"Those who work for public organs from Central level to grassroots level are more or less endowed with power, and thus are more likely to be wealthy through robbing the Government or stealing from the people. Without maintaining diligence, frugality, integrity and righteousness and impartiality, they are easily spoiled and become robbers in the eyes of the people."

---

[12] Collection of Ho Chi Minh works (2000), 495.

[13] Collection of Ho Chi Minh works (2000), 490.

[14] Collection of Ho Chi Minh works (2000), 490.

At the subjective level, "appropriation is caused by the lack of moral consciousness and egoism" among public servants and cadres. Ho Chi Minh
writes: "Egoism is such an effective virus that causes various illnesses, for instance sluggishness, cynicism, greed, opportunism, abuse of authority, misappropriation, debasement, wastefulness and extravagance. It also diminishes
solidarity, self-discipline and ignites whimsicality, the defiance of State and
Party's policies, and inhibits revolutionary and popular efforts. By and large,
egoism may lead to various frauds." Ho Chi Minh says that abuse of power is
the root of misappropriation and extravagance. All of these bad practices are
the enemies of the people, army and Government. Insidious as they are, for
they carry no weapons and yet penetrate our organizations to disrupt our tasks,
dishearten and demoralize our men, and prevent them from practicing diligence, frugality, integrity and righteousness. They are "internal invaders" and
enemies within. Therefore, "the battle against misappropriation, extravagance
and abuse of power is as important and volatile as military battles. This is a
battle in ideological and political fields."

These practices can also be caused by the lack of knowledge and education
and generally the inadequate management of the state. Therefore, to combat
them, it is necessary to improve both the moral quality of public servants and
administration and organization of the state.

Ho Chi Minh's Viewpoints on Anti-Corruption Solutions

Having been aware of the insidious nature as well as the causes of misappropriation, extravagance and abuse of power, Ho Chi Minh proposes a set of solutions to prevent these acts.

In preventing these practices, Ho Chi Minh is particularly concerned about
improving overall awareness among the masses. That is, "to make the masses
aware of the danger of misappropriation, extravagance and abuse of power; to
transform hundreds of vigilant eyes and ears into omnipresent supervisors who
prevent the occurrence of these acts."[15] To prevent misappropriation, extravagance and abuse of power, the masses supervise public servants by quickly
identifying illegal behaviors and criticizing and denigrating their bad conducts. Thorough supervision of the masses over public servants through different methods is an efficient way to prevent these practices. In addition, timely

[15] Collection of Ho Chi Minh works (2000), 576.

comments and complaints made by the masses help relevant authorities to quickly discover bad behavior and produce appropriate penalties. Ho Chi Minh says that misappropriation and extravagance are caused by egoism and abuse of power. This literally means to focus on appropriating and self-indulgence without any concern for moral improvement and professional performance, to be ignorant of the aspirations and demands of subordinates and citizens, and a general avoidance of supervision and criticism. The prevention of egoism and abuse of power is most useful in combating misappropriation and extravagance. Ho Chi Minh instructs that:

"Our Party should do its best to educate its members about communist ideals, missions and policies and about their tasks and ethical requirements."[16]

A public official is supposed to be aware of his position as 'servant' of the people and revolutionary goals, to put his own interests below that of the revolution, the Party and the people, be devoted and thorough in his tasks, be open to the masses, respect and promote people's mastery and improve the collective spirit and self-discipline. He must continuously pursue personal growth and improve his knowledge through various ways from reading books to learning from his superiors, subordinates and the populace.

According to Ho Chi Minh, a public servant must be a good example of dedication, purity, resilience and morality; and follow diligence, frugality, integrity and righteousness. Ho Chi Minh writes:

"To maintain purity and stay away from corruption, it is necessary to practice the four virtues on a regular basis, namely diligence, frugality, integrity and righteousness."[17]

He further explains:

"Diligence means to be productive in personal duties, whatever they are. Frugality means economical use of time. Integrity means to avoid misappropriation and protect public and common properties at all cost. Righteousness means to evade every bad practice and follow every good practice."[18]

He then requires and instructs public officials to practice these virtues and consider them must-have qualities of a revolutionary servant. Second, it is

---

[16] Collection of Ho Chi Minh works (2000), 439.

[17] Collection of Ho Chi Minh works (2000), 347.

[18] Collection of Ho Chi Minh works (2000), 392.

necessary to practice democracy and maximize the people's mastery by leaning on them. Ho Chi Minh writes:

"What is democracy? It means the people are masters. So what are the President, Ministers, Deputy Ministers and other public members? Servants! They are servants of the people and not revolutionary elite. The maintenance of democracy is the key to every difficulty".

He emphasizes that only when the entire population takes part in realizing and implementing the motto "the people know, the people discuss, the people perform, and the people check" can misappropriation, extravagance and abuse of power efficiency and actively be solved. President Ho Chi Minh asks the people to fulfill their mastery. He claims that "corruption among officials is caused by ignorance among people", therefore, the people must be aware of their power and know how to supervise public servants in practicing their integrity. When a house is robbed, everyone will be informed and all village members go out to catch the robber. Likewise, when a public possession is lost, everyone is responsible for informing on the culprit and punishing him because everyone is charged with protecting public properties. State properties are infrangible and thus their misuses mean the violation of common interests and an enemy. Public officials must do their best to maintain integrity. They must practice collective criticism and self-criticism to clear themselves of any desire for misappropriation, extravagance and abuse of power. A nation that knows how to maintain frugality and integrity is rich in both material and spiritual aspects and deserves to be regarded as civilized. He continuously emphasizes: "persistent anti-misappropriation is a common mission of the Party and the people". To this end, the Party launches the "Three pros and three cons", in which "the improvement of enthusiasm, consolidation of financial management and technical reforms" are the pros and "misappropriation, extravagance and abuse of power" are the cons (this campaign was launched in the 1960s).

Third, it is necessary to make constant state reforms and train and improve professional skills of public servants. This is a basis to develop a cost-effective and efficient government that fulfills and represents the people's power (through measures, policies and regulations) under their supervision; and also contributes to democratization and enhanced transparency. All during his presidency, Ho Chi Minh successfully trained ethical and capable public officials who were indeed "servants" of the people and devoted to the construction of a state of the people, by the people and for the people. He himself is the best example of a morally-conscious person who practices "diligence, frugality, integrity, righteousness and impartiality" and combines words and deeds.

While Ho Chi Minh has a "reservoir of affection" for the entire Party, people and army, he stops at nothing to realize his resolute and unyielding anti-corruption project. President Ho Chi Minh, having been through "sleepless" nights, decided to execute Colonel Tran Du Chau, a quartermaster general who misused a large amount of the army's funds in trivial pursuits, while the entire population was struggling to expel the French colonists. This case is but a past event yet retains its value today.

Ho Chi Minh's Anti-Corruption Ideas in the Development of Vietnamese Rule of Law Today

Thanks to the party-led renovation, Vietnam has gained important economic achievements. Socio-economic developments improve living standards while national security is ensured. Nevertheless, we are faced by serious challenges and difficulties. One of the obstacles to renovation is corruption. Corruption and extravagance are becoming more complicated and lasting, causing indignation among the people and huge losses for the state, deflecting the integrity of party members and public officials and compromising social justice and equality.Being aware of this situation, party and state have released many resolutions to reduce corruption and gained preliminary results. However, corruption has become more prevalent than before and appears to expand to every sector, industry and area. Clearly, a better understanding of the nature and causes of corruption is necessary in order to create better solutions. Among anti-corruption solutions, preventive measures are also important due to the following reasons:

- First, if applied on a regular basis, these measures can produce a range of effects. By regularly and continually performing these measures, it is possible to attack corrupt behaviors at their root.
- Second, preventive measures can reduce the consequences of otherwise irreversible corrupt acts. Prevention means proactive anti-corruption and can minimize possible damage. This includes not only economic loss, which is numerical, but also the degradation of morality and in a broader sense, in-

fringement of the laws and social justice, which causes skepticism among the people towards s state and party and our project of renovation.
- Third, the study and application of preventive measures contribute to the overall renewal and improvement of state management and governance in particular and socio-economic renovation in general.

Regarding Party Members and Public Officials

Every success in the national liberation and renovation in the past and present is attributed to the Communist Party's leadership. Its strength is reflected in the individual strength of its members. More than anyone, party members are supposed to be the pioneers of anti-corruption, especially with respect to those who currently hold important positions in the state. Anti-corruption is a battle against the temptation of material gains which becomes even more influential and powerful under the impact of a market economy. The ethical, political and ideological education of party members should not merely stops at decisions and resolutions but has to become a regular and important task of the party's organs and every conscious member.

The party has to instruct and supervise each member in improving his moral quality by fulfilling particular tasks and roles. Political education and moral improvement should not stop at slogans and have to include practical criteria based on which every party member can self-improve and party organs can evaluate its members plus provide necessary support.

Promote the Supervision of Party Members

This is especially important. What is needed is improved coordination between the party and state organs in managing public servants, as the party members account for most of the positions in the state, especially at senior level. The management of party members refers to an overall system of management, including recruitment, nomination, appointment and evaluation during their term. Mismanagement of party members easily enables possible opportunists to infiltrate the party and state and even claim the highest positions to pursue their personal gains. This is an especially complicated issue that requires a substantive understanding of the danger of irresponsible management and possible solutions in case there are errors.

Include Criticism and Self-criticism into Regular Party Activities

Criticism and self-criticism are useful weapons of the party. "The Party should not seek to hide its mistakes or avoid criticism. The Party has to admit its mistakes and correct them to ameliorate and give example for public officials. It has to perform self-criticism and self-correction (...) The Party has to say no to self-indulgence, self-interests, arrogance and exaggeration."[19] Criticism and self-criticism have been overall underrated and in some cases even neglected and bypassed. Every party member has to be conscious of his responsibilities and of self-criticism as an instrument to improve his own moral conducts and a weapon to prevent bad practices and opportunistic ideas. Moreover, not a few public officials and party members are aware of their responsibility to make honest and sincere feedback and criticism to the party and their comrades as pioneers of the working class. In some cases, criticism is misused as a tool in power struggle and conflict of position. These are disgraceful acts that need to be corrected so that criticism and self-criticism can contribute to improving and consolidating the morale of the party and preventing corruption.

Improving Public Awareness

This is what currently concerns the entire society and tests the ability of party and state in maintaining confidence among the populace. It is impossible to ask for popular confidence if a lawbreaker, especially a party member who produces corrupt behaviors, remains unpunished despite repeated accusation against him. Furthermore, a legal system is no longer legal if it allows important figures in the party and state to escape their punishment for having spread corruption within their own sector. It is understandable that the party aims to sustain political stability, but this does not mean we should ignore or tolerate those who spoil the party's image by disobeying the law and ignoring public interests. Public officials and servants, especially those higher-up, are put under the party's leadership and management. Thus, the party itself is in charge of punishing dishonest acts or irresponsible behaviors that can lead to corruption. A strict posture towards flawed party members increases the confidence in it and is also a useful preventive measure.

---

[19] Collection of Ho Chi Minh works (1995), 267–268.

Regarding State Organs

Adjusting and improving state policies and regulations, especially on economic and financial management and public asset management is an efficient way to prevent corruption. As mentioned above, corruption tends to develop in particular socio-economic conditions. Loopholes in policies are the best perpetrator of corrupt behaviors. Thus, it is necessary to adjust and complete the system of state's policies, rules and regulations and to provide sufficient, clear and accessible regulations, first of all on economic, financial, land, public asset and service management. In addition, these policies and regulations have to be upheld and protected from being exploited by opportunists to acquire illegitimate rights and benefits.

Other tools are: promotion of state reforms by delegating clear and proper tasks for public officials, improving administrative reforms, removing unnecessary red tape and bureaucratic rules for businesses and citizens and publicizing administrative procedures. These measures are well recognized but it takes a step-by-step process to produce favorable results. The state, especially its administrative system, is gaining membership and becoming more and more complicated in terms of its functions and tasks due to objective reasons such as population growth and continuous expansion of socio-economic areas, thanks to technological advances. However, the fact remains that the quantity of administrative officials is not matched by their performance. This is a thought-provoking issue. The growing number of public organs as well as their functions and missions is sometimes not in line with socio-economic requirements or not based on scientific forecasting, instead it results from subjective calculation or even from the parochial thinking of certain local authorities. Therefore, it is necessary to reform the state by simplifying its organizational structure and clarifying relevant responsibilities of each administrative officer. In addition, unnecessary and opaque bureaucratic rules make way for the development of authoritative and haughty behaviors to the point where they become natural and public. Despite our efforts and solutions to improve administrative procedures as one of the strategic aspects of renovation, results are still limited. It is therefore necessary to further promote these reforms by regularly checking and removing unnecessary procedures that threaten public interests at every level and in every sector, especially the areas that most likely produce corruption.

The wage system must be reformed along with the improvement of the livelihood of salaried employees. Other measures include the punishment of corrupt behaviors and the improvement of political awareness, discipline and professional capacity among public officials and cadres. These are also important issues, because after all, any system or policy is created by human beings and the first reason to enter the workforce is for one's living, even for public servants. Justice is the first requirement of every public servant. But one cannot maintain justice if one is burdened with survival needs. It is unreasonable for us to ask for heartfelt service from public officials if they do not earn enough for their living. Therefore, while regularly educating officials about their responsibility, we have to accelerate the reforms of the wage system. The wage reform policy is gaining popularity among the population and expected to become one of the useful measures to prevent corruption.

The compliance with the regulations of party and state on the conduct of public officials is also an efficient anti-corruption solution. The state must make sure this requirement is followed by every public official and servant, and the managers of state organs must regularly enforce their subordinates to efficiently abide by these regulations. In addition, enumeration of assets (e.g. real estate, income sources, and valuables) must be maintained to effectively manage the income of each public official and quickly expose illegitimate income sources. However, it has to be carefully carried out so as to avoid being exploited to cause divisions within State organs.

Other important issues are: further promote supervision and inspection to spot and prevent corrupt behaviors, maintain constant control and inspection of government officials and public authorities, especially those who own a great deal of assets and human resources or have close links with businesses and citizens, to prevent bureaucratic and haughty behaviors, and to make timely correction to any loophole and weakness in administrative policies that can lead to corruption. Inspection, examination and supervision are among the most efficient and proactive anti-corruption solutions. President Ho Chi Minh once said: "Ninety percent of our governing mistakes results from inadequate inspection and examination. Proper supervision helps reduce possible mistakes in the future."[20]

Our current system of inspection and examination is still underdeveloped. There are far too many agencies, and their inspection and examination is underperformed. These basic problems require effective solutions that are cur-

---

[20] Collection of Ho Chi Minh's works (2000), 489.

rently under way while the Law of Inspection is being verified by the National Assembly. However, to improve the performance of inspection it is necessary to combine different methods in the overall system of supervision and inspection, which eventually would contribute to the efficiency of State management and promote the people's mastery. An informed understanding of Ho Chi Minh's ideas on the management of public officials and on the training and handling of Party members is also a preventive measure against corruption. Ho Chi Minh emphasizes:

"Public officials are main actors of public administration and every success or failure depends on their quality."[21]

Corrupted officials violate moral principles and deserve to be regarded as incompetent. Therefore, it is necessary for managers to understand their subordinates so as to appoint them appropriate positions. If the appointment of officials is not based on professional skills or moral qualities but on personal affiliation, if it is not based on collective interests but on personal and "partisan" relations, then these officials will not only fail to accomplish their tasks, they will form parochial and inner circles by whatever means to take in personal gains and tread on collective interests. Therefore the selection of public officials has to be impartial, for it not only affects the officials in question but also the collective power represented by the Party and State. In reality there have been many cases in which by relying on petty tricks to acquire position, authority, power and money, public officials propagate bad practices among their peers and facilitate the spreading of corruption.

The nomination of public officials must be unbiased and objective and help expose those who take advantage of collective ideals to project their own interests, who only serve their own interest groups under the guise of common development while spreading corruption. We must base on rational criteria to appoint public officials who are not only devoted to their professional tasks but are brave enough to say no and even stand up against corruption.

---

[21] Collection of Ho Chi Minh's works (1995), 487.

Conclusion

President Ho Chi Minh is a perfect example of a moral, diligent, frugal, righteous and impartial character. In light of the current diffusion of corruption, the usefulness and importance of Ho Chi Minh's principles become even more apparent. To follow his anti-corruption ideas is the responsibility of every public official, party member and citizen so that we can reduce as much dangerous threat to our national development as possible in this epoch of integration and development. The relentless combat against sectarianism and provincialism helps us to timely anticipate and handle misappropriation and corruption among public organs.

Harmful practices such as misappropriation and corruption currently manifest themselves under nuanced and sophisticated forms. Therefore, the party members must resolutely and determinedly avoid these practices and protect the common properties of the people, at the same time they should focus on productive and entrepreneurial efforts and contribute to socio-economic improvement. Misappropriation and corruption are contrary to revolutionary ethics, so the party members must consistently follow Ho Chi Minh's ethical standards so that transparency and solidarity among the party, state and collective organizations are upheld, and the populace has full confidence in our common project of national renewal and development.

References

Cao Van Thong/Ngoc Quoc Thai (2011): Supervision as a System to Prevent Authoritarianism in the Ruling party (Công tác giám sát góp phần ngăn ngừa nguy cơ của Đảng cầm quyền). Hanoi.

Communist Review Issue 20 (July 2002): Frugality and the Struggle against Misappropriation, Extravagance and Abuse of Power According to Ho Chi Minh's Ideas (Thực hành tiết kiệm, chống tham ô, lãng phí, chống bệnh quan liêu theo tư tưởng Hồ Chí Minh).

Communist Review issue 31 (November 2003): Scientific Conference: The reforms of the Party and anti-corruption: Experiences and solutions. (Hội thảo khoa học và thực tiễn: Xây dựng chỉnh đốn Đảng, chống tham nhũng: Kinh nghiệm và giải pháp).

Culture and Information Publisher (ed.) (1998): General Vietnamese Dictionary. Hanoi.

Ho Chi Minh (1980): The practice of frugality and the prevention of misappropriation, extravagance and abuse of power (Thực hành tiết kiệm và chống tham ô, lãng phí, chống bệnh quan lieu). Hanoi.

Le Doan Hop (2003): Some opinions on corruption and anti-corruption (Một số ý kiến về tệ nạn tham nhũng và việc chống tham nhũng). Journal of Research exchanges issue 11.

National Politics Publisher (ed.) (1995): Collection of Ho Chi Minh works. Fourth volume. Hanoi.

National Politics Publisher (ed.) (2000): Collection of Ho Chi Minh works. Sixth volume. Hanoi.

National Politics Publisher (ed.) (2000): Ho Chi Minh Collection of works in CD. Hanoi.

Nguyen Dinh Gam (2002): The issue of corruption: causes and safeguard measures. (Tệ nạn tham nhũng: Căn nguyên sâu xa và biện pháp phòng chống). Journal of State and law issue 1.

Nguyen Huy Tan (2003): Towards efficient anti-corruption efforts among the People's Public Security. (Thực hiện lời dạy của Bác Hồ. Góp phần nâng cao hiệu quả công tác đấu tranh chống tham nhũng trong lực lượng Công an Nhân dân). Journal of Research Exchanges issue 11.

Nguyen Khac Bo (2002): Anti-corruption: immediate and long-term solutions (Chống tham nhũng, giải pháp trước mắt và lâu dài). Journal of Law and Democracy issue 4.

Nguyen Thi Doan (2002): Improve inspection among the Party to prevent and reverse corruption. (member of the Party's Central Committee, Vice President of the Central Inspection Committee). Communist Review, issue 12.

Pham Ngoc Hien/Pham Tuan Anh (2012): Questions and answers on anti-corruption (Hỏi – Đáp về phòng, chống tham nhũng). Hanoi.

Tran Nghi (2014): Ho Chi Minh's ideas on the law and its application in the renovation of Vietnam (Tư tưởng Hồ Chí Minh về pháp luật và việc vận dụng trong sự nghiệp đổi mới ở Việt Nam). Hanoi.

Tran Quang Nhiep (2002): The Press in Our Struggle against the Abuse of Power and Corruption Today (Báo chí trong cuộc đấu tranh chống quan liêu, tham nhũng ở nước ta hiện na). Communist Review, Issue 11. April.

Vo Nguyen Giap (2000): Ho Chi Minh's ideology and the revolutionary path of Vietnam (Tư tưởng Hồ Chí Minh và con đường cách mạng Việt Nam). Hanoi.

Rule of Law and Codes of Trust. Interdependencies between Legal and Social Institutions: A Case Study of China

Michael Baurmann/Liu Mengyue

Introduction

Formal state institutions like the political and legal order consist of rules that are formally codified and enforced by organizations with coercive power, while informal social institutions refer to the unwritten norms which are enforced outside the officially sanctioned channels. The research on social capital and its impact on the working of a political and legal order focuses on the relations between these two types of institutions. It has one basic message: for a political and legal order to work well and sustainably it is not only dependent on a smartly crafted institutional design with a well-constructed system of incentives, formal controls and coercive mechanisms; at least as important are the supporting social institutions and informal norms which motivate and encourage citizens to cooperate with each other individually and collectively and to contribute voluntarily to the thriving of their political order and its institutions and organs.

This research has provided evidence that well-functioning interpersonal relations and widespread social networks in the private contexts of a vibrant civil society are necessary foundations for the development of essential social virtues such as the capacity to create new relationships ("sociability"), the readiness to participate actively in societal affairs, the commitment to support political and legal institutions and to contribute one's share to those public goods which cannot be provided by formal institutions.[1]

"Trust" is a key factor in this context. Only if people trust each other will they be ready to cooperate with their fellow-citizens, to do business with them even when transactions involve risks or work together in a collective enterprise to create common goods in their mutual interest. Only if citizens trust their politicians and civil servants will they support them in their ruling and administrating duties and follow their orders and decisions willingly. And only if politicians and civil servants trust their citizens in turn will they be ready to rule by argument and persuasion rather than by control and sanctions.

The lesson social capital theory teaches us is that the formation and distribution of these different variants of trust are rooted in the informal social institutions and culture of a society and cannot be created artificially by political fiat. But we must be aware of the fact that the "codes of trust" in a society can vary greatly and that it makes a huge difference if people restrict their relationships of trust to a well-defined group with a clear demarcation towards outsiders or if they are also ready to place trust in people who are connected with them only by "weak ties".

We will start with a short recapitulation of the arguments in favour of the relevance of trust and social virtues for the working of a political and legal order and why the social capital of a society is a main factor in the production of such attitudes and virtues. We then explain why it is of central importance to distinguish between different variants of social capital and to be aware of a "black" and a "white list" of social capital. On the basis of a differentiated picture of the relation between formal state institutions and informal social institutions, we will discuss and illustrate the topic with the example of Chinese economic history over the last 40 years – and conclude with some general remarks.

---

[1] See Banfield (1958); Putnam (1993); Putnam (2000); Putnam (2001); Baurmann (1999); Baurmann (2000); Baurmann (2002); Baurmann (2006); Baurmann (2008); Ostrom/Ahn (2003).

Economising on Virtue or Taking Virtue Seriously?

Trustworthiness and virtuousness are valuable and possibly also scarce goods. It is therefore expedient to be sparing with them. This principle of "economising on virtue"[2] not only applies to the relationship between single individuals but, as the Scottish moral philosophers have taught us, should also be a guideline for the creation of societal and political institutions. The market serves as a paradigmatic example of an arena where the participants' virtues and morals are largely dispensable, and yet where the result of their actions serves everyone's interest and, thereby, the public welfare. Institutions of this kind relieve individuals of the burden of moral duties and reduce the need for social norms as well as for investments to enforce them.

The classical authors of the Scottish Enlightenment were optimistic that this principle could also be transferred to political institutions. Even within the difficult realm of state power, it seemed possible to invent institutions through which an "invisible hand" would aggregate the general pursuit of individual interests to a common good.[3] This prospect was particularly attractive as one could discard the – possibly futile – Platonic task of controlling the personal ambition of state rulers by instructing them in virtuousness and morality. If, instead, there were ways of shaping the institutional framework of political action so that it would be to the rulers' own advantage to take care of their subjects and the common weal, then trust in politics would become independent of trust in the character of the politicians.

The hope of being able to rely on the "morality" of the political institutions rather than on the morality of the politicians still plays a prominent role in modern political science and social theory and, moreover, in public opinion too. Especially the modern democratic state with its institutionalized possibility of voting politicians out of office, its protection of basic rights, and its ingenious system of the separation of powers and "checks and balances" seems to be the perfect example of a system which by means of cleverly constructed mechanisms prevents state rulers from misusing their power for their own private aims.

---

[2] See Brennan/Hamlin (1995).

[3] See Hirschman (2013).

In recent years, however, the insight has grown among social theorists that the principle of "economising on virtue" has its limits and that we cannot solve all the problems of social and political order by well-designed institutions and their incentives.[4] The functioning of a well-ordered political and legal system is, to a large extent, not only dependent on the behaviour of politicians or civil servants acting directly under the rules of state institutions, but also on the attitudes and the spontaneous behaviour of the citizens outside formal institutions. Many social scientists today believe that because of this a well-ordered society and its political institutions must be rooted in genuine social virtues and trustworthiness of its members which cannot be traced back to rational opportunistic behaviour under some artificially created extrinsic incentives.[5]

However, there can be no doubt that formal state institutions and the incentives they create matter and that different institutions will produce different outcomes. Institutional rules influence the behaviour of actors inside and outside the institutions. But the effects of institutional design are dependent not only on the properties of the formal institutions themselves. Every state institution is embedded in an environment of informal social institutions and the overall impact of a state institution is not the result of an endogenous equilibrium produced only by the incentives of this institution and the given preferences of the actors. This impact is always a result of an equilibrium which emerges from the characteristics of the formal institution *and* exogenous forces and conditions. So the same institutional system can have very different outcomes depending on the social context in which it is implemented. The "rules of the game" always include more than deliberately created rules of formal institutions. "Design principles" for formal institutions are clearly relevant for institutional stability and performance – but their exact consequences are not context-independent.[6]

Emphasizing that social virtues are important for making a political order work is therefore not tantamount to assuming that political and legal institutions and their design are irrelevant. To some degree the opposite is true: social virtues do not make formal institutions superfluous, but can serve as a basis for

---

[4] See Baurmann (2000).

[5] See Putnam (1993), (2000); Fukuyama (1995a); Pettit (1997); Brennan/Hamlin (2000); Dekker/Uslaner (2001).

[6] See Ostrom (1990), Ostrom (2005).

making these institutions even more successful. We can reach more efficient equilibria by institutional devices if we can rely on the trustworthiness and intrinsic motivation of the actors: it becomes easier to create and change formal institutions, the demand for hierarchy and control in institutions decreases, the tension between formal und social institutional processes diminishes, institutional norms and rules are more readily followed and the commitment to collective decisions under institutional rules increases.

If the outlined thesis is right, the working of a well-ordered society demands a stable equilibrium between proper institutional design and a suitable social environment in which supporting social virtues play a central role. Political and legal institutions can bring about a lot of things – but whether they do so in a desirable way is greatly influenced by factors outside these institutions themselves. The efficiency of state institutions, their stability, their legitimacy and conformity to their norms and rules can only be realized if they are properly implanted in their social soil. It is true that societies can be changed and shaped with the help of state institutions, but how successful this is and what kinds of institutions are necessary cannot be answered in general terms. We cannot simply replace the moral fabric of a society and its spontaneous forces by the incentives of a cleverly designed institutional framework. The working of a society cannot only be based on extrinsically motivated compliance with formal rules but also requires an intrinsically entrenched commitment to fundamental social norms: we have to take virtue seriously!

Bowling Together: Making Democracy Work

The view that social virtues are essential prerequisites of a good society and a legitimate political order has a long history. The same is true of a family of theories about the factors which promote the desired virtues of citizens. These theories, which go back to Aristotle, were ingeniously renewed in Tocqueville's analysis of democracy in America and in our time have been put in the context of social philosophy by the communitarians.[7] In the last twenty years, however, a new and promising variant of these theories has been developed by the political scientist Robert Putnam in his pioneering books Making Democracy Work (1993) and Bowling Alone (2000) which initiated a large number

---

[7] See MacIntyre (2007); Etzioni (1993).

280

of theoretical and empirical studies on the social and cultural fundaments of a well-functioning society.

In a nutshell, these theories share the assumption that social virtues are the product of a particular sort of interpersonal relationship between the members of a society. According to this assumption these civic relationships outside the state domain constitute a special area of a "civil society" whose dynamics are rooted in the aspirations and values of the citizens as private actors. As participants in this kind of private relationship, people will develop capacities and behavioural dispositions which promote their general sociability and cooperativeness and which are therefore beneficial to the society as a whole and will spill over into the public sphere.

To Aristotle this function is fulfilled by friendships which motivate individuals to behave altruistically towards each other and to jointly promote the values of their community. Tocqueville extended Aristotle's view to include all personal relationships which are part of a collective enterprise that people privately and voluntarily initiate to realize a common aim. From his observations he draws the conclusion that by taking part in such associational groups, individuals will overcome short-sighted egoism and will learn to cooperate, to contribute to collective goods, trust each other, and peacefully solve issues of common interest. For Tocqueville the concrete aims, sizes and structures of associational groups are secondary. Whether they are established to build a bridge for a village, to come together to pray or to collect money for a hospital, they will all have beneficial influences on the behaviour and character of their members by turning them into persons who feel responsible for their fellow-citizens and the common welfare.

Whereas the communitarians in some respect go back to Aristotle in emphasizing the importance of common values, uniform convictions and shared traditions as the basis of social virtues, the modern theories in the political and social sciences are more in the spirit of Tocqueville focussing as they do on the variety and diversity of associational activities. They have coined the term "social capital" to summarize the different forms of association which can be produced through the private initiative of the citizens. The exponents of social capital theory believe that there are manifold kinds of social relationships which – although maybe to different degrees – have the capacity to create those special bonds between their participants which promote the development of social virtues: from the weak ties of loose social networks in neighbourhoods, from bowling and bird-watching, soccer-clubs and bible-circles to political parties, NGOs and spontaneous social movements.

According to this view, well entrenched interpersonal relations and widely spread social networks are not only important to provide individuals with access to different kinds of valuable resources.[8] Being embedded in stable social institutions should also teach the virtues of sociability and the general capacity to create and maintain reciprocal and cooperative relationships, to participate in common tasks and adhere to the principles of fairness. Without being able to overcome the free-rider problem, to act successfully as a collective and feel committed to the rules of a group, most joint enterprises would not get off the ground. Acting in social networks should moreover foster friendly and altruistic personal relationships and thus a general emotional commitment. The norms and rules in networks would honour and sanction personal trustworthiness thereby laying the ground for mutual trust in a society.[9]

The crucial premise of social capital theory is, however, that there is indeed a spill-over, a transfer from the context of the social institutions of privately organized associational life to the society as a whole. But if individuals in a small village learn to behave fairly towards other village members, if they feel an emotional commitment to them and prove themselves to be trustworthy neighbours, will they consequently also be fair, altruistic and trustworthy as citizens of a large society? The exact mechanisms by which membership in associations of civil society leads to a high level of general sociability and widely spread trust are not yet clearly understood. We must gain more insight into which forms and elements of private associations and networks promote the desirable transfer and which do not. Of course, there is undeniable empirical evidence that there are important differences between various forms of social capital in this respect and that not every joint activity is conducive to society and its institutions as a whole.

---

[8] See Coleman (1988); Granovetter (1973), Granovetter (1985).

[9] See Gambetta (1988); Misztal (1996); Fukuyama (1995a).

Making Democracy Worse: the Dark Side of Social Capital

Timothy McVeigh and his co-conspirators in the Oklahoma City bombing were members of a bowling league: they were not, unfortunately, "bowling alone". Osama Bin Laden was not acting as an isolated mad man, but was firmly embedded in a well-functioning network of internationally acting terrorists. The so-called Islamic State is not held together by its imitation of state institutions but is based on the unfortunately quite effective social institutions of a deviant community. These extreme examples make clear that successful cooperation to achieve a common aim, or solidarity in a group of like-minded people who may also be emotionally committed and develop stable trust relationships is not automatically desirable for people outside the group or the political order of a society. The collective good for the group could be a public bad for the community. Even when we think of less dramatic possibilities than in the Oklahoma City bombing or in the case of Al Quaida, differential mobilization of the population by ethnic, racial, religious, or other ascriptive criteria can lead to very particularistic demands and will undermine rather than support a society as a whole.[10] A rich network of associational activities and stable social institutions alone are no guarantee of a flourishing society and stable state institutions. They can be both a source of trust and a source of distrust. Instead of promoting sociability and cooperative capacities, they can produce insurmountable conflicts by shaping and organizing antagonistic interests and locking them in an inextricable equilibrium of continuous power struggle and mutual hostility.

Putnam claims as a central result of his studies in Italy that the malfunctions of state institutions in Southern Italy were chiefly a consequence of a low level of social capital.[11] To generalize this correlation would be misleading. It is not the case that poorly performing societies with defective state institutions always display a low level of social capital. The stability of autocratic and despotic regimes often has two faces: on the one side there may be a fragmented civil society in which more or less isolated individuals live within weak social networks and must endure an underdeveloped associational life – a situation which is often the intentional outcome of a political strategy of the rulers who

---

[10] See Hardin (1995).

[11] See Putnam (1993).

want to prevent the emergence of a strong civil society. But on the other side the members of the ruling oligarchy themselves may be integrated in a social and political network which guarantees a sufficient degree of mutual trust and reciprocity inside the political elite to enable the efficient realization of their collective goods. On this basis the commitment among them can be strong enough to overcome short-term opportunistic and selfish behaviour and achieve beneficial cooperation – which does not exclude the fact that the aim of this cooperation is to suppress and exploit the rest of the society. This also applies to the notorious example of the Mafia: Mafia *is* a form of social capital as it embodies a highly efficient social network, creates strong norms of honour and reciprocity, and successfully overcomes collective action problems of all.[12]

High levels of social capital can also be a difficult obstacle in the transitional phase from traditional societies to modern democracies. Afghanistan and Albania, for example, are not societies with an especially low level of social capital. In both societies there are at least partially well-functioning social networks, relations of emotional commitment, trust and reciprocity, and the capacity for collective action embodied in traditional structures of families, kinship, clans, and tribes – all of them embedded in a highly respected social and religious tradition which contains values and norms with a considerable degree of legitimacy. The problem here is clearly not a problem of lacking social capital – the problem is the lack of the *right kind* of social capital. Social capital of a traditional sort may be very efficient in promoting cooperation and trust in certain groups, but at the same time it can be also very efficient in preventing cooperation and trust *outside* these groups. It is a long-held and quite common opinion that China provides another example of a kind of social capital that bars the way to progress by privileging only closed and traditional communities and thereby preventing the development of a modern market economy. We will come back to this prejudice soon.

We have to acknowledge that social capital can have a dark, even sinister side.[13] Networks, reciprocity, trust, emotional commitment and altruistic behaviour are good only in the right context. Indeed, some of the communities that have been able to educate their members successfully to behave unselfishly

---

[12] See Gambetta (1993).

[13] See Hardin (1995); Levi (1996); Portes/Landolt (1996); Adler/Kwon (2000).

and to sacrifice their individual interests to the common cause are responsible for the largest catastrophes in the history of mankind.

But also less dramatic excesses prove that well-developed forms of social capital could make a political order and societal life worse instead of making it work. Nepotism, corruption, rent-seeking, or partisanship are all forms of behaviour which are detrimental and destructive to a society. *And* they are all forms of behaviour which are, as a rule, more successful if carried out in a group as a collective enterprise than as an individual effort (see Baurmann 2005). Not surprisingly we find that empirically all manner of social capital is built around those activities – ranging from loose networks which bring a few people together for a short period of time, to small associations with horizontal relations between members connected by trust and reciprocity, up to large organisations with formal rules and a strict hierarchy. The more developed and the more efficient those forms of social capital are, the worse for outsiders and for society as a whole.

The dark side of social capital is not always connected with obviously condemnable behaviour such as trying to bribe or seek rents at public expense. Negative externalities whereby social capital is used to facilitate collusion among a group can also be generated when particularistic demands are put forward which cannot always be judged as morally wrong at the outset. Mobilization of people to realize their religious visions or to promote the interests of their race or ethnicity can be rooted in moral convictions and personal virtues and can create social capital in a paradigmatic form. Groups and associations like these will often embody dense social networks, high levels of personal trust, altruistically driven reciprocity and generosity, and a strong intrinsic motivation to make sacrifices for the common good.

These forms of social capital will, nevertheless, more often subvert rather than strengthen a society. The reason for this is obvious: associations like these are not "bridging" and "outward-orientated", but centred around people of the same kind or origin and promoting goods which are exclusively valuable to the members of the group. The more successful these associations are, the less their members will have the incentive to cooperate and bargain with other groups on a common basis, but will see the chance to enforce their particularistic interests at the expense of others. Thus social capital in this variant erects barriers of mistrust between people instead of uniting them and contributes to aims and goods which can very easily conflict with the aims and goods of the society as a whole. Associational groups of this kind will trigger a vicious circle because they undermine shared interests in a society and thereby create incentives for other groups – who, by themselves, would have no genuine reason to develop in this way – to concentrate exclusively on *their* members and *their* particularistic interests as well.

Social networks, emotional commitment and trust alone are therefore not sufficient for a desirable spill-over effect beyond group boundaries. Social capital can also have a dark side as it can embody networks which are not bridges bringing different kinds of people together to promote joint interests, but instruments of separation erecting borders and barriers, and providing an exclusive resource to a special group. Instead of encouraging reciprocal and trustworthy behaviour beyond the confines of a group or association, social capital can contribute to a restriction of reciprocity and trust and lead to an increase in opportunism and distrust outside the respective groups. Social capital can lack positive spill-over effects because it only promotes commitment to the "club" good of a group rather than to the public good of the society as a whole.[14] Emotional commitment internally to a group can be combined with antipathy towards outsiders and trust could remain particularistic and only encompass the members of one's own group. Clusters of this kind will more likely embody "bonding" than "bridging" social capital and be networks in which the internal strong ties are fostered by the homogeneity of their members. From this "black", negative list results a "white", positive list with those attributes which prima facie can contribute to a spill-over of the social capital of specific groups and communities that is valuable to the society at large.[15] Thus it is decisive that social networks are not exclusive resources and instruments of separation by which artificial borders are erected against goods and services. The different clusters must instead be embedded in a comprehensive network by which "bridges" are built between the different groups thereby unfolding a potential of inclusion.[16]

We can conclude that the relation between the formal institutions of a political and legal order and the informal social institutions which create the social capital of a society is more complex and differentiated than it may ap-

---

[14] See Stolle (1998).

[15] See Stolle/Rochon (1998); Warren (2001); Paxton (2002).

[16] Baurmann (2006); (2008); Granovetter (1973).

pear at first sight: social institutions can support state institutions in motivating people to behave in ways that are conducive to the stability and flexibility of the formal institutions of a society – this was the main focus of early social capital theory. But social institutions can also erode state institutions in motivating people to behave contrary to the rules and laws that are enacted by political and legal organs. Social institutions can compete with state institutions by creating social relationships and social norms as alternatives to the existing laws and institutions. And social institutions can substitute state institutions if state institutions are defective or too weak to enforce a political or legal order.

We would like to discuss this more complicated picture by means of a concrete and highly interesting example: the example of China and its social, political and economic history over the last 40 years.

Guanxi as the Chinese Social Capital

After the Cultural Revolution the Chinese people found themselves in a dreadful situation and realized that they could not count on the Communist state for a better life. They then began to revive the resources of traditional social institutions in China which are based on personal networks and emotional bonds. Such relationships are defined as *guanxi*. The influential Chinese anthropologist, Fei Xiaotong, characterizes guanxi as a "differential mode of association" which he illustrates with the image of "concentric circles formed when a stone is thrown into a lake".[17] The closer persons are to the actor in the centre, the more easily the actor will trust them and treat them preferentially. But unlike familism or other particularistic relationships which are firmly embedded in kinship, affinity or geographical origin, guanxi is an open and flexible institution. Under market conditions it is a rule that the wider one's social network is, the easier it is to get access to profitable economic transactions.

For this reason the Chinese exploit every chance to extend guanxi in various ways: social occasions such as birthdays, weddings or funerals are taken as opportunities to enhance existing guanxi relations. Mutual friends function as "trust intermediaries" and form bridges to new guanxi partners. Simultaneously the Chinese nowadays are ready to turn away from persons who have earned

---

[17] Fei (1992), 63.

a bad reputation even when they are genetically or geographically close. So it is still accurate to state that in the networks of guanxi people are treated particularistically in regard to their position in "the differential mode of association". But these networks can expand dynamically and the position of people in them can change depending on their compliance to the rules of guanxi.

Some scholars consider guanxi as a kind of instrumental relationship which depends mainly on mutual material interests.[18] But it is an essential feature of guanxi that its instrumental functionality is inseparably linked with its expressive components, especially *renqing* (personal feeling) and *mianzi* (face).[19] It is an efficient strategy in China to utilize the rules of renqing and mianzi as ways and means of influence and manipulation, especially when people with few economic and political resources try to fraternize with people of a higher social rank. This strategy is successful because no matter how economically wealthy or politically powerful certain persons are, they have to be responsive to the requests from their friends and partners in order to maintain renqing and mianzi. The instrumental value of guanxi depends on the fact that Chinese people are willing to invest economic and political resources in the maintenance of guanxi not only for the material profit of long lasting cooperation, but also out of moral commitment and for nurturing a favorable personal reputation. Therefore, instead of being either an instrumental or an expressive social relation guanxi should be understood as a "mixed tie" of instrumentality and expressivity.

It is widely accepted that in China guanxi is the most valuable social capital in everyday life.[20] However, it is quite controversial which effect guanxi has at a wider societal level. According to Max Weber,[21] the inward feature of Chinese social networks erects borders and barriers between groups rather than bridging them. And this is why a modern market economy could not be born in China. Contemporary social scientists such as Fukuyama hold the same

---

[18] See Sun (1996).

[19] Reqing refers to the expressive feelings between interacting individuals, e.g. empathy. Mianzi refers to personal dignity and reputation. One can lose mianzi by either refusing to do a favour for friends or being refused by friends. More information of renqing and mianzi see Hwang 1987.

[20] See Yang (1994).

[21] Weber (1968).

opinion. He argues that guanxi is responsible for the small scale of business and the widespread corruption in public sectors in China.[22] From this perspective guanxi actually destroys the foundation of a well-functioning society and its institutions instead of promoting it.

However, the development of China in the last 30 years tells a much more differentiated story. The Chinese economy has been growing at an average of almost 10 % since the beginning of the economic reforms in 1978 – three times the global average. It is hard to believe that a society with a serious shortage of mutual trust and limited skills of cooperation is capable of achieving such an astounding success. For this reason some scholars admit that guanxi actually contributes to the efficiency of economic transactions in China.[23] Moreover, the extremely adverse political and legal environment at the beginning of the reforms[24] suggests that the boom of the Chinese private economy in the 1980s is to a great extent to be attributed to social factors – more specifically, to the social institution of guanxi rather than to political and legal institutions of the state.

Therefore, instead of assigning guanxi exclusively and statically to the "black" or "white" list of social capital, we will analyze its development as an adaptation to a dynamic social and institutional framework. Guanxi is not a static institution and its role as social capital has undergone significant changes during the last decades of Chinese history. Especially its relation to the political and legal institutions has altered significantly and developed from an institution that promoted the establishment of an efficient market economy in confrontation with the political system to an institution that strengthens corrupt relations between entrepreneurs and state officials and weakens economic productivity. This historical clue will help us to gain a better understanding of guanxi as social capital and its complex interdependencies with the political and legal institutions in China.

---

[22] Fukuyama (1995a), Fukuyama (1995b).

[23] See Wong/Chan (1999); Wong/Leung (2001); Yeung/Tung (1996).

[24] In the 1980s there was not only no formal protection of private property rights, but the Communist Party of China (CCP) also imposed extensive restrictions on the private sector. Any economic activity crossing these lines would be punished in the name of "speculation". We will discuss this later in this paper.

Evolving the Chinese Market Economy

According to theories in the tradition of institutional economics well-defined property rights are the prerequisite of a flourishing market economy. In a society without an effective legal order and enforceable rules everybody is involved in "the war of all against all" and thus any form of efficient economic exchange is hampered. The exit option from such a "Hobbesian jungle" is to establish powerful state institutions that can guarantee a stable order of cooperation. Seen from this perspective, the economic performance of a society depends vitally on the efficacy of coercive instruments of the state in protecting private property and punishing those who disobey the laws. Douglass North consequently assumes that the rise of the Western World would not have been possible without its efficient institutional protection of private property.[25]

However, the growth of the Chinese private economy is quite different from its western counterparts. At the beginning of the economic reform in the 1970s the CPC (Communist Party of China) decided to shift its focus from political campaign to centrally administered economic development. State-owned enterprises were the main concern and as at that time the Party had no intention of encouraging private enterprises or a market economy in general. Consequently, during the 1970s and 1980s no laws were enacted in order to protect market contracts or private property. If Chinese citizens wanted to conduct private transactions at that time, they had to act in a "Hobbesian jungle" where opportunist behaviour or the breach of contracts was not prevented or punished by formal institutions.

But not only "predation" in the "Hobbesian jungle" threatened the first generation of Chinese entrepreneurs. There was also discrimination and persecution by state organs – the "Leviathan". Heavy tax was imposed on private enterprises and time-consuming bureaucratic procedures had to be followed. Private entrepreneurs were not allowed to employ more than seven employees before 1987 and, in addition, their economic activities were discreetly controlled by the authority. Any private transactions not complying with these prescriptions would be punished as "crimes of speculation", a kind of crime that was codified in 1979 and eliminated only in 1997. According to the study

---

[25] North/Thomas (1973).

by Xiaobo Wu[26] around 30,000 people were convicted of the crime of speculation in 1982, most of whom were successful private entrepreneurs. Obviously, the original purpose of the Party was to protect the state-owned and collective economy from competition in the market. The fact that the private economy finally grew "out of the plan" (see Naughton 1995) was unexpected and unwanted.

Therefore, rebutting conventional wisdom, the legal institutionalization of private property followed the growth of the private economy in China, not the other way round.[27] In order to understand the Chinese economic "miracle", it is necessary to focus on the social institutions that made private economic activity and the development of markets possible without legal authorization and a formal protection of property rights.

The greatest challenge to the first generation of Chinese entrepreneurs was to protect private property from the threat of "Leviathan", namely from the Communist state and its jurisdiction. Hundreds of thousands of entrepreneurs were doing business "illegally" at risk of imprisonment. In view of this difficult situation, Chinese entrepreneurs came up with organizational innovations to feign collective ownership which could save them from prosecution by the state. The two most important innovations were shareholding corporatives and "red hat" enterprises. In a shareholding corporative several families joined together to run a business. All the family members were owners as well as the employees of the corporative. A "red hat" enterprise was a private enterprise that was registered as a collective one. Nominally these enterprises belonged to the local governments but were actually under the control and part of the "informal" property of individuals. In both cases the enterprises founded by private citizens were disguised as being in collective ownership.

That does not mean that faked collective ownership was without dangers and risks. As a new form of economic organization, a shareholding corporative was not clearly defined as a collective enterprise by the central authority until 1990. Thus its survival and development relied mainly on the local policies of the cadres on-site. In the same way "red hat" enterprises were neither clearly encouraged nor forbidden by the CPC, leaving the local governments plenty of room for dealing with this novel form of economic business at their own dis-

---

[26] Wu (2007), 85.

[27] See Li/Li/Zhang (2000); Lin (1989); Naughton (1995); Nee/Opper (2012).

cretion. As Donald Clarke remarks, local party officials and bureaucrats could easily regain the actual control over these enterprises by changing their policies. The private owners of the enterprises would be demoted "to mere employees with no right to a return on the capital that they had invested".[28] However, local cadres normally did not exploit the situation for their private gains but instead protected and encouraged these institutional inventions in many areas from below. Because of this support from local governments, shareholding corporative and "red hat" enterprises became very successful and popular all over the country in the 1980s. More remarkably, they contributed a great part to the national economic growth although the policies of the central government in that period were extremely unstable and unpredictable.[29]

Why were the local cadres in fact willing to help private entrepreneurs despite their extremely dominant position in relation to these entrepreneurs? The crucial factor was their joint embeddedness in the social institution of guanxi and their subjection to the same social forces created by this institution. Unlike economic or political power, the social power of guanxi is generated by personal interactions in everyday life. It is a binding social obligation for Chinese to maintain affective and reliable relationships with their relatives, friends and partners via regular gift-giving and invitations to banquets. Through these frequent exchanges and their contribution to stable interpersonal ties and reciprocal commitments an effective social power is created which can trump political and economic power. Especially in smaller towns and villages this power can be particularly strong because people are closely connected through kin, marriage and long-lasting personal acquaintance.

Therefore, in the aftermath of the Cultural Revolution rural cadres found it more and more difficult to maintain and make use of their formal power. They were integrated in the social institutions of their communities and social pressure caused them to accept bargains and compromises with villagers who were their relatives and friends. When state policies came into direct conflict with the interests of the communities, the cadres usually chose to protect the interests of local people by deceiving the state officials. Observing this phenomenon Yun-xiang Yan concludes: "the new pattern of political behavior among the rural cadres might create an informal mechanism to counterbalance and resist

[28] Clarke (1991), 305.

[29] See Nee/Opper (2012); Tsai (2007); Whiting (2006).

state control of society and the negative effects of central policy".[30] Similarly, Yusheng Peng (2004) found a solid and positive correlation between the solidarity of kinship and the prosperity of private economy in Chinese villages: the more closely villagers are socially connected to each other, the more likely local cadres submit to the social norms of guanxi and the better the local economy develops. The fact that local cadres in rural areas are particularly committed to their fellow-citizens due to the strength of social networks in these areas can partly explain why in the early 1980s private entrepreneurship was developing most vibrantly in the poorest and most rural regions of China.[31]

In dealing with local cadres Chinese entrepreneurs successfully utilized the norms and rules of guanxi. For example, instead of offering direct bribes, private entrepreneurs tried to produce or intensify emotional bonds between the cadres and themselves via gift-giving and invitations to banquets, which gave rise to obligations and indebtedness. The skills and techniques of creating genuine guanxi relationships are known in China as guanxixue (guanxi studies) which refers to the capability of establishing and manipulating guanxi for one's own purposes. With this capability private entrepreneurs could influence relevant cadres even when they had no relationship of blood and affinity. As Mayfair Yang observes:

"Gift-giving creates a microcosmic world in which hierarchical relations are to a certain extent reversed. Donors become the moral superiors of recipients, who now owe favors to their donor. Symbolic capital compensates for the lack of material, office, or political capital. Thus face and the morality of reciprocity, obligation, and indebtedness become in a sense the ammunition of the weak. This mobilization of the forces of gift morality effects a subtle displacement of the potency by diversifying the state economy's principle of classification and distribution by rank."[32]

From this point of view guanxi was the most powerful "weapon of the weak" (Scott 1985). Through a sophisticated use of this weapon officially discriminated private entrepreneurs successfully created a "microcosmos" in which they could counter the political power of the central authority as well as avoid the possible economic extortion by the local governments. Guanxi helped them to

---

[30] Yan (1995), 230.

[31] In regard to the robust development of the private economy in the rural areas of China see Huang 2008.

[32] Yang (1994), 206.

create a small safe environment in an unfriendly political and legal institutional framework and to achieve a thriving private economy in China.

In a similar way the "microcosmos" of guanxi also helped the first generation of Chinese entrepreneurs to deal with the second challenge they faced in the early years of the private economy in China, namley to secure their economic transactions against fraud and deception by private parties without any legal protection. As already emphasized, if the Chinese wanted to conduct private transactions at this time, they had to act in a world where opportunist behaviour or the breach of contracts would hardly be punished by the formal institutions of a legal order. But the norms and rules of guanxi were not only strong social forces that integrated state officials in an efficient network of mutual trust and commitment, they also created social capital that provided a dense web of stable social relations in which economic exchange could successfully take place without the protective shield of institutionalized property rights and a reliable contract law. Stable interpersonal relations and reciprocal commitments which are created by guanxi produce binding obligations and affective ties between entrepreneurs and state officials but also between the private actors on the market in their economic transactions.

Establishing the Chinese Market Economy

In the 1980s the Chinese private entrepreneurs had achieved tremendous success and changed the whole economic landscape of China. Realizing reluctantly that the bottom-up privatization had greatly stimulated the national economy despite its inconsistency with the Communist ideology, the central authority began to legalize the private firms and to gradually establish a market economy from the end of the 1980s. For example, in 1987 the restriction of a maximum of seven employees in private firms was removed and in 1997 the crime of "speculation" was eliminated from criminal law. The property rights of private entrepreneurs were officially admitted and protected by the state authority, thus rendering fake collective ownerships superfluous.[33] Some scholars believed that guanxi would lose its importance once the formal protection of private property became available (Guthrie 1998). This prediction failed. De-

---

[33] See Kung (1999).

spite the dramatic changes in the formal institutional environment in China, guanxi still plays an important role in everyday life and economic contexts.[34] Still today foreign investors are advised to learn the rules of guanxi – namely the rules of mianzi and renqing – if they want to build trust relationships with their Chinese partners (Buckley/Clegg/Tan 2006).

The persistence of guanxi results from two facts. Firstly, although the protection of private property rights was finally added in a constitutional amendment in 2004, the enforcement of formal laws in China is still weak, costly and unreliable. To press a charge against a person for a criminal or civil offence and realize a conviction is time-consuming and incalculable, especially when government officials are involved.[35] It is more efficient and less risky to resolve conflicts or problems via personal networks rather than through formal procedures.

The second reason is that even in a developed market economy guanxi can still contribute significantly to a well-functioning and sustainable order of economic cooperation. It has often been argued that guanxi as a social institution is incompatible with a modern market because guanxi mechanisms are restricted to local networks that divide markets into small segments. These restrictions would prevent the advantages of an efficient division of labour and large companies with economies of scale would not be feasible.[36] However, as Yang suggests, guanxi should be recognized as "a multifaceted ever-changing set of practices".[37] On the one hand, market relationships are structured by guanxi, yet on the other hand, the dynamics of markets force guanxi to evolve. After the successful establishment of a market economy the main challenge of Chinese entrepreneurs is not the *intensity* of guanxi but its *extensity*: the larger and wider social networks of persons become, the more chances they will have at the marketplace to establish profitable and stable economic relationships. Under these conditions ties of kinship and affinity alone could no longer satisfy private entrepreneurs who wanted to expand their business and to seize the opportunities a growing market offers.

---

[34] Su/Littlefield (2001); Yang (2002).

[35] Nee/Opper (2012), 7-8.

[36] Fukuyama (1995b); Weber (1968).

[37] Yang (2002), 459.

The most practical way to enlarge one's networks is to use the social capital of an existing guanxi. For example, one can establish guanxi with a stranger via a mutual friend. A person will trust a stranger if a mutual friend forms a bridge and a bond between them: all persons in this new triangle have to respect the mianzi of each other because humiliating the new acquaintance – e.g. by refusing a request – will also hurt the old friend and if one owes a renqing-favor of his or her friend, he or she will usually feel responsible for the newly introduced stranger. In this way trust and commitment can be transferred by intermediaries from one relationship to another. Mianzi and renqing function as universal media which can flow from hand to hand thereby creating widespread and inclusive social and economic networks.

Therefore, even in a modern market economy guanxi as a social institution is effective in promoting the social virtues of cooperation and trustworthiness and thereby reducing the costs and risks of economic exchanges and promoting the overall functionality of a market. Some scholars thus assume that guanxi-mediated market processes are to be seen as a genuine alternative to the western market system. Moreover, with regard to low transaction costs and strong commitment guanxi may be even more efficient than the western style market mechanisms.[38]

Given the ongoing weakness of legal institutions and the high degree of adaptability of guanxi to the demands of modern markets it makes sense for Chinese entrepreneurs to stick to the traditional social institutions when looking for security and protection of their interests. The more entrepreneurs try to solve problems via personal ties, the more refined their skills of guanxi become. And the greater the resources of guanxi which are accumulated, the more reluctant they will be to resort to formal procedures. In this way the social institution guanxi has managed successfully to substitute suboptimal and defective formal institutions and fulfil functions that from a standard point of view are the exclusive responsibility of state organs.

---

[38] See Lovett/Simmons/Kali (1999).

Undermining the Chinese Market Economy

However, guanxi has also revealed dark sides as social capital. In supporting economic transactions it strengthens social virtues of cooperation, facilitates mutual trust between exchange partners and increases the level of sociability. But when political agents are involved, guanxi tends to establish patron-client relationships which jeopardize economic efficiency by distorting market mechanisms and favouring preferential intervention. Actually, pursuing political patronage via guanxi is not a new phenomenon concomitant with the market economy in China. This strategy was already widely utilized in socialist factories in Mao's era when the workers tried to build affective personal ties with their leaders for the sake of political, material and career advantages.[39] In the 1980s, as already described above, Chinese peasant entrepreneurs successfully forced local cadres to provide a "political shelter" against the state with the help of personal connections in clan and kinship.[40] But while in Mao's era patron-client relationships actually supported the CPC in incorporating the society into the communist system,[41] and in the 1980s stimulated the economic growth of the whole country by establishing competing social institutions that promoted the emergence of markets, patron-client relationships based on the guanxi culture have now become negative factors that hinder the further political and economic development of China.

As the institutional environment changed, political favours that were formerly used for securing private property or protection against state control came to signify new messages for the market participants: the opportunity for additional personal advantages that could be gained through corruption in politicized markets. For example, on the stock and real estate markets which are strictly constrained by the government, market participants are tempted to establish reliable guanxi with relevant cadres in order to gain more profit through their special protection. With the help of cadres one can acquire a personal fortune by buying personal stocks with public funds or renting land at extremely low costs.[42] The seductive prospects of realizing huge profits by

---

[39] See Walder (1986).

[40] See Peng (2004).

[41] Walder (1986), 123.

[42] Gong (1997), 279.

the circumvention of market mechanisms motivate many Chinese entrepreneurs to invest in the competition for political power instead of in the competition for customers thereby destroying the most important foundation of the "wealth of nations".

Obviously, in this "power game"[43] only a small fraction of the participants can win, while most of them will lose. But, as Chenting Su and James Littlefield observe, "even though power is quite scarce in today's China, the populace is still actively having a hand in carving up monopolized interests by means of their specific qinyou[44] guanxi web".[45] Why are the Chinese still clinging to such ineffective competition even though the overall return from this form of guanxi is dramatically decreasing? The reason is the social embeddedness of corruption. Even though the purposes and consequences of patron-client relationships in China have changed, renqing and mianzi are still the most important norms of these relations. Thus, political power in China is not arbitrarily abused but distributed according to the rules of guanxi. This means that the relation between entrepreneurs and cadres is not simply an exchange of money and favors. One famous example is Lai Changxin, the central figure in an enormous corruption scandal that exploded in the Chinese city of Xiamen in 1998. Having started from a lower social class Lai successfully built guanxi connections with dozens of local cadres. With their help he quickly became the most powerful and wealthy man in Xiamen by smuggling luxury cars and entire tanker-loads of oil into China. Mark Granovetter, inspired by the story of Lai, comments:

"Elaborate systems of gift giving, banquets, entertainment, and favors keyed to the highly particular needs of officials are developed. Whereas a cash payment to the official would be considered an insult, the banquets and special favors can be thought of as a form of deference, which the higher-status person can imagine is owed to him."[46]

The social embeddedness of corruption has two effects. Firstly, the role of guanxi in patron-client relationships provides chances even for those people who come from lower classes. As the story of Lai tells, access to higher-ranking cadres is not exclusive to social elites. Anyone who acquires sufficient skills of

---

[43] See Hwang (1987).

[44] Qinyou is a Chinese word meaning relatives and friends.

[45] Su/Littlefield (2001), 205.

[46] Granovetter (2007), 158.

guanxi has the chance to improve his or her social status. Because of the wide range of social networks, most Chinese can establish guanxi even with high profile cadres via intermediaries. Secondly, guanxi restrains cadres from abusing their political power ad libitum. Cadres do not only value financial returns but also their personal reputation in the relevant social networks. They like to think that they are not actually bribed but simply receive gifts from friends and returned favours. Because of these social and moral constraints, the behaviour of cadres in China is predictable and maneuverable which is different from the corruption in Africa where officials exploit their power arbitrarily and without scruples.[47]

Therefore, even though most Chinese acknowledge the notorious deficiency of their political and legal institutions, they are quite confident that they have sufficient skills and capacities to utilize their guanxi resources and take advantage of the deficient political system to secure their personal interests (see Sun 1996, 30). In this way guanxi not only undermines the mechanisms of a market economy but also discourages people from demanding further institutional development. This is one reason why, contradictory to the prognoses of many scholars,[48] China has failed to evolve into a democratic society after its astounding economic achievements and instead become a "capitalism without democracy" (Tsai 2007).

Interdependencies between Legal and Social Institutions

The experience of China supports social capital theory in its central claim that political and legal institutions are not the only forces that affect the trajectory of societal development but that social institutions like guanxi have a strong impact on the dynamics of a society and the performance of the formal state institutions. However, the Chinese case also makes clear that the relation between the formal institutions of the state and the informal institutions of social capital are complex and diverse. As we have seen, social norms that are enforced by guanxi relationships in everyday life can neutralize the economic and political advantages of the ruling powers and provide ordinary citizens with

---

[47] See Heberer (2005), 334.

[48] Hu (2000); Lollar (1997).

opportunities to initiate a progressive development of the economic system. However, the same social institution can in other contexts discourage the potential challengers of a political order and undermine economic efficiency and progress.

To achieve a more differentiated picture of the possible relations between formal state institutions and informal social institutions it is helpful to adapt a fourfold table proposed by Gretchen Helmke and Steven Levitsky.[49] They suggest using two dimensions: whether a social institution is convergent or divergent in relation to state institutions which are, in turn, divided into effective and ineffective institutions with respect to their more or less successful enforcement:

Table 4: Interdependencies between Legal and Social Institutions

	Effective state institutions	Ineffective state institutions
Convergent social institutions	*Supporting*	*Substituting*
Divergent social institutions	*Eroding*	*Competing*

Source: Helmke/Levitsky (2004), 728 (slightly changed)

This typology can enhance our analysis of institutional development. We can recapitulate the institutional evolution in China with its ongoing changes between formal and informal institutions by using this table with the different outcomes it signifies.

In Mao's era (1949–1976) the most important formal institution in China was the Communist political system whose rules and norms were strictly enforced. Many Chinese people were convinced that the CPC would establish a wealthy communist society. Social institutions like universalistic comradeship were promoted and widely accepted for the purpose of the realization of a Communist society. In the spirit of comradeship study groups were established for studying and spreading Marxist-Leninist theory and the thoughts of Mao Zedong, and "revolution groups" were established for promoting the class campaigns. These social institutions were convergent with effective state insti-

---

[49] Helmke/Levitsky (2004).

tutions and supported the CPC in reshaping China into a Communist state. They later developed into the radical political movement of the Cultural Revolution.

After the disastrous economic failure of the Communist system the Chinese became tired of political movements and sceptical about the economic prospects of a centrally planned command economy. Chinese people started to revitalize traditional social institutions and developed the social capital of guanxi independent of the state. As mentioned above, on the basis of this social capital private entrepreneurs invented "shareholding cooperatives" and "red hat enterprises" in the 1980s in order to broaden their business and avoid being accused of the "crime of speculation". These practices did not openly contradict the laws and on the surface were compatible with the legal order. But they violated the "spirit" of the laws and the original intention of the CPC which at the beginning of the reform tried to restrict the development of a private economy. Eventually the people managed to establish informal property rights on the basis of a working social institution that successfully confronted the state institutions. With the help of guanxi, divergent social institutions were established that started to undermine and erode the state control of the economy.

After the market economy was finally introduced as the fundament of the national economy, laws were enacted for the protection of private property and the enforcement of contracts. However, guanxi was not completely replaced by formal rules and institutions because of their weak and uncertain enforcement. Chinese entrepreneurs therefore still use guanxi to ensure economic transactions and create stable business relations. Guanxi is a convergent social institution in this case because it is compatible with formal rules and procedures but also a substitute for state institutions which are not effective enough to create a sufficiently stable environment for economic actions.

What we see now, however, is the transformation of guanxi into a new form of divergent and competing social institution. In the 1980s guanxi relations with political cadres were used to gradually establish a market economy and thereby promote economic efficiency. Today guanxi networks in the political realm are used more and more as instruments for rent-seeking and receiving privileges, to circumvent market competition or evade legal prescriptions. This development endangers economic productivity and undermines the efficiency of market mechanisms – just the contrary effect guanxi had in the era of the development of a market economy in China.

Many social scientists acknowledge that a gradual process of reform is the secret of China's success.[50] At the beginning Chinese entrepreneurs tried to circumvent formal rules that restricted private economic activity. They revitalized and renewed the social institutions of guanxi for this purpose. These social institutions successfully eroded the Communist economic order and managed to compete directly with the political and legal institutions as the state's power waned. Finally, the relevant laws were changed in acknowledgment of the factual developments. In this way the radical institutional changes in China were realized piece by piece through the institutional inventions from below and the official recognition from above. Thus, bottom-up initiative, experimentation, learning, and adaptation form the core of the institutional changes in China.

However, this is not the whole story and not the only lesson Chinese history taught us about the relationship between formal state institutions and informal social institutions. The chain of causes must be analysed not only from social capital to legal and political institutions but also vice versa. If our analysis is correct and the dark side of guanxi as social capital is gaining momentum in China as an effective instrument of socially embedded corruption then this development must be combatted by enforcing an efficient rule of law.

As we said at the outset, the overall state of a society is always an equilibrium between the forces of formal and informal institutions. But if a society is in the grip of the dark sides of social institutions, a new and improved equilibrium cannot be initiated without the intervention of the legal and political institutions of the state – which is especially challenging if these institutions are not supported by convergent social institutions: that is the message from social capital theory that remains valid.

Insofar it is not surprising that China has failed to stimulate a new round of effective political and legal reforms up to now. Public authorities are often compromised via guanxi and most Chinese still believe that they can take advantage of the *status quo* using their guanxi skills and resources. Further institutional reforms will not happen before most Chinese realize that only a small amount of players can win in the "power game" but that all could benefit from

---

[50] Jefferson/Rawski (1994); Naughton (1995); Rawski (1999).

302

a firm rule of law. At this point one must hope that social capital will enter the stage once again in its heroic role and that Chinese citizens will create a social force to influence state policies to the better. Because of the strict control of the government, there are few civil organizations similar to such associations in Western democracies, but citizens in China are as always connected via personal ties and social networks in their guanxi relations. Maybe guanxi will again demonstrate its flexibility and adaptability and acquire a new meaning in shaping the social fabric of an independent civic realm in which the interests and preferences of citizens are formed and articulated. In this way a civil society of its own kind may be realized in China, different in its foundation and profile from Western society but perhaps as powerful and beneficial as it was during the realization of a market economy in the face of counteracting political forces.

Conclusion

We started our paper with a theoretical discussion of social capital. In order to gain a more complex and appropriate understanding of social capital and its dimensions and impacts, we referred to the Chinese experience of the last 40 years. The tremendous success China has achieved as well as the huge challenges it now faces could in great part be attributed to Chinese-style social capital: guanxi, which exerts both a positive and negative influence on the transition of Chinese society. We learn from this study that first, social capital cannot be viewed simply as an exclusively benign social resource, second, that the societal impact of social capital not only depends on its own features but also on its economic and political context, and, finally, that a promising and underexposed field of research lies in the dynamic interaction between formal institutions such as the rule of law and social capital as a social institution: how they conflict, coexist and adapt to each other. Insight into this process may improve our understanding of institutional change and the determining factors of its notorious path dependency.

References

Adler, Paul S./Kwon, Seok-Woo (2000): Social Capital: The Good, the Bad, and the Ugly. In: Lesser, Eric E. L. (ed.): Knowledge and Social Capital. Boston. 89–115.

Banfield, Edward C. (1958): The Moral Basis of a Backward Society. New York.

Baurmann, Michael (1999): Solidarity as a Social Norm and as a Constitutional Norm. In: Bayertz, Kurt (ed.): Solidarity. Dordrecht. 243–272.

Baurmann, Michael (2000): Legal Authority as a Social Fact. In: Law & Philosophy (19), 247–262.

Baurmann, Michael (2002): Vertrauen und Anerkennung. In: Maurer, Andrea/Schmid, Michael (eds.): Neuer Institutionalismus. Frankfurt. 107–133.

Baurmann, Michael (2005): Korruption, Recht und Moral. In: von Alemann, Ulrich (ed.): Dimensionen politischer Korruption. In: Politische Vierteljahresschrift, Sonderheft 35, 164–182.

Baurmann, Michael (2006): Markt und Soziales Kapital. In: Ballestrem, Karl K. G./Gerhardt, Volker (eds.): Politisches Denken Jahrbuch. Berlin. 129–155.

Baurmann, Michael (2008): Political Norms, Markets and Social Capital. In: Kühnelt, Jörg (ed.): Political Legitimization without Morality? Dordrecht. 161–180.

Brennan, Geoffrey/Hamlin, Alan (1995): Economizing on Virtue. In: Constitutional Political Economy 6(1), 35–56.

Brennan, Geoffrey/Hamlin, Alan (2000): Democratic Devices and Desires. Cambridge.

Buckley, Peter J./Clegg, Jeremy/Tan, Hui (2006): Cultural Awareness in Knowledge Transfer to China: The Role of Guanxi and Mianzi. In: Journal of World Business 41(3), 275–288.

Clarke, Donald C. (1991): Regulation and Its Discontents. Understanding Economic Law in China. In: Stanford Journal of International Law 28, 283–322.

Coleman, James (1988): Social Capital in the Creation of Human Capital. In: American Journal of Sociology 94, 95–120.

Dekker, Paul/Uslaner, Eric M. (eds.) (2001): Social Capital and Participation in Everyday Life. New York.

Etzioni, Amitai (1993): The Spirit of Community: Rights, Responsibilities, and the Communitarian Agenda. New York.

Fei, Xiaotong (1992): From the Soil: The Foundations of Chinese Society. Berkeley.

Fukuyama, Francis (1995a): Trust: Social Virtues and the Creation of Prosperity. New York.

Fukuyama, Francis (1995b): Social Capital and the Global Economy. In: Foreign Affairs, 89–103.

Gambetta, Diego (ed.) (1988): Trust: Making and Breaking Cooperative Relations. New York.

Gambetta, Diego (1993): The Sicilian Mafia: The Business of Private Protection. Cambridge.

Gong, Ting (1997): Forms and Characteristics of China's Corruption in the 1990s. Change with Continuity. In: Communist and Post-Communist Studies 30(3), 277–288.

Granovetter, Mark (1973): The Strength of Weak Ties. In: American Journal of Sociology 78(6), 1360–1380.

Granovetter, Mark (1985): Economic Action and Social Structure: The Problem of Embeddedness. In: American Journal of Sociology 91(3), 481–510.

Granovetter, Mark (2007): The Social Construction of Corruption. In: Nee, Victor/Swedberg, Richard (eds.): On Capitalism. Redwood City. 152–172.

Guthrie, Douglas (1998): The Declining Significance of Guanxi in China's Economic Transition. In: China Quarterly 154, 254–282.

Hardin, Russell (1995): One for All: The Logic of Group Conflict. Princeton.

Hirschman, Albert O. (2013): The Passions and the Interests. Political Arguments for Capitalism Before its Triumph. Princeton.

Heberer, Thomas (2005): Korruption in China. Dimensionen politischer Korruption, Beiträge zum Stand der internationalen Forschung. In: von Alemann, Ulrich (ed.): Dimensionen politischer Korruption. In: Politische Vierteljahresschrift, Sonderheft 35, 328–349.

Helmke, Gretchen/Levitsky, Steven (2004): Informal Institutions and Comparative Politics: A Research Agenda. In: Perspectives on Politics 2(4), 725–740.

Hu, Shaohua (2000): Explaining Chinese Democratization. Westport.

Huang, Yasheng (2008): Capitalism with Chinese Characteristics. Entrepreneurship and The State. Cambridge.

Hwang, Kwang-kuo (1987): Face and Favor: The Chinese Power Game. In: American Journal of Sociology 92(4), 944–974.

Jefferson, Gary H./Rawski, Thomas G. (1994): Enterprise Reform in Chinese Industry. In: The Journal of Economic Perspectives 8(2), 47–70.

Kung, James Kai-Sing (1999): The Evolution of Property Rights in Village Enterprise. In: Oi, Jean J. C./Walder, Andrew A. G. (eds.): Property Rights and Economic Reform in China. Redwood City. 95–122.

Levi, Margaret (1996): Social and Unsocial Capital: A Review Essay of Robert Putnam's Making Democracy Work. In: Politics & Society 24(1), 45–55.

Li, Shaomin/Li, Shuhe/Zhang, Weiying (2000): The Road to Capitalism. Competition and Institutional Change in China. In: Journal of Comparative Economics 28(2), 269–292.

Lin, Cyril Zhiren (1989): Open-ended Economic Reform in China. In: Nee, Victor/Stark, David/Selden, Mark Stark (eds.): Remaking the Economic Institutions of Socialism. Redwood City. 95–136.

Lollar, Xia Li (1997): China's Transition Toward a Market Economy, Civil Society, and Democracy. Bristol.

Lovett, Steve/Simmons, Lee C./Kali, Raja (1999): Guanxi Versus the Market: Ethics and Efficiency. In: Journal of International Business Studies 30(2), 231–247.

MacIntyre, Alasdair (2007): After Virtue. Indiana.

Misztal, Barbara A. (1996): Trust in Modern Societies: The Search for the Bases of Social Order. Cambridge.

Naughton, Barry (1995): Growing Out of the Plan: Chinese Economic Reform, 1978–1993. New York.

Nee, Victor/Opper, Sonja (2012): Capitalism From Below. Cambridge.

North, Douglass Cecil/Thomas, Robert Paul (1973): The Rise of the Western World. A New Economic History. Cambridge.

Ostrom, Elinor (1990): Governing the Commons: The Evolution of Institutions for Collective Action. Cambridge.

Ostrom, Elinor (2005): Understanding Institutional Diversity. Princeton.

Ostrom, Elinor/Ahn, T. K. (eds.) (2003): Foundations of Social Capital. Cheltenham.

Paxton, Pamela (2002): Social Capital and Democracy: An Interdependent Relationship. In: American Sociological Review 67, 254–277.

306

Peng, Yusheng (2004): Kinship Networks and Entrepreneurs in China's Transitional Economy. In: American Journal of Sociology 109(5), 1045–1074.

Pettit, Philip (1997): Republicanism: A Theory of Freedom and Government. Oxford.

Portes, A./Landolt, P. (1996): The Downside of Social Capital. In: The American Prospect 26, 18–22.

Putnam, Robert D. (1993): Making Democracy Work: Civic Traditions in Modern Italy. Princeton.

Putnam, Robert D. (2000): Bowling Alone. The Collapse and Revival of American Community. New York.

Rawski, Thomas G. (1999): Reforming China's Economy: What Have We Learned. In: The China Journal (41), 139–156.

Scott, James C. (1985): Weapons of the Weak: Everyday Forms of Peasant Resistance. New Haven.

Stolle, Dietlind (1998): Bowling Together, Bowling Alone: The Development of Generalized Trust in Voluntary Associations. In: Political Psychology 19(3), 497–525.

Stolle, Dietlind/Rochon, Thomas R. (1998): Are All Associations Alike? Member Diversity, Associational Type, and the Creation of Social Capital. In: American Behavioral Scientist 42(1), 47–65.

Su, Chenting/Littlefield, James E. (2001): Entering Guanxi: A Business Ethical Dilemma in Mainland China? In: Journal of Business Ethics 33(3), 199-210.

Sun, Liping (1996): "Guanxi", Social Relationship and Social Structure. In: Sociological Studies 5, 20–30.

Tsai, Kellee S. (2007): Capitalism without Democracy: The Private Sector in Contemporary China. New York.

Walder, Andrew G. (1986): Communist Neo-traditionalism: Work and Authority in Chinese Industry. Berkeley.

Warren, Mark R. (2001): Dry Bones Rattling: Community Building to Revitalize American Democracy. Princeton.

Weber, Max (1968): The Religion of China. Confucianism and Taoism. New York.

Whiting, Susan H. (2006): Power and Wealth in Rural China. The Political Economy of Institutional Change. New York.

Wong, Y. H./Chan, R. Y. (1999): Relationship Marketing in China: Guanxi, Favouritism and Adaptation. In: Journal of Business Ethics 22(2), 107–118.

Wong, Y. H./Leung, Thomas K. (2001): Guanxi: Relationship Marketing in A Chinese Context. New York.

Wu, Xiaobo (2007): Thirty Years of Chinese Business. Beijing: Zhongxin Press.

Yan, Yun-xiang (1995): Everyday Power Relations: Changes in a North China Village. In: Walder, Andrew A./Walder, G. (eds.): The Waning of the Communist State. Berkeley. 215–241.

Yang, Mayfair (2002): The Resilience of Guanxi and Its New Deployments: A Critique of Some New Guanxi Scholarship. In: The China Quarterly (170), 459–476.

Yang, Mayfair M. (1994): Gifts, Favors, and Banquets: The Art of Social Relationships in China. London.

Yeung, Irene Y.M./Tung, Rosalie L. (1996): Achieving Business Success in Confucian Societies. The Importance of Guanxi (Connections). In: Organizational Dynamics 25(2), 54–65.

The Role of the Press in the Construction of a Legitimate State in Vietnam Today

Nguyen Thi Thuy Hang/Phan Duy Anh

Introduction

The construction of state legitimacy has been for a long time now an inevitable trend in democratic politics in the modern world. Vietnam is not an exception to this general trend. In Vietnam's revolutionary reality, especially since the beginning of the renovation process in 1986, the question of how to construct a socialist and legitimate state of the people, by the people and for the people has been a regular issue, simultaneously a political objective and an urgent requirement of societal practice. The Vietnamese Communist Party is theoretically aware of the necessity to develop legitimate state patterns. It has led and mobilized many resources to enhance state legitimacy, including the press in particular, because it is "a sharp tool in attitude and culture of Party and State, and social and political organizations; both a voice of the party, the state, organizations and the people's forum."

An important characteristic of Vietnam's political system is the existence of only one ruling party. Therefore the establishment and development of legitimacy are under the leadership of the Communist Party which deeply influences the Vietnamese state: the party determines the principles of the state's organization and leads the entire governmental structure on a strategic level. The state at the same time is an agency of people's power which is led by the Party through basic principles for policies, but also by defining directives and conceptualizing laws. All these elements of the party's policies, including the further development of a socialist legitimate state of the people, by the people and for the people, are communicated to the Vietnamese population mainly through mass media, especially through media like the Party's newspapers. In this article, we summarize the results of a survey we conducted on important official gazettes: People Newspaper, Communist Magazine, and Electronic Newspaper of the Vietnam Communist Party, from January to August2014. These eight months anteceded the XI Congress term, an important period of time during which the issue of socialist legitimate state construction was intensively covered by the media. The first half of 2014 was also part of a so called "speeding- up- year" in order to achieve the goals of the Five-Year-Plan (2011–2015) and the first year to apply the Amended Constitution of 2013.

Let us briefly characterize these official gazettes. People Newspaper is

"a voice of the Party, the State; an honest voice of the Party and State within the country and in world opinion, etc.; simultaneously a people's forum, reflecting thoughts, needs, proposals and initiatives and experiences of the people and organizations, etc.; a political and ideological flag of the Party in the press arena of the country, the daily communication bridge of the Party, State with the masses."[1]

Communist Magazine is a theoretical and political agency of the Center of the Vietnamese Communist Party. Electronic Newspaper of the Vietnam Communist Party is

"a voice of the Party, State and Vietnamese people on the internet; an electronic information source of Center of Vietnamese Communist Party; a center integrating and exploiting information from the electronic information page of the Departments of Center Party, Center Office, Provincial committee of the Party, City committee of the Party, Party committee under Center; an information and communication portal between the Party and People."[2]

People Newspaper, Communist Magazine, and Electronic Newspaper of the Vietnam Communist Party belong to three different types of gazettes but they are significant for the Communist Party's and Vietnam's press agencies in general. Both, official party documents and the Constitution, assure that the Vietnamese State is a contract of its citizens as a socialist legitimate state of the people, by the people and for the people. In this state, all power belongs to the people. This means that democracy is the core of state-legitimacy in Vietnam. To develop it further a process is encouraged to institutionalize people's power

---

[1] Vietnamese Communist Party (2007), 398.

[2] http://dangcongsan.vn/cpv/Modules/News/gioi_thieu.aspx.

by laws in the state apparatus. The goal is to provide maximum benefits for the people. All activities of the state apparatus must abide by the Constitution and laws and must be guided by the spirit of the law. Every staff officer who is working in the state apparatus is required to be a man of "morals" and "talent" to meet the need of the task of socialist legitimate state construction. These issues are fundamental contents of articles writing about the legitimate state in Vietnam.

The paper uses both qualitative methods and quantitative methods, such as the participant observation and statistical methods. We collected 766 articles writing about the construction of a legitimate state in Vietnam from People Newspaper, Communist Magazine and Electronic Newspaper of the Vietnam Communist Party from January to August 2014, then classified and analyzed three main roles of the press First, the press on extending democracy, promoting the voice of the people; second, the press on the renovation and improvement of the state apparatus; and third, the press on improvements of staff, cadres and civil servants.

The Press on Extending Democracy, and Promoting the Voices of the People

In a democracy power belongs to the people and is exercised by it. This power is expressed in various areas of which the possession and control of state power is a central one. Democracy and law are two parts of a whole, as democracy is under the provision of law and an integral part of the entire legal framework. Legitimate state power belongs to the people; its exercise is a way of democratic expression itself. Democracy is only possible under the legality and humanity of a legitimate state. History has proven that "no legitimate state, no democracy". Democracy is based on laws as a fundament of democracy and tools to further improve it. The process to expand and implement social democratization is a process of developing and perfecting laws. To improve the legitimacy of the state is therefore directly related to the process of democratization.

In Vietnam, state power is delegated by the people, therefore, the nature of the relation between people's and state's power is the key issue of democratization. Under the Vietnamese Constitution the people decides about areas, purposes and ways of how state power is exercised. There are various ways of state power control, depending on location, function and task of each governmental organization. The control of state power by the mass media plays a decisive role. On the one hand the Vietnamese population is constantly provided with information about the government, as the state must publicize its activities. The 4th President of the United States of America James Madison once said: "A popular government, without popular information, is but a prelude to a farce or tragedy, or perhaps both."[3] On the other hand, the mass media create forums for the people to express their demands and thoughts.

Reporters and journalists with modern facilities are highly capable of detecting and reflecting people's expectations regarding state and society. Due to the starting process of further democratization in Vietnam, the above mentioned gazettes have begun to provide more information about governmental activities (reflected in the People's Daily newspaper by providing more information about activities of the leaders of party and state). They have also published/uploaded more articles than previously on democratic theory, and about opinions and expectations from the public. From January until August 2014, all three newspapers have posted a total of 162 articles on democratic theory and public opinion: People Newspaper has posted 96 articles (accounting for 60.5 %), Communist Magazine with 6 articles (accounting for 3.7 %) and Electronic Newspaper of Vietnam Communist Party with 58 articles (accounting for 35.8 %).

On behalf of the Communist Party's Theoretical Agency, Communist Magazine has always published profound research by scientists and politicians on democratic theory in Vietnam, such as "The leadership of the Communist Party of Vietnam – the decisive factor for democracy in our country today" (February 2014), "Enhancing the Party's leadership for the people to participate in building the Party, a clean and strong government" (April 2014). People Newspaper and Electronic Newspaper of Vietnam Communist Party have also given special importance to post articles on democracy: for example "Democracy" or "Anti-democracy" (People Newspaper, 10 June), or "Meditations on all Abnormal Phenomena" (Electronic Newspaper of the Vietnam Communist Party, 19 August). As can be seen from these articles, in terms of perception, the current cadres and civil servants and the different social classes have increasingly understood the relevance of the democratic issue, particularly

---

[3] Tran Ngoc Duong (2011), 368.

expressed in expanding freedom of speech, and thought, thereby, improving the democratization process of the society.

The press not only transmits theoretical information on democracy, but also is a public forum. Through the press, for example People Newspaper, the people can raise their voices on diverse problems. From January to August 2014, People Newspaper has posted 94 articles containing opinions and messages of its readers. The articles' contents reflect opinions about national policies regarding the state apparatus and its democratization: "Delayed enforcement, civilian damages" (14 August), "Government fails, people suffer" (1 August), "Ill management in medication" (5 July), "The people are thirsty for clean water beside the abandoned waterworks" (20 June), "Must choose officers for reception of citizens" (31 May).

Electronic Newspaper of the Vietnam Communist Party is an e-paper and therefore another "young" newspaper in the system of Vietnam's revolutionary press. From January to August 2014, it posted 54 articles containing opinions and messages of the people: "Reception of citizens and '4-imploration' story" (25 July), "A story about the mirror at 'One-door Department'" (24 April), "Clarifying the 'allegations' about bidding" (24 April). Published opinions about the implementation conditions, unreasonable aspects when making policies or shortcomings in the operation of state agencies play an important role. For management agencies this is a step forward to adjust and improve policies and activities of the state soundly and effectively.

As can be seen from the press, democratic awareness of all social classes in Vietnam has been improved. The articles represent opinions of the people about all aspects of life, but especially in political life they introduce new values in political culture: further democratization by enhancing communication and behavioral skills in a democratic sense. The Vietnamese citizens have realized that democracy today not only is expressed through methods of work itself, but also through a bilateral style and behavior: public officers and party members to citizens and vice versa.

The growing relevance of the press as a common public forum has clearly demonstrated that there is an increase in political participation and democratization in Vietnam. The population nowadays is more aware of its rights and responsibilities as citizens under law. Simultaneously, it also indicates that the freedom of speech which is guaranteed by the constitution is increasingly exercised in reality. This all proves that power increasingly belongs to the people.

The Press on Renovation and Improvement of the State Apparatus

One basis of renovation policies is the improvement of the governmental structure, an issue which is connected with the implementation of legitimate administrative procedures. The entire governmental structure and each of its measures must follow the Vietnamese Constitution and the laws. In this sense 2014 was an important year, because the Amended Constitution of 2013 was put into effect. In this process the mass media played a key role, as they not only provided information about the Amended Constitution but also mirrored opinions about the reform process. The mass media can help to discuss and improve legal regulations and can enhance awareness of civic responsibility, and improve general knowledge about the renovated legal system. As a bridge between people, party and state, gazettes like People Newspaper, Communist Magazine and Electronic Newspaper of the Vietnam Communist Party dealt intensively with the Amended Constitution and its content. From January until August 2014, a total of 112 articles on legal topics were published in these newspapers: People Newspaper posted 36 articles (accounting for 32.1 %), Communist Magazine 8 articles (accounting for 7.2 %) and Electronic Newspaper of Vietnam Communist Party 68 articles (accounting for 60.7 %).

The gazettes predominantly published treatises which presented deeper analysis about the content of the Amended Constitution to improve common knowledge about the changes occurring, such as: "Continuously build and perfect the socialist legitimate state under the spirit and contents of the new constitution" (Communist Magazine, March 2014), "Congress on the Constitution (Amended)" (People Newspaper 12 March), "Some new points of the Constitution (Amended) about Government" (People Newspaper 25 March), "Enforcement of human rights in the Constitution" (Electronic Newspaper of Vietnam Communist Party 28 March). Besides, the press focused on observing critically the activities to implement or reform specific state agencies, an important part of the entire reform process. In this way, the press played an important role to bring the Amended Constitution into real life.

As information about the previously prevailing legal norms as well as the changes in the Amended Constitution, the gazettes created favorable conditions and presented a platform for the readers to discuss the ongoing renovation process including specific laws on Thrift Practice, Combat of Waste, Disaster Management, Land, Health Insurance etc. Besides, the press was also a channel for people to raise their voices about the inadequacies of the current legal system. For example, the article "Soon 'remove' the inadequacies in wrong compensation" (People Newspaper 12 February), dealt with large inadequacies in the Law on State Compensation Liability – persons claiming compensation had to identify the officers responsible for the damage already at the beginning of the compensation request. Law enforcement in fact demonstrated that these regulations were a big obstacle to the implementation of the new liability law, especially for ordinary people. Another article "Breaking 'barriers' in administrative implementation of investment" (People Newspaper 26 February) demonstrated the inadequacies in the implementation process of administrative procedures for investment projects which are stipulated by the Law on Investment. This is another example for the continuous efforts of state and party to improve law enforcement through publications by gazettes.

Considering the different branches of state power, legislative, executive, and judiciary, the Vietnamese press has always reported intensively about the holder of legislative power, the National Assembly News about the National Assembly is conducted regularly by the press. Due to the specific activities, members of the National Assembly mostly work concurrently; activities mainly take place when the National Assembly convenes, which is also the period of most of the press' publications.

During the sessions of the National Assembly, its Standing Committee and other Committees of the National Assembly, many press agencies and journalists were mobilized to report. According to our survey, from January until August 2014, all three newspapers published 277 articles about activities of the National Assembly. In which, People Newspaper posted 90 articles (accounting for 32.5 %); Electronic Newspaper of the Vietnam Communist Party has conducted 185 articles (accounting for 66.8 %) and Communist Magazine has posted 2 articles (accounting for 0.7 %). Therefore, reporting about the National Assembly is not the main content of the magazine. Its task is rather to provide the members of parliaments with information. Through transmitting information the press agencies have drawn the attention of the public to the activities of the National Assembly. Especially, information published about the daily sessions of the National Assembly helped the people to understand the ongoing political changes., and enabled the Vietnamese citizens to monitor these, and to ascertain opinions which were posted. During the seventh session of the National Assembly XIII (20 May to 24 June 2014), People Newspaper and Electronic Newspaper of Vietnam Communist Party published 35 typical comments of citizens about the content of the sessions. These comments on the one hand created more public awareness of the National Assembly's activities, and helped to improve the law making process of the parliament on the other hand.

The administrative function of state agencies covers nearly every area of the society. Therefore it is an urgent task to promote the reform of Vietnam's administration and of its administrative procedures in particular. The latter are currently given a lot of attention, as administrative procedures as well as any other legal provisions are not only implemented to manage the administration but must create conditions for citizens, and organizations to exercise their rights and obligations. Until now, for many reasons, administrative procedures have always been causing much inconvenience as cumbersome and complex regulation has been one of the reasons for corruption, and authoritarianism. Therefore, posting articles related to the reform of administrative procedures has always been emphasized by the press since the beginning of the reform process in Vietnam. From January until August, 2014, People Newspaper and Electronic Newspaper of Vietnam Communist Party released 41 articles on this problem. Some striking ones are: "Remove difficulties in settling administrative procedures" (People Newspaper 3 January), "Publicize the whole process of settling administrative procedures" (People Newspaper 8 February), "Administrative procedures, easier said than done" (Electronic Newspaper of the Vietnam Communist Party 20 February), "Enhance responsibilities of the head in controlling administrative procedures" (Electronic Newspaper of the Vietnam Communist Party 15 August). The articles highlighted the inadequacies in enforcing the current administrative procedures, and proposed solutions for further reform such as reducing the number of administrative levels, improving the cooperation between different state agencies, creating a more favorable environment for production and business and for the citizens to claim their legal rights.

To defend justice, and to protect human rights, an objective requirement is to improve the judiciary in Vietnam. Judicial reform is necessary, as with the ongoing changes many new challenges for the Vietnamese court system have emerged, for example in the areas of market economy, international integration, and economic relations. Vietnam must undergo on the one hand a reform process to ensure favorable legal environments for economic activities, for the protection of property rights, and business freedom, and generally for the legal interests of investors, business and citizens. In addition, on the other hand, law enforcement must be improved to fight crime and law violations more effectively. Therefore, the press agencies have always focused on the publication of information on judicial reforms. From January to August, 2014, the gazettes published 27 articles on judicial reform, in which, People Newspaper posted 7 articles, Electronic Newspaper of Vietnam Communist Party posted 19 articles and Communist Magazine posted 1 article. The main contents throughout these articles were the objectives of the judicial reform to build a strong, democratic, systematic and clean judiciary in order to protect justice and human rights.

With a total of 457 articles published in the operational information on many aspects of the reform process from January to August 2014, People Newspaper, Electronic Newspaper of Vietnam Communist Party, Communist Magazine – the important press agencies of Vietnam's revolution press – provided information on the activities of the state to citizens. The press became a forum to transmit public opinion to the state, thereby contributing to promote innovative activities.

The Press on Human Resources

Human resources in the state apparatus have an important role in determining its effective and efficient operation. President Ho Chi Minh said:

"Staff is persons who bring the policies of the government and its organizations to the people. If staff is bad, good policies can not be done".4 "Staff is the line of the machine. If the line is not good, no matter how good the engine is running, even running the whole machine, it is still paralyzed."[5]

Human resource management plays a significant role in building a socialist legitimate state of the people, by the people and for the people. Therefore, staff and civil servants must meet the requirements associated with it, and possess professional capacities for their mission. They must be dedicated and hard-

---

[4] Ho Chi Minh (2011), 265.

[5] Ho Chi Minh (2011), 68.

working; responsible and possess a work ethic while performing duties in their assigned tasks; comply with the provisions of the law with self-awareness and strict discipline; have respect for citizens and their legal rights; be citizen-centered; listen to opinions and aspirations of the people and learn from the people in a modest manner, etc. Creating human resources for the civil service is not only a task of the political system, but an outcome of their interaction with the masses.

As a medium of information between party, state, and people, the press has always focused on reflecting activities of staff work, and have been a forum of expression of popular opinion about human resources of party and state. From January to August, 2014, People Newspaper, Communist Magazine and Electronic Newspaper of the Communist Party published 147 articles on staff and work-related issues. In which, People Newspaper posted 107 articles (accounting for 72.8 %), Electronic Newspaper of Communist Party posted 37 articles (accounting for 25.2 %), and Communist Magazine posted 3 articles (accounting for 2 %).

First of all, we must affirm that the press plays a significant role in detecting and posting information about positive examples of "Servants of the people." People Newspaper greatly emphasized this matter, and gave many examples of positive voices about good public officers. From January to August, 2014, at the beginning, with the column "People's servants" and then after "The jobs for the people", it published articles about 28 typical examples of staff. Some outstanding articles namely "Take the good to remove the bad" (16th May) about the head of a small village – Nguyen Hoang Khanh at Phu Thanh, Mai Dam town, Chau Thanh District, Hau Giang Province – who is always at the forefront of building mass movements to protect national security, "a staff who has always earned the people's trust."[6] The article: "The son of the mountain village" (12th June) about Le Hong Thanh, lieutenant-colonel, captain of the criminal police of Yen Chau district, who is a typical example of "a citizen-centered style, having the same food, the same house, and working and producing with compatriots"[7] of a people's police.

We can conclude that that many arcticles mention the positive sides of cadres and civil servants. These human resources are well trained, and retrained

---

[6] Thanh Phong (2014), 8.

[7] Duc Tuan (2014), 4, 8.

both in political theory and professional knowledge regarding policies and laws, they meet certain levels of assigned work. A part of the contemporary human resources in Vietnam's administration quickly adapt to the new requirements and challenges in the process of the state reform. The articles describe the majority of human resources in public service as of high political quality, with good work-ethics, citizen-centered, and abiding by guidelines, policies and laws.

However, in comparison with the requirements for human resources in the socialist legitimate state of the people, by the people and for the people, the cadres and civil servants today also revealed many weaknesses and inadequacies. Both are reflected in the mass media by the popular voice. From January to August 2014, People Newspaper published 27 articles which reflected people's opinions about the shortcomings of cadres and civil servants in a special column: "troublesome jobs in the eyes of the people". Some remarkable articles such as: "It is such a lack of responsibility to the people" (published 12th June) about the shirking of responsibilities by staff at General Hospital in Quang Nam area and Da Nang Eye Hospital where five patients suffered infections after eye surgeries. Article "Lack of responsibility towards the people" (4 July) about insensitivity, irresponsibility of some officials of Nam Hung commune, Nam Truc District, Nam Dinh Province in the treatment policy for people with meritorious services who fought in the country's armed forces.

Through the common reflections via forums of the press it can be seen that many weaknesses and shortcomings exist among the current cadres and civil servants: professional qualifications are still incommensurate to meet the job requirements; the initiative and sense of responsibility for assigned work is still low, lax discipline; limited management and operating skills. A number of cadres and civil servants are incapable, fraudulent, corrupt, harassed, lacking in impartiality and objectivity in handling affairs, irresponsible towards the people's work; a number of key officials at the local level seem to be confused, embarrassed, passive with weak skills and spirit when problems arise.

Besides posting assessments of public human resources, the press has also emphasized reporting about staff work in order to reflect existing disadvantages, but also to detect innovation in administration and its procedure, especially assessment of work on the local level and job rotation for officers. From January to August 2014, People Newspaer published 31 articles on staff work, which mainly reflected innovation on the local level. However, many shortcomings of staff work are still existing in general. Typical articles are: "Identifying expressions of "Group's Benefits" in staff organization work and solutions" (Communist Magazine, May 2014), "good and bad in staff rotation" (People Newspaper October 2014), "How to make personnel work reasonable/sensible" (People Newpaper 28 June), "The paradox in the management and use of cadres and civil servants in Hanoi" (People Newspaper 30 August), "Is it true that talents are like autumn leaves?" (Electronic Newspaper of the Communist Party 28 April).

In these articles the shortcomings of local committees, branches and units are decribed: they do not really care for human resources, do not actively plan their development or if only in a perfunctory way, especially not for leaders and managers, do not properly consider job rotation from the central to local levels. Structures of the administrative service including the organization of personnel is often irrational.

It can be seen from the chart that from January to August 2014, People Newspaper, Communist Magazine and Electronic Newspaper of the Communist Party published a total of 766 articles on issues of the legitimate state in Vietnam today (People Newspaper with 358 articles, Communist Magazine 20 and Electronic Newspaper of Communist Party 388 articles published). Electronic Newspaper of Communist Party has the highest number of articles because it is a daily online newspaper. Communist Magazine has the lowest number because it is a theoretical monthly magazine.

The number of articles on human resources is the highest, expressing the importance of this issue, while the number of articles on extending democracy, promoting the voices of the people is at least comparable to other ones. It is not easy to write on theoretical issues in daily newspapers. The number of articles on renovation and improvement of the state apparatus is high, including all typical divisions of power such as the legislature, executive and judiciary.

Table 5: Selected Newspapers on Improvements of the Legal State

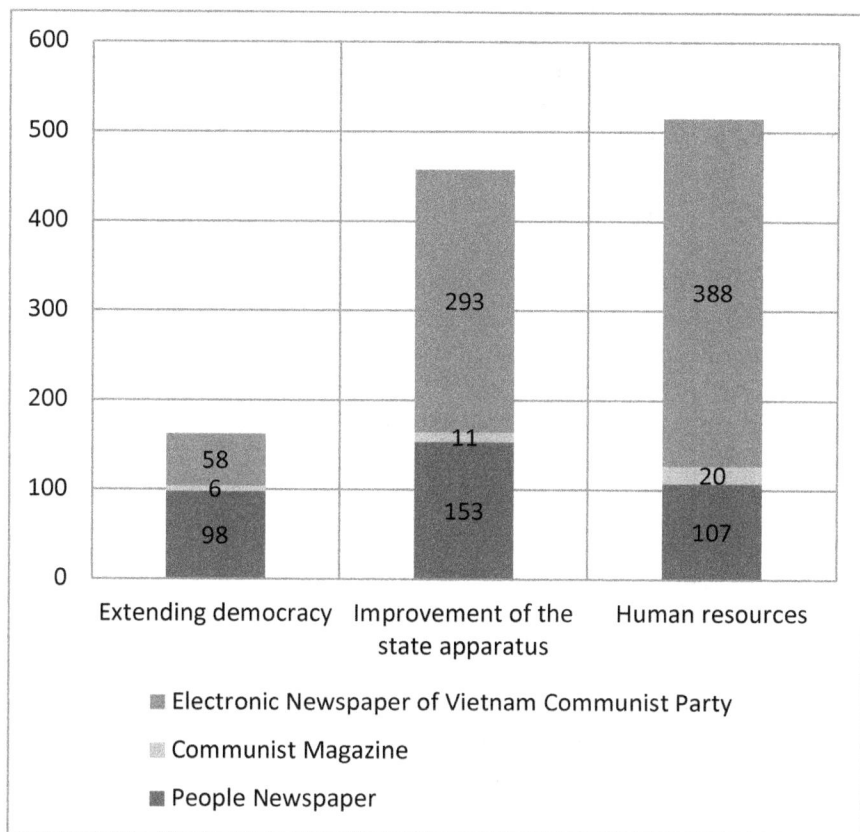

Source: Own data analysis

Conclusion

It can be seen that there are three main roles of the press in the construction of a legitimate state in Vietnam today. First, the press gives information in order to help people understand the concept of the legitimate state, and especially the characteristics of the socialist and legitimate state of the people, by the people and for the people in Vietnam. Second, the press advocates the general line and policies of party and state, and mobilizes citizens to participate in building the legitimate state. Third, the press is a forum for people to express their opinions, and to monitor the state apparatus as well as the staff and civil servants in the process of building the legitimate state in Vietnam.

However in the entire reform process, the press in Vietnam has some limitations. Firstly, information about the rule of law is plentiful today, but not really presenting the full picture. The difficulties and challenges in building the legitimate state has not been analyzed sufficiently. Besides, although the press has often been reflecting the negative sides of the state apparatus, it has not dared to speak out some problems. Moreover, the mistakes mentioned in the press mostly come from low-level officials, less from high-level ones. It is a requirement for the press to broach the issue of administrative reform more intensively, as well as to communicate more the values of the rule of law. The central goal is to mobilize citizens and to engage them in the construction of a socialist and legitimate state of the people, by the people and for the people in Vietnam.

References

Bui Xuan Duc (2007): Innovate, improve state apparatus in the current period. Hanoi.

Dang Dinh Tan (2006): People monitoring the elected agencies in Vietnam during the renovation period. Hanoi.

Duc Tuan (2014): The son of the mountain village. People Newspaper, 12th June 2014.

Ho Chi Minh. National Political Publishing House (ed.) (2011): The Complete Collection. Vol. 5. Hanoi.

http://dangcongsan.vn/cpv/Modules/News/gioi_thieu.aspx

Le Huu Nghia/Bui Dinh Bon (2013), Competence and responsibility of the ruling party and the State in implementing people's power. Hanoi.

Le Minh Quan (2011): On the process of democratization of socialism in Vietnam today. Hanoi.

Le Minh Thong (2011): Innovate, perfect apparatus of socialist legitimate state of the people, by the people, for the people in Vietnam today. Hanoi.

Leonard, Thomas M. (ed.) (2006): Encyclopedia of the developing world. New York.

Nguyen Duy Quy (2008): Thinking innovation and innovation process in Vietnam. Hanoi.

Nguyen Quoc Pham/Do Thi Thach (2012): New Perspectives on socialism and building socialism in Vietnam. Hanoi.

Nguyen Van Manh (2010): Construction of socialist legitimate state in Vietnam – theoretical and practical. Hanoi.

Ta Ngoc Tan (2001): Mass Communications. Hanoi.

Thanh Phong (2014): Take the good to remove the bad. People Newspaper, 16th May 2014.

Tran Ngoc Duong (2011): Some issues on assignment, coordination and control of the power in constructing socialist legitimate state in Vietnam. Hanoi.

Vietnamese Communist Party (ed.) (2007): The Complete Collection of Party Documents. Vol. 53. Hanoi.

On the Civil society and the State of Law in Vietnam

Phan Xuan Son

What is a Civil Society?

"Civil society" is called "xã hội công dân" in Vietnamese, "Société civile" in French and "Zivilgesellschaft" in German. Among them, "civi"", and "civile" are all adjectives that mean "belonging to the citizens, of the citizens' affairs." For example, civil law means "dân luật", civil rights means "quyền công dân" and civic liberty means "tự do công dân" in Vietnamese.[1] Society may mean "association", "union", "community", "organization" and "company". Its meaning is identical to that of "société" in French. Therefore, civil society is an assembly of citizens in the form of an "organization", "community", "company", "group", "association", "union" or "cooperative".

When translated into Vietnamese it can be understood as either "xã hội công dân" (society of citizens) or "xã hội dân sự" (society for civil affairs). Both terms have their equivalent meanings in English. In the former case, civil society refers to the organizations, communities and networks of citizens. The latter term emphasizes that these organizations, communities and unions are related to the affairs of the citizens (civil affairs).

However "dân sự" (công việc của dân) in Vietnamese can have multiple meanings. First of all, depending on the contexts, "dân" can mean "citizens", "people" or "subject" ["ordinary person/people", "ordinary subject/s", which

---

[1] Encyclopedia Publisher (2005): Từ điển Anh-Việt (English-Vietnamese Dictionary). Hanoi. 166.

refer to a person or a group of people that are not the state (e.g in feudal periods)]. "Sự" means affairs or matters. However when combining "sự" with "dân", the resulting "dân sự" refers to the affairs of "dân" (which means people, citizens or subjects) which are different from and independent of those of the state. Meanwhile, the concept of "civil society" in the first place implies an organization and community of citizens who possess legal and political status in relation to the state. While "Dân sự" is sufficient to distinguish "civil affairs" (việc dân) with those of the state, it fails to indicate what political and legal relations the citizens in question have with the state. In other words the concept of "xã hội công dân" (society of citizens) is created as soon as people in societies acquire their rights and obligations, and after the introduction of capitalist states of law. On the other hand, "xã hội dân sự" refers to a non-state and civil sector and does not specify the relations between this sector and the state. A comparison can be made between "Xã hội dân sự" and "Xã hội công dân" and "Kinh tế hàng hóa" (commodity economy) and "Kinh tế thị trường" (market economy) in economics, respectively. "Xã hội dân sự" denotes a general non-state sector in society, while "xã hội công dân" refers to this sector but only after the introduction of the capitalist states of law (not heretofore). This difference is primarily caused by the Vietnamese language. In English, Russian, France and other languages there is no such a case and only the equivalent of "xã hội công dân" in Vietnamese exists.

Thus while "xã hội dân sự" conveys a broader meaning, its political and legal connotations are opaque. Its counterpart "Xã hội công dân" indicates the following main connotations:

- It is a sector of citizens (e. g. a community or organization) in a society, which can be considered the first legal stratum. It means that without his/her civil rights and obligations and citizenship as regulated by the law of a nation, a person is not included in this concept.
- The citizens organize themselves into a "society" (e. g. an association, union, or community) that operates under the state of law and is legitimate. This is the second legal stratum. As a result, illegal organizations do not belong to this concept.
- Civil organizations and communities are multiple hence their relations have to be regulated by the law, which is the third legal stratum. These constitute other indirect connotations of "civil society" such as civilization and urban dwellers.

Therefore, it is my recommendation that "xã hội công dân" should be used to connote "civil society" instead of "xã hội dân sự".[2]

Why is there a Civil Society?

Looking at the ideological, theoretical and practical development of the state of law, it can be said that: The sovereignty of citizens over the state is an objective reality, as citizens decide the form and organization of a state by authorizing their power to a number of representatives who run it on their behalf. The sovereignty of citizens over the state is a prerequisite of the state of law.

The sovereignty of citizens is manifested in economic, political and social terms as follows:

-   Citizens have their respective economic status, based on a particular ownership of the means of production and possessions.
-   Citizens are permitted to organize and contribute to overall affairs of the state (which are read as the right to elect, self-nominate and participate in state management).
-   Citizens are allowed to supervise the activities of state authorities.
-   Citizens have the right to express their will and realize their interests or those of their community (political rights such as freedom of association and assembly, of demonstration and speech, freedom of religion and belief).
-   Although part of it is delegated to the organization of the state and fulfilment of public functions, the power of citizens is fundamentally preserved and is supreme.
-   The evolution of mankind is simultaneously an ongoing struggle to claim civil sovereignty. While this struggle has gained significant achievements, civil sovereignty remains a critical issue to be solved along with social development.

To oppose and remove feudal authoritarianism and safeguard the liberal rights of people, thinkers influenced by Enlightenment insist on a civil society as a basis of the state of law. The concept of civil society as an independent entity in relations to the state is criticized zed in the history of Western ideas, and though it is defined in different ways by thinkers from France and Germany,

---

[2] Hereafter referred to as "civil society".

there is a common attempt to clarify the problematic and complicated relations between public and private sectors, individuals and society, social ethics and individual interests, and between personal desires and social concerns. Despite these varying trends, the idea of civil society appeals to many ideologists, who considered it to be a collection of the desires of both society at large and each individual. Civil society, therefore, includes a wide range of moral ideas on social order, or at the very least harmonizes the conflict between the personal needs and interests with those of the society at large.

The concept of civil society stems from the theory of natural law, although its development is increasingly sophisticated, even present in certain aspects of medieval Christian ideology. The ideological history of civil society begins with philosophers from the Age of Enlightenment to Karl Marx and the subsequent political and legal ideologists. The social need for civil society is the need to revert to manageable aspects of social life which emphasizes voluntary civil unions. Civil society in modern capitalist states is a part of the communal process of continuous struggle for freedom, equality and justice, avoiding being compromised by both the market and the state.

Civil Society in Marxism

According to Marx, the term civil society was introduced in the 18th century, when ownership relations had evolved beyond their communal form as in ancient and medieval times. Marx claimed that family and civil society were the prerequisites of the state:

"Family and civil society are the bearers of the state (in the widest sense – PXS); they are the existence of will, they are the state's mode of existence. Family and civil society form the state."[3]

Marx's notion has a great significance in terms of methodology in thinking on the state and choosing a model for social development. According to Marx, civil society is not within the political realm, but all of its activities affect the state. Because of this, the institutions (organizations) of civil society bear certain political forms. As such, in building a civil society, it is necessary to recognize its independence and objective role for the state (i.e. assigning various fields of human activity) on the one hand, and recognize its political forms on the other hand.

---

[3] Marx/Engels (1995), 314–315.

In terms of freedom, it transforms the society's supreme bodies into its dependents, and even nowadays whether a state is free or not depends on "the extent by which the state's freedom is limited"[4] by such forms. "It is the individual as a member of civil society who, therefore, is the basis, the premise of a political state. The state acknowledges this accordingly in terms of human rights."[5]

Civil Society as a "Non-state" Area

Marx held that, "political emancipation means freeing civil society from politics, even from the appearance of a certain universal content."[6] At that point, "man, as a member of civil society, the apolitical man must appear as a natural man."[7] Thus, the birth of civil society, the "political emancipation or turning of man into a member of civil society, an egoistic and independent individual on the one hand, and into a citizen of the state, a legal entity on the other hand"[8] is major historical progress in medieval times, when social life is uniform to political life.

On the Importance of Civil Society

Karl Marx wrote, on the importance of civil society, that "civil society is the actual center, the actual arena of history in its entirety,"[9] and that "political revolution is a revolution of civil society."[10] This shows that any modern political party or a modern social force striving for victory must win the ultimate battle in civil society. Although Marx studied civil society in his contemporary historical context, the universal values of his standpoint remain in effect until today. When addressing civil society, Marx confirmed that it is the fruition of the capitalist development (in Marx's time, capitalism is the highest socio-

[4] Marx/Engels (1995), 554.

[5] Marx/Engels (1995), 554.

[6] Marx/Engels (1995), 554.

[7] Marx/Engels (1995), 554.

[8] Mác/Ăngghen toàn tập, tập 1, CTQG, H, 1995, tr.557.

[9] C. Mác-Ph. Ăngghen, Tuyển tập, tập 1, Nxb Sự thật, Hà Nội, 1980, tr. 299. (Hệ tư tưởng Đức).

[10] Mác/Ăngghen toàn tập, tập 1, nxb CTQG, H, 1995, tr.554.

economic form), but he remained faithful to the term "in any era"; as long as the state exists, civil society will be its basis. Civil society, wrote Marx, "always refers to a social organization that stems directly from production and commerce and, in any era, is the basis of the state and of the ideological superstructure as well."[11]

Definition

Civil society is a system of civil organizations, communities and their relations, operating within the national law in order to realize individuals and characters, connecting individuals to the social system, and strengthening and protecting communal interests. At the same time and through organizations and communities, civil society coordinates with the state, ensuring that the relations between the state and society remain balanced, stable, and optimal for sustainable development and social progress.

The Structure of the Civil Society

In terms of institutions (organizations), it includes all unions, associations, interest-based leagues (economic, political, cultural, professional, scientific, educational, entertaining, etc.). It would be insufficient, however, to refer to institutions without mentioning their interrelations, their coordinating mechanisms and other organizational and operational principles.

The Position of the Civil Society in the Social System

Civil society refers to the institutions that "stand next to" (in the words of Karl Marx) those of the state (e.g. parliament, government, president, the judicial body, local administrations, etc.). In other words, the institutions of civil society are relatively independent; they do not depend on and are not state organizations, nor are they manufacturers or businesses.

The Characteristics of a Civil Society's Activities

Important factors to characterize institutions of the civil society are a common identity of the respective group or community, (financial) self-reliance, self-management, voluntarism, and diversity in organizational forms. Depending

---

[11] C.Mác/Ph.Ăngghen: Tuyển tập, tập IV, Nxb Sự thật, Hà Nội, 1984, tr. 362.

on the model of the political system, civil society's organizations can be within or outside of the political system.

Functions of Civil Society

Some basic functions of the civil society are:
- Socializing individuals, realizing personalities, connecting individuals to the social system, strengthening and protecting the communal interests.
- Providing a basis for the state and coordinating with it, supplementing and replacing it (in certain areas, usually where the state cannot perform with higher efficiency than civil society), verifying, and perfecting the state activities, thereby balancing and stabilizing state and social activities.

Nowadays, the civil society is among the three most fundamental pillars of social development: If a market economy is the prerequisite for national development, and a state of law is what directly determines development, then the civil society is a guarantee for development. The final goal of a modern civil society is the development and perfection of individuals, which is the condition for the development of community, society, and humanity. In terms of development, civil society is the place where a nation's social capital is formed, accumulated and preserved. The development of civil society aims at humanity's common progressive values, while at the same time depends on the periodic characters and specific historical backgrounds of each nation; it depends also on the forms and types of state and on their political system.

In summary, a civil society is a voluntary collective realm of activities whose purpose is to share common benefits, goals, and values. Theoretically, their organizational forms differ from those of the state, family, and the market; although in reality, the frontiers between the state, civil society, family, and the market are often complicated, ambiguous, and reciprocal. The nature of civil society, as addressed above, is the relationship between individuals , between individual and community, and between individual and the state, in other words citizens in their forms of community.

Models of Civil Society

There is a wide range of models of civil societies, and they can be summarized into three major types:
- The liberal model understands the civil society as opposition to the state, and is observable in countries like the US, or UK.

- The democratic socialist model sees the civil society as a unifier of state and society. Its proponents are modern democratic socialist parties, mainly from Scandinavia and Germany. This model is reflected in the definition of the "social state". The state is concerned with all social groups, and builds interactions and unity between itself and civil society.
- Whether a specific Soviet civil society actually exists or not has long been a subject of debate between international and Soviet scholars. In general, most scholars recognize its existence, but due to a lack of official acknowledgement and proper regulative legislations, Soviet civil society has suffered from a number of derailments and weaknesses.

Studying the issue of the civil society provides us with a methodological basis to study international socio-political entities in general and those in Vietnam in particular.

Negative Manifestations of Civil Society

Beginning with the development of production and division of labor, social structures diversified increasingly in terms of professions, interests, and value orientations. The formation of groups with different interests is hence inevitable. However, it is not inevitable that a certain group is only pursuing its own interests and violating those of other groups and/or the state; this stems from egoistic goals. "Interest group" is a group that seeks to maximize its own interests and, in the process, violates the common interests of society or those of other groups. Interest groups cause social fragmentation and corrupt social unity and consensus. Should all groups act in such a way, then the civil society "becomes a battlefield where everyone is against everyone" (Hegel).

Due to limited resources and lax organization, many civil society organizations seek for sponsorship from business or foreign entities, thus creating financial dependence. These organizations fail to achieve their intended goals on the one hand, and become dependent on, or are even used to accomplish the wicked purposes of economic or political forces on the other hand.

Some domestic civil society organizations may be formed "unnaturally" as partners of foreign NGOs, which are also formed in order to realize the malicious goals of certain forces. Without adequate legislation to prevent such organizations, social insecurity may ensue, especially in the context of global integration when the freedom of speech, freedom of press, and freedom of assembly are not only universal values but also binding requirements in international commitments. Even though a civil society may be considered a place "external to politics", a number of groups have been shifting towards the political realm for the sake of self-interest rather than the benefits of its members. These groups rely on sacred values and sentiments, such as national and ethnic bonds, religious beliefs, human rights and dignity etc. to promote hate, violence, and hostility against the state, with measures ranging from peaceful to radical that far exceed the scope of a civil society organization.

Quite a large number of such groups have been prepared to act as "insiders" for foreign enemies. Some with economic influences may utilize money or other substances to seduce high-ranking political figures, manipulate the policy making process to serve their own interests, violating the principle of non-profit. For organizations with state funding (several socio-political and other social organizations), they tend to foster superficiality, authoritativeness, and derailing from the nature of civil society.

There are limitations and negativities to every realm and aspect of social life. In the case of a market economy, it is the willingness to sacrifice everything for "maximum profit", even if it means the compromise of national interests, a widened rich-poor gap, foul play in business, and illegal competition. Even in a state of law, such plights as bureaucracy, corruption, policy exploitation and manipulation, and abuse of power persist.

These negativities (or shortcomings) of a market economy, of a state of law, or of a civil society as aforementioned are understandable and have yet to be eradicated. But they cannot derail the developmental orientation of the Vietnamese people, and cannot eclipse the benefits of market economy, state of law, and civil society; and as a result, we should not be "afraid" of a market economy, state of law, and civil society. It is necessary for the state to introduce a legislative system to regulate and manage civil society. Only after clear legislation is created can we limit or eradicate organizations that undermine state and society.

What are the Characteristics of the Vietnamese Civil Society?

Universality and Particularity

The theoretical issues discussed above on civil society and socio-political organizations will serve as a basis for us to examine the civil society in Vietnam. In Vietnam, the system of social and socio-political organizations, despite their being atypical, bear the trait of universality. It means that they are created and exist firstly because of the inherent needs of the civil society itself; even during the era of national liberation, participating in socio-political organizations was an urgent need of all societal classes. Moreover, historical areas notwithstanding, the people's need to assemble into groups is greatly diverse, especially in the modern era, and this requires a corresponding shift in the political thinking of the state, stemming from the needs, desires and benefits of the people.

As such, it is reasonable to say there is in fact a civil society in Vietnam. In terms of organization, there are around 500 organizations (associations) operating nationwide; around 3.000 operating locally, and tens of thousands more on the district and grass root levels. They are structured as follows:

-   Socio-political: The Vietnam Fatherland Front (VFF) and other socio-political organizations are within the political system and act as the core of Vietnamese civil society. The VFF is a socio-political organization with some 50 member groups and many prominent individuals, among these are five socio-political organizations that have been codified by the constitution and by law.
-   Economic: productive, business and service associations (professional associations) such as associations for steel, cement, construction, architecture, sugar cane, coffee and cocoa, rice export, etc.
-   Scientific and technological: union of scientific and technological associations, private research groups, etc.
-   Social: socio-professional organizations, groups concerning common interests, charity, humanitarian aid, hospitality, gender, etc.
-   Non-governmental organizations (NGOs) in Vietnam.

Among these organizations are their coordinative relations, principles, and mechanisms. Of course, the criteria for classifying these organizations are only relative. In Vietnam, the creation of the socialist republic is closely related to a struggle for national independence and de colonization. The VFF and other socio-political organizations were formed under the mobilization and arrangement of the Communist Party of Vietnam, intertwined with it in that struggle and answering to its leadership. In other words, the sense of citizenship and political awareness had matured along with the struggle for national liberation. In that process, the formation of social and socio-political organizations bore the trait of collectivism as Vietnamese people from all walks of life were mobilized against imperialism and feudalism, and the interests of all classes were first and foremost connected with the process of political struggle. Such positions and features strengthened when the CPV became the ruling party and are persisting until today. In the new context, although the VFF and other socio-political organizations retain their political functions, their social capacity is increasingly expanding and diversifying. This proves that the VFF and other socio-political organizations play a crucial role as core forces of Vietnam's civil society.

Challenges for the Civil Society

When civil societies first exist as representatives of and protectors of the interests of a certain class or group in their relations with the politically/economically dominant lords, or even with the state, they are not immediately recognized as legal. Because of certain interests, the state often prohibits the existence and activities of these organizations. Despite its prominence in the 18th and 19th century, the term "civil society" from time to time ceased to be widely used. At times, the major theories of Western thinkers focused only on the complex relationship between the state and the market. As such, "society" was no longer under the spotlight. After the collapse of the Soviet Union and Eastern European socialist states, people began to doubt the "role" of civil society. However, in contrast to that skepticism, scholars found that the USSR and Eastern European states did not accept the civil society, that these states were highly centralized with a too feeble civil society, unlike Western states with the same level of development. Perhaps it was this that caused those states to collapse.

However, studying the experiences with the respective civil society is adequate not only for Eastern Europe but also for developing nations. The EU shows great interest in this matter. The "Civil Dialogue", initiated with the 1990 Commitment, was its first attempt to facilitate social institutions – so that actors from governments and business lobbies are not the only audible agents in the policy making in Brussels. The EU has also commenced the regulation of frequently conflicting interests among NGOs and other civilian groups. There has been a shift in the awareness in the EU, which now holds that state governments and international institutions should be more open toward civil society institutions.

It is industrialization that encourages the assembly of groups, of organizations with large numbers of people and collectivism, privately at first but publicly later on. These organizations are formed to counter the power of laissez-faire ideologists and business owners, and consist of labor unions, farmer and consumer associations. The unions' activities range from demanding higher wages, fewer working hours, benefits for laborers, job insurance, enterprise management, and production contracts. They consist of workers that are not insured, who are individually poorer and weaker than the entrepreneurs. Whether a union could stand firm depends on their unity.

At first, unions were suspected of violating the scope of legal operation. Early 19th century English labor law only allowed workers to individually sign contracts with entrepreneurs, in which each party was considered an equivalent contractual party.. But in reality, since workers' capacity to negotiate is smaller than that of business owners, employees tried to balance the deal by unifying into a coherent front to ask for better terms. The employers, in turn, asked for state intervention to prohibit such associations. The British Parliament responded with a series of new legislations and declared that any association founded as a way to achieve equal standing in a collective negotiation with business owners would be illegal. The situation was much more dire in France, where there was a time when the state imposed heavy punishment on the unions which were considered rebellious. In the US, unions were also considered criminal organizations.

But with the development of the industrial society, the state could no longer resist the pressure of labor unions and the struggle by members of the "middle class". The existence of labor unions and of other civil society organizations was tolerated, accepted and then acknowledged. But Western democracies, even having accepted the legitimacy of these groups, still eradicated groups that are deemed "suspicious" or "disrupting to the social order". The skepticism of nations toward civil organizations was not demonstrated solely by absolute prohibition. It also introduced rules and limitations to impinge or control the operation of these organizations. Hence, civil organizations depended on many bindings: on their objectives and those of the state. They sometimes had to adapt to the established institutional and structural forms. In some countries, while socio-political organizations are not meant to be formed as opposition, the government's policies and agendas put them in an oppositional stance with the state.

In the West, socio-political organizations can freely be formed and operate within the law today as a result of long lasting political conflicts. In developing countries, where many incompetent governments exist, governments usually do not take interest groups seriously or are tired of them, because of the fact that they often have to listen to the comments, criticisms and condemnations made by these groups about their incompetence. But their voices are the vein of society whose resonance can still be heard by governments. In a number of cases, governments must adjust their policies because of the criticisms by interest groups. The recommendations by environmental groups, for instance, initially irritated most countries' leaders, but in time they gradually had to pay greater attention to ecological matters, which have become a global responsibility.

How Does the State of Law Manage the Civil Society in Vietnam?

First of all, it is necessary to reaffirm that the civil society is an objective social structure rather than a political instrument that can be freely utilized or disposed of. Past experiences have shown that state regimes which are "hostile" toward the existence of a civil society will eventually be toppled it.. In recent decades, the world witnessed various "color revolutions" which caused many regimes to topple, even resulting in the complete collapse of governmental order or entire states. Among the causes are weaknesses, or even a complete lack of a civil society in those countries. The inadequacy of civil society in those countries drives their state regimes toward authoritarianism (which in turn would further undermine civil society). This leads to the degradation of the state itself. The systems of government in those countries were sluggish, nepotistic, corrupted, dictatorial and authoritarian; their economic and socio-cultural performances were bad, the country was internationally isolated; and its people discontent. Even a small number of groups can suffice to take advantage of this discontent, and in coordination with external intervention they can mobilize the people to instigate protests or anti-state violent subversion, despite the great cost it would incur. If a civil society is strong enough, it may prevent the state from becoming so degraded that subversion becomes inevitable, and it would also help to prevent and preclude domestic and foreign conspiracies driven by self-interest.

The civil society is the source of human and social capital of Vietnam in general, and of the party and the state in particular. Loosening state management over civil society will deprive us of the human resources and social capital needed for the construction of a state of law and to foster national development as desired.

In the past struggle for national independence, each particular action had to be in the service of the supreme interest of the nation. National independence was the precondition for any further achievement in the realm of interests of the diverse social classes and groups. But today, as the national independence of Vietnam is secured, the further development of Vietnam must take a step forward. Today the ultimate goal – national development – can only be achieved by realizing the interests of various social classes and groups. In the contemporary history of Vietnam we can observe two different trends with reverse priorities: In the past: "no country – no home", and now "prosperous people – powerful nation". Thus, the existence of civil society is first and foremost determined and promoted by the interests of its members (i.e. citizens, participants).

Due to the complexity of socio-economic life and the diversity of needs and interests, the assemblage of civil society organizations must be correspondingly diversified, from the VFF and socio-political organizations to socio-professional organizations, clubs, NGOs, etc. As a result, diversifying the forms of civilian assemblage is a condition for the success of and also a guarantee of the party's leadership in the future.

The state manages civil society through legislations, policies, and other tools. At present, it has promulgated a number of laws regarding the civil society in Vietnam, but there is still a lack of adequate legislations, even the most basic ones, for the management of the civil society. This lack creates more difficulties for governance, especially for functional authorities, which due to having no relevant legislations to refer to, have problems and uncertainties in how to deal with legal (registered) and illegal (unregistered) organizations. The registration itself is difficult. Which organization can register, and which cannot? Why so? Currently, even those that can register have only registered in documents, by which they state their purposes and principles. But civil society is not a single organization and cannot be limited within purposes and principles; it has a much larger scope and is related to factors like governance, political and social system, other associations and the general provisions of civil rights. Since there is no association law yet, the state is unable to manage these affairs, and sanctions for the organizations' wrongdoings cannot be imposed. In reality, state agencies were unable to determine whether protesting against China's placement of an oil rig on Vietnam's continental shelf, or the declaration of a group to form an organization, is illegal or not (provided that their purposes and principles are not unconstitutional).

Past experiences in economic development also showed that when we had no intention of building a market economy, there was no law on economic activities, and state authorities were unable to determine whether the conducts of Ba Thi, Kim Ngoc, or those who traded goods between provinces, were against the law. We can only imagine the challenge that the authorities had to face when pursuing and confiscating inter-provincial shipments back then, or when the confiscated goods from petty merchants or bought from state-owned shops were just resold on the street with a higher price ("con phe", as it was called)! Not to mention issues related to tariff and penalties. The lack of legislation is also what has been challenging Thailand's authorities in the recent cases of surrogate pregnancy. But as soon as there are clear guidelines and legislations, things become much easier.The same is true for state governance and civil society. Civil organizations or communities operating legally shall have permission to do whatever is not prohibited by the law, and those who violate the law must face legal punishment. This requires an imperative perfection of the legal system on civil society, in which association law holds a key role.

The perfection of the legal system on civil society will not only reflect the fact that state governance capacity has met the demands of objective reality, helping authorities do their lawful assignments, but also guarantee civil rights, security, order, and promote social development. Currently, due to the lack of legislation, civil society organizations operate in a disorganized manner, in which some even take advantage of legal ambiguity to conduct anti-state activities, producing serious harm to national development. Authorities are faced with multiple difficulties when dealing with such groups; this unknowingly casts upon them a sense of "allergy" or prejudice toward civil society. When legal clarity is present, these challenges will largely be overcome. It is foreseeable, though, that after such legislations are enacted, many new civil society associations and organizations will be established, just like the mushrooming of enterprises after the introduction of the Law on Enterprises. Just as in the case of the market economy, legitimate and effective organizations that operate legally persist, while the rest go into "bankruptcy". Only after such a period can we hope for a true civil society in Vietnam.

It is also necessary to note that the legal system, especially association law, will concern a number of extra-governmental organizations that include political parties, socio-political organizations, and other social organizations. Therefore, we should have a clear definition and distinction between these forms of organization:

- Political party refers to political entities whose purpose is to take over control of the government and exercise state power. Such great purpose usually impels parties to have a coherent organization, high level of discipline, and principles that are faithful to their ideals, guidelines, and strategies.
- Socio-political organizations are groups that operate for the benefits of particular social groups and communities, through measures that can have influence on the government and political parties (without having a goal for taking over governmental control or participation).
- Social organizations are groups of members who strive to achieve common purposes of the group, society, or the community without goals to have direct influence, impact on the policy making process of the state or political parties (e.g. association for gardening, charity, poetry etc.).

Of course, such distinction is also relative. When there are changes in the socio-economic situation, social needs, or purposes and methods of operation in accordance with the national legal context, a social organization may turn into a socio-political one, and a socio-political organization may turn into a political party. In Russia, following the collapse of the Soviet Union, hundreds of political parties came into being. Most of them have ceased to exist, and some went on to become social organizations. This is a noteworthy issue in the governance of Vietnam regarding its civil society.

Recommendations

- Awareness: Conducting research, exchange between leaders, managers, scholars, and citizens in order to have an accurate and scientific awareness of civil society.
- The demand for a civil society in Vietnam is great and objective. The Communist Party should advocate the construction, development, and guidance of the Vietnamese civil society.
- The National Assembly should quickly embark on proper legislation regarding civil society, with priorities on association and demonstration law to provide a basis for state governance of the civil society.

References

Đào Trí Úc (n.y.): Bước đầu tìm hiểu về xã hội công dân (A preliminary research on civil society, research project at Institute level of the Institute for State and Legal studies). Hanoi.

Encyclopedia Publisher (2005): Từ điển Anh-Việt (English-Vietnamese Dictionary). Hanoi.

Hall, John R. (1995): Civil society. Theory, History, Comparison. Cambridge.

Lê Văn Quang/Văn Đức Thanh (eds.) (2003): Quan hệ giữa nhà nước và xã hội dân sự Việt Nam-Lịch sử và hiện tại (The relationship between state and civil society in Vietnam – Historical and current issues). Hanoi.

Lipson, Leslie (1965): Những tranh luận lớn về chính trị (The great issues of politics: an introduction to political science, translated by the Vietnamese Insitute for Political Science). Englewood Cliffs.

Meny, Yves (1991): Chính trị học so sánh (Comparative Political Science, translated by the Institute for Political Science). Paris.

Phan Xuân Sơn (ed.) (2003): Các đoàn thể nhân dân với việc đảm bảo dân chủ cơ sở hiện nay (Civil organizations and the maintenance of grassroots democracy today). Hanoi.

Phan Xuân Sơn/Quan điểm của (2005): C.Mác về Xã hội công dân (K. Marx's ideas on Civil Society). In: Journal of Theoretical Discussions, Danang, 6th issue (73).

Seligman, Adam B. (1995): The Idea of Civil Society. Princeton.

Truth Publisher (ed.) (1995): Mác/Ph. Ăngghen. Toàn tập ((Marx and F. Engels, collected works). Tập IV (4th volume). Hanoi.

Truth Publisher (ed.) (1995): Mác/Ph. Ăngghen. Toàn tập (Marx and F. Engels, collected works). Tập I (1st volume). Hanoi.

The State of Law in Vietnam: Understandings, Prospects and Challenges

Vu Cong Giao

The Concept of the State of Law

The idea of the state of law emerged long ago in human history. As early as in antiquity, philosophers like Socrates (469–399 B.C.), Aristotle (384–322 B.C.), and Cicero (106–43 B.C.) described the characteristics of a state ruled by law. For instance, in Plato's Crito Socrates expresses that an individual must always adhere to the state and state law.[1] Aristotle also affirms: "A state is stable only when men are equal to law,"[2] meanwhile Cicero believes that: "we are in bondage to the law in order that we may be free".[3] Those ideas are reinforced by European and American thinkers such as St. Thomas Aquinas (1225–1274), John Locke (1632–1704), Charles de Montesquieu (1698–1755), Jean-Jacques Rousseau (1712–1778), Immanuel Kant (1724–1804), Thomas Jefferson (1743–1826), Thomas Paine (1737–1809), John Adams (1735–1826), Georg Wilhelm Friedrich Hegel (1770–1831) then becoming a legal theory, particularly in the period of Enlightenment. The idea of the rule of law was also regulated in a number of legal documents in some countries in medieval times. For example, the well-known Great Charter Magna Carta (1285) of England stipulated that:

---

[1] Stephens (1985), 3–10.

[2] www.quotationspage.com/quote/28897.htm.

[3] quotes.liberty-tree.ca/quote_blog/Marcus.Tullius.Cicero.Quote.7330.

"No free man shall be seized or imprisoned, or stripped of his rights or possessions, or outlawed or exiled, or deprived of his standing in any way, nor will we proceed with force against him, or send others to do so, except by the lawful judgment of his equals or by the law of the land."[4]

As time went on, many definitions of the state of law have been proposed each of which defined some certain properties of the rule of law. For instance, Anthony Kennedy, Chief Justice of the United States, has said:

"When we talk about the rule of law, we assume that we are talking about a law that promotes freedom, that promotes justice, that promotes equality."[5]

The Oxford dictionary provides a shorter definition of the rule of law:

"The restriction of the arbitrary exercise of power by subordinating it to well-defined and established laws."[6]

Besides, there have been some more detailed definitions, for example, according to the World Justice Project (WJP):

"State of law is a framework of rights and rules that created the foundation of social justice and prosperity. This is a system in which no entity, including the government, can stand above the law; where laws protect fundamental rights; and where everyone has rights to access to justice."[7]

According to the Secretary General of the United Nations:

"The rule of law refers to a principle of governance in which all persons, institutions and entities, public and private, including the state itself, are accountable to laws that are publicly promulgated, equally enforced and independently adjudicated, and which are consistent with international human rights norms and standards. It requires, as well, measures to ensure adherence to the principles of supremacy of law, equality before the law, accountability to the law, fairness in the application of the law, separa-

---

[4] Magna Carta, article 39, at: http://www.historylearningsite.co.uk/magna_carta-transcript.htm.

[5] See also: ABA, What is rule of law, http://www.americanbar.org/content/dam/aba/migrated/publiced/features/Part1DialogueROL.authcheckdam.pdf.

[6] http://www.oxforddictionaries.com/definition/english/rule%2Bof%2Blaw___1?q=-rule+of+law.

[7] http://worldjusticeproject.org/what-rule-law.

tion of powers, participation in decision-making, legal certainty, avoidance of arbitrar-iness and procedural and legal transparency.'[8]

Although the content and the way of expression are somewhat different, how-ever, to some extent, those above-mentioned definitions of the rule of law focus on the relationships between people and government. This is the core relation-ship and the foundation of every society derived from nature and the demands of existence of human society. The nature of this relationship, as succinctly summed up by James Madison – one of the founders of the U.S. Constitution:

"If men were angels, no government would be necessary. In framing a government which is to be administered by men over men, the great difficulty lies in this: You must first enable the government to control the governed; and in the next place, oblige it to control itself."[9]

Nevertheless, it is necessary to confirm that the state of law is not a kind of state but a way of organizing a state as well as managing the society based on a democratic platform. In that sense, the rule of law is attached to and placed on a foundation of democracy. Democracy, therefore, is both the result and the condition of the state of law. The latter cannot exist under a non-democratic regime. That explains why in mankind's history, the idea of the rule of law emerged from ancient times, but not until the establishment of the capitalist state did it become a reality. As a way of managing the state on the foundation of democracy, the rule of law must be built and operated on the basis of demo-cratic principles. According to WJP, those principles are:

- The government and its officials and agents as well as individuals and pri-vate entities are accountable under the law.
- The laws are clear, publicized, stable, and just; are applied evenly; and pro-tect fundamental rights, including the security of persons and property.
- The process under which laws are enacted, administered, and enforced is accessible, fair, and efficient.
- Justice is delivered timely by competent court system.[10]

---

[8] Report of the Secretary-General on the Rule of Law and Transitional Justice in Con-flict and Post-Conflict Societies (S/2004/616), http://www.unrol.org/files/2004%-20report.pdf.

[9] Madison (1788).

[10] http://worldjusticeproject.org/what-rule-law.

Also, World Justice Project determines the criteria for evaluating the rule of law which include:[11]

- Limited Government Power: This criterion requires that powers and duties of the state bodies must be clearly defined in law and controlled by different checks and balances mechanisms in order to prevent the abuse of power including the organization of state power in accordance with the principle of separation of powers.
- Absence of Corruption: This criterion requires that the state does not accept and shall take all measures to combat corruption.
- Order and Security: This criterion requires the state to protect the rights, freedom, life and property of the citizens by means of prevention of all forms of crime and violence and lead the state under these dimensions: absence of crime, absence of civil conflict including terrorism, and armed conflict, and absence of violence as a socially acceptable means to redress personal grievances.
- Fundamental Rights: This criterion requires the state to respect, protect and ensure fundamental human rights embodied in the Universal Declaration of Human Rights.
- Open Government: This criterion requires the state to act on the principles of openness, transparency, accountability, promotion of contact, participation, cooperation and accessible possibility to the government of the people.
- Regulatory Enforcement: This criterion requires law must be strictly and timely enforced without unreasonable delay or improper interference. The government must pay compensation if damage is caused during the application of law.
- Civil Justice: This criterion requires the state to ensure that people have the ability to peacefully and effectively resolve conflicts, conflicts within the community (civil conflict) through formal judicial authorities but not some kind of self-administered justice by means of violence.
- Criminal Justice: This criterion requires the state to have an effective criminal justice system to prevent crime, ensure the order and security of society. This system must be independent from any external interference, but must ensure that human rights in criminal proceedings as well.

---

[11] http://worldjusticeproject.org/what-rule-law.

- Informal Justice: This criterion requires the state to encourage the type of traditional justice (unofficially) as customary laws, local laws, reconciliation team to solve small conflicts within the community. However, unofficially justice must also comply with standards such as impartiality, efficiency and respect human rights.

Understandings and Characteristics of the State of Law in Vietnam

The idea of the rule of law was introduced to Vietnam in the early 20th century through revolutionaries and patriots like Phan Boi Chau, Phan Chu Trinh, Nguyen Ai Quoc. For instance, in his writings and speeches, Phan Chu Trinh heightens the role of a constitution and sees it as a legal instrument to limit the military monopoly and other abuses of power by the Eastern autocratic monarchies. He says

"Basing on the ideas of a person or a court to rule a country then that country is no more than a flock who are prosperous, happy or hungry all depending on the generosity of the shepherds. But a state built by the people means that people create by themselves constitution, laws, and institutions to serve the general concerns of people."[12]

For Nguyen Ai Quoc, the influence of Western ideas on the rule of law can be seen clearly in the document called "Claim of the people of Annam" (in French: Revendications du peuple annamite) which was sent to the Versailles Conference in 1919, the seventh demand of that document called for a replacement of the regime of arbitrary decrees by a regime of law. Following the success of the August Revolution, the Declaration of Independence of 1945 and the 1946 Constitution more clearly showed Ho Chi Minh's idea on the rule of law while confirming the natural equal rights of humans which set the foundation for the independence of the people (Declaration of Independence) and helped to build a new Vietnam with a decentralized mechanism to control the power in a state characterized by the principle of the separation of powers, and a mechanism for the rights and obligations of citizens (1946 Constitution).

Since its foundation in 1930, the Communist Party of Vietnam has stressed the goal of building a democratic state under the doctrine of Marxism-Leninism, i.e. a state led by the proletariat class (workers, peasants) to exercise

---

[12] Nguyễn Văn Dương (1995), 815–816.

a dictatorship of the proletariat over the exploiting classes (bourgeoisie, land-lords)to enforce basic human rights. For example, in the Brief Political Program published in 1930, the party defined its objectives:

- to overthrow the French imperialism and feudalism,
- to achieve full sovereignty of Vietnam,
- to build up a government controlled by workers, peasants and militants,
- to organize a workers and peasants army in order to ensure these aims,
- To realize goals like the freedom of association, equal rights of men and women, mass education, and reforms in industry and agriculture.[13]

The idea to build a proletariat state was then clearly pointed out in many party documents, especially in those of the 6th National Party Congress (1976) stating that:

"the socialist state is the state of the proletariat, an organization performing the collective ownership of the working class and working people, an organization through which the party implements its leadership in the process of social development."

This idea was then embodied in the constitutions promulgated after 1946 with different levels and ways of expression, particularly in the 1980 constitution which states that: "The Socialist Republic of Vietnam is the state of proletariat" (article 2), "In the Socialist Republic of Vietnam the collective ownership is the working people including the working class, collective peasant class and socialist intelligentsia and other working people, among them the core alliance of workers and peasants is led by the working class" (article 3).

Since the 6th Party Congress (1986), interpretation and viewpoints of the party on the proletariat state have been gradually changed. During the 6th National Party Congress, although the term "proletariat state" was still used and confirmed that it is a model of a transitional state:

"Our state is the instrument of the socialist collective ownership in which the working class and working people organize organs of political power. In the transitional period, that is the proletariat state conducting the socialist democracy."[14]

However, the interpretation of the function and mission of the proletariat state was renewed:

---

[13] Communist Party of Vietnam (1998), 2–3.

[14] National Political Publishing House (2000), 124.

"Under the leadership of the party, the state function is institutionalized by law, rights, benefits and obligations of working people and economy and society are ruled by law. The state at the same time must ensure the really democratic rights of working people, and firmly punish those who violate the people's right."[15]

In this case, the term "dictatorship" (to administer the state and society mainly based on guidelines, resolutions of the party) was eased and replaced by law. In addition, democratic rights were stressed more. This shows a positive movement toward the advance of the state of law approved by its superiority and rational elements in the world. The process was then promoted in the following party congresses. The 7th National Party Congress stressed the importance of democratic practices by defining socialist democracy as the quintessence of the renewal process. The strengthening of the political system became both an objective and a motivation of Doi Moi. To innovate and strengthen the political system, the party advocates to continue promoting administrative reforms to reach the following aims: The state is of the people, by the people and for the people; the state put under the leadership of the party administers the society by law and is organized and operated according to the principle of democratic centralism; the state implements unified but decentralized power; the state structure is downsized and operated effectively.[16]

The state of law became politically fundamental for the national renovation process in the transitional period to socialism. Since then the Communist Party has continued to outline innovations for governance, for example in the 6th and 7th Party Congresses. They emphasized the role of the state in managing the society by law and created a general model for the organization of state power in Vietnam under which it is unified but assigned to three aspects: legislative, executive and judiciary.[17]

Expressing these ideas in such important documents demonstrates significant changes in the basic policy of the Communist Party when innovating the organization and operations of the state following the jurisdiction principle. This is considered premise for the Conference of the Central Party Committee (the 7th Party Congress), the term "the state of law" was officially introduced

---

[15] National Political Publishing House (2000), 125.

[16] National Political Publishing House (2000), 297.

[17] National Political Publishing House (2000), 327.

and views, principles and content of building the state of law was firstly defined in a more comprehensive way stating that the state of law of Vietnam is:

"The state of the people, by the people and for the people; the state administers all fields of the society by law and leads the country to a socialism-oriented development. The rule of law in Vietnam is built on the basis of strengthening and expanding its national unity, the alliance of working class and peasant class is seen as the core foundation and put under the leadership of the party."[18]

Thus, the conference defined the very basic denotation of the term "the socialist rule of law in Vietnam". However, not until the 8th Conference of the Central Party Committee in 1995 (the 7th Party Congress) guidelines, solutions of innovation and perfection of the state toward a state of law were specified. In this conference, five central views on building the socialist state of law were identified:

- Building the socialist state of law of the people, by the people and for the people, the alliance of working, peasant class and intelligentsia is seen as the core foundation of Vietnam and put under the leadership of the Communist Party. The state fully implements the people's democratic rights, keeps the social order and exercises control over all acts violating the interests of the motherland and the people.
- State power is unified with the assignment and close coordination between state agencies in implementing the three powers: legislative, executive and judiciary.
- Putting into effect the principle of democratic centralism in the organization and operation of the Socialist Republic of Vietnam.
- Strengthening socialist legislation; building a state of law in Vietnam to control the society by law and improvements in education and socialist morality.
- Securing the leading role of the party in the Vietnamese State.

The above-mentioned views on building the socialist state of law were then confirmed and specified in the 8th (1996), 9th (2002) and 10th (2006) National Congress of the Communist Party of Vietnam. Most recently, the 11th National Congress of the Communist Party of Vietnam has stated:

"continue to promote and perfect socialist rule of law as well as ensure the state is really of the people, by the people and for the people and put under the leadership of

---

[18] National Political Publishing House (2000), 329.

the party; the state implements effectively the economic and social management func-
tions, at the same time properly resolves the relationship between the state and other
institutions within its political system, with the people and with the market."

The congress also identified one of the most important instruments to build
and perfect the socialist state of law:

"to research and to supplement specific institutional and mechanism operations to
ensure the principle that all state power belongs to the people, and the principle of
state power is unified with the assignment, coordination and control among agencies
in the implementation of legislative, executive and judiciary; to enhance the role and
effectiveness of economic management of the state in accordance with the requirements
of economic development of the socialist-oriented market; to continue to improve the
legal system, mechanisms and policies to effectively operate the economy and imple-
ment international commitments, protect national interests; to urgently study, modify
the Constitution (1992) amended and supplemented in 2001 in order to be consistent
with the new situation."[19]

In order to meet the demand of the changes in the party's concept of the rule of
law, article 2 of the Vietnamese Constitution , which was amended in the
2001, states: "The Socialist Republic of Vietnam is a socialist-law-governed
state of the people, by the people and for the people. All state power belongs to
the people; the foundation is the alliance of the working class with the peasantry and the intelligentsia. State power is unified with the assignment and coordination among agencies in the implementation of legislative, executive and
judiciary". This is the first time the term "the rule of law" as well as the nature
of the socialist state of law in Vietnam was officially confirmed in the Constitution of Vietnam.

The 2013 constitution continued to reaffirm that statement of the 1992
constitution, also in article 2, one important word was added i.e., "The Socialist Republic of Vietnam is a socialist-law-governed state of the people, by the
people and for the people. The Socialist Republic of Vietnam is owned by the
people; all state power belongs to the people; the foundation is the alliance of
the working class with the peasantry and the intelligentsia. State power is
unified with the assignment, coordination and control among agencies in the
implementation of legislative, executive and judiciary." By adding the term
"control", the 2013 constitution marked a huge step in accepting reasonable
elements of state power control under the separation of powers model (alt-

---

[19] National Political Publishing House (2011), 246–247.

352

hough this principle has not been accepted) that is commonly applied in many countries all over the world.

Based on the above ideas, it can be seen that since the foundation of the Communist Party of Vietnam, it has continually focused on building a model for a state and a law system which is compatible with the political goal of the party: to build a socialist government in Vietnam. The party's interpretation, awareness, and policies on this matter have gradually changed over the past years during which the biggest changes have been recorded since its launch of Doi Moi (1986). So far, the views of party and state on a socialist state ruled by law or a socialist legal state have been clearly shaped, whereby the socialist state rule of law includes the following basic characteristics:[20]

- The state is of the people, by the people, for the people; the people are the owner of the state.
- The state is organized and operated on the basis of the constitution; the state respects and protects the constitution.
- The state governs the society by law, and ensures the predominant position of law in social life.
- The state respects and protects human and civil rights.
- The state is organized on the basis of unified state power with the assignment, coordination and control among agencies in the implementation of legislative, executive and judiciary in accordance with the inspection and supervision of the implementation of state power through social organizations.
- The state is led by the only political party called the Communist Party of Vietnam.

These characteristics point out that the party's views and understandings of Vietnam have approached but not yet been completely updated with the common view on the rule of law of the international community. For instance, the first and the fourth characteristics are the most compatible meanwhile the fifth one only reaches the basic level of compatibility as according to the common agreement of the international community, one of the characteristics of a state of law is the principle of separation of powers which was not reflected in the 5th characteristic.

---

[20] Nguyen Van Manh (2012), 17–21.

Nevertheless, the biggest gap is shown in the last characteristic. If the socialist state of law in Vietnam is based on the leadership of one political party then a fundamental attribute of the rule of law, according to the common conception in the world is pluralistic politics in which political freedom i.e., freedom of association is guaranteed and civil society is protected and encouraged to be active.

Advantages and Challenges in Promoting the Rule of Law

The Vietnamese Constitution of 2013 creates fundamental advantages to promote the building of the state of law in Vietnam. In this constitution, one chapter and twenty seven articles were cut, only seven former articles remained, twelve articles were added, one hundred and one articles of the 1992 Constitution were amended; the 2013 Constitution contains many new provisions some of which are both direct and indirect prospects to promote the building of the state of law. However, in order to realize that vision it is required to overcome many challenges that can be generalized as follows.

The goal of building a socialist state ruled by law has been identified in the 2001 revision of the 1992 Constitution and embodied again in the 2013 Constitution pointed out in article 2 (The Socialist Republic of Vietnam is a socialist law-governed state of the people, by the people and for the people. State power is unified with the assignment, coordination and control among agencies in the implementation of the legislative, executive and judiciary); article 6 (Organizations and members that belong to the party operate within the framework of the constitution and law); article 8 (The state is organized and operated by constitution and law, society is governed also by constitution and law); articles 94, and 96 (The government implements the execute power and is responsible for protecting human rights and civil rights); article 102 (The people's court performs judicial authority and is responsible for the protection of justice as well as human rights); article 107 (The People's Procuration is responsible for protection of human rights and civil rights). These regulations are still general, however, they require amending the related laws, and thereby the organizational structure and operation of the state to be changed in a way that comes closer to the principles of the rule of law.

However, to implement those above-stated innovations is not easy. As mentioned previously, the views, and perceptions of a socialist state of law in Vietnam are still not fully compatible with the common view of the world. There is still a difference between the conception of a socialist state of law with the common perception of the rule of law in two important points: organizational centralization of state power and political institutions. Therefore, the first and the most important challenge in promoting the rule of law in Vietnam is to deeply understand their nature and attributes.

More specific challenges relate to the implementation of the assignment, coordination and control between the legislature, executive and judiciary in the context that state power in Vietnam is considered to be unified and centralized in the National Assembly as well as ensured by a Communist Party of Vietnam which is on the one hand the sole head of state and society, and on the other hand is answerable to the people and subject to the supervision of the people (article 4 of 2013 constitution). These are also the issues that contain theoretically unclear, even contradictory factors, and in fact, they have not ever been implemented and regulated in our law system.

By reaffirming and clarifying the people's sovereignty (mentioned in the constitutions of 1959, 1980, 1992), the 2013 Constitution also creates great opportunities for the expansion of democracy – the basis of the rule of law in a number of regulations: It is stated in the preamble (people are the actors who build, implement and protect the constitution); in article 2 (people are the owners of the country, all state power belongs to the people); in article 4 (the party, party organizations and party members are subject to the supervision of the people and responsible for their decisions); in article 6 (the way the people implement state power is direct and representative democracy); in article 70 ("The National Assembly is the only organ with constitutional power" no longer exists); in article 120 (regulates a referendum on the constitution). These new amendments together with the capitalized term "People" indicate that the role of people's power is solemnly acknowledged in the 2013 Constitution. They also show the shift in the main features of the state to the idea that the state is a social contract in which people are establishing subjects; people empower and work out mechanisms to control the operation of the government created by them. These changes promise to promote the expansion of democracy in our country in the coming years.

However, the expansion of democracy may encounter many challenges. Currently, in Vietnam, there is still no clear legal framework and effective implementation of democratic rights, in particular the absence of a series of legal foundations for a democratic society, including the law on political parties, the law on association, protest law, law on referendum, and the law on access to information. The legal framework of a representative democracy (the law on election of deputies to the National Assembly and the law on election of deputies to the People's Council) exists but contains many obsolete provisions and needs to be modified to be compatible with the new situation (e.g., regulations on candidates, nomination, negotiation of candidates). Although direct democracy was firstl introduced and emphasized in the 2013 Constitution, there is still not any specific law and the concept itself has not really been clarified in our country.

The 2013 Constitution also creates opportunities for a state governance reform which is indeed related directly to the building of the state of law. Series of newly added or amended regulations express the efforts of law -makers in forming a new framework for the governance of the country e.g., article 2 (control function among agencies in the implementation of the legislative, executive and judiciary); article 55 and 112 (decentralization between central and local level under a development model allowing local government to have its own budget); article 117 and 118 (two independent constitutional authorities are established: the National Election Council and the State Audit); article 9 (the role of criticism and supervision of the Vietnam Fatherland Front and its members is clarified). These new revisions promise to promote reforms toward building transparent governance, efficiency and accountability and meet the demands arising from the process of democratization, and international integration of Vietnam.

Despite that, there are also challenges in the reformation of national governance. Only criticism and monitoring issues of the Vietnam Fatherland Front and its members have been regulated,[21] other significant issues that reflect a framework of national governance reform added in the 2013 Constitution i.e., a mechanism of mutual control between the legislature, executive and judiciary; separation of powers between the central and local level according to a development model; organization and operation of two independent constitu-

---

[21] See Politburo of the Communist Party of Vietnam (2013).

tional bodies as the National Election Council and State Audit have not yet been specified in our country, as this requires the new promulgation and revision of many related laws.

However, the biggest difficulty is not the legislative issue, because Vietnamese law makers and legal experts are qualified to build a legal framework for transparent governance, efficiency and accountability, but the obstacles to the establishment and operation of institutional control and power monitoring. This is expressed in the regulation of the Constitutional Council – an independent constitutional institution, upon which almost all Vietnamese legal experts agree, the role of which is as a strong agency to control power; however, it was removed from the 2013 Draft Constitution (amended version). Another example is the building of the Law on Criticism and Supervision of the Vietnam Fatherland Front and its member organizations (to codify the Regulation on supervision and social criticism of the Vietnam Fatherland Front, mass organizations of the Politburo) has been delayed, despite of the fact that it has long been proposed by the Front itself. In short, the novelty and complexity of institutional controls, power supervision along with their potential conflicts with the closed mode of operation of the current state institutions show that the reform of the framework of governance under the 2013 Constitution of our country will not be easily and quickly completed.

The 2013 Constitution creates an unprecedented opportunity to complete the constitutional framework of human, and civil rights – one of the factors and basic foundation of the rule of law. Human rights institutions and citizen rights are mostly amended and supplemented in the 2013 Constitution. The amendments and supplements represent a new approach closely associated with common human recognition as well as the standards of international law on human rights. That is shown as follows.

In the former 1992 Constitution, chapter 5 called "Rights and responsibilities of the citizen" is now changed to chapter 2 and renamed "Human rights, rights and responsibilities of citizen". The former term "Rights and responsibilities of citizen" does not completely encompass the content of the chapter, this change also confirms the important role of this institution within the constitution, at the same time being with compatible general trends in the world.

Human and citizens' rights are no longer seen equally (as shown in the 1992 Constitution) but these two terms are used for institutional rights, e.g., equality before the law; business freedom; private ownership of property and productive assets; rights in scientific research and technology, literary and artistic creation and to receive the benefits from such activities; the right to the protection, and health care; freedom of belief and religion; the right to inviolability of the body, health, honor and dignity protected by law are stipulated in the 1992 Constitution only for citizens. However, the 2013 Constitution stipulates that this applies to everyone. Therefore, not only Vietnamese citizens but foreigners living in Vietnamese territory are also protected.

Three obligations of the state are acknowledged in accordance with international human right law: respect, protect and guarantee human rights (in article 3 and 14 of the 2013 constitution meanwhile, the obligation to respect was only referred to in article 50 of the 1992 Constitution). This change not only ensures the harmonization with international human rights law, but also forms the institutional basis that binds constitutional agencies to fully and seriously implement the obligation in human rights, citizen rights in reality, especially the dual obligation of protection and guarantee.

The principle of limited power is defined for the first time (paragraph 2, article 16) which has been outlined in international human rights law and in the constitution of a number of countries. The constitutional principles have important implications, because: This clarifies the spirit of international human rights law, that means the state must respect, protect and guarantee human rights but also set and apply the limits for a number of rights in order to perform the functions of the state's social management, ensure the rights and interests of the community and the rights and legitimate interests of other individuals. It prevents the potential abuse of state power to violate human rights; this is done through the stipulation of strict conditions for the limitation of rights. It prevents inordinateness in the extreme uses and actions in the enjoyment of rights.

Adding some new rights which have not been addressed in the 1992 and previous Constitutions of Vietnam that include: right to life (article 21); cultural rights (article 41); the right to determine ethnicity, native language, choose the language of communication (article 42); right to live in a healthy environment (article 43); citizens cannot be deported and handed over to other states (article 17 paragraph 2); the right to have legal residence (article 22); the right to social security (article 34). These new rights expand the scope of constitutional protection for human rights, citizen rights in both civil and political fields (article 21, 17, 42) as well as in economic, social, cultural fields (Article 41, 42, 43, 22, 34) and meet the new demands on human rights emerging in the context of industrialization, modernization and international integration of our country.

Most of the recognized articles in the 1992 Constitution are strengthened (specified or detailed in separate articles):
- equality before the law (article 16),
- prohibition of torture, violence, coercion, and corporal punishment (article 20 paragraph 1),
- privacy and residence (articles 21 and 22),
- access to information (article 25),
- participation in state governance and social affairs (article 28),
- gender equality (article 26),
- voting in a referendum (article 29),
- procedural fairness (article 31),
- private property (article 32),
- labor and employment (article 35).

The revised rules also contribute to enhancing the level of compatibility of the rule of human rights, civil rights in the 2013 Constitution which is compatible with the contents of international treaties on human rights to which Vietnam is a member and with provisions on human and civil rights in the constitutions of democratic countries.

However, there are still many challenges in the assurance of human and constitutional rights of citizens in the 2013 Constitution. The first obstacle is that the 2013 Constitution does not regulate the direct effect of constitutional rights. This means that many important rights, especially civil and political rights as freedom of association, meeting, demonstration, the right to vote in the referendum will have to wait for the National Assembly to enact laws and for the government to issue decrees to guide the implementation.

The second obstacle is that there is still no clear legal and effective mechanism for the protection of constitutional rights. As the Constitutional Council has not yet been established, there is no possibility to prevent and effectively deal with the documents and decisions that violate the constitutional rights (unconstitutional) of the legislature, executive and judiciary. Similarly, the proposal of a national human rights agency is ignored causing the elimination of people's opportunity to be protected by an independent constitutional agency. Currently, through the mechanism for resolving complaints and denunciations designed as "to be a judge of one's own case" (complaints and denunciations are solved by the authorities which themselves create the complaints and denunciations in the first place or by their higher authorities) and through the judicial system that is lacking in independence, the ability to solve and compensate properly the violation of human rights, citizen rights, especially civil rights, and politically sensitive rights is limited.

The third major obstacle relates to unreasonable regulations applied to issues of national security in order to restrict rights (article 14) including the broad and vague prohibition of the abuse of human and citizen rights to violate national interests, legitimate rights and interests of others (article 15). In fact, these rules have been misused to violate constitutional rights. In the context of the judicial system which is not acting in the defense of justice together with the lack of an independent institution in human rights protection namely the Constitutional Council and a national human rights body, the ability to stop the abuses described above will be very difficult.

References

ABA: What is rule of law, http://www.americanbar.org/content/dam/-aba/migrated/publiced/features/Part1DialogueROL.authcheckdam.pdf.

Communist Party of Vietnam (ed.) (1998): Party Documents. Complete Collection. Hanoi.

http://worldjusticeproject.org/what-rule-law.

http://www.oxforddictionaries.com/definition/english/rule%2Bof%2Blaw___1?q=rule+of+law.

Madison, James (1989): The Structure of the Government Must Furnish the Proper Checks and Balances Between the Different Departments (Federalist Paper No. 51, 1788): In: Hamilton, Alexander/Madison, James/Jay, John: The Federalist Papers. New York.

Magna Carta, article 39th, at: http://www.historylearningsite.co.uk/magna-_carta-transcript.htm.

National Political Publishing House (ed.) (2000): Documents of Party Congresses in Doi Moi period (the 6th, 7th, 8th and 9th Congresses). Hanoi.

National Political Publishing House (ed.) (2011): Documents of 9th Party Congress. Hanoi.

Nguyễn Văn Dương (ed.) (1995): Selected Works of Phan Chu Trinh. Da Nang. 815–816. Cited according to Phan Đăng Thanh, Constitutional Thought of Phan Chu Trinh, at: http://www.na.gov.vn/Sach_QH/Ban-%20ve%20lap%20hien/Chuong1/5.htm.

Nguyen Van Manh (2012): Building the Socialist Rule of Law-Based State of the People, by the People, for the People. Hanoi.

Politburo of the Communist Party of Vietnam (2013): Regulation on Supervision and Social Criticism of the Vietnam Fatherland Front, Mass Organizations Issued together with Decision 217-QD/TW, December 12, 2013 of the Politburo of the Communist Party of Vietnam. Hanoi.

Quotes.liberty-tree.ca/quote_blog/Marcus.Tullius.Cicero.Quote.7330.

Report of the Secretary-General on the Rule of Law and Transitional Justice in Conflict and Post-Conflict Societies (S/2004/616), http://www.unrol.org/-files/2004%20report.pdf.

Stephens, James (1985): Socrates on the Rule of Law. In: History of Philosophy Quarterly. Vol. 2, No. 1. 3–10.

www.quotationspage.com/quote/28897.htm.

List of Tables